# Housing Inequality in Chinese Cities

In recent decades, Chinese cities have experienced profound social, economic and spatial transformations. In particular, Chinese cities have witnessed the largest housing boom in history and unprecedented housing privatization. China now is a country of homeowners, with more than 70 per cent of urban residents owning homes, higher than many developed countries.

This book shows how China's spectacular housing success is not shared by all social groups, with rapidly rising housing inequality, and residential segregation increasingly prevalent in previously homogeneous Chinese cities. It focuses on the two extremes of the residential landscape, and reveals the stark contrast between low-income households who live in shacks in so-called 'urban villages' and the nouveaux riches who live in exclusive gated villa communities. Over four parts, the contributors look at the degree to which inequality affects Chinese cities, and the extent of residential differentiation; housing for the urban poor, and in particular, housing for migrants from rural China; housing for the rapidly expanding Chinese middle class and the new rich; and finally, governance in residential neighbourhoods.

*Housing Inequality in Chinese Cities* presents theoretically informed and empirically grounded research into the polarized residential landscape in Chinese cities, and as such will be of great interest to students and scholars of Chinese studies, urban geography, urban sociology, and urban studies.

**Youqin Huang** is Associate Professor in the Department of Geography and Planning at the State University of New York at Albany, USA.

**Si-ming Li** is Chair Professor of Geography and Director of the David C. Lam Institute for East-West Studies at Hong Kong Baptist University.

# Routledge contemporary China series

# Housing Inequality in Chinese Cities

Edited by Youqin Huang and Si-ming Li

Routledge
Taylor & Francis Group

LONDON AND NEW YORK

First published 2014 by Routledge

2 Park Square, Milton Park, Abingdon, Oxon OX14 4RN
711 Third Avenue, New York, NY 10017, USA

*Routledge is an imprint of the Taylor & Francis Group, an informa business*

First issued in paperback 2017

*British Library Cataloguing in Publication Data*
A catalogue record for this book is available from the British Library

*Library of Congress Cataloging-in-Publication Data*
Housing inequality in Chinese cities / edited by Youqin Huang and Si-ming Li.
pages cm. – (Routledge contemporary China series; 115)
Includes bibliographical references and index.
1. Housing–China. 2. Urban poor–Housing–China. 3. Urban policy–China. 4. Urbanization–China. 5. Equality–China. I. Huang, Youqin. II. Li, Si-ming.
HD7368.A3H68 2014
363.5'10951091732–dc23
2013028892

ISBN: 978-0-415-83428-5 (hbk)
ISBN: 978-1-138-06922-0 (pbk)

Typeset in Times New Roman
by Cenveo Publisher Services

# Contents

# Figures

xiv *Figures*

# Tables

# Contributors

**Huimin Du** is a PhD candidate in the Department of Geography at Hong Kong Baptist University. Her research focuses on housing inequality, village-in-the-city, migration, and mobility in China.

**Qiang Fu** is currently a PhD candidate in the Department of Sociology and a PARISS fellow at Duke University. Since the summer of 2009 he has conducted field research on homeowners' associations and neighborhood governance in urban China. His work has appeared in journals such as *Environment and Planning A*, *International Journal of Urban and Regional Research*, *Chinese Sociological Review*, and *Child Indicators Research*.

**Guillaume Giroir** is a professor in the Department of Geography of China at the University of Orléans (France). His current research interests focus on the natural reserves, the wine, and the gated communities in China. He is a consultant for several companies interested in the luxury Chinese market. He is writing a book on the sustainable development in China.

**Brenda Madrazo Gonzalez** is a PhD student in the Faculty of Geosciences at Utrecht University, the Netherlands. Her research focuses on urban development and housing inequality in China.

**Xiong He** is an associate professor in the Department of Urban Economics and Management at Zhongnan University of Economic and Law, Wuhan, China. His research focuses on urban development in China.

**Youqin Huang** is an associate professor in the Department of Geography and Planning at State University of New York at Albany. Her research focuses on housing, migration/mobility, neighborhood change, and urbanization in China. She is the co-author of *China's Geography: Globalization and the Dynamics of Political, Economic and Social Change* (Roman & Littlefield Publishers, 2011), and *The Emergence of New Urban China: Insiders' Perspectives* (Lexington Books, 2012). She has also published many papers in leading journals in geography, urban studies, housing, and China.

**Limei Li** is an associate professor at Shanghai Key Lab for Urban Ecological Processes and Eco-Restoration, East China Normal University, Shanghai. She works on the social geographies of Chinese cities, including housing consumption and residential differentiation, migrants, and citizenship.

**Si-ming Li** is currently Chair Professor of Geography and Director of David C. Lam Institute for East-West Studies, Hong Kong Baptist University. He specializes in Urban Geography and is currently studying urban housing and spatial transformation in Chinese cities and housing policy in Hong Kong.

**Zhilin Liu** is an associate professor in the School of Public Policy and Management, Tsinghua University. Her main research interests are in affordable housing policy, urban planning and governance, sustainable development, and new institutional theory.

**Yu-Ling Song** is an associate professor of Geography at National Chang-hua University in Taiwan. In recent years she has published work on displaced residents in Shanghai. She is currently undertaking research into the housing choice of the middle class in Beijing and Shanghai.

**Xiaoyi Sun** is a PhD candidate of the Department of Public Policy, City University of Hong Kong. Her research focuses on neighborhood governance and homeowner activism in urban China. She has published in academic journals such as *Journal of Public Management* and *Journal of Social Sciences*.

**Lili Wang** is currently a PhD student in the Department of Geography of the Ohio State University. She uses multiple urban theories – urban political economy, urban political ecology, ordinary urbanism, and cyborg cities – to investigate the Chinese city in transition.

**Ya Ping Wang** is Chair Professor in global city futures at Urban Studies, School of Social and Political Sciences, the University of Glasgow. Previously he was Professor in Urban Studies at the School of Built Environment, Heriot-Watt University in Edinburgh. His research focuses on urbanisation, housing, land development, planning, and rural migrant living conditions in Chinese cities. He is the author of *Urban Poverty, Housing and Social Change in China* (Routledge, 2004), co-author of *Housing Policy and Practice in China* (Macmillan, 1999, with A. Murie), and *Planning and Housing in the Rapidly Urbanising World* (Routledge, 2007, with P. Jenkins and H. Smith). His research projects and fieldworks were supported by the ESRC, DFID, British Academy, Leverhulme Trust, British Council, and Lincoln Institute of Land Policy.

**Yujun Wang** is an assistant professor in the Department of Sociology, Renmin University of China. Her main research interests are in social stratification, economic sociology, social demography, and research methods.

**Yunyan Yang** is a professor in the Department of Urban Economics and Management at Zhongnan University of Economic and Law in Wuhan, China. His research focuses on migration and regional development in China.

**Chengdong Yi** is a professor in the Department of Urban and Real Estate Management at Central University of Finance and Economics, Beijing, China. His research focuses on housing market and policies and urban spatial structure.

**Ngai Ming Yip** is a professor in the Department of Public Policy, City University of Hong Kong. He has published extensively on the neighborhood and housing issues in China and other Asian countries, which includes an edited book *Neighborhood Governance in Urban China*, published in 2013.

# Part I
# Housing inequality and residential differentiation

# 1 Housing inequality, residential differentiation, and social stratification

## Chinese cities in the early twenty-first century

*Youqin Huang and Si-ming Li*

## Introduction

The 2008 global financial and housing crisis has brought housing to the forefront of social and economic debates again. Meanwhile, rising social inequality in the neoliberal era has caused much anger from the public, which was epitomized by the global spread of the "Occupy Wall Street" movement. Housing inequality, a long-held central concern of socio-spatial studies, has re-energized scholars and policy makers who are determined to understand "the housing question" in the new era. It is in this global context that this book focuses on housing inequality in China, where profound social, economic and spatial transformations are taking place at unprecedented scales and speeds under privatization, marketization and neo-liberalization, notwithstanding the continuing domination of the (Chinese Communist) Party-State in charting the developmental trajectories at all levels of territorial governance.

For decades, China was known for its welfare-oriented housing system under which public rental housing was allocated among urban residents. (In the country-side, there is a different housing system, where villagers built their own housing on collectively owned land.) While housing shortage and residential crowding were prevalent in Chinese cities, relative homogeneity in housing conditions and neighborhood compositions set China apart from other developing countries where appalling housing inequality underpinned by prevalence of slums and widespread squatting seems to be inevitable. Yet, China today is a very different country. On the one hand, China has experienced spectacular success in housing development in recent decades. In the first decade of the twenty-first century, the number of housing units built in China was roughly twice the total stock of housing units currently in Spain or the UK, or about the same as Japan's current total stock (Economist Intelligence Unit, 2011). With the unprecedented housing boom, Chinese households are enjoying much better and larger housing than before. Per capita residential floor space in Chinese cities increased from 4 m$^2$ in 1980s to 31 m$^2$ in 2010. While it is still far below the level in the US, it is on par with many developed countries such as Japan and countries in Europe. China is also becoming a nation of home-owners, with 75 per cent of urban households (85 per cent of all households nationwide) owning their flats/houses in 2010, compared to only 20 per cent in 1980. Moreover, more than 15 per cent of urban households owned multiple homes in

2007 (Huang and Yi, 2011). Dominated by public rental housing only three decades ago, China now has a higher rate of homeownership than many developed countries. For a significant percentage of Chinese nationals, the "Chinese Dream" of access to decent housing under owner occupation is now realized.

However, at the same time millions of urban poor continue to be denied basic housing. Many have to live in boxy rooms in crumble shacks and low-rises in dusty suburban villages and tiny dark dorms in bomb shelters and basements under glossy apartment buildings (Wu, 2002; Wu, 2004; Solinger, 1999; Ma and Xiang, 1998; Huang and Yi, 2013). Reminiscent of worker insects in a colony and mice in underground cellars, they are called "ant tribe" (*yizu*) and "mouse tribe" (*shuzu*), respectively. The Chinese Dream is far beyond their imagination and reach. Meanwhile, the new *nouveaux riches* live in exclusive gated villa communities that are on par with upscale gated communities in the West (Giroir, 2006; Huang, 2005; Wu, 2005). The Chinese urban residential landscape, alongside the social, economic and political landscapes, is becoming increasingly complex and polarized and challenging our perception and understanding of Chinese cities.

## Housing reform and housing inequality

As an important component of China's overall institutional transition, housing reform in Chinese cities was launched nationwide in 1988 after experiments in several cities. Despite its slow start, the housing reform has profoundly changed the way housing is produced and consumed in urban areas. First of all, the existing public rental housing stock was privatized. Sitting tenants were given the option of either purchasing their dwellings at heavily subsidized prices, depending on their status in the respective work units such as seniority, years of service and job rank, or paying increasingly higher rents which would eventually reach market levels. The great majority of existing public housing was thus sold, especially after the 1998 housing reform under which sitting tenants were given the last chance to buy at heavy discounts. This privatization of public housing contributes significantly to the high rate of homeownership in Chinese cities. More than 40 per cent of homeowners in 2000 and a quarter of homeowners in 2010 in Chinese cities owned previously public housing, often known as "reform housing" (*fang gai fang*) (Yi and Huang, 2012). At first, reform housing was conferred only partial property rights and reselling was subject to strict restrictions. But such restrictions were gradually lifted in the early 2000s (Li and Yi, 2007b); as such, the bulk of reform housing has since been commodified.

Second, private developers were allowed to invest in residential real estate. Massive private housing, called "commodity housing" (*shang ping fang*), has been developed with both domestic and foreign investment. While some commodity housing is for rent, most is for sale due to higher profit margins and shorter investment cycle in the owned sector. Catered to different social strata, there is a wide range of commodity housing, with high-rise apartments, multi-story townhouses, and luxurious villas. At the lower end is subsidized, price-controlled commodity housing called "economic and comfortable housing" (ECH, *jing ji shi yong fang*), also known as "affordable housing" and "economic and comfortable housing" in the literature, which was designated as the main housing type for low- and middle-income urban households in 1998, but was recently redefined as low-income housing in 2007 (Huang, 2012). Local municipal governments usually provide cheap land to developers and set the prices of the housing units built, while qualified residents purchase the housing units with partial property rights that constrain them from profiting from their housing.

The privatization and commodification drive has been accompanied by promotion of homeownership. Both the existing public housing and newly developed private housing is predominately for sale. The government also established a Housing Provident Fund (HPF), which mandated employees to save part of his/her salary, matched by employer's contribution, for future home purchase. Contributors can take loans from the HPF with lower interest rates (Li and Yi, 2007a). Commercial mortgage is also available, although until recently its role has been relatively small, probably reflective of the high saving rates and the high incidence of inter-generational wealth transfer in China (Li and Yi, 2007a). The State Council (1998) officially ended public provision of housing in 1998, and in 2003 "ordinary commodity housing" was defined as the main housing type for urban households (State Council, 2003). Since then China has entered a period of accelerated housing marketization. With massive investment by property developers, private housing has become the main housing source; at the same time housing prices have skyrocketed. According to the housing price-income ratio, China is ranked in the category of "severely unaffordable" (Man *et al.*, 2011). Housing affordability has become the topmost concerns among low- and middle-income households.

Third, concomitant with the weakening of the *danwei* or work-unit system, the main vehicle through which healthcare, retirement benefits and other social welfare provisions were extended to urban households, from the mid-1980s onwards the Chinese government gradually withdrew from social service commitments. Neoliberal critiques such as the inherent rigidities, inefficiencies and financial unsustainability of state provision of social services dominated policy discourses in China for much of the 1980s and 1990s, even though the term neoliberalism was probably not known to the reformers until quite recently. Under such a circumstance, social welfare provision including low-income housing has been neglected in the hot pursuit of high economic growth by both the central and local government. The development of "Cheap Rental Housing" (*lian zu fang*) – low-income rental housing – stagnated, and covered only a tiny fraction of the poorest urban households, while the construction of ECH – subsidized homeownership – has actually declined (Huang, 2012). Aggravating the very limited low-income housing provision are rampant problems in its distribution, with unqualified middle-high income households occupying especially subsidized housing in the owned sector such as ECH. Faced with increasing discontent and potential social instability, the Chinese government has revived the low-income housing programs in recent years, especially since 2010, by pumping billions of RMB (Renminbi, the Chinese currency; at current rate of exchange US$1 = RMB6.2 approximately) into low-income housing and setting up ambitious targets for local governments (Huang, 2012). While this is an encouraging development, the result is yet to be seen, as there are many structural problems that prevent local governments from full commitment in low-income housing.

Under privatization, marketization and neo-liberalization, the housing gap in Chinese cities between the rich and the poor has reached unprecedented levels. While housing inequality also existed in the socialist era, it has risen rapidly to a whole new level in the reform era (Logan *et al.*, 1999; Wang, 2005; Huang and Jiang, 2009; Logan *et al.*, 2010; Sato, 2006; Li, 2012). The rising housing inequality has to be seen in the context of increasing social inequality in former socialist countries that are experiencing market transition, including China (Szelenyi, 1983; Bian and Logan, 1996; Rona-Tas, 1994). With its physical form, housing inequality is arguably the most vivid manifestation of social and economic inequality (Szelenyi, 1978).

At the early stage of the housing reform, it has been found that the usual determinants of housing consumption in market economies such as life-cycle factors and household income were not important; instead, institutional factors such as *hukou* or household registration status, the nature and rank of work unit, and political status such as occupational rank and membership in Chinese Communist Party (CCP) were more important to account for differentiations in housing consumption (Li and Yi, 2007b; Li, 2000b; Li, 2000a; Wang and Murie, 2000; Wang *et al.*, 2005; Logan *et al.*, 1999; Zhou and Logan, 1996; Huang, 2003; Huang and Clark, 2002; Huang and Yi, 2011; Huang and Jiang, 2009; Li and Li, 2006). In general, people with urban local *hukou* status, high job rank, CCP party membership, and those working in high-ranking state/government agencies enjoyed better housing and were more likely to be homeowners. They were also the same privileged group who were more likely to access better housing in the socialist era. In fact, these people gained windfall in conjunction with the privatization of public housing, making them the largest winners of the reform (Logan *et al.*, 2010). In other words, housing privatization has exacerbated housing inequality rooted in the socialist housing system.

With accelerated housing privatization and marketization since 1998, market forces such as income and wealth are becoming increasingly more important; yet, institutional forces continue to shape housing inequality. On the one hand, housing inequality similar to market economies in the West is emerging in Chinese cities, with the rich consuming larger and better housing, owning more homes, and living in better neighborhoods than the poor. In both suburbs and inner cities, upscale housing developments have been developed like the bamboo shoots after the spring rain, catering to the growing housing need of the new rich and rapidly expanding middle class of professional and managerial workers (Huang, 2005, 2006). Meanwhile, tens of millions of low-income households who cannot move up the housing ladder have to be contented with rundown tenements in dilapidated neighborhoods in the inner city, or rudimentary housing lacking modern facilities in workers' villages built in the socialist era, or substandard and legally dubious housing in former suburban villages that are now engulfed by the rapidly expanding city.

On the other hand, housing inequality in relation to institutions and mechanisms instated in the earlier years of the People's Republic of China continues and is even exacerbated, due to the "commodification of political power" and persistent political power under the one-party state (Bian and Logan, 1996; Rona-Tas 1994). The privileged not only have higher income which allows them to access better housing on the market but also continue to receive housing subsidies from the work units. It is not uncommon for high-ranking officials and employees in large public work units such as universities and central government agencies/party organizations to own multiple housing units, with some subsidized and others from the market (Huang and Yi, 2010, 2011). In contrast, low-income urban households and rural–urban migrants cannot even afford to rent a small apartment and have to live in illegal housing in migrant enclaves and basements. Once praised by scholars who visited China behind the bamboo curtain in the pre-reform times for their relative homogeneity and classlessness (Ma, 1979), Chinese cities today are among the most unequal places in the world.

## Housing as a mechanism for social and spatial stratification

The concept of housing class was first put forward by Rex and Moore (1967) and subsequently developed further by Pahl (1969) and others (e.g. Harloe 1977) to underscore the struggles behind the claim to subsidized housing in Britain. It was formulated at a time when the welfare state managed to shift social conflicts tied to class struggles in the sphere of production to struggles primarily in the sphere of consumption (Harvey, 2005). While closely related to income and occupation, the most often examined dimensions of social stratification, housing as a process, mechanism, and institution also serve distinctive stratifying functions. In China where the labor market either does not exist or is subject to all kinds of restraints and distortions the concept of housing class or stratification manifested in the realm of housing assumes special relevance. There is an emerging body of research on housing stratification in Chinese cities. The usual approach is to study housing consumption for different social strata (e.g. (Bian and Liu, 2005; Liu and Dai, 2005; Liu and Hu, 2010). But housing differentiation is also studied as a way to define social strata. For example, Li (2009) divided urban households into six different strata based on the types of housing they live in, Zhang (2009) divided households into the strata of homeowners, housing borrowers, and renters, while Liu and Mao (2012) further divided homeowners into those with subsidized homeownership, market homeownership, inherited homeownership, and those with multiple homes.

As was evident from the discussion above, a major factor contributing to housing stratification in Chinese cities today is the persistence of work-unit based housing subsidies and the *hukou* system. First, resourceful work units continue to provide housing subsidies to their employees. In addition, many work units continue to build workers' housing and purchase commodity housing in bulk and then re-distribute this housing to their employees at discounted prices. For this the Chinese central government has repeatedly issued circulars to forbid work units from engaging in housing development and distribution of subsidized housing. Among them are State Council No. 18 Circular of 2003, Ministry of Housing and Urban and Rural Development (MOHURD) No. 196 Circular of 2006 and State

Council No. 24 Circular of 2007. In other words, employees of resourceful public work units continue to be privileged in accessing better housing and attaining homeownership (Li and Li, 2006; Huang and Clark, 2002). Furthermore, within a given work unit those possessing redistributive powers were able to purchase better quality reform housing with greater discounts. Subsequent conferment of full property rights to these properties enables them to trade up on the housing ladder. Moreover, through inter-generational transfer, the politically privileged often help their children to purchase up-market housing in good neighborhoods (Li and Yi, 2007a; Huang and Yi, 2011; Huang and Yi, 2010), and hence enhance the latter's life chances. Housing inequality therefore contributes significantly to unequal wealth accumulation not only for the present generation but also for the next one.

Empirical evidence also reveals that the politically privileged are more likely to own multiple homes (Huang and Yi, 2011, 2010). Often the privatized public housing unit is retained in theory as the primary residence for access to premier schools and hospitals, which is based on the district or sub-district of *hukou* registration. The other home is likely to be an up-scale suburban condominium apartment or townhouse where the family spends most of the time. The phenomenon of *renhufenli* or separation between official (*hukou*) and actual residence not only applies to long-distance migrants from rural areas. It is also common for urban households with the proper *hukou* status in the city (Li and Li, 2010). Contrary to the market transition thesis of Victor Nee (1989), which postulates that stratification in relation to access to political resources will decline with the maturation of the market, in China politically based housing stratification in conjunction with the system of state work units is further consolidated during the reform era (Huang and Jiang, 2009). Moreover, given the differential access to quality education, health care and social services delivery as well as high-status employment opportunities between localities, housing stratification heavily impinges on an individual's and his/her family's social and economic wellbeing.

The persistent *hukou* system is of even greater importance in housing strata delineation for migrants without the local *hukou*. They are largely excluded from subsidized housing such as CRH and ownership-oriented ECH, although there are signs that more inclusive allocation policies have been instituted since 2010 (Huang, 2012). Beginning from the early 1990s, one after another former rural villages which are now engulfed by urban developments have been turned to migrant enclaves, variously know as "urban villages" (Wu, 2004; Wu, 2002; Du and Li, 2010; Wang *et al.*, 2010; Wang, 2005; Ma and Xiang, 1998). Because of the *hukou*-based land tenure system, urban villages generally remain outside the purview of the municipal authority and are therefore not provided with proper municipal services, such as hygiene and education provisions. Migrant children are often denied access to local public schools, and even if they are allowed to enroll they have to pay prohibitive high tuitions and fees. Moreover, migrants' general lack of financial means and limited spatial knowledge severely constrain their activity space and social networks in the city. For many the urban village that they live in is practically identical to the city itself; as such the village assumes particular significance in determining their life experiences and life chances.

In more recent times an increasingly large number of migrants have infiltrated inner-city neighborhoods in both the pre-1949 city and former work-unit compounds as many former inhabitants have traded their substandard privatized public housing flats for much more spacious and better equipped ones in newly constructed gated communities in suburbs (He, 2013). A process of filtering not dissimilar from that in cities in the United States in the 1960s and 1970s is taking place in urban China today, although the central city–suburban dichotomy is much less visible in Chinese cities largely due to municipal government-induced gentrification (He, 2010). In comparison with living in urban villages, residence in inner-city neighborhoods has a number of advantages, not the least proximity to the city's best health care services and schools as well as a much larger pool and variety of employment opportunities. It also enables the migrant to have a more holistic understanding of the city, including the city's history and geography. But this also means that the residences of the migrants are much more scattered, and the kinship and place of origin-based social support is much more difficult to come by. In addition, like living in urban villages, residence in dilapidated tenements and under-maintained housing in former work-unit compounds is subject to the constant threat of forced relocation without compensation, given the scale and pace of redevelopment activities in Chinese cities. Moreover, migrants are looked down upon by the locals wherever they live.

On the other hand, with mature housing and labor market, the market mechanism has played an role in shaping housing consumption and housing stratification. With newly granted freedom of housing choice and residential mobility, households with financial means, the number of whom is increasing by leaps and bounds in line with China's almost incessant double-digit growth over the past thirty years, are able to move up the housing ladder, socially and spatially. For China's rapidly expanding middle class of professional and managerial workers and *nouveaux riches* of entrepreneurs and politically connected individuals, ownership in the commodity housing sector is now the norm. On the supply side, the real estate industry was identified as an economic pillar by the central government in conjunction with the 1998 housing reform (Li, 2005). At the municipal level the local government, developers and financial institutions have constituted a strong growth coalition, tapping the immense rent gaps between the rising market land price and the cost of land requisition both for central-city "brownfield sites" and for agricultural lands on the urban fringe (Li, 2005; Lin, 2007). For more than two decades cities in China have practically been huge construction sites. The largest metropolises in particular are expanding both horizontally and vertically at miraculous pace. Urban sprawl characterized by never-ending freeways and auto-based commuting for the first time has become seemingly unstoppable in China today.

There is evidence that the newly formed homeowners class is becoming increasingly more vocal and willing to act collectively to protect its property rights and economic interests (Davis, 2007; Davis and Lu, 2003; Pow, 2010; Tomba, 2005;

Read, 2008). There is also a strong desire among homeowners to distinguish themselves from others through housing consumption and lifestyle, including the quest for privacy and escape from state surveillance (Tomba, 2004; Read, 2008; Zhang, 2010; Pow, 2009). Homeownership is a vehicle toward "paradise" and "good life." At the same time, however, the state has tried to re-assert its control over society in the context of continual disintegration of work-unit compounds and growing awareness of citizenship; the latter is facilitated by the formation of online communities. Grassroots representation of the Party-State including the street (sub-district) office and residents' or neighborhood committees has been empowered to oversee neighborhood and sub-district level social services delivery and to organize community-based activities. In suburban housing estates as well as redeveloped inner-city apartment complexes a new form of sometimes uneasy local governance consisting of the property management company, often a subsidiary of the developer, the homeowners' association, and the residents' committee and street committee has emerged.

## Major policy concerns

The unprecedented housing inequality discussed above has become a major source of social discontent and political instability in China. For this, recently the central government has revived its commitment to low-income housing, and set ambitious targets for, and pumped billions of RMB into, low-income housing development (Huang, 2012). For example, the government added 5.8 million new units in 2010, and aimed to add another 36 million units of new affordable housing over the period of 2011–2015. Yet, local governments are much less committed to building affordable housing due to emphasis on economic goals. Moreover, affordable housing is off limit to migrants without the local *hukou*. Leaving out such a large segment of the poor clearly defies the ultimate purpose of low-income housing policy – social justice. With about one-third of urban residents being migrants without legal resident rights such as access to subsidized housing, arguably urbanization in China is far from "complete." Premier Li Keqiang recently proposed to accelerate urbanization to drive economic growth, and it is expected that another 300–400 million migrants will flock to Chinese cities in the next fifteen years. Such a huge population without access to decent housing will be an immense de-stabilizing force. It is imperative that the government has to gradually lift the institutionalized housing discrimination and incorporate migrants into its low-income housing system. After benefiting from cheap migrant labor for decades, it is time for the government to shoulder some housing responsibility for them. In addition to directly providing low-income housing to poor migrants, the government should actively involve the private sector to expand affordable housing provision.

In comparison with the owned sector, the formal rental housing market is very much underdeveloped in China. Institutional infrastructures protecting the right of both the landlord and the tenant are grossly inadequate. Moreover, with high profit margins, developers have focused on upscale housing for sale. The very limited rental housing provided by developers is often high-end serviced apartments for the elite. There is a need for the government to further develop the legal and other institutional frameworks to help expand the rental sector. The government recently required developers to provide low-income housing in proportion in some of their private housing development – so-called *"pei tao jian she"* (or inclusionary housing) (State Council, 2007). While encouraging, its impact has so far been minimal. Policy incentives such as tax breaks, low-interest loans, and cheaper land should be given to encourage developers to provide low-end rental housing for the urban poor and migrants. In addition, the government should formalize the housing provision by rural collectives and suburban villagers and encourage them to provide decent affordable housing. "Urban villages" have been a major provider of low-end rental housing to the urban poor and migrants. Yet with the constant threat of being demolished by the local government for land, villagers are often unwilling to invest heavily to improve housing conditions and neighborhood infrastructure. Reforms are needed for the collectively owned land in "urban villages" to protect villagers' land tenure and motivate them to provide more decent and affordable housing

Favoritism, nepotism and discriminatory practice underpin China's market transition and permeate China's nascent urban housing market, other than *hukou*-related matters. The market-oriented reform in fact has substantially enhanced the power-based allocation of housing that characterized the former socialist redistributive economy. More specifically, the immense transfer of wealth in association with the privatization of former public housing invariably favored the elites. Moreover, irrespective of the formal proclamation of ending the welfare allocation of housing in 1998, many of those holding political power and working in resource-rich state-owned enterprises continue to be offered favorable housing deals such as price discounts as well as information on highly sensitive matters such as proximity to planned subway lines and refuse dumps. Many continue to receive large housing subsidies. Such institutionalized privileges that the elites enjoy not only are unnecessary but also breed corruption and should be abolished. What is really needed is a need-based housing subsidy allocation system so that the urban poor, with and without the local urban *hukou*, are entitled to decent and affordable housing.

The concern for favoritism, nepotism and discriminatory practice goes much deeper than the persistence of housing inequality under the former socialist redistributive economy. More specifically, there has been prevalent and irregular transfer of wealth from the state to private hands. Similar to what happened in other former socialist economies, large numbers of China's *nouveaux riches* have accumulated their wealth by exploiting policy loopholes and taking advantage of *guanxi* networks with government agencies and major state-owned-enterprises so as to acquire sensitive information and secure highly profitable business deals. The immense wealth, often accumulated through not-so-legitimate means, enables and encourages conspicuous consumption of luxurious goods, including luxurious housing. Today, all of the world's major designer brands are eyeing on this rapidly expanding market. Even though the size of the capitalist class may be small, their chase for super-deluxe housing and purchase of housing for speculative gains are likely to have diverted developers' attention from producing housing for the mass. Contributing to such distortion in housing demand is China's rather irregular and rudimentary taxation system. For example, while the government has recently raised the taxes and fees for housing transactions in order to cool down the property market, to date there is no property tax in China. This encourages the owning of multiple homes mainly for speculative purpose by the super-rich, as it does not cost much to maintain them once these homes are purchased while the housing price has been skyrocketing.

The percentage of owning multiple homes in Chinese cities is higher than that in many developed countries (Huang and Yi, 2011). It is not uncommon for the rich to leave multiple apartments unoccupied, a clear waste of scarce housing resource; at the same time large numbers of urban poor have to stay in make-shift structures in construction sites or share a room in dilapidated tenement flats or endure health, fire and crime hazards in substandard urban village housing. Recently, the Chinese government has introduced financial tools such as a higher down payment and a higher mortgage interest rate for the purchase of second and multiple homes in order to curtail housing speculation (Central Bank of China, 2007). So far, however, the policy has not been very successful, as the new rich who are well connected to local governments and banking institutions often can circumvent the use of mortgage loans and yet raise enough cash to purchase housing properties. The government should consider alternative policies such as the introduction of property tax and taxation on vacant housing properties to avoid wastage and the concentration of precious housing resources into the hands of a few. Introducing the property tax has the added advantage of alleviating municipal governments' heavy reliance on land leasing revenues; the latter is arguably the main consideration behind forced land requisition of both brownfield and greenfield sites, and residential relocation upon wholesale redevelopment of inner-city neighborhoods.

## Chapter highlights

The twelve chapters, which are divided into four parts, try to further tackle, from a variety of angles and disciplinary vantages, the extent and nature of housing inequality and housing stratification in urban China today.

Part I provides an overall account of the degree of housing inequality and the extent of residential differentiation in Chinese cities. First, Si-ming Li and Huimin Du, based on household surveys conducted in Guangzhou, estimate the Gini coefficient and the Theil Entropy Index of housing consumption. The result reveals worsening housing inequality in the latter part of the first decade of the twenty-first century; further, in an increasingly marketized setting, household income has become the most important variable explaining variations in housing consumption. However, institutional variables pertaining to the former socialist planned economy, particularly *hukou* status, continue to act as major discriminatory factors structuring individual households' access to housing.

Next, Youqin Huang, Chengdong Yi, Yunyan Yang and Xiong He study the case of Wuhan and find significant inequalities in housing consumption and housing access between population groups defined by mobility and *hukou* status. Furthermore, there is a moderate degree of residential segregation and isolation between these population groups. A dual mechanism in which both market forces and socialist legacy is at work.

The nature of residential differentiation in urban China is further analyzed by Brenda Madrazo Gonzalez' chapter. Employing survey data gathered in Nanjing, Gonzalez identifies four different types of neighborhoods, namely, traditional, work-unit, commercial and urban village. Each is characterized by a distinctive spatial structure, built environment and change in socioeconomic composition. Yet, inequality within a given type is high, and could even be higher than inequality between neighborhood types.

Part II focuses on housing for the urban poor, especially housing for migrants from the rural areas. Ya Ping Wang, Huimin Du and Si-ming Li situate the Chinese case by reference to the debate on formal versus informal housing, both in developing countries and in advanced industrialized nations. They argue that the formation and evolution of informal housing in China, particularly in urban villages, is a highly intricate and dynamic process, and has played an important part in China's phenomenal urban transformation. Extreme care should be exercised in any attempts to restructure and integrate such housing to the formal housing provision system.

The issue of formal versus informal housing is further taken up by Zhilin Liu and Yujun Wang, who examine migrants' sense of attachment to the city of current domicile. Their analysis reveals that migrants who are able to get access to formal housing tend to be more attached to the destination city and are likely to express settlement intention, after controlling for socio-demographic attributes, migration experience and variables gauging social interaction.

Compared to migrants, the urban poor with local registration are qualified for housing subsidies from the local government. Yet, the lack of affordable housing and housing poverty remain acute among the urban poor after decades of housing marketization and privatization. Chengdong Yi and Youqin Huang evaluate the effectiveness, efficiency and equity of the Cheap Rental Housing system in Beijing. Despite significant improvement in recent years, they argue that the system of CRH lacks effectiveness, demonstrated by its extremely low coverage. The goal of providing housing subsidies to all needy households has not been achieved yet in Beijing. In contrast, efficiency and equity seems to be less problematic in CRH, with the majority of subsidies provided through monetary "rent subsidies" and the policy design embodying both vertical and horizontal equity although not always the case in implementation.

Contrasting the above, Part III turns its attention to China's rapidly expanding middle class and the rich. The architectural supremacy and aristocracy implied by naming luxurious gated communities as châteaux, which have become very popular in China, intrigues Guillaume Giroir. He points out that while this growing feudalism is apparently at odds with a still communist China, the Chinese Communist Party being a Chinese cultural product is characterized by a power structure not dissimilar to that of Imperial China. But obviously this conspicuous spatial expression of the super-rich exacerbates the feeling of injustice among those who have to struggle with their daily existence.

The bulk of commodity housing development subsequent to the 1998 housing reform is not for the super-rich but for China's growing middle class of young and highly educated professional and managerial workers. Yu-ling Song alerts us to the danger of stigmatizing the urban middle class as a homogeneous group. There is obvious inequality between individuals within this class, especially in respect to how they accumulate wealth through home purchase. Yet, apparently all bear the same stigma under the "social justice" principle and are given the same social responsibility, which render many of them feel uneasy.

Quite expectedly, the urban middle class is also characterized by their knowledge and possession of state-of-the-art information technology. As far back as the late 1990s and early 2000s the young middle class were actively involved in virtual communities of various kinds. Limei Li and Si-ming Li study how private home-ownership paves the way for the development of neighborhood-based online forums, which serve a variety of functions, not the least the defense against encroachment of legitimate property rights by estate management firms and local governments.

Part IV studies the issue of governance in China's commodified residential neighborhoods in greater detail, focusing on the role of homeowners' associations. First, Qiang Fu details the establishment, development and conflicts of homeowners' associations in Chinese cities. Fu points out that an essential mechanism for building civil society is the formation of network relations between civic organizations and other parties. However, there is a mismatch between homeowners' associations in China and the standard of civil society as it is generally understood in the West. This calls for a re-orientation of neighborhood relations in urban China.

Next, Xiaoyi Sun and Ngai Ming Nip study how, in the case of Shanghai, the municipal government has provided incentives to strengthen the role of residents' committees, a constituent component of the Party-State at the neighborhood level, in urban China's increasingly privatized urban space, particularly in up-market gated commodity housing estates.

Finally, Lili Wang, based on extensive studies of online news reports and published works, provides a historical account of the conflicts around living space in urban China, and tries to contextualize such conflicts in respect to the commodification of land and housing as well as community maintenance, the transformation of community governance, and the establishment of property ownership.

## References

Bian, Y. and Liu, Y. (2005) Social stratification, housing property rights and housing satisfaction (Shehui fenceng, zhufang chanquan he juzhu zhiliang). *Sociological Research (Shehuixue Yanjiu)*, 3, 82–98.

Bian, Y. and Logan, J. R. (1996) Market transition and the persistence of power: the changing stratification system in urban China. *American Sociological Review*, 739–58.

Central Bank of China (2007) A notice about strengthening mortgage management for commercial real estate (Guangyu jiaqiang shangye xing fangdichan xingdai guanli de tongzhi).

Davis, D. S. (2007) Chinese homeowners as citizen-consumers. *Consumer Culture and its Discontents*.

Davis, D. S. and Lu, H. (2003) Property in transition: Conflicts over ownership in post-socialist Shanghai. *European Journal of Sociology*, 44, 77–99.

Du, H. and Li, S.-M. (2010) Migrants, urban villages, and community sentiments: a case of Guangzhou, China. *Asian Geographer*, 27, 93–108.

Economist Intelligence Unit (2011) Building Rome in a day: the sustainability of China's housing boom. Available from www.eiu.com (accessed 30 January, 2014).

Giroir, G. (2006) The Fontainebleau villas (Shanghai), as globalized golden ghetto in a Chinese garden. In Wu, F. (ed.) *Globalization and the Chinese City*. London/New York: Routledge Curzon.

Harloe, M. (1977) *Captive Cities: studies in the political economy of cities and regions*. London: John Wiley & Sons.

Harvey, D. (2005) *A Brief History of Neoliberalism*. Oxford: Oxford University Press.

He, S. (2010) New-build gentrification in Central Shanghai: demographic changes and socioeconomic implications. *Population, Space and Place*, 16, 345–61.

He, S. (2013) Evolving enclave urbanism in China and its socio-spatial implications: the case of Guangzhou. *Social & Cultural Geography*, 14(3): 243–75.

Huang, Y. (2003) Renters' housing behaviour in transitional urban China. *Housing Studies*, 18, 103–26.

Huang, Y. (2005) From work-unit compounds to gated communities: housing inequality and residential segregation in transitional Beijing. In Ma, L. J. C. and Wu, F. (eds) *Restructuring the Chinese City: changing society, economy and space*. London and New York: Routledge.

Huang, Y. (2006) Collectivism, political control, and gating in Chinese cities. *Urban Geography*, 27, 507–25.

Huang, Y. (2012) Low-income housing in Chinese cities: policies and practices. *The China Quarterly*, 212, 941–64.

Huang, Y. and Clark, W. A. (2002) Housing tenure choice in transitional urban China: a multilevel analysis. *Urban Studies*, 39, 7–32.

Huang, Y. and Jiang, L. (2009) Housing inequality in transitional Beijing. *International Journal of Urban and Regional Research*, 33, 936–56.

Huang, Y. and Yi, C. (2010) Consumption and tenure choice of multiple homes in transitional urban China. *European Journal of Housing Policy*, 10, 105–31.

Huang, Y. and Yi, C. (2011) Second home ownership in transitional urban China. *Housing Studies*, 26, 423–47.

Huang, Y. and Yi, C. (2013) An Invisible Slum: The Production of an Underground City in Beijing. *Manuscript*. Not yet published.

Li, L. and Li, S.-M. (2010) The impact of variations in urban registration within cities. *One Country, Two Societies: Rural–Urban Inequality in Contemporary China*. Cambridge, MA: Harvard University Press, 188–215.

Li, Q. (2009) Housing status groups in transitional Chinese cities (Zhuanxin shiqi chengshi zhufang diwei qunti). *Jiangsu Social Science (Jiangsu shehui kexue)*, 4(1): 42–53.

Li, S.-M. (2000a) Housing consumption in urban China: a comparative study of Beijing and Guangzhou. *Environment and Planning A*, 32, 1115–34.

Li, S.-M. (2000b) The housing market and tenure decisions in Chinese cities: a multivariate analysis of the case of Guangzhou. *Housing Studies*, 15, 213–36.

Li, S.-M. (2005) China's changing urban geography: a review of major forces at work. *Issues & Studies*, 41, 67–106.

Li, S.-M. (2012) Housing inequalities under market deepening: the case of Guangzhou, China. *Environment and Planning A*, 44 (12), 2852–866.

Li, S.-M. and Li, L. (2006) Life course and housing tenure change in urban China: a study of Guangzhou. *Housing Studies*, 21, 653–70.

Li, S.-M. and Yi, Z. (2007a) Financing home purchase in China, with special reference to Guangzhou. *Housing Studies*, 22, 409–25.

Li, S.-M. and Yi, Z. (2007b) The road to homeownership under market transition Beijing, 1980–2001. *Urban Affairs Review*, 42, 342–68.

Lin, G. C. (2007) Chinese urbanism in question: state, society, and the reproduction of urban spaces. *Urban Geography*, 28, 7–29.

Liu, Z. and Dai, J. (2005) Living resources and social stratification – a study on social stratification in central Chinese cities (Shenhuo ziyuan yu shehui fengceng – yixiang dui zhongguo zhongbu chengshi de shehui fengceng yanjiu). *Jiangsu Social Sciences (Jiangsu Shehui Kexue)*, 1, 133–8.

Liu, Z. and Hu, R. (2010) Urban housing stratification: analysis based on 2006 CGSS (Chengshi zhufang de jianceng fenghu: jiyu CSSS 2006 diaocha shuju de fengxi). *Society (She hui)*, 30(5): 164–92.

Liu, Z. and Mao, X. (2012) Housing stratification in urban China: a case study based on a 1000-household survey in Guangzhou in 2010 (Zhongguo chengshi zhufang fengceng: jiyu 2010 nian Guangzhoushi qianhu wenquan diaocha). *China Social Sciences (Zhongguo shehui kexue)*, 2, 94–112.

Logan, J. R., Bian, Y. and Bian, F. (1999) Housing inequality in urban China in the 1990s. *International Journal of Urban and Regional Research*, 23, 7–25.

Loagn, J. R., Fang, Y. and Zhang, Z. (2010) The winners in China's urban housing reform. *Housing Studies*, 25, 101–17.

Ma, L. J. (1979) The Chinese approach to city planning: policy, administration, and action. *Asian Survey*, 19(9): 838–55.

Ma, L. J. and Xiang, B. (1998) Native place, migration and the emergence of peasant enclaves in Beijing. *China Quarterly-London*, 155, September issue 546–81.

Man, J. Y., Zheng, S. and Ren, R. (2011) Housing policy and housing markets: trends, patterns and affordability. In Man, J. Y. (ed.) *China's Housing Reform and Outcomes*. Cambridge: MA: Lincoln Institute of Land Policy.

Nee, V. (1989) A theory of market transition: from redistribution to markets in state socialism. *American Sociological Review*, 54(5): 663–81.

Pahl, R. E. (1969) Urban social theory and research. *Environment and Planning*, 1, 143–53.

Pow, C.-P. (2009) *Gated Communities in China: the politics of the good life*. London/New York: Routledge.

Pow, C.-P. (2010) Special entitlement: "gated communities" and the emerging middle-class in Shanghai (Tequan jingguan: Shanghai de xinxing Zhongchanjieji). In Su, Y., Feng, S. and Han, C. (eds) *Social Classes in Transitional China (Zhongguo shehui zhuanxing zhongde jieji)*. Beijing: Social Sciences Academic Press (China).

Read, B. L. (2008) Property rights and homeowner activism in new neighborhoods. In Li, Z. and Aihwa, O. (eds) *Privatizing China: socialism from afar*. Ithaca, NY: Cornell University Press.

Rex, J. and Moore, R. (1967) *Race, Community and Conflict*. Oxford: Oxford University Press.

Rona-Tas, A. (1994) The first shall be last? Entrepreneurship and communist cadres in the transition from socialism. *American Journal of Sociology*, 100(1): 40–69.

Sato, H. (2006) Housing inequality and housing poverty in urban China in the late 1990s. *China Economic Review*, 17, 37–50.

Solinger, D. J. (1999) *Contesting Citizenship in Urban China: peasant migrants, the state, and the logic of the market.* Berkeley, CA: University of California Press.

State Council (1998) Guowuyuan guanyu jingyibu shenhua chengzhen zhufang zhidu gaige jiakuai zhufang jianshe de tongzhi (A Notification from the State Council on Further Deepening the Reform of Urban Housing System and Accelerating Housing Construction). Beijing.

State Council (2003) Guowuyuan guanyu cujin fangdichan shichang chixu jiankang fazhan de tongzhi (Notice from State Council about Promoting the Continuously Healthy Development of Real Estate Market). Beijing.

State Council (2007) Guowuyuan guanyu jianjiu dishouru jiating zhufang wennan de ruogan yijian (Several Suggestions from State Council About Solving Housing Problems for Low-income Households). Beijing.

Szelenyi, I. (1978) Social inequalities in state socialist redistributive economies. *International Journal of Comparative Sociology*, 19, 63–87.

Szelenyi, I. (1983) *Urban Inequalities under State Socialism*. Oxford: Oxford University Press.

Tomba, L. (2004) Creating an urban middle class: social engineering in Beijing. *The China Journal*, 1–26.

Tomba, L. (2005) Residential space and collective interest formation in Beijing's housing disputes. *The China Quarterly*, 184, 934–51.

Wang, Y. P. (2005) Low-income communities and urban poverty in China. *Urban Geography*, 26, 222–42.

Wang, Y. P. and Murie, A. (2000) Social and spatial implications of housing reform in China. *International Journal of Urban and Regional Research*, 24, 397–417.

Wang, Y. P., Wang, Y. and Bramley, G. (2005) Chinese housing reform in state-owned enterprises and its impacts on different social groups. *Urban Studies*, 42, 1859–78.

Wang, Y. P., Wang, Y. and Wu, J. (2010) Housing migrant workers in rapidly urbanizing regions: a study of the Chinese model in Shenzhen. *Housing Studies*, 25, 83–100.

Wu, F. (2005) Rediscovering the 'gate' under market transition: from work-unit compounds to commodity housing enclaves. *Housing Studies*, 20, 235–54.

Wu, W. (2002) Migrant housing in urban China: choices and constraints. *Urban Affairs Review*, 38, 90–119.

Wu, W. (2004) Sources of migrant housing disadvantage in urban China. *Environment and Planning A*, 36, 1285–304.

Yi, C. and Huang, Y. (2012) Housing Consumption and Housing Inequality in Chinese Cities during the First Decade of the 21st Century. *Manuscript*.

Zhang, J. (2009) A study on housing stratification among young employees in Lanzhou City (Lanzhoushi chengshi qingnian zhigong zhufang fengceng zhuangkuang yanjiu). *China Youth Studies (Zhongguo qingnian yaniu)*, 7, 64–7.

Zhang, L. (2010) *In Search of Paradise: middle-class living in a Chinese metropolis*. JSTOR, Cornell University Press.

Zhou, M. and Logan, J. R. (1996) Market transition and the commodification of housing in urban China. *International Journal of Urban and Regional Research*, 20, 400–21.

# 2 Residential change and housing inequality in urban China in the early twenty-first century

## Analysis of Guangzhou survey data[1]

### Si-ming Li[2] and Huimin Du[3]

## I. Introduction

The turn of the century witnessed fundamental changes in the way urban housing in China was produced and allocated. In order to minimize the impacts of the Asian Financial Crisis of 1997–98, the Chinese government under Premier Zhu Rongji identified real estate development and auto production as two economic growth engines or driving forces because of their extensive multiplier effects (Li, 2005). Concomitantly, Zhu pronounced to end the welfare allocation of housing, under which state work units had acted as the main provider of urban housing since the founding of the People's Republic (Li and Yi, 2007a). From then onwards, the great majority of urban households have had to rely on the market for housing access (Li and Yi, 2007a).

These policy initiatives have proved exceedingly successful. Investments in urban real estates have since increased by leaps and bounds. Sprawling gated commodity housing estates proliferate not only in suburban areas, rapidly engulfing valuable farmlands, but also in the inner-city core and former work-unit compounds in association with urban redevelopment projects of unprecedented scales. At the same time, auto production and sales have also experienced phenomenal growth. In 2009, China overtook the United States to be the world's number one nation in car production and sales (Li, 2009). Today, along with a spacious home in a well-managed housing estate, the private car is among the most sought-after consumption items for China's rapidly expanding urban middle class and *nouveaux riches*. Of course, car ownership further fuels suburbanization and urban sprawl, besides aggravating the chronic congestion and severe air pollution that are plaguing all major cities in the country these days.

In the early days of the reform, irrespective of the rhetoric of privatization and commodification, the role of state work units in urban housing provision in fact expanded, and housing continued to be allocated to the workers according to established guidelines, such as occupational rank and seniority in the workplace as well as the position of the work unit in the state administration hierarchy (Wu, 1996; Li, 2000). With the gradual implementation of the 1998 reform, the last two years of the twentieth century saw massive disposal of work-unit housing and housing managed by the municipal housing bureau to sitting tenants via heavily discounted sales. Variously, such housing is known as *fanggaifang* or reform housing. In the early 2000s these housing units were allowed to enter the market, without the need to pay the concerned work units the difference between the discounted and market price. Clearly, a major result of the 1998 housing reform was the conferment of windfall profits to those who already received housing benefits and the perpetuation of established patterns of housing inequalities characterizing the pre-reform and early-reform periods.

At the same time, China's accession to the World Trade Organization (WTO) in 2001 accelerated the transition to a market economy. Associated with market deepening is widening income spreads and wealth re-alignment, both of which have profound implications for housing consumption and residential differentiation. The world's largest transnational corporations (TNCs) have since flocked to the Middle Kingdom, both for establishing production bases and for penetrating into China's vast and rapidly growing domestic market. Under the policy of "to become large and strong" so as to better withstand the encroachment of TNCs from the outside, large numbers of China's state-owned enterprises, which are listed on the stock exchange of Hong Kong, Shanghai and New York, have also been transformed into transnational corporations, with the implied substantially enlarged spreads in remuneration packages.

Local governments in China have played a pivotal role in fostering China's economic miracle. The quest for world city status by municipal governments throughout the country via massive investments in urban infrastructures and generous incentives offered to local and foreign investors (Wu, 2000), in particular, has provided further impetus to polarized urban and economic growth. Irrespective of the continual dominance of the (Chinese Communist) Party-State and the persistence of labor and housing market segmentation in association with the discriminatory household registration or *hukou* system, elements of neoliberalism permeate the Chinese political economy and society.

While factors affecting housing inequalities under the former socialist planned economy were in a sense fossilized with the discounted sale of work-unit housing, new entrants to the housing market, particularly the young households who have to satisfy their housing needs and aspirations in the private market, are subject to very much the same kinds of income and wealth constraints prevailing in most market economies. Surely they are presented with much larger choice sets. However, unlike their parents who were entitled to housing benefits and who were conferred homeownership under the housing reform, for the younger generations homeownership attainment and living in a decent home is tied to the ability to earn high incomes and accumulate substantial wealth. The latter factors also determine to a significant extent access to mortgage loans. Of course, in a society where family values are sacrosanct, parental contributions could be of great importance (Li and Yi, 2007b; Li, 2010). This further complicates the housing consumption scene in Chinese cities.

In socialist redistributive economies where monetary income shows little variation, housing inequality is arguably the most important manifestation of social and economic inequality (Szelenyi, 1978). But at least cadres and workers live in the same work-unit compound and at times even in the same apartment block. However, in market economies residential differentiation and segregation with contrasting built environments between high- and low-status social areas is more or less the norm. In the case of China, market or income- and wealth-based housing inequalities are built upon inequalities arising from differential access to political and economic resources between cadres and ordinary workers under the former socialist redistributive economies. This renders the issue of housing inequalities highly complicated and a major source of social discontent.

For this the Chinese government has over the past few years introduced a series of measures to cool down the property market, including restricting the purchase of second homes; in some cities the local authorities forbid people without the proper residential status to buy homes within their jurisdictions. In addition, after almost thirty years of privatization and commodification rhetoric, provision of social or public housing once again tops the policy agenda. A prerequisite to appropriate policy formulation is a firm grasp of the real situations. Yet, the great majority of studies on housing access and inequality in Chinese cities, such as Logan *et al.* (1999), Logan and Fang (2010), and Li (2000), are based on data generated before the full implementation of the 1998 housing reform. To our knowledge, the only statistical work gauging China's housing inequality in what can be termed the full marketization stage of the housing reform is Li (2012). This study shows that in Guangzhou there was only modest increase in housing inequality up till 2005. However, arguably at that time the full implications of the 1998 reform still had to be revealed. A more updated analysis is therefore useful.

To do this, in this chapter we employ survey data collected in Guangzhou in 2010 to examine changes that had taken place in the first decade of the twenty-first century. In the next section we describe the dataset and outline the analytical procedures employed in measuring household consumption of individual households as observed in the 2010 Guangzhou survey; the latter involves the estimation of a hedonic price equation. Based on these measures we then compute two commonly employed inequality measures, namely, the Gini Coefficient and Theil Entropy Index. Section III provides key statistics on the attributes of the sampled housing units. Also, the resultant hedonic price regression is presented and discussed. Section IV reports the findings of inequality measures computation, as well as that of a regression analysis trying to identify the major factors underlying variations in housing consumption and hence housing inequality in Guangzhou at the time of survey. Section V concludes the paper.

## II. Data and methodology

### Data

The 2010 Guangzhou survey, which was undertaken in the latter part of the year, aimed to represent all households of the city living in permanent residential structures. The survey covers the original eight urban districts of the city prior to the redrawing of district boundaries in 2005, plus the newly incorporated district of

Luogang in the east and the northern part of Panyu District in the south, where massive real estate developments have taken place in recent years (see Figure 2.1).

The survey was targeted at the head of household and conducted through indoor interview. A pilot survey was administered in August 2010 to ascertain the feasibility of the survey and the validity of the questionnaire. In addition to inquiring the socio-demographic attributes of the respondent and the household,

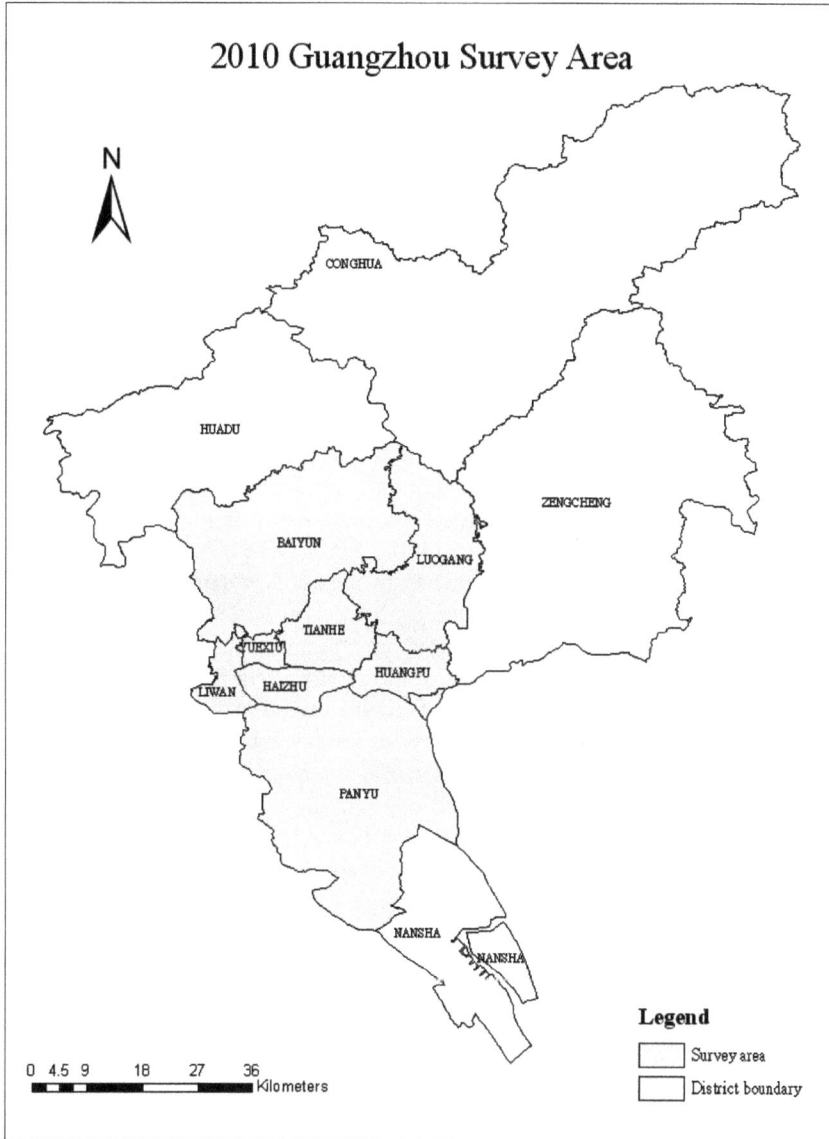

*Figure 2.1* Survey area.

the questionnaire also included a wide range of questions on the respondent's residential and employment characteristics and histories. A multi-stage probability proportion to size (in respect to the number of households) sampling strategy was adopted, with urban districts, *shequ* or communities (formerly known as *jiedao*, which are broadly equivalent to census tracts in American cities), and residents committees or neighborhoods being the three geographical-administrative levels for selecting the sampled housing units, equivalently, households. A total of 1250 households were interviewed.

## Methodology

Housing is a multi-dimensional good, characterized by spatial fixity and a high degree of durability. What is valuable to one household may not be of much use to another. In urban economics theory such as the classic land use models of Alonso (1964), Mills (1972) and Muth (1969), it is often assumed that the amount of housing service yielded by a certain dwelling per unit of time, usually indexed by the letter h, can nonetheless be measured by reference to a single numéraire, even though it is a composite good. In particular, under competitive equilibrium h is proportional to and therefore can be measured at any given point in time by the rent or market price of the dwelling, the latter being the sum of future discounted rental incomes (Olsen, 1987). The market clearing price summarizes how much the occupying household or household at the margin attaches value to the housing unit.

A housing unit is an expensive asset; in premier cities such as Guangzhou and Shanghai a 60 m$^2$ apartment is easily worth more than one million Renminbi or RMB, the Chinese currency, or more (at the current rate of exchange RMB 1 = USD 0.16 approximately). Home purchase involves all kinds of considerations and is often a once-for-life decision. Among these are: whether the housing unit concerned suits the need of the household in respect to location, size and internal design; whether the purchase is made at the right time in respect to home price movement; and whether the household is eligible for mortgage loan and has saved enough for the down-payment. Even renting involves the signing of a binding contract between the landlord and the renter for a rather long period of time. Moreover, moving house, the major form of adjusting housing consumption by a household (Brown and Moore, 1970; Hanushek and Quigley, 1979), is also costly both in monetary and psychological terms. For a given housing unit, transaction in the form of change in ownership or entering a new lease agreement only takes place infrequently. Over the interval between transactions the dwelling experiences ageing; at the same time market conditions and hence the market-clearing price may also experience drastic changes.

All these complicate the use of dwelling price as a measure of housing consumption. In distinction from measuring income and hence income inequality, constructing comprehensive and comparable measures of housing consumption and hence inequality is not a straightforward proposition. In the case of Chinese cities, the construction of housing inequality measures is further complicated by the presence of a plethora of housing tenures as a result of the incremental market reform (Li and Yi, 2007a). These include not only renting and owning in the open market but also various forms of subsidized rental occupancy and ownership. The latter include privatized work-unit housing or reform housing and compensation housing provided by the developer in conjunction with redevelopment projects. In addition, there is housing built by local villagers in villages-in-the-city on (former) city outskirts, which in theory should only be for the villagers' own consumption (Wang *et al.*, 2009).

In this study we follow the procedures outlined in Figure 2.2 to arrive at a set of comparable housing service measures, which are given by the market-equivalent price values for different dwellings. In particular, we first estimate a hedonic price regression; the latter provides the latent market values of individual housing attributes, such as location, size, dwelling age, estate management and neighborhood characteristics (Linneman, 1980; Rosen, 1974). The regression is based only on transactions in the commodity housing or open market sector. Then, the resultant price equation is used to estimate how much each of the dwellings in the sample was worth in the marketplace at the time of survey, regardless of housing tenure. These market-equivalent values form the basis for the computation of the Gini Coefficient and the Theil Entropy Index, the two most commonly employed indices of inequality. Finally, the market-equivalent values of individual dwellings are regressed against a set of household demographic and socio-economic attributes in order to reveal which factors are of importance in governing housing inequality in Guangzhou today.

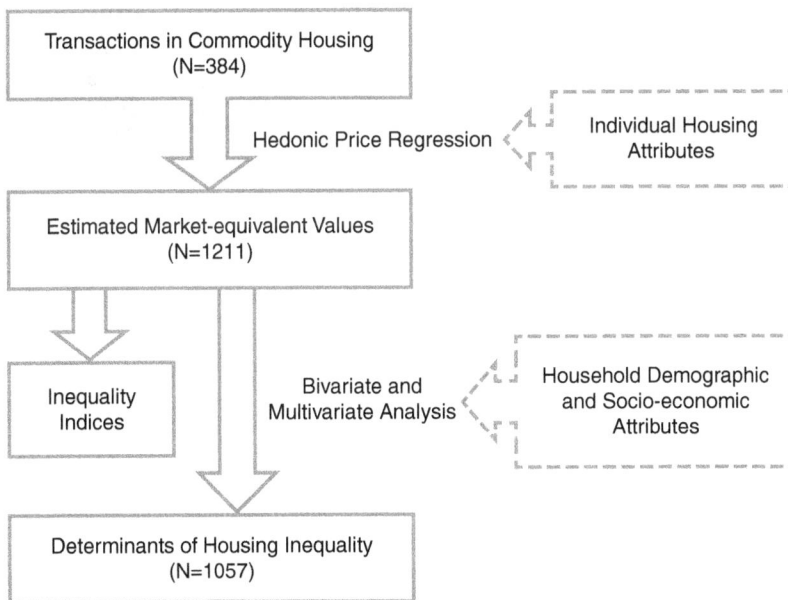

*Figure 2.2* Analytical procedures.

## III.  Sampled housing units and hedonic price regression

### *The sampled housing units*

To provide an overview of the current situation of housing consumption in Guangzhou, summary statistics of selected attributes of the sampled housing units are given in Table 2.1. In order to better understand the nature of housing consumption variations, we also make occasional reference to cross-tabulations, which in the interest of space are not shown in the table.

By design, the location distribution of the housing units in the sample is roughly in proportion to that of the total stock of housing in the city. Reflecting the rapid urban expansion, only 28.1 per cent of the sampled dwellings are found in the old inner-core districts of Yuexiu and Liwan. Cross-tabulation with dwelling age shows that the majority of the sampled housing units in these two districts were built in the 1980s or before – 60.8 per cent for Yuexiu and 58.6 per cent for Liwan. The districts of Haizhu, Tianhe and Panyu, located just outside the old urban core, have been the main foci of commodity housing development since the 1990s. They respectively account for 18.0, 19.8 and 15.9 per cent of the housing units in the sample.

*Table 2.1* Summary statistics

| | Commodity housing | | All housing units | |
|---|---|---|---|---|
| | *Mean* | *Std. deviation* | *Mean* | *Std. deviation* |
| *Floor area* | 91.76 | 28.29 | 71.75 | 43.61 |
| *No. of rooms* | 2.64 | 0.73 | 2.24 | 1.19 |
| *Floor height* | 7.02 | 5.22 | 4.99 | 4.06 |
| *Monthly management fee* | 119.47 | 86.65 | 60.47 | 72.04 |
| *Dwelling price (10,000 RMB)* | 45.59 | 28.14 | 28.66 | 29.68 |
| *Dwelling rent* | 900 | 787 | 731 | 779 |
| | *Percentage* | | *Percentage* | |
| *Location* | | | | |
| Inner core | 13.3 | | 28.0 | |
| Haizhu | 14.0 | | 18.0 | |
| Tianhe | 27.8 | | 19.8 | |
| Baiyun/Huangpu/Luogang | 20.6 | | 19.3 | |
| Panyu | 24.3 | | 15.9 | |
| *Recreation facilities* (1 = present) | 59.1 | | 28.7 | |
| *Lift* (1 = present) | 50.4 | | 23.3 | |
| *First-hand purchase* (1 = yes) | 70.9 | | 79.2 | |
| *Dwelling age* | | | | |
| Built before 1990 | 10.3 | | 37.7 | |
| Built 1990s | 32.3 | | 33.3 | |
| Built 2000s | 57.4 | | 29.0 | |
| *Year of purchase* | | | | |
| Purchased before 2000 | 12.3 | | 32.7 | |
| Purchased 2000–2004 | 42.6 | | 25.4 | |
| Purchased after 2004 | 45.1 | | 41.9 | |

With respect to tenure mix, rented units constitute 41.0 per cent of the sample. Of these units, only 26.4 per cent remain in the traditional public rental sectors, i.e. renting from work units and the municipal housing bureau, whereas 67.7 per cent are rented housing in the private market. In the more outlying districts of Panyu and Luogang, a substantial proportion of private renting involves renting in urban villages. However, even within the old urban core districts of Yuexiu and Liwan, 56.7 per cent and 70.8 per cent, respectively, of the rented units are under private rental occupation. It is likely that many of these dwellings are privatized public housing now rented to migrants and other low-income groups. Cross-tabulation with *hukou* status shows that 37.4 per cent and 29.6 per cent of the respondents in Yuexiu and Liwan, respectively, do not hold the local *hukou*. Evidently, with the great majority of urban housing having been privatized and marketized, urban-bound migrants in Guangzhou have now infiltrated the inner-city core. Increasingly, the spatial demographics in Chinese cities today as exemplified by the filtering process appear to resemble those that took place in cities in the West in the immediate post-war years.

As for the owned units, which account for 59.0 per cent of the sample, slightly more than half (56.3 per cent) are commodity housing. Subsidized ownership, which includes reform housing, compensated housing in relation to redevelopment projects, and economic and comfortable housing, constitutes 16.4 per cent, 8.3 per cent and 6.9 per cent of the owned units, respectively. Reflecting the extensiveness of the village-in-the-city or urban village phenomenon in Guangzhou, 12.1 per cent of owner-occupiers in the sample reside in self-built housing.

In terms of dwelling size, the sample mean floor area is 71.8 m², with a standard deviation of 43.6 m². The corresponding coefficient of variation (CV) is therefore 0.68. Slightly less than one-half of the sampled households live in flats of 45–90 m² in size. But cases on either extreme are also common, with 10.1 per cent residing in flats of less than 30 m² and 12.1 per cent in flats larger than 110 m². As can be expected, a disproportionate number of smaller units (<70 m²) is found in the old urban districts of Yuexiu and Liwan, whereas a disproportionate number of larger units (>70 m²) are located in the more outlying districts.

Living in multi-story apartment building is the norm in Guangzhou. The mean height of buildings reaches 4.99 stories. Yet, residential structures up to nine stories built in the 1980s or before are often not equipped with lifts. Also, while large-scale housing estates with landscaped gardens and sports and other recreational facilities dominate the landscape in suburban areas, stand-alone residential buildings without facilities are common in the inner-city core districts. In the sample, 32.6 per cent belong to the latter category.

The substantial difference in amenities provided within the dwelling as well as in the neighborhood is reflected in the large variations in housing price and rent as well as in the management fee paid. Regarding the former, within the commodity housing sector, the mean price paid by the owner-occupiers is RMB 438,500 with a standard deviation of RMB 288,810, which gives a CV of 0.66. The mean rent of private housing at the time of survey was RMB 900 per month with a standard deviation of RMB 787; thus the corresponding CV is 0.87. Regarding the latter, the mean management fee in the commodity housing sector stands at RMB 117 per month, with a standard deviation of RMB 86. For the rest of the sample, which comprises various forms of subsidized housing, the mean management fee is much lower, at RMB 33, and the standard deviation is RMB 37.

### Hedonic price regression

The house price data reported above refers to the price paid by the occupying household at the time of transaction. To arrive at a set of comparable prices, we estimate how much the dwellings are worth in the marketplace at the time of survey. This is achieved by regressing the reported transaction price in the owned-commodity housing sector against a set of housing and location attributes. A number of specifications have been tried, and the one given in Table 2.2 is adopted for further analysis. In this specification the dependent variable is the logarithm of transacted home price, as reported by the respondent. The set of independent variables consists of the following: location (in relation to the inner-core districts of Yuexiu and Liwan), log floor area, log number of rooms, presence

*Table 2.2* Hedonic price equation based on owned commodity housing transactions

Dependent variable: Log home price (10000RMB)
$R^2 = 0.677$; N = 384

|  | Unstandardized coefficients | Standardized coefficients | t | Sig. |
|---|---|---|---|---|
| (Constant) | −2.218 |  | −4.328 | .000 |
| *Location* (0 = Inner core) |  |  |  |  |
| Haizhu | .188 | .094 | 2.175 | .030 |
| Tianhe | .002 | .001 | .022 | .983 |
| Baiyun/Huangpu/Luogang | .004 | .002 | .050 | .960 |
| Panyu | −.240 | −.153 | −2.747 | .006 |
| *Ln floor area* | 1.149 | .493 | 8.280 | .000 |
| *Ln N rooms* | −.131 | −.056 | −1.078 | .282 |
| *Recreation facilities* (1 = present) | .109 | .079 | 2.014 | .045 |
| *Floor height* (0 = <5) |  |  |  |  |
| Floor 5–9 | −.005 | −.004 | −.099 | .921 |
| Floor 10+ | −.051 | −.023 | −.578 | .564 |
| *Lift* (1 = present) | .063 | .047 | 1.094 | .275 |
| *First-hand purchase* (1 = yes) | −.095 | −.064 | −1.620 | .106 |
| *Dwelling age* (0 = before 1990) |  |  |  |  |
| Built 1990s | .188 | .130 | 2.437 | .015 |
| Built 2000s | .295 | .217 | 3.320 | .001 |
| *Year of purchase* (0 = before 2000) |  |  |  |  |
| Purchased 2000–2004 | .312 | .230 | 3.810 | .000 |
| Purchased 2005+ | .730 | .539 | 8.268 | .000 |
| *Management fee* (0 = <50RMB) |  |  |  |  |
| Fee 50–99 | .062 | .041 | .903 | .367 |
| Fee 100–199 | .182 | .130 | 2.229 | .026 |
| Fee 200+ | .368 | .205 | 3.658 | .000 |

of lift, presence of recreation facilities in the estate, floor height of the dwelling unit, whether the purchase is first-hand, dwelling age, the year in which the purchase took place, and management fee per month. Note that this specification is the same as the one reported in Li (2012), which makes use of survey data collected in 2001 and 2005 in Guangzhou employing almost identical sampling strategies. This enables ready comparison between the present and the Li (2012) study and hence the depiction of trends emerging in the first decade of the twenty-first century.

The regression model, which is given in Table 2.2, yields a rather high $R^2$ of 0.677, based on 384 observations. In general the coefficient estimates, whether in terms of sign or magnitude, appear quite reasonable. First, let us examine location variations in home price. With the massive investments in urban infrastructures, including the extension of the metro rail networks, the construction of new sports facilities in conjunction with the holding of the 2010 Asian Games, and the completion of the new Guangzhou Opera House and the 600-meter Guangzhou TV Tower in Zhujiang New Town of Tianhe District, the relative advantages of individual locations in the city have experienced marked changes. More specifically, the old inner-core districts of Yuexiu and Liwan have experienced relative declines.

This is evident from the hedonic price equation. For example, residential units in Haizhu today command a premium of 19 per cent over the traditional inner-core districts. In recent years Haizhu District, where the prestigious Sun Yat-sen University is located, has experienced major facelifts. Almost all former industrial sites have been redeveloped to pricy commodity housing estates. Apartments on the bank of the Pearl River, in particular, have become some of the most sought-after premises in the city. Also, no discernible differences in home prices are found between Tianhe and the two traditional core districts. The same is observed for the outlying districts of Baiyun, Huangpu and Luogang, although home prices in the suburban Panyu District, which is separated from the core areas of the city by the Pearl River, are lower than those in the old inner-core districts by 24.5 per cent, *ceteris paribus*.

Next, we examine the two variables related to dwelling size, specifically, floor area and number of rooms (both in logarithmic scale). The inclusion of both is to discern effects due to variation in internal design. Perhaps because of collinearity, only the former is significant. The result shows that doubling the floor area results in slightly more than doubling the value of the dwelling; in other words Guangzhou households are willing to pay a premium for larger dwellings.

The regression equation also shows that provision of recreation facilities in the estate or neighborhood adds value to a dwelling; so is the presence of lift service in the residential block. Clearly, both the presence of such facilities implies the need for the payment of higher estate management fees. The regression result also shows that households in Guangzhou are quite receptive to paying higher estate management fees if this means better management and maintenance: the higher the management fee, the higher the home price, other variables being constant.

Li (2012), based on 2001 and 2005 survey data, found that higher floor commands a premium over lower floor. Yet, this relationship is not evident in the present sample. Maybe this is due to the relative lack of sampling variation in this variable – some 90 per cent of the housing units analyzed by the regression model are on the ninth floor or below. Similarly, unlike the findings given by Li (2012), in the 2010 Guangzhou sample first-hand purchase (transaction in the primary market) tends not to command a premium. In fact the coefficient estimate is negative in sign, although statistically insignificant. In China, most homes sold by the developers are not fitted with kitchen or bathroom fixtures; nor are they provided with wooden or tile floors. Maybe as the housing market matures, homebuyers begin to appreciate the added fixtures that homes in the secondary market provide, which easily cost hundreds of thousands of RMB. Of course, more works are needed to ascertain this change in consumer preference.

The findings for dwelling age and the year of purchase are in line with expectation and those reported in Li (2012). Dwellings built in the 2000s are about 11 per cent more expensive than those built in the 1990s, which are in turn more than 19 per cent more expensive than those built even earlier, other things being constant. Also, reflecting the rapid increase in home price in recent years, the findings show on average a person had to pay more than 40 per cent more for purchase made after 2005 than that made a few years earlier for an otherwise identical housing unit.

## IV.  Inequality indices and determinants of housing inequality

### *Inequality indices*

The high $R^2$ and the reasonableness of the coefficient estimates in general give credence to the use of the hedonic price equation given in Table 2.2 in computing the Gini Coefficient and the Theil Entropy Index. The former, being in the 0 (absolute equality) to 1 (absolute inequality) range, is perhaps the most commonly employed inequality index and is readily comparable over time and across different places. On the other hand, the latter is additively decomposable with respect to any socio-economic or demographic categorization of the subjects under investigation (Conceição and Ferreira, 2000). As such, it can be used to analyze the relative contribution of a given socio-economic or demographic variable to the overall inequality of the sample.

The procedure of computing the respective inequality indices is as follows. First, the market-equivalent value of a given dwelling at the time of survey is calculated by inserting the observed values of the individual housing attributes to the regression equation and setting the value for "purchased 2005+" at 1 (i.e. the price of the dwelling if it were to be traded at the time of survey) and "first-hand purchase" at 0 (as the dwelling can now be transacted in the secondary market). The computation procedure is applied to all housing units in the sample, whether they belong to the owned commodity housing category or not. The underlying assumption is that the estimated hedonic price equation describes the relationship between the price and the attributes of all dwelling units in the City of Guangzhou. A total of 1250 market-equivalent home values are thus computed for subsequent analysis.

The Gini Coefficient thus derived is 0.368, and the Theil Entropy Index is 0.226. Li (2012) reports that in Guangzhou the Gini Coefficient for the years 2001 and 2005, which were computed by the same procedures, are 0.321 and 0.332, respectively. Correspondingly, the Theil Entropy Index for 2001 and 2005 given by Li (2012) are 0.167 and 0.177. In other words, the 2010 Gini Coefficient is 10.8 per cent higher than the 2005 one and 14.6 per cent higher than the one in 2001; whereas, the 2010 Theil Entropy Index is 27.7 per cent higher than the 2005 index, and 35.3 per cent higher than the 2001 one.

Both measures point toward the same trend: while the increase in housing inequality in the first five years of the first decade of the twenty-first century was quite modest, the second half of the decade witnessed much greater increases. This finding is in line with the trend of market deepening alongside the staged implementation of the 1998 urban housing reform and China's accession to the WTO in 2001, the full effects of which would not have been felt until the latter part of the decade due to inertia and time lag. Between the two, the Theil Entropy Index indicates a substantially higher rate of increase.

## Determinants of inequality in housing consumption

### Decomposing the Theil Index

The Theil Entropy Index is additive decomposable with respect to any given categorization of the observations into a number of groups. For instance, the Theil Index on housing inequality reported above can be decomposed with respect to tenure status so as to assess how much the overall level of inequality is attributed to the sum of inequalities within each tenure mode and how much is attributed to inequality between tenure modes (Conceição and Ferreira, 2000). In most market economies, ownership generally is associated with higher level of housing consumption. Access to homeownership, in turn, is very much dependent on the household's position in the socio-economic ladder, as gauged by income and wealth, although life-course considerations also contribute significantly to the preference for homeownership (Clark and Dieleman, 1996).

In China, the complex tenure mix which comprises both market and subsidized renting and ownership of various forms is likely to complicate the picture. While ownership of newly built commodity housing, which is usually of better quality, is likely to be income and wealth dependent, ownership of reform housing, a substantial portion of which was commodity housing bought by individual work units, has more to do with a person's position in the administrative and Chinese Communist Party (CCP) hierarchy as well as seniority in the work unit (Li, 2000). Access to economic and comfortable housing, variously termed affordable housing, has been an issue of much debate (Wang, 2011). It was planned to cover the great majority of low- and lower-middle-income households. However, the scale of the program has been too small to achieve this. In fact, in many cities the 2000s witnessed further dwindling of the program. Moreover, affordable housing dwellings tend to be quite large in size and are beyond the means of low- and lower-middle-income households.

The 2010 Guangzhou sample reveals substantial variations in housing consumption both within given tenure modes and between tenure modes. The former contribute 64.5 per cent to the overall Theil Index, whereas the latter 34.5 per cent (see Table 2.3). As can be expected, owned commodity housing has the highest mean market-equivalent price, RMB 570,808. Economic and comfortable housing and self-built housing have quite high mean prices, too, which stand at RMB 466,652 and RMB 473,782, respectively. Reform housing, with a mean price of RMB 297,551, is of relatively poor quality. All forms of rental housing are of poor quality. The mean price for work-unit and housing bureau rental housing units is RMB 254,389 and RMB 240,562, respectively. The lowest mean price – RMB

*Table 2.3* Decomposition of the Theil Index

|  | Entropy index | % contribution | Predicted mean home value [1] |
|---|---|---|---|
| *a. By tenure status* |  |  |  |
| Rent work-unit | 0.194 | 3.80 | 25.44 |
| Rent housing bureau | 0.215 | 2.50 | 24.06 |
| Rent market | 0.218 | 15.11 | 21.64 |
| Rent free | 0.192 | 1.13 | 38.61 |
| Rent compensated | 0.026 | 0.07 | 19.48 |
| Owned commodity | 0.087 | 18.92 | 57.08 |
| Owned reform | 0.060 | 1.98 | 29.76 |
| Owned compensated | 0.133 | 2.85 | 39.41 |
| Economic and comfortable housing | 0.052 | 1.15 | 46.67 |
| Self-built housing | 0.425 | 17.02 | 47.38 |
| Within group |  | 64.51 |  |
| Between group |  | 34.51 |  |
| *b. By occupational group* |  |  |  |
| Senior professional | 0.090 | 1.53 | 63.90 |
| Junior professional | 0.138 | 18.28 | 49.05 |
| Clerk and skilled | 0.163 | 11.79 | 37.12 |
| Manual worker | 0.213 | 11.47 | 26.83 |
| *Geti* (proprietor of small business) | 0.325 | 34.78 | 36.87 |
| Others | 0.140 | 1.74 | 42.41 |
| Within group |  | 79.60 |  |
| Between group |  | 9.97 |  |
| *c. By age group* |  |  |  |
| Young | 0.200 | 31.66 | 35.52 |
| Middle | 0.250 | 57.24 | 40.77 |
| Old | 0.187 | 10.20 | 38.28 |
| Within group |  | 99.11 |  |
| Between group |  | 0.88 |  |
| *d. By* hukou *status* |  |  |  |
| Local | 0.186 | 61.60 | 44.58 |
| Non-local | 0.248 | 27.47 | 27.20 |
| Within group |  | 89.07 |  |
| Between group |  | 10.64 |  |

Note: (1) The unit is 10000 RMB.

194,766 – is that of resettlement housing, which is occupied by those who are affected by demolition. With regard to within mode inequality, among all tenure modes, self-built housing, which can be huge mansions as well as shabby huts, gives the highest within group Theil Index – 0.43 – whereas reform housing and economic and comfortable housing exhibit the smallest within mode inequalities, with the Theil Index standing at 0.06 and 0.05, respectively. Quite surprisingly, renting in both the private market and public sectors yields very similar Theil Index scores, all of which are close to the overall index.

In China, it may be argued that the single most important factor that affects an individual's life chance is *hukou* status (Chan, 2010). Public housing, whether rental or for ownership, is off limits to migrants without the local *hukou*. But even in the open market, home purchase and access to mortgage finance are often conditioned upon the possession of the local *hukou* and a stable and decent job. The latter, again, is *hukou* dependent. In the 2010 Guangzhou sample, households with local *hukou* on average lived in dwellings worth RMB 445,811; however, those without local *hukou* on average lived in dwellings only worth RMB 271,997. The difference between local and non-local *hukou* holders is large. However, inequalities within given *hukou* groups are also substantial. This is especially the case for migrant households, many of whom are in fact quite well off. Decomposing the Theil Index by *hukou* status shows that within group variations contributes to 89.1 per cent of the overall score.

In a market setting, the ability to consume decent housing of course depends to a large extent on the individual's income, which in turn is a function of occupational status. In socialist redistributive economies, monetary income may not be an important factor; occupational status, however, remains important; in fact it directly affects a person's access to scarce resource, including housing (Szelenyi, 1978). In the 2010 Guangzhou sample, high-status cadres and senior professionals enjoyed the highest mean level of housing consumption (RMB 638,969). They are followed by other professional workers (mean = RMB 490,534). Unskilled laborers had the lowest mean consumption level (RMB 268,306). While difference in housing consumption between occupational groups is evident, there exist substantial housing inequalities within given occupational groups, probably reflecting the mixing of hierarchical ordering of jobs according to state and CCP administrative structure, on the one hand, and market considerations, on the other. Decomposing the Theil Index reveals that the latter contribute 79.6 per cent of the overall inequality score.

In Western cities, preference and needs, which are closely related to a person's position in the life course and the stage of the family life cycle, are often more important than affordability in housing consumption decisions (Clark and Dieleman, 1996). However, in Guangzhou today life course as indexed by age of the head of household does not seem to have much influence on the level of housing consumption. A decomposition of the Theil Index by three age groups, young, middle and old, shows that 99.1 per cent of the overall inequality level is due to within group variations. One possible explanation is that parents in China, many of whom have enjoyed subsidized homeownership, are prepared to extend substantial financial support to their grown-up children to assist home purchase (Li and Yi, 2007b). This has accelerated the housing ladder climb for the younger generation.

*Multivariate analysis*

We can continue to decompose the Theil Index exercise with respect to other variables or categorization schemes to further elucidate the nature of housing inequality in Chinese cities. But some of the variables of interest, such as household income and education attainment of the head of household, are closely related to each other and to the variables discussed above, for instance occupational status and *hukou*. Also, while it is possible to add variables in a classification scheme to act as statistical controls, the exercise will become highly cumbersome and data demanding. A more straightforward approach is to regress the computed market-equivalent home values or levels of housing consumption against a set of socio-economic, demographic and institutional variables in order to analyze the factors underlying variations in housing consumption and hence housing inequality. The results are given in Table 2.4.

*Table 2.4* Determinants of housing inequality

Dependent variable: Log market-equivalent home price (10,000RMB)
$R^2 = 0.466$; N = 1057

|  | Unstandardized coefficients | Standardized coefficients | t | Sig. |
|---|---|---|---|---|
| (Constant) | −.542 |  | −1.548 | .122 |
| Ln age of head | .013 | .006 | .182 | .855 |
| Local hukou (1 = yes) | .331 | .212 | 7.516 | .000 |
| Membership in CCP (1 = yes) | .075 | .031 | 1.206 | .228 |
| Ln household size | .199 | .114 | 4.382 | .000 |
| Education (0 = Primary or less) |  |  |  |  |
| Junior secondary | .150 | .089 | 2.250 | .025 |
| Senior secondary | .149 | .092 | 2.163 | .031 |
| College or higher | .326 | .204 | 4.008 | .000 |
| Occupational status (0 = Manual worker) |  |  |  |  |
| Senior professional | .183 | .039 | 1.509 | .132 |
| Junior professional | .060 | .035 | 1.051 | .293 |
| Clerk and skilled | .006 | .003 | .104 | .918 |
| Geti (proprietor of small business) | .141 | .086 | 2.025 | .043 |
| Nature of work unit (0 = Party, government and kindred organizations) |  |  |  |  |
| State enterprise | −.038 | −.020 | −.635 | .525 |
| Private enterprise | .072 | .043 | 1.228 | .220 |
| Foreign enterprise | −.219 | −.049 | −1.936 | .053 |
| Collective | −.021 | −.005 | −.205 | .838 |
| Individual enterprise | −.139 | −.086 | −1.740 | .082 |
| Ln household income | .373 | .410 | 13.613 | .000 |

Previous studies, the great majority of which employed data collected before or just after the 1998 housing reform, generally found that the usual determinants of housing consumption in market economies, including age of the household head and other variables characterizing a person's life course and the family life cycle, and personal and household income, lack statistical significance. Instead, variables gauging the broader political and social settings, such as work-unit characteristics, including the type of industry to which the work unit belongs, rank of the work unit in the state administrative hierarchy, membership in the CCP, and *hukou* status, account for the bulk of variance in urban housing consumption and hence inequality (Li, 2000; Logan *et al.*, 1999; Logan and Fang, 2010; Huang and Jiang, 2009).

The 2010 Guangzhou survey was conducted more than a decade after the pronouncement of the 1998 housing reform, which theoretically ended the welfare allocation of urban housing. It may be expected, then, that life course and income variables would have gained importance. At the same time, however, the selling of work-unit housing to sitting tenants and the irregularities in the sale of economic and comfortable housing tends to perpetuate former patterns of housing inequality. Also, in the sample, renting from work units and the municipal housing bureau still accounts for 10.8 per cent of the observations. Moreover, despite the attempts to reform the household registration or *hukou* system in recent years, *hukou* status continues to be one of the most important discriminatory factors constraining an individual's access to local amenities, including employment opportunities and housing (Li *et al.*, 2010; Chan, 2010). All these suggest that market considerations are not the sole factors underlying housing consumption in this "full marketization stage" of China's housing reform (Li and Yi, 2007a).

The regression analysis yields a reasonably high $R^2$ (0.466) for studies employing micro-level data. Moreover, the parameter estimates are largely in line with the above discussion. After thirty years of market-oriented reform, household income has now become the single most important determining factor of housing consumption according to the beta or standardized coefficient estimate, which is 1.93 times the beta of the next most important variable, *hukou* status. The implied income elasticity of demand for housing service is 0.37. Considering that the income variable used is current rather than permanent income or income in the absence of stochastic variation, the income elasticity estimate obtained is not much lower than those reported for Western cities, which are in the region of 0.6–0.8 (Olsen, 1987).

As for *hukou* status, the result shows that availability of local *hukou* is associated with average housing consumption 33.1 per cent higher than that of households without local *hukou*, other variables being constant. The third most important variable according to the beta estimate is household size, which is related to the family life cycle. However, the magnitude of influence is quite modest. Doubling the size of household is associated only with 19.9 per cent increase in the level of housing consumption, suggesting the controlling effect of income. In line with the result of the bivariate analysis discussed above, age of the household head is not significant.

Education attainment, which underlies a person's position in the job hierarchy as well as preference formation, is of major significance, even after controlling for the income variable. Individuals with college or above education consume, on average, 32.6 per cent more housing than people with primary or less education, other variables being constant. The bivariate analysis reported earlier shows substantial differences in housing consumption between occupational groups. However, probably because of the close relationship between education and occupational status, the latter variable is not significant. Likely because of the same reason, CCP membership, which is closely related to education and occupational status, is not significant either. Nature of work unit, i.e. whether the work unit is a private or state-owned enterprise or a government and related organization, also fails to show statistical significance, after controlling for income, education, *hukou* status and other variables.

These findings clearly point towards an obvious conclusion. In a system of housing provision primarily based on market forces, household income or affordability has become the single most important factor determining the level of housing consumption in Chinese cities. As such, the causes of income inequality are also the most important causes underlying housing inequality in urban China today. While this is not dissimilar from the situation in market economies in the West, in China income and by implication also *hukou* and occupational status are intricately tied to the complex political and social networks of power relationships and resource controls in the Chinese state (Khan and Riskin, 2001). Given that such networks and relationships are deeply rooted in the country's political economy and can hardly be altered in any fundamental way, at least in the near future, the recent re-emphasis on social housing so that the link between income and housing consumption can be weakened is a sensible policy to address housing inequality.

## V.  Summary and conclusion

Based on a household survey conducted in 2010 and using the method of hedonic price regression, market-equivalent housing consumption is derived for all 1250 housing units in the sample. This is used to compute the Gini Coefficient and Theil Entropy Index, two most commonly employed measures of inequality. The results are compared with those of a previous study (Li, 2012). An accelerated increase in housing inequality in Guangzhou since 2005 is revealed. Both bivariate analysis by way of Theil Index decomposition and multivariate analysis of the housing consumption data derived from the hedonic price regression show that the most important factors underlying housing inequality today are household income, *hukou* status and household size. In this sense, the nature of housing inequality in China becomes increasingly akin to that in most market economies. The regression result also reveals the lack of significance for work-unit related variables such as occupational rank and nature of work unit, and also membership in the CCP, after controlling for income, *hukou* status and household size. This notwithstanding, one cannot jump to conclusion that factors governing housing inequality in the former socialist political economy are no longer relevant. It may very well be the case that the effects of above-cited factors today are manifested primarily through their effects on the income variable.

# Notes

1 The authors would like to thank Professor Wangbao Liu of South China Normal University for helping with the Guangzhou 2010 survey, which provides the main corpus of data for the present study. Financial support of the Hong Kong Research Grant Council is gratefully acknowledged (Grant No. GRF HKBU 245511).
2 Si-ming Li, Chair Professor in the Department of Geography, and Director of the David C. Lam Institute for East-West Studies, Hong Kong Baptist University, Hong Kong. Email: lisiming@hkbu.edu.hk
3 Humin Du, PhD candidate, Department of Geography, Hong Kong Baptist University, Hong Kong. Email: helenduhuimin@gmail.com

# References

Alonso, W. (1964) *Location and Land Use*. Cambridge, MA: MIT Press.
Brown, L. A. and Moore, E. G. (1970) "The intra-urban migration process: a perspective", *Geografiska Annaler B*, 52: 1–13.
Chan, K. W. (2010) "Fundamentals of China's urbanization and policy", *China Review*, 10 (1): 63–94.
Clark, C. A. V. and Dieleman, F. M. (1996) *Households and Housing: Choice and Outcomes in the Housing Market*. New Brunswick, New Jersey: Rutgers – the State University of New Jersey.
Conceição, P. and Ferreira, P. (2000) The young person's guide to the Theil Index: suggesting intuitive interpretations and exploring analytical applications, University of Texas Inequality Project, Working Paper 14.
Hanushek, E. A. and Quigley, J. M. (1979) "The dynamics of the housing market: a stock adjustment model of housing consumption", *Journal of Urban Economics*, 6 (1): 90–111.
Huang, Y. Q. and Jiang, L. W. (2009) "Housing inequality in transitional Beijing", *International Journal of Urban and Regional Research*, 33: 936–56.
Khan, A. R. and Riskin, C. (2001) *Inequality and Poverty in China in the Age of Globalization*, Oxford; New York: Oxford University Press.
Li, F. F. (2009) China leads the world in auto sales, production. *China Daily*, December 8. Last accessed June 18, 2012 from http://www.chinadaily.com.cn/business/2009-12/08/content_9135316.htm
Li, S. M. (2000) "Housing consumption in urban China: a comparative study of Beijing and Guangzhou", *Environment and Planning A*, 32: 1115–34.
Li, S. M. (2005) "Perspectives on China's urban space," *Issues and Studies*, 41 (4): 67–106.
Li, S. M. (2010) "Mortgage loan as a means of home finance in urban China: a comparative study of Guangzhou and Shanghai", *Housing Studies*, 25 (6): 857–76.
Li, S. M. (2012) "Housing inequalities under market transition: the case of Guangzhou", *Environment and Planning A*, 44: 2852–66.
Li, S. M. and Yi, Z. (2007a) "The road to homeownership under market transition: Beijing, 1980–2001", *Urban Affairs Review*, 42: 342–68.
Li, S. M. and Yi, Z. (2007b) "Financing home purchase in China, with special reference to Guangzhou", *Housing Studies*, 22: 409–25.
Li, L. M., Li, S. M. and Chen, Y. F. (2010) "Better city, better life, but for whom?: the hukou and resident card system and the consequential citizenship stratification in Shanghai", *City, Culture and Society*, 1: 145–54.
Linneman, P. (1980) "Some empirical results on the nature of the hedonic price function for the urban housing market", *Journal of Urban Economics*, 8: 47–68.

Logan, J. R., Bian, Y. J. and Bian, F. Q. (1999) "Housing inequality in urban China in the 1990s", *International Journal of Urban and Regional Research*, 23: 7–25.

Logan, J. R. and Fang, Y. (2010) "The winners of China's urban housing reform", *Housing Studies*, 25: 101–17.

Mills, E. S. (1972) *Studies in the Structure of Urban Economy*. Baltimore, MD: Johns Hopkins University Press.

Muth, R. (1969) *Cities and Housing*. Chicago: University of Chicago Press.

Olsen, E. O. (1987) "The demand and supply of housing service: a critical survey of the empirical literature", in Mills, E. S. (ed.) *Handbook of Regional and Urban Economics*, Vol. 2, Amsterdam; New York: North-Holland, pp. 989–1022.

Rosen, S. (1974), "Hedonic prices and implicit markets: product differentiation in pure competition", *The Journal of Political Economy*, 82: 34–55.

Szelenyi, I. (1978) "Social inequalities in state socialist redistributive economies: dilemma for social policy in contemporary socialist societies in Eastern Europe", in Etzioni, A. (ed.) *Policy Research*. Leiden, the Netherlands: E J Brill, pp. 63–87.

Wang, Y. P. (2011) "Recent housing reform practice in Chinese cities: spatial and social implications", in Man, J. Y. (ed.) *China's Housing Reform and Outcomes*. Cambridge, MA: Lincoln Institute of Land Policy, pp. 19–46.

Wang, Y. P., Wang Y. L. and Wu J. S. (2009) "Urbanization and informal development in China: urban villages in Shenzhen", *International Journal of Urban and Regional Research*, 33 (4): 957–73.

Wu, F. L. (1996) "Changes in the structure of public housing provision in urban China", *Urban Studies*, 33 (9): 1601–27.

Wu, F. L. (2000) "Place promotion in Shanghai, PRC", *Cities*, 17 (5): 349–61.

# 3 Mobility, housing inequality and residential differentiation in transitional urban China

## A case study of Wuhan

*Youqin Huang, Chengdong Yi,*
*Yunyan Yang and Xiong He*

## Introduction

Chinese cities have made spectacular achievement in housing in recent decades, with the rate of homeownership increased from 20 per cent in the 1980s to 70 per cent in 2010, and per capita residential floor space increased from 4 m$^2$ to 29 m$^2$ during the same period (Huang and Clark, 2002; Yi and Huang, 2012). Yet this dazzling housing improvement has not been enjoyed by all social groups, and housing inequality has become unprecedentedly evident in this formerly socialist country. At the same time, China is on the move with increasingly high mobility. Hundreds of millions of migrants are moving into cities due to the rapid urbanization, while urban residents are moving within cities for better housing or to give way to urban redevelopment. Thus a massive social and spatial sorting of households and neighborhoods is taking place in previously homogenous cities. Wealthy "gated communities" with multi-million dollar villas and dilapidated "migrant enclaves" with crowded shacks are now emerging side by side in major Chinese cities (Huang, 2005). This chapter studies the patterns and dynamics of housing inequality and residential differentiation in Chinese cities by taking a case study of Wuhan.[1]

In the socialist era, urban housing was a welfare benefit provided by local governments (through municipal housing bureaus) and state employers (called work units), and the allocation of public rental housing was based on a set of non-monetary factors such as seniority, job rank, marital status and household size (Huang and Clark, 2002; Wang and Murie, 1999; Li, 2000a; Li, 2000b). While there were evidences for housing inequality (Logan *et al.*, 1999), the overall level of housing consumption was very low (Huang, 2003), and the degree of housing inequality was relatively low. Residential pattern was characterized by relatively homogeneous work-unit compounds surrounding old neighborhoods in central cities; and industry and occupation, instead of income and housing quality, were the main factors differentiating social space (Yeh *et al.*, 1995).

Launched nationwide in 1988, the housing reform aims to introduce market mechanisms into the housing system, and it has fundamentally changed housing provision and consumption. While public housing is privatized through subsidized sale, new private housing by developers – called "commodity housing" – becomes an increasingly important part of the housing stock. In 1998, the State Council

(1998) officially ended the provision of public housing, which further encouraged the massive provision of private housing and forced households to purchase housing from the private sector. Different types of private housing ranging from villas, regular commodity housing, to subsidized commodity housing (called "economic and comfortable housing") have been provided to cater for different strata of urban population.[2] Having suffered from severe housing shortage and the lack of housing choice for decades, urban households in Chinese cities embrace newly built private housing and homeownership in an unprecedented housing boom. With 70 per cent in cities and 85 per cent nationwide, the rate of homeownership in China now is higher than in many developed countries. Yet, housing inequality is rising rapidly, and a socio-spatial sorting of urban households and neighborhoods are taking place in Chinese cities. A previously homogeneous society characterized with public rental housing and work-unit compounds are being transformed into an unequal society with privately owned housing and vastly differentiated neighborhoods.

Despite significant housing inequality and residential differentiation in Chinese cities, empirical studies have been sketchy, mainly because of the lack of systematic data on housing. The 2000 census is the first census with housing information; yet its micro-level data has not been available to the public except a handful of scholars. The latest 2010 census includes housing information as well; yet the Chinese government has not released aggregated data for all cities, let alone micro-level data. Using questionnaire survey data for specific cities and the 2000 census data, several studies have helped us understand housing inequality in China (Logan and Bian, 1999; Wang and Murie, 2000; Huang, 2005; Huang and Jiang, 2009; Li and Huang, 2006; Li and Wu, 2006; Li and Wu, 2008; Logan *et al.*, 2010); yet, much is still unknown due to the complexity of the housing system. Furthermore, in spite of the profound neighborhood changes in Chinese cities, the spatial impact of housing reform, especially on the urban social-spatial structure, is still a gap in the literature. In this chapter, we aim to study the patterns and dynamics of housing inequality and its geography by taking a case study of Wuhan.

## Research context and hypotheses

Housing inequality and residential segregation is one of the central topics in social sciences. Despite the longstanding debate on what is the main driving force, scholars generally agree that a set of factors including socio-economic status, racial discrimination, personal preference, and urban economic structure contributes to housing inequality and residential segregation in the US (Massey and Denton, 1993; Massey and Denton, 1987; Denton and Massey, 1991; Clark, 1986; Galster, 1988). During suburbanization, affluent middle class, dominantly whites, move to suburbs with better housing, leaving the poor in inner cities with generally worse housing condition. While recent gentrification in some urban neighborhoods has improved housing and neighborhood condition in inner cities, it has not fully changed the inner city–suburb contrast. Yet, much of the existing literature focuses on market economies, while we know relatively little about housing inequality and residential segregation in other economies such as socialist and transitional economies.

Although housing was considered a welfare benefit in socialist economies, there was significant housing inequality. As housing was provided mainly through work units, large, high-ranking state owned work units were more resourceful thus could provide better housing to their employees than smaller non-state work units (Logan *et al.*, 1999; Szelenyi, 1983; Walder, 1986; Bian, 1994). Within a work unit, people with political power such as those with higher job rank, seniority and political status tend to access better housing. Spatially, housing inequality is manifested with old one-story courtyard houses in the inner city, surrounded by work-unit compounds with uniform public housing (Huang, 2005; Wang *et al.*, 2005; Wang and Murie, 2000). Old housing in inner cities was often managed by municipal housing bureaus and provided to urban residents whose work units could not provide housing. While centrally located, it was often dilapidated, crowded, and lacked modern facilities. In contrast, public housing in work-unit compounds was built in the socialist era by work units for their employees. Although often utilitarian, they were close to the workplace and relatively better in quality. Furthermore, cadres, professionals and employees in high-ranking work units often lived in better neighborhoods such as those close to key schools, and with access to gardens/parks (Logan and Bian, 1993).

The housing reform in urban China aims to introduce market mechanisms into the welfare-oriented housing system. In addition to privatizing existing housing stock and developing new private housing (Wang and Murie, 2000; Li, 2000a; Huang and Clark, 2002), households are given freedom to choose their housing and neighborhood. Consequently, residential mobility has been rising significantly (Li *et al.*, 2005; Huang and Deng, 2006), and a socio-spatial sorting is in process, which has resulted in significant housing inequality and residential differentiation in Chinese cities. Huang (2005) offered a conceptual framework that incorporated both market mechanisms and persisting socialist institutions to understand housing inequality and residential differentiation in transitional Chinese cities. With the lack of reliable data on income in China, housing consumption is becoming an important indicator for social stratification (Bian and Liu, 2005). People with political power and access to previous public housing also enjoy better housing in the reform era due to heavy subsidies during privatization of public housing, and they are the biggest winners in China's housing reform (Logan *et al.*, 2010), while rural-to-urban migrants tend to suffer housing poverty (Sato, 2006; Wu, 2002). Housing inequality between different socio-economic and institutional groups was further aggravated by housing reforms in the late 1990s (Huang and Jiang, 2009).

Spatially, differentiated neighborhoods are replacing relatively homogeneous work-unit compounds. In Shanghai, neighborhoods are being sorted, regrouped and differentiated, with some in the central areas gentrified, others deteriorating, and the suburbs becoming increasingly heterogeneous (Li and Wu, 2006). Yet, residential differentiation in Shanghai is based more on housing tenure instead of socio-economic status (Li and Wu, 2008). In Beijing, there is significant residential differentiation at neighborhood level with upscale housing and low-income housing communities emerging; yet at the city level, mixing is still prevalent (Huang,

2005), in contrast to the inner city–suburb divide in the West. Meanwhile, with ample affordable housing, suburban villages in large cities like Beijing are becoming "migrant enclaves" (or "urban villages") with distinctive migrant residents and rural landscape (Ma and Xiang, 1998).[3]

These studies have shed important light on housing inequality and residential differentiation in Chinese cities. Yet, much is still unknown due to its complexity and changing nature. Existing research also focuses on first-tier large coastal cities such as Beijing, Shanghai and Guangzhou that tend to enjoy preferential policies (Huang, 2005; Huang and Jiang, 2009; Li and Wu, 2008; Li, 2009). This chapter aims to contribute to the emerging body of literature on housing inequality in transitional economies by conducting a case study of a second-tier inland city – Wuhan – and by adopting a perspective of mobility.

Mobility is a driving force and utilizing vehicle for socio-spatial sorting in Chinese cities. Since housing reform, spatial mobility has been rising significantly, with an influx of rural-to-urban migrants and massive residential mobility within cities (Li, 2004; Li, 2003; Huang and Deng, 2006). Because of the persistence of the Household Registration (hukou) System, an institution that defines a person's socio-economic status and access to welfare benefits in China (Cheng and Selden, 1994), mobility cannot be separated from a person's hukou status. Based on mobility and hukou status, there are eight sub-populations in Chinese cities: non-movers (people who are registered at where they live and have not moved since their birth); residential movers (people who are registered in the city they live but have moved within the city boundary); permanent migrants (people who are registered in the city they live but came from places outside of the city); and temporary migrants (people who are registered elsewhere, and came from places outside of the city). Each can be further divided based on whether they have agricultural or non-agricultural hukou (Table 3.1). These groups enjoy different housing entitlements, and thus have different housing consumptions and residential patterns.

Non-movers with non-agricultural hukou, the dominant group in most Chinese cities, are the most privileged group regarding housing rights. They are entitled to housing subsidies in both public and private sector, and they can access any type of housing. They mostly lived in public rental housing in the socialist era, and thus enjoyed heavy subsidies during privatization of public housing and became homeowners en masse. Yet, their housing conditions vary significantly depending on their socio-economic and political status and the nature of their work units (Huang and Clark, 2002; Huang, 2003; Li, 2000b; Logan *et al.*, 1999; Bian and Logan, 1996). While the better-off households and the younger generation may live in private housing estates, most live in either old housing neighborhoods in inner cities or work-unit compounds in suburbs where housing condition tends to be inferior to that of newly built private housing.

In contrast, non-movers with agricultural hukou – suburban villagers – are subject to the rural housing system. While they are entitled to build housing on collectively owned land (called "self-build housing") and purchase commodity housing, they are not qualified for housing subsidies. Thus they mostly live in self-build housing, which may be large in size but often poor in quality. They concentrate in scattered

Table 3.1 Housing entitlement and housing consumption for social groups defined by mobility and hukou

| Groups by mobility | Hukou status | Housing entitlement | Housing condition | Neighborhood |
|---|---|---|---|---|
| Non-movers (Never moved) | Non-agricultural hukou registered locally | All public and private housing; qualified for housing subsidies | Vary; high rate of homeownership, especially of public housing | Old neighborhoods in inner cities; work-unit compounds and private housing estates in suburbs |
| | Agricultural hukou registered locally | No public housing; no housing subsidies; self-build housing, commodity housing | Often large houses with poor quality and facility, high rate of homeownership | Urban/suburban villages |
| Residential movers (Moved within the city, voluntarily or involuntarily) | Non-agricultural hukou registered locally | All public and private housing; qualified for subsidies | Vary, but tend to live in larger and newer housing; high rate of homeownership | Suburban private housing complex; affordable housing, resettlement community |
| | Agricultural hukou registered locally | Resettlement housing | Lower end among private housing | Resettlement community |
| Permanent migrants (Moved from a place outside of the city, with local hukou) | Non-agricultural hukou registered locally | All public and private housing; qualified for housing subsidies | Vary, but tend to live in larger and better housing; high rate of homeownership | Work-unit compounds; suburban commodity housing complex; affordable housing |
| | Agricultural hukou registered locally | Self-build housing, commodity housing; no subsidies | Often large houses with poor quality and facility | Urban/suburban villages |
| Temporary migrants (Moved from a place outside of the city, without local hukou) | Non-agricultural hukou registered elsewhere (urban migrants) | No public housing; no housing subsidies; private housing except economic and comfortable housing; temporary housing by work-units (e.g. dorms) | Depends on income; mostly rental | Urban/suburban villages; dorms; commodity housing complex |
| | Agricultural hukou registered elsewhere (rural migrants) | Same as above | Poor, mostly rental | Urban/suburban villages; factory dorms |

villages at the urban fringe, where residential crowding and lack of public services are prevalent (Deng and Huang, 2004).

Residential movers are local residents who moved within the city either voluntarily or involuntarily. This is becoming an increasingly large group with massive housing construction and urban renewal in recent decades. Voluntary residential movers, regardless of their hukou status, are often better-off households who either can afford to trade up on the housing ladder, or benefit from new subsidized housing (such as economic and comfortable housing) provided by work units. Thus they tend to live in newer and larger housing, have a higher rate of homeownership, and concentrate in suburban private housing estates. For those who moved involuntarily due to urban renewal in inner cities or urban expansion at the suburbs, they often live in resettlement housing estates in marginalized locations with relatively poor housing condition.

With rapid urbanization, there are also massive influxes of migrants into Chinese cities. "Permanent migrants" are those with hukou registered at the destination city while "temporary migrants" are those with hukou registered elsewhere. These two migrant groups have very different housing entitlements and housing conditions. Permanent migrants with non-agricultural hukou tend to have higher human capital endowments than local urban residents, thus they often live in larger and better housing with a higher rate of homeownership. Permanent migrants with agricultural hukou are a very small group, and they enjoy similar housing entitlement as non-movers with agricultural hukou. Temporary migrants are the most disadvantaged group regarding housing entitlement, as they are generally not allowed to access subsidized housing, and collectively owned land for housing construction at the destination city. They can only access housing in the private sector, which tends to be more expensive, and temporary housing by their work units such as dorms. Thus they often concentrate in private rental housing in sub(urban) villages and quarter housing such as factory dorms. They can be further divided into those with non-agricultural hukou and those with agricultural hukou, with the former usually possessing higher human capital endowments and enjoying better housing conditions than the latter.

Thus we hypothesize that there is significant housing inequality between groups defined by mobility and hukou status. While residential movers enjoy the best housing condition due to the trade-up process, temporary migrants, especially those with agricultural hukou, lie at the bottom of the housing ladder. In contrast to temporary migrants' disadvantaged position in the housing system, permanent migrants share more similarities with non-movers than temporary migrants. Spatially, we hypothesize that these groups are sorted into different parts of the city, and there is a fairly high degree of residential segregation and isolation between them. The following empirical analysis aims to test these hypotheses.

## Empirical analysis

### *The study area, data and research design*

Wuhan is the capital of Hubei province and the largest city in central China. The population was 8.3 million in 2000 and 9.8 million in 2010 (NBSC, 2000;

NBSC, 2012). Located along the golden waterway of the Yangtze River, Wuhan has always been an important commercial center and industrial base in history. Yet, compared to first-tier coastal cities such as Guangzhou and Shanghai, Wuhan's development lagged behind in recent decades mainly due to the government's economic development policies that have favored the east coast. In this regard, Wuhan is typical of Chinese inland cities and shares more similarities with many other Chinese cities than major coastal cities.

With its convenient transport and a vast populous hinterland, Wuhan has experienced an influx of migrants in recent decades. There were 1.1 million migrants in 2000 and 2.8 million migrants in 2010 in Wuhan, accounting for 11.8 per cent and 28.3 per cent of its total population, respectively (NBSC, 2012). While lower than that in first-tier cities such as Beijing, Guangzhou and Shanghai, the share of migrants in Wuhan is one of the highest among second-tier cities. Wuhan is also a research/education center with many universities and research institutes, and a provincial capital with many provincial government agencies. Thus in addition to typical rural-to-urban migrants, Wuhan also attracts a large volume of educated/skilled migrants and college students. Meanwhile, many local residents have moved within Wuhan, either for better housing or to give way to urban development. Similar to many other Chinese cities, Wuhan has experienced an unprecedented housing boom and urban development in recent decades with massive new private housing development, large-scale urban renewal, and infrastructure development, all of which lead to high residential mobility in the city. Thus, Wuhan serves as an excellent context to study the impact of mobility on housing inequality and residential differentiation.

As most large Chinese cities, Wuhan is composed of an urban core, a suburb that has close economic ties to the urban core, and rural counties. Since rural counties have a significant share of rural population who are subject to a different housing system, they are excluded from the following analysis. Thus the study area includes seven urban districts (Jiang'an, Jianghan, Qiaokou, Hanyang, Wucang, Qingshan, and Hongshan district), and two suburban districts (Dongxihu and Hannan district). Based on the history of urban development in Wuhan, we further divide the study area into four zones: old city, new city, inner suburb, and far suburb (see Figure 3.1)[4] (Yang *et al.*, 2004). The development of Wuhan has gone through three main phases. The first phase was during the nineteenth century and the first half of the twentieth century, when Wuhan developed rapidly as one of the port cities in China for international trade. Hankou developed rapidly as a trade center, Hanyang became an important industrial base, and Wuchang was established as a political and military center. These "three towns" form the "old city" in Wuhan, which is characterized with pre-1949 dilapidated public housing but with easy access to employment and services. The second phase was during the socialist era (1950s–1970s), when Wuhan received massive state investment in heavy industries, infrastructure, and education/research due to its favorable location in national defense. Consequently, Wuhan expanded rapidly, forming the "new city" area with large state-owned enterprises and universities, and corresponding public rental housing compounds for state

*Figure 3.1* Sub-districts and the four sections in Wuhan.

employees. During the reform era, Wuhan has experienced a new level of rapid growth, with new private housing districts and economic develop zones established often in previously rural areas, forming the inner suburb and far suburb that is characterized with the juxtaposition of newly built private housing estates and suburban villages with self-build housing.

The 2000 Census is the first Chinese census that collected housing information. In addition to conventional socio-demographic information, in the short form it collected basic housing information, including floor space, number of rooms and facilities. In the long form, which was administrated to randomly selected ten per cent of households, additional housing information was asked, such as housing type/tenure. In this research we mainly use one per cent random sample of the long-form dataset of the 2000 Census for Wuhan.

Despite that the 2000 census data is somewhat dated and many changes have taken place since 2000, it remains one of the most systematic data on housing, which has many superior qualities than small-scale surveys conducted by individual scholars. Due to limited access to 2000 census data in China, scholars have not fully studied housing consumption in 2000. More importantly, the year of 2000 represents the early stage of marketization and privatization as the State Council (1994, 1998) deepened housing reform in 1994 and ended the provision of public housing in 1998. Thus this analysis of 2000 census data can reveal the impact of the first stage of housing reform and serve as a baseline for changes after 2000. The latest 2010 census also collected housing information; yet, the micro-level data is not available to the public, which prevents us from studying changes over time. We have access to some aggregated data of 2010 census and the 2012 Migrant Dynamic Survey in Wuhan, both of which will be used to offer some insights of changes since 2000 after a detailed analysis of 2000 census data.[5]

In the 2000 census, households are grouped into "collective households" (jiti hu) and "family households" (jiating hu); yet housing information is collected only for family households.[6] Thus analyses on housing will focus on family households only. In addition, we exclude the following groups from housing analyses: 1) household heads who are younger than 16 years old as they are not allowed to work legally and are often not considered independent decision-makers for housing; 2) residents with agricultural hukou registered locally as they are subjected to the rural housing system; and 3) people engaging in agriculture. This filtering process results in 13,229 family households. Yet, when we analyze population composition and distribution, every person is included, and the sample size is 49,851 persons (see Table 3.2).

According to Table 3.2, more than 70 per cent of the population in Wuhan moved during 1995–2000, and about 14 per cent of the population were residential movers, 35 per cent were permanent migrants, and another 23 per cent were temporary migrants. This indicates a very high mobility in Wuhan with a large influx of migrants from outside, and a large number of local residents moving within Wuhan city. While more than half of temporary migrants had agricultural hukou, the majority of permanent migrants and residential movers had non-agricultural hukou, similar to non-movers. Among family households, permanent migrants, residential movers and non-movers virtually all had non-agricultural hukou due to the above-mentioned filtering process.

*Table 3.2* Population and household classification in Wuhan, 2000

| Categories | Total population (%) | | Family households (%) | |
|---|---|---|---|---|
| Non-movers | 28.0 | | 19.3 | |
| Agricultural hukou | | 6.4 | | 0.0 |
| Non-agricultural hukou | | 21.6 | | 19.3 |
| Residential movers | 13.9 | | 15.0 | |
| Agricultural hukou | | 1.7 | | 1.4 |
| Non-agricultural hukou | | 12.2 | | 13.6 |
| Permanent migrants | 34.6 | | 43.0 | |
| Agricultural hukou | | 2.9 | | 0.0 |
| Non-agricultural hukou | | 31.8 | | 43.0 |
| Temporary migrants | 22.7 | | 22.5 | |
| Agricultural hukou | | 12.9 | | 12.3 |
| Non-agricultural hukou | | 9.8 | | 10.2 |
| Others | 0.8 | | 0.2 | |
| Total | 100.0 | | 100.0 | |
| Total frequency | 49,851 persons | | 13,229 households | |

*Table 3.3* Housing consumption for different groups in Wuhan, 2000 (family households only)

| | Per capita floor space (m²) | Gini coefficient | Have private kitchen (%) | Gas or electricity for cooking (%) | Have tap water (%) | Have hot water for bathing (%) | Have private bathroom (%) | Facility index |
|---|---|---|---|---|---|---|---|---|
| Non-movers | 19.1 | 0.37 | 79.6 | 94.6 | 99.6 | 47.1 | 38.1 | 3.87 |
| Residential movers | 23.0 | 0.32 | 85.1 | 95.6 | 99.8 | 64.9 | 62.2 | 4.28 |
| Permanent migrants | 18.6 | 0.32 | 87.1 | 95.9 | 99.7 | 64.7 | 57.1 | 4.27 |
| Temporary migrants | 15.5 | 0.43 | 57.5 | 81.9 | 98.0 | 28.3 | 29.8 | 3.26 |
| Others | 19.1 | n.a. | 82.6 | 95.7 | 100.0 | 56.5 | 56.5 | 4.11 |
| All | 18.7 | 0.36 | 79.3 | 92.8 | 99.4 | 53.8 | 48.6 | 3.99 |

### Housing consumption and housing inequality in 2000

Housing consumption varies significantly by mobility and hukou status (Table 3.3). Residential movers consumed the largest per capital floor space, followed by non-movers, permanent migrants, and then temporary migrants. According to the Gini coefficient (scaled 0–1 with 1 indicating the maximum inequality), the overall inequality in per capita floor space was moderate (0.36); yet there were significant differences between groups, with the largest inequality among temporary migrants (0.43), and the lowest among residential movers and permanent migrants. This shows that temporary migrants are a much more diverse group than the other groups regarding housing consumption. Housing facilities also varied between groups. While tap water and gas/electricity for cooking were almost universal, temporary migrants were the least likely to have private kitchen (57.5 per cent), private bathroom (29.8 per cent), and hot water (28.3 per cent), while residential movers and permanent migrants tended to live in housing most likely to be equipped with all these facilities. Not surprisingly, the facility index (scaled 0–5) was the highest for residential movers and permanent migrants, and lowest for temporary migrants, with non-movers lying in between.[7] In sum, temporary migrants had the worst housing condition but highest within-group inequality, while residential movers enjoyed the best housing condition and the lowest inequality.

Due to the transitional nature of the housing system, there are different types of housing. Overall, about 40 per cent of households purchased previously public housing, another 25 per cent lived in public rental housing, and 5.7 per cent purchased economic and comfortable housing, all of which are heavily subsidized (Table 3.4). In other words, more than 71 per cent of households still lived in subsidized housing after more than a decade of housing reform. Yet, housing access varies significantly between migrant groups. Residential movers and permanent migrants were the most likely to purchase public housing and live in public rental housing, making them the most likely to live in subsidized housing (65.9 per cent and 87.6 per cent respectively). Not surprisingly, residential movers were the most

Table 3.4 Housing access and homeownership by hukou and mobility in 2000 (family households only)

| % | Self-build housing | Purchase commodity | Purchase economic | Purchase public | Rent public | Rent private | Others | Total | Rate of home-ownership | Subsidized housing |
|---|---|---|---|---|---|---|---|---|---|---|
| Non-movers | 30.1 | 2.5 | 4.5 | 27.3 | 30.0 | 1.7 | 4.1 | 100 | 64.4 | 61.8 |
| Residential movers | 2.2 | 16.1 | 13.6 | 32.4 | 19.9 | 9.3 | 6.3 | 100 | 64.3 | 65.9 |
| Permanent migrants | 6.6 | 2.3 | 4.7 | 58.7 | 24.2 | 0.7 | 2.9 | 100 | 72.3 | 87.6 |
| Temporary migrants | 8.1 | 5.4 | 3.7 | 16.5 | 27.8 | 26.3 | 12.4 | 100 | 33.7 | 48.0 |
| Agricultural hukou | 7.3 | 3.2 | 1.3 | 1.7 | 26.5 | 43.2 | 17.1 | 100 | 13.5 | 29.5 |
| Non-agricultural hukou | 8.9 | 7.7 | 6.1 | 31.3 | 29.1 | 9.2 | 7.7 | 100 | 54.0 | 66.5 |
| Other | 13.1 | 4.4 | 4.4 | 43.4 | 13.1 | 17.5 | 4.4 | 100 | 65.3 | 60.8 |
| Total | 10.9 | 5.0 | 5.7 | 39.9 | 25.4 | 7.4 | 5.6 | 100 | 61.5 | 71.0 |

likely to purchase newly developed commodity and economic and comfortable housing. In contrast, temporary migrants, especially those with agricultural hukou, were the most likely to rent private housing but the least likely to purchase subsidized housing such as public and economic and comfortable housing. In general, temporary migrants were not allowed to purchase subsidized housing. But our data show that 16.5 per cent of temporary migrants purchased public housing and 3.7 per cent purchased economic and comfortable housing. A close look at them shows that they predominately had non-agricultural hukou and were from rural counties of Wuhan that were outside of our study area. Thus these temporary migrants most likely were employees of state-owned enterprises located in suburban rural counties who were working in the city, and they were qualified for purchasing subsidized housing through their work units. More than two-thirds of these migrants also had spouses with local non-agricultural hukou. Thus they could also purchase subsidized housing through their spouses.[8] About 28 per cent of temporary migrants rented public housing, mostly likely rental housing provided by work units.

Housing in Chinese cities can be owned with different bundles of property rights depending on how households accessed their housing. Households who purchased public housing and economic and comfortable housing at heavily subsidized prices have only partial property rights, while those who purchased commodity housing at market prices have full property rights.[9] With different types of homeownership in mind, the overall rate of homeownership was about 62 per cent in Wuhan, lower than the average rate of all cities in China (72 per cent) in 2000. Permanent migrants had the highest rate, followed by non-movers, residential movers, and temporary migrants, especially those with agricultural hukou who had the lowest rate of homeownership.[10] Temporary migrants were clearly in a disadvantaged position regarding homeownership, as they were generally not allowed to purchase housing with subsidies. Yet, there was a large difference between temporary migrants with agricultural and non-agricultural hukou, with the latter clearly more likely to be homeowners and more likely to purchase public and economic and comfortable housing. As discussed earlier, temporary migrants with non-agricultural hukou were mostly state employees from rural counties in Wuhan, thus they were not very different from non-movers regarding housing access except they were slightly more likely to rent private and purchase commodity housing, while less likely to live in self-build housing. Thus housing subsidy was still very much a privilege for people with non-agricultural hukou.

### Modeling housing consumption in 2000

To determine factors affecting housing consumption, OLS regressions on floor space ($m^2$) and facility index were conducted. The independent variables include socio-economic variables such as age, $age^2$, education, occupation, marital status, and household size, and institutional variables such as hukou status (agricultural vs. non-agricultural hukou), mobility (non-movers, residential movers, permanent migrants, temporary migrants), migration time (moved five years ago, and moved in the last five years), and residential location (old city, new city, inner suburb, far suburb). In addition, households can access housing through spouses, thus spouse's education, occupation, and hukou status are included as well.

According to Table 3.5, first of all, socio-economic variables are significant to housing consumption, demonstrating the working of housing markets similar to the West. Older, married, and better-educated people, people with leading positions and professional occupations, and larger households generally live in larger and better housing. Secondly, institutional variables are significant, indicating the persistency of socialist institutions in housing consumption. People with non-agricultural hukou

*Table 3.5* OLS regressions on floor space and facility index in Wuhan, 2000 (family households only)

| Independent variables | Floor space | | Facility index | |
|---|---|---|---|---|
| *Socio-economic variables* | | | | |
| Age | 1.03 | *** | 0.04 | |
| Age² | −0.01 | *** | 0.00 | *** |
| Household size | 4.20 | *** | 0.09 | *** |
| Years of education | 1.40 | *** | 0.06 | *** |
| Occupation (Reference: manufacture worker) | | | | |
| Head/manager | 12.80 | *** | 0.21 | *** |
| Technician/professional | 9.20 | *** | 0.23 | *** |
| Staff and clerical worker | 9.31 | *** | 0.21 | *** |
| Service and sales worker | 0.55 | | −0.05 | |
| Unemployed and others | 1.61 | | −0.06 | * |
| Marital status (Reference: singles) | | | | |
| Married | 0.65 | | 0.19 | ** |
| Divorced | −0.75 | | 0.17 | ** |
| Spouse's education | −0.09 | | 0.00 | |
| Spouse job (Reference: others) | | | | |
| Managerial or professional | 1.97 | * | 0.05 | |
| *Institutional variables* | | | | |
| Hukou type (Reference: agricultural) | | | | |
| Non-agricultural hukou | 13.68 | *** | 0.81 | *** |
| Spouse's hukou (Reference: agricultural hukou) | | | | |
| Non-agricultural hukou | −15.87 | *** | −0.19 | *** |
| No spouse or spouse has no hukou | −16.22 | * | −0.11 | |
| Mobility (Reference: non-movers) | | | | |
| Permanent migrant | n.a. | | n.a. | |
| Temporary migrant | −2.25 | | −0.20 | *** |
| Residential movers | 7.21 | ** | 0.42 | *** |
| Migration time (Reference: no move) | | | | |
| Moved 5 years ago | 0.29 | | 0.26 | *** |
| Moved in the last 5 years | 1.61 | | −0.06 | |
| Residence (Reference: old city) | | | | |
| New city | 8.47 | *** | 0.34 | *** |
| Inner suburb | 15.19 | *** | 0.21 | *** |
| Far suburb | 15.82 | *** | −0.20 | * |
| Constant | −18.36 | *** | 0.84 | *** |
| Sample size | 10,606 | | 10,389 | |
| Adjusted R square | 0.16 | | 0.22 | |
| Durbin-Watson | 1.58 | | 1.46 | |

Notes: * significant at 90% level; ** significant at 95% level; *** significant at 99% level.

enjoy much larger and better housing than those with agricultural hukou. Residential movers live in larger and better housing than non-movers, demonstrating the trade-up process, while temporary migrants live in smaller housing with poorer facilities than non-movers, demonstrating again the former's disadvantaged position in urban housing. Established migrants (who moved five years ago) live in better housing than those who did not move, which demonstrates migrants' housing improvement as their duration in cities increases. Not surprisingly, people living in new city and inner suburbs consume significantly larger and better housing than those in old city. People living in far suburbs also live in larger housing but with worse facilities than in old city, probably due to a large share of self-build housing in suburban villages.

To model housing tenure, a variable with six categories, we conducted a series of logistic regression, in each of which "rent public housing" is treated as the reference category.[11] Public rental was the dominant housing tenure in socialist urban China, and it remains an important reference point in 2000. Again both socio-economic and institutional variables are significant to housing tenure (Table 3.6). For example, older and better-educated people, and large households are more likely to be homeowners than renting public housing. Heads/managers are more likely to own commodity and economic and comfortable housing on the one hand, and rent private housing on the other hand probably due to their high job mobility. Technicians/professionals, and staff or clerical workers are more likely to own commodity housing, economic and comfortable housing and public housing, while services and sales workers are also more likely to rent private housing.

People with agricultural hukou are less likely to own any type of housing, but more likely to rent private housing than those with non-agricultural hukou. Compared to non-movers, residential movers are more likely to own private housing and public housing than public rental, but less likely to live in self-build housing. Migrants (both permanent and temporary) are less likely to live in self-build housing, purchase economic and public housing than non-movers. Temporary migrants are also more likely to own and rent private housing than non-movers. Established migrants are more likely to be homeowners, which again shows migrants' housing assimilation over time. Compared to those living in the old city, households living in the new city, inner and far suburbs are more likely to live in every other type of housing than public rental, indicating public rental is concentrated in the old city.

### *Residential pattern and residential differentiation in 2000*

In addition to different housing consumption, groups defined by mobility also lived in different parts of the city (Table 3.7). Overall, about 29 per cent of total population lived in the old city, 49 per cent in the new city, while only 14 per cent in inner suburbs and 8.1 per cent in far suburbs. Among the three migrant groups, residential movers and permanent migrants were much more likely to live in the new city that was characterized with decent housing and proximity to city centers, while temporary migrants were the most likely to live in inner and far suburbs. Considering both housing quality and distance to the city center, temporary migrants were at spatial disadvantage by concentrating in suburbs.

Table 3.6 Multiple Binary Regressions on housing tenure in Wuhan, 2000 (Reference: rent public housing)

| Variables | Self-build housing | Purchase economic | Purchase commodity | Purchase public | Rent private |
|---|---|---|---|---|---|
| *Socio-economic variables* | | | | | |
| Age | 0.08 *** | 0.05 * | 0.02 | 0.13 *** | -0.06 * |
| Age² | 0.00 *** | 0.00 | 0.00 | 0.00 *** | 0.00 |
| Household size | 0.23 *** | 0.17 *** | 0.21 *** | 0.14 *** | -0.04 |
| Years of education | -0.08 *** | 0.11 *** | 0.13 *** | 0.10 *** | -0.02 |
| Occupation (Reference: manufacture worker) | | | | | |
| Head or managerial | 0.05 | 0.76 ** | 1.17 *** | 0.12 | 0.45 * |
| Technician or professional | -0.55 * | 0.22 | 0.41 | 0.32 ** | -0.47 |
| Staff or clerical worker | -0.17 | 0.53 ** | 0.47 * | 0.35 ** | -0.31 |
| Service and sales worker | -0.11 | 0.06 | 0.22 | -0.38 *** | 0.43 ** |
| Unemployed or others | 0.20 | 0.07 | 0.50 ** | -0.11 | 0.21 |
| Marital status (Reference: singles) | | | | | |
| Divorced | 0.03 | 0.13 | -0.22 | -0.01 | -0.39 |
| Married | -0.11 | 0.27 | -0.09 | -0.01 | 0.19 |
| Spouse's education | 0.00 | -0.04 * | -0.01 | -0.02 | -0.03 |
| Spouse job (Reference: no) | | | | | |
| Managerial or professional | -0.29 | -0.47 | -0.25 | -0.22 * | -0.24 |
| *Institutional variables* | | | | | |
| Hukou (Reference: non-agricultural hukou) | | | | | |
| Agricultural hukou | -0.28 | -1.28 *** | -1.07 *** | -2.11 *** | 1.27 *** |
| Spouse's hukou (Reference: non-agricultural) | | | | | |
| Agricultural hukou | 0.39 ** | 0.51 ** | 1.03 *** | 0.66 *** | 0.11 |
| No hukou or missing | 1.42 *** | 0.92 *** | 1.86 *** | 1.17 *** | -0.17 |
| Mobility (Reference: non-movers) | | | | | |
| Residential movers | -2.31 *** | 1.12 *** | 2.08 *** | 0.47 *** | 1.49 *** |
| Permanent migrants | -2.72 *** | -1.25 *** | -0.08 | -0.92 *** | -0.42 |
| Temporary migrants | -2.84 *** | -1.30 *** | 0.50 * | -1.35 *** | 1.49 *** |

(continued)

Table 3.6 Multiple Binary Regressions on housing tenure in Wuhan, 2000 (Reference: rent public housing) (continued)

| Variables | Self-build housing | Purchase economic | Purchase commodity | Purchase public | Rent private |
|---|---|---|---|---|---|
| Migration time (Reference: no move) | | | | | |
| Moved 5 years ago | 1.25 *** | 1.15 *** | 0.12 | 1.49 *** | −0.21 * |
| Moved in the last 5 years | n.a. | n.a. | n.a. | n.a. | n.a. |
| Residence (Reference: old city) | | | | | |
| New city | 0.22 * | 0.87 *** | 0.12 | 0.75 *** | 0.22 |
| Inner suburb | 2.16 *** | 2.10 *** | 1.71 *** | 0.42 ** | 1.32 *** |
| Far suburb | 2.18 *** | 2.07 *** | 1.91 *** | 0.44  0.58 | |
| Constant | −2.92 *** | −6.39 *** | −6.70 *** | −6.15 *** | −1.09 |
| Sample size | 4,574 | 3,926 | 3,838 | 8,231 | 4,126 |
| Chi-square | 1,628 | 891 | 1,090 | 2,543 | 1,542 |
| −2 Log likelihood | 3,962 | 2,866 | 2,360 | 8,458 | 2,849 |
| Cox & Snell R square | 0.30 | 0.20 | 0.25 | 0.27 | 0.31 |
| Nagelkerke R square | 0.43 | 0.33 | 0.42 | 0.36 | 0.48 |

Notes: * significant at 90% level; ** significant at 95% level; *** significant at 99% level.

*Table 3.7* Population distribution by mobility and hukou, 2000

| % | Old city | New city | Inner suburb | Far suburb | Total % | Total N |
|---|---|---|---|---|---|---|
| *Residential movers* | 24.7 | 54.7 | 16.3 | 3.8 | 100 | 6,911 |
| *Permanent migrants* | 28.4 | 59.5 | 6.9 | 5.2 | 100 | 17,262 |
| *Temporary migrants* | 30.7 | 40.6 | 21.4 | 7.3 | 100 | 11,308 |
| *Non-movers* | 31.8 | 38.7 | 15.5 | 14.0 | 100 | 13,962 |
| *Others* | 20.6 | 33.6 | 22.1 | 23.8 | 100 | 408 |
| *Total* | 29.3 | 48.6 | 14.0 | 8.1 | 100 | 49,851 |

Figure 3.2 shows the percentage of three migrant groups out of total population of sub-district, the smallest spatial unit released by the Chinese government. With massive urban renewal in the old city and development in the new city such as the development of the Qingshan Hong Steel City, the percentage of residential movers was the highest in sub-districts surrounding the old city with large-scale residential development such as Changqing, Beihu and Hongshaxiang Residential Quarter. More than one-third of residential movers in Wuhan moved due to demolition and relocation. Similarly, the percentage of permanent migrants was higher in sub-districts surrounding the old city, and sub-districts with major universities and provincial government agencies. This was a result of the development of the University City and the High-tech Science Park and job transfer of government officials. In contrast, temporary migrants concentrated in inner suburbs due to their proximity to employment centers in the old city and new city, and availability of cheap rental housing in (sub)urban villages. It is clear the distribution patterns for three types of migrants are different but spatially complementary.

Housing consumption varies across space. According to Figure 3.3, households living in suburbs had larger per capita floor space and were more likely to be homeowners. Yet households living in the old city such as the central city of Hankou and the new city with large state work units such as Qingshan Hong Steel City were more likely to live in subsidized housing. This in part was a result of the spatial pattern of housing development over time as the old city was dominated by old public housing managed by the municipal housing bureau, the new city was dominated by public housing built during the socialist era, and the suburbs were dominated by newer private housing.

When we consider the origin and destination of movers, Figure 3.4 shows the schematic spatial pattern of migration among those who moved in the last five years as only these recent movers had origin and destination information. It is clear that residential movers moved mainly from the old city to new city, and from far suburb to inner suburb. The majority of permanent migrants (80 per cent) settled down in the new city, with a smaller percentage in the old city. In comparison, a much larger proportion of temporary migrants (34 per cent) settled in the old city and inner suburbs (20 per cent). This migration pattern shows that Wuhan in 2000 was still at its early stage of suburbanization with local movers and permanent migrants moving to the new city, while temporary migrants filled in the old city and suburbs. It also shows the attractiveness of the new city with decent housing

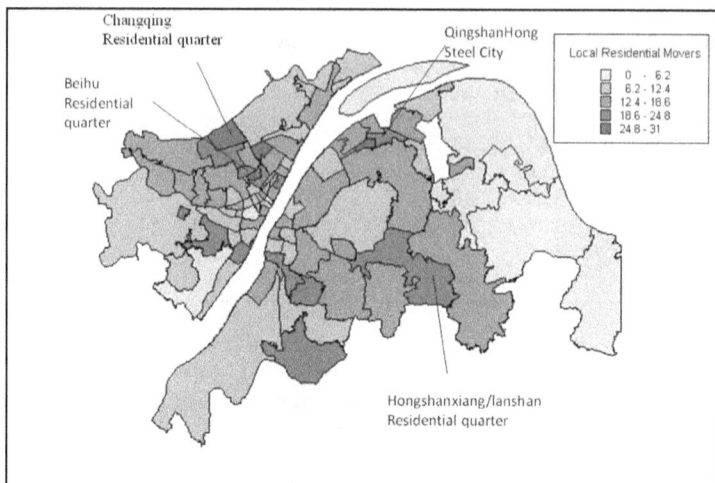

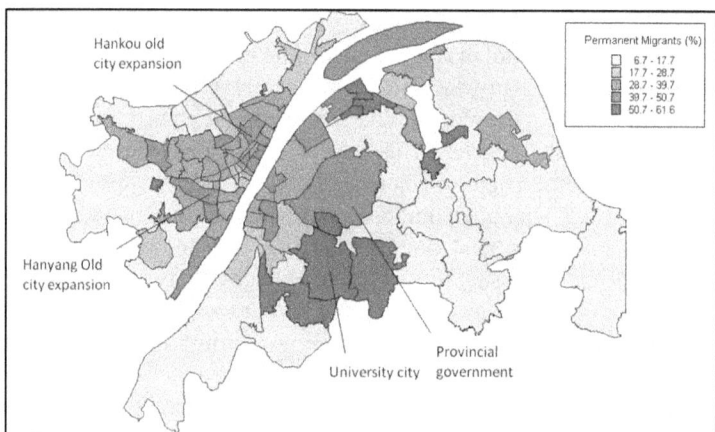

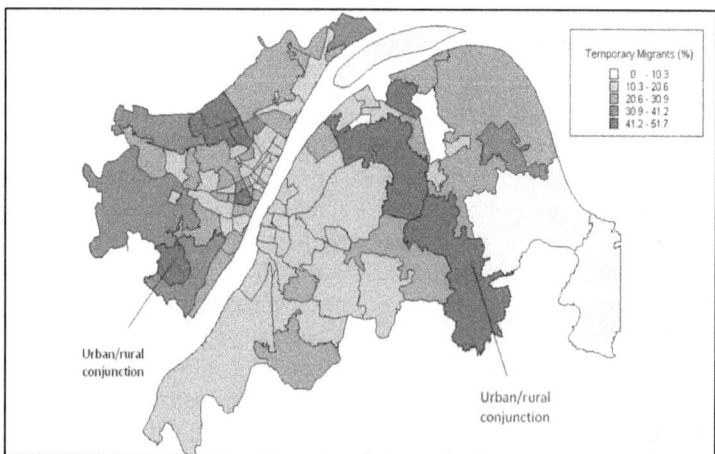

*Figure 3.2* Residential patterns of three groups by mobility (percentage out of total population in sub-district).

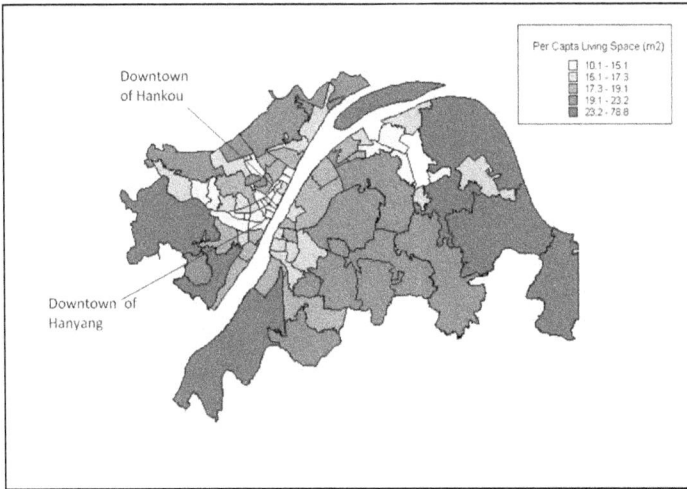

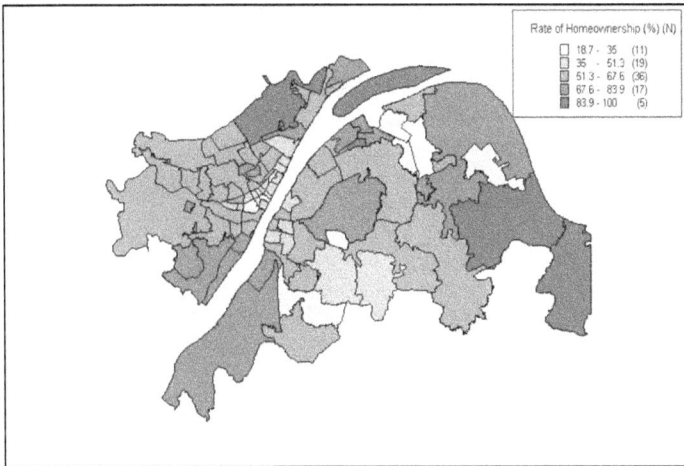

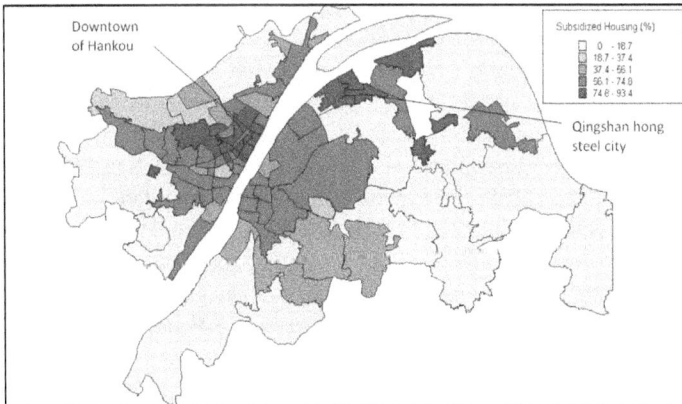

*Figure 3.3* The spatial pattern of housing consumption.

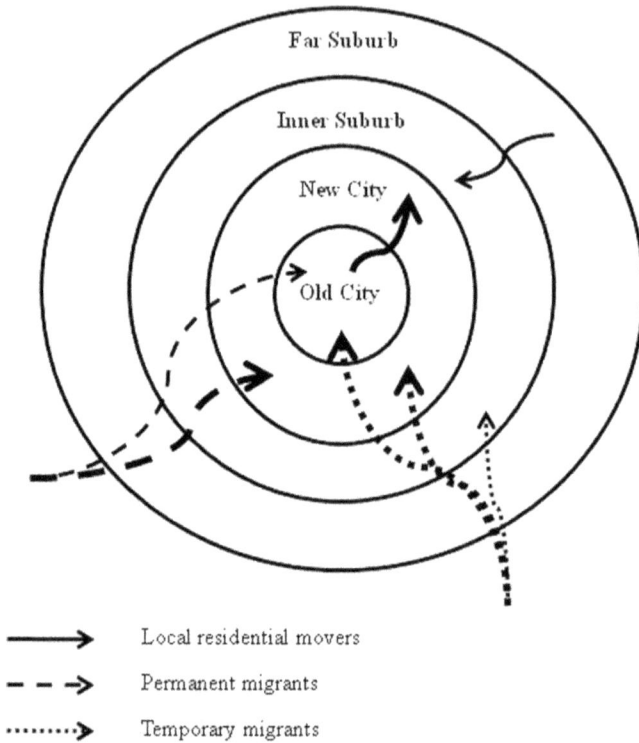

Far Suburb

Inner Suburb

New City

Old City

⟶ Local residential movers

- - ⟶ Permanent migrants

·······⟶ Temporary migrants

Note: The line width of flows indicates large vs. small volume of migrants.

*Figure 3.4* A schematic pattern of mobility in Wuhan.

and relative proximity to the city center so that well-off households such as residential movers and permanent migrants tended to move to the new city.

With obvious residential differentiation and sorting, the question is how severe is the degree of residential differentiation in Wuhan. Residential segregation has been measured using a variety of measures over the years (Massey and Denton, 1988; Duncan and Duncan, 1955; Lieberson *et al.*, 1981). We use two commonly used indices – index of dissimilarity (D),[12] and index of isolation (P).[13] According to Massey and Denton (1988), the index of dissimilarity (scaled 0–1) measures the evenness in residential patterns of two exclusive groups, and the percentage of one group that has to move across borders of small spatial units (e.g. sub-district) in order to match the residential distribution in a larger geographic area (e.g. city), while the index of isolation measures the degree of isolation (scaled 0–1) among group members. When the index of dissimilarity is below 0.3, the degree of segregation is considered low, 0.3–0.6 is considered moderate, while 0.6+ is considered high (Massy and Denton, 1988). So overall, the degree of residential segregation was relatively low for all four groups in Wuhan (D is between 0.20 and 0.25) according

*Table 3.8* Segregation indexes for different geographic units

| | Index of dissimilarity | | | | Isolation index | | | |
|---|---|---|---|---|---|---|---|---|
| Geographic unit | Residential movers (RM) | Permanent migrants (PM) | Temporary migrants (TM) | Non-movers (NM) | RM | PM | TM | NM |
| Wuhan | 0.20 | 0.25 | 0.23 | 0.23 | 0.17 | 0.40 | 0.28 | 0.34 |
| Old city | 0.16 | 0.17 | 0.25 | 0.12 | 0.13 | 0.36 | 0.30 | 0.32 |
| New city | 0.16 | 0.20 | 0.15 | 0.21 | 0.18 | 0.45 | 0.21 | 0.26 |
| Inner suburb | 0.20 | 0.28 | 0.20 | 0.25 | 0.19 | 0.23 | 0.38 | 0.36 |
| Far suburb | 0.53 | 0.30 | 0.31 | 0.36 | 0.26 | 0.29 | 0.27 | 0.57 |

to the Western standard (Table 3.8). Yet, there were significant spatial variations. In the far suburbs, D is higher than 0.3 for all groups, indicating a moderate but higher degree of segregation than the rest of the city. This was especially the case for residential movers as D is 0.53, approaching the 0.6 benchmark. This was probably due to uneven housing development in the far suburbs such that residential movers concentrate in some sub-districts with new housing developments.

The isolation index shows that migrants (permanent and temporary) and non-movers were moderately isolated, and a large share of social contact was among its own group members, while residential movers were the least isolated. Surprisingly, permanent migrants had a higher degree of isolation than temporary migrants (0.4 vs. 0.28). This was probably due to the fact that permanent migrants were mostly college students and government employees who concentrate in University City and where the provincial government was located. Spatially, there was also a large degree of variations. Non-movers in far suburbs (0.57), permanent migrants in old city (0.36) and new city (0.45) and temporary migrants in inner suburbs (0.38) had the highest degree of isolation. Compared to a high degree of segregation only in far suburbs, high degree of isolation might occur in any part of the city, depending on the specific group. It is interesting to note that temporary migrants, often compared to illegal immigrants in the West, were not a group with the highest degree of segregation and isolation. This shows that the difference between temporary migrants and the others is based mainly on class (instead of race or ethnicity) and housing access (due to hukou status). Instead of racial discrimination and ethnic avoidance, housing affordability and housing entitlements are the main reasons for the relatively low degree of residential segregation and isolation in Chinese cities.

## Changes since 2000

The first decade of the twenty-first century is a decade of profound housing marketization. Ideally a comparison between the 2000 and 2010 census would reveal the changing pattern of housing inequality and residential differentiation. Unfortunately, the Chinese government has not released the micro-level data for the 2010 census. We only have limited aggregated data of the 2010 census and a migrant survey in

2012 in Wuhan. Instead of different migrant groups, we only have data on temporary migrants, through which we aim to offer some insights of changes since 2000.

In 2010, there were 2.15 million temporary migrants in the study area, accounting for more than one-third (34.1 per cent) of its total population. The share of temporary migrants in 2010 was much higher than that in 2000 (22.7 per cent, see Table 3.2), indicating a rapid increase of temporary migrants in Wuhan during 2000–2010. In particular, temporary migrants increased rapidly in old commercial districts, such as Jianghan district and Qiaokou district (21 per cent increase) and inner suburban districts such as Hongshan (21 per cent) and Dongxihu district (31 per cent). In 2010, they became the majority group (more than 50 per cent of the total population) in 16 per cent of all sub-districts, with the mean of 31.5 per cent and the standard deviation of 18.3 per cent.

Spatially, 70 per cent of temporary migrants settled in seven urban districts, and they mainly concentrated in three types of communities (see Figure 3.5): 1) Commercial districts in the old city. As local residents moved out of the old city for better housing in the new city and suburbs, migrants moved into old cities often for job opportunities in services/sales and affordable old housing. Many migrants also lived in businesses where they worked during the day. For example, in Hanzheng sub-district in Hankou district, one of the famous commercial districts in Wuhan, 63.6 per cent of its population was temporary migrants in 2010. 2) Suburbs with "urban villages." Not different from before, inner suburbs with "urban villages" offer migrants not only affordable housing but also relative proximity to urban centers, thus they are popular destination for migrants. For example, in Hongshan sub-district (Hongshan district), 65 per cent of its population was migrants due to a large stock of affordable housing in urban villages and decent transport to cities.

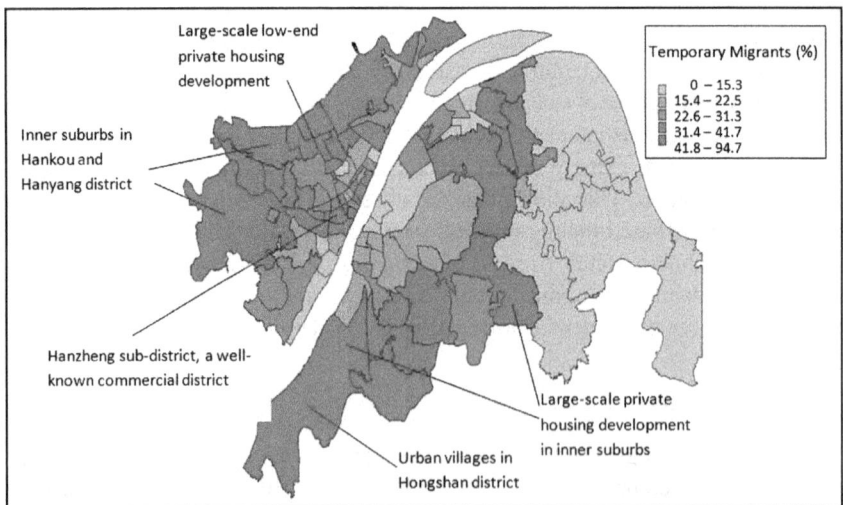

*Figure 3.5* Percentage of temporary migrants out of total population by sub-district in 2010.

3) Suburbs with large low-end private housing development. Wuhan has experienced a housing boom in the last decade with many large-scale private housing developments in suburbs, some of which can accommodate about 300,000 people (e.g. Xinhua Garden and Nanhu Garden). In addition to local residents, these large housing estates attracted well-off migrants to purchase private housing. In many of these sub-districts migrants accounted for more than 50 per cent of the total population; in Changfeng sub-district in Qiaokou district, migrants accounted for more than 80 per cent of its population. Compared to 2000, the concentration of temporary migrants in ownership-oriented house estates in suburbs is a new phenomenon.

Due to massive development of private housing in suburbs, housing consumption in Wuhan has improved significantly during 2000–2010. Per capita floor space increased from about 18.7 m² in 2000 to 28.2 m² in 2010. Unfortunately, we do not have access to housing information for different migrant groups in 2010. Yet, it is fair to assume all groups improved housing consumption due to trickle-down process, although gains might vary significantly between groups. According to the 2012 Wuhan Migrant Dynamic Survey, 73.5 per cent of temporary migrants lived in private rental housing, 8.0 per cent purchased homes, 8.2 per cent lived in employer-provided housing, while only 0.1 per cent lived in government-subsidized cheap rental housing. Compared to 2000, temporary migrants were more likely to live in private rental housing, while less likely to live in subsidized housing by the government or employers in 2010. This is a result of further housing marketization during 2000–2010.

## Conclusion and discussion

In the last three decades, Chinese cities have been experiencing profound social, economic and spatial transformation. We argue that mobility, together with hukou status, offers a useful lens to understand the socio-spatial sorting in Chinese cities. In contrast to the conventional dual division of urban residents and migrants, we divide the urban population into four major groups based on mobility: non-movers, residential movers, permanent migrants, and temporary migrants; each can be further divided based on their agricultural or non-agricultural hukou. Despite maturing housing markets, each group has different housing entitlements thus different housing consumption and residential patterns.

Using the 2000 census data, we show that overall there was a moderate degree of housing inequality and residential differentiation in Wuhan. Yet, housing inequality and residential differentiation varied significantly between groups and across space, and in some cases they have already reached an alarmingly high level. While residential movers lay at the top of the housing ladder, temporary migrants lay at the bottom of the housing ladder; yet interestingly the latter was not the most segregated and isolated group. In fact residential movers and non-movers in the far suburbs were more segregated, and permanent migrants in the new city were more isolated. While the exact reasons are difficult to pinpoint with the existing data, uneven housing development and functional zoning in suburbs have contributed to their higher degree of segregation and isolation. Permanent migrants shared more similarities with non-movers than temporary migrants. This demonstrates migrants' housing assimilation after they obtain local registration (or citizenship), which is different from immigrants in Western countries where race/ethnicity seems to have more lasting impact on housing attainment. It is clear that both market mechanism and socialist legacy shaped housing consumption in 2000. Yet, there are signs of further housing marketization and urbanization in the following decade, as there was a rapid increase in the volume of temporary migrants, and they were more likely to live in private housing in 2010.

The relatively low degree of housing inequality and residential differentiation in 2000 shows that the socio-spatial sorting in Wuhan was still at its early stage. At the same time, it shows that housing entitlement defined by hukou status and mobility is more important to housing inequality, and uneven housing development is more important to residential segregation than racial discrimination and ethnic avoidance as is the case in the West. The policy implication is that further hukou reform and proper urban planning and housing development would significantly reduce housing inequality and segregation in Chinese cities. Finally, this research shows once again the disadvantaged position of temporary migrants in the housing system. While the Chinese government has renewed its commitment in low-income housing in recent years (Huang, 2012), it focuses on urban residents with local hukou status. To reduce housing inequality, the Chinese government has to grant similar housing rights to temporary migrants by providing housing subsidies to qualified migrants on the one hand and encouraging the market provision of decent affordable housing to migrants on the other hand. Otherwise, the "housing divide" between migrants and local urban residents will never converge.

## Notes

1  We use "residential differentiation" instead of "residential segregation" because: 1) residential sorting is still at a relatively early stage in Chinese cities; 2) neighborhood sorting in Chinese cities is often based on social economic status, which may change over time, instead of race/ethnicity as in other countries due to the dominate ethnic Han population in China.
2  "Economic and comfortable housing" is provided by developers on government-provided land, and sold with government regulated prices to qualified urban households.
3  "Migrant enclaves" or "urban villages" are previously suburban villages that are engulfed by urban development. Because of the dual land system in China, land in these villages is collectively owned (compared to state-owned urban land), and villagers are entitled to build housing for self-occupancy, but now increasingly for rents. Constrained in housing options, migrants tend to concentrate in these villages for affordable housing.
4  The basic spatial unit in Chinese cities – sub-district (jian dao) or towns – is used for zoning. There are 35 sub-districts in the old city, 40 in the new city, 14 sub-districts or towns in inner suburbs, and 26 in far suburbs.
5  In 2012, the National Population and Family Planning Committee conducted a Migrant Dynamic Survey, which was a nationwide multi-stage stratified random sample of temporary migrants aged 15–59 without local hukou, who have left their hukou registration places for more than one month. The sample size for Hubei Province was 3,986 and for Wuhan city was 2,227.
6  People living in collective households are mainly students and factory workers living in dormitories and quarter housing.

7  An index scaled 0–1 is assigned to each facility, with 1 for the best/private facility, 0.5 for mediocre or shared facilities and 0 for no such facility. Then five indexes are summed to form the facility index.
8  Similarly, temporary migrants are generally not allowed to have self-build housing in cities. Yet our data show that 8 per cent of temporary migrants live in self-build housing. Most of them are villagers from suburban counties in Wuhan who are qualified for self-build housing. While one-third of them still have agricultural hukou, two thirds of them have already changed to non-agricultural hukou during rural-to-urban conversion (nong zhuan fei).
9  "Full property rights" include right of occupancy, the right to extract financial benefits, the right to dispose through resale and the right to bequeath it to others (Davis, 2003). "Partial property rights" means homeowners only have the right of occupancy and use-right, and they are not allowed to sell their homes on the market for profit within the first five years unless they pay the difference between discounted and market prices.
10  Temporary migrants may own homes at their hometowns. Yet this research focuses on their housing consumption in Wuhan.
11  Instead of one multinomial logistic regression, a set of binary logistic regressions was conducted due to small cell frequencies for some groups. Previous studies such as Logan *et al.* (2009) have adopted the same strategy in such a context.
12  It is calculated using the following: $D = \dfrac{1}{2}\sum_{i}\dfrac{t_i \mid p_i - P \mid}{TP(1-P)}$, where $t_i$ and $p_i$ are the total population and the "minority" proportion of district i for indices for the city (or sub-district i for indices for districts), and T and P are the population size and minority proportion of the whole city (or district).
13  The index of isolation index is calculated using the following: $_xP_x{}^* = \sum_{i}(\dfrac{x_i}{X})(\dfrac{x_i}{t_i})$, where $x_i$ and $t_i$ are numbers of population X and the total population in district i for indices for the city (or sub-district i for indices for districts), and X is the total number of population X city-wide (or district-wide).

# References

Bian, Y. (1994) *Work and Inequality in Urban China*. Albany, NY: State University of New York Press.

Bian, Y. and Liu, Y. (2005) Social stratification, housing property rights and housing satisfaction (Shehui Fenceng, Zhufang Chanquan He Juzhu Zhiliang). *Sociological Research (Shehuixue Yanjiu)*, 3, 82–98.

Bian, Y. and Logan, J. R. (1996) Market transition and the persistence of power: the changing stratification system in urban China. *American Sociological Review*, 739–58.

Cheng, T. and Selden, M. (1994) The origins and social consequences of China's hukou system. *The China Quarterly*, 139, 644–68.

Clark, W. A. V. (1986) Residential segregation in Americancities: a review and interpretation. *Population Research and Policy Review*, 5, 95–127.

Davis, D. (2003) From welfare benefit to capitalized asset. In Forrest, R. and Lee, J. (eds) *Chinese Urban Housing Reform*. London and New York: Routledge, pp. 183–96.

Deng, F. F. and Huang, Y. (2004) Uneven land reform and urban sprawl in China: the case of Beijing. *Progress in Planning*, 61, 211–36.

Denton, N. A. and Massey, D. S. (1991) Patterns of neighborhood transition in a multiethnic world: US metropolitan areas, 1970–1980. *Demography*, 28, 41–63.

Duncan, O. D. and Duncan, B. (1955) A methodological analysis of segregation indexes. *American Sociological Review*, 20, 210–17.

Galster, G. (1988) Residential segregation in American cities: a contrary review. *Population Research and Policy Review*, 7, 93–112.

Huang, Y. (2003) A room of one's own: housing consumption and residential crowding in transitional urban China. *Environment and Planning A*, 35, 591–614.

Huang, Y. (2005) From work-unit compounds to gated communities: Housing inequality and residential segregation in transitional Beijing. In Ma, L. J. C. and Wu, F. (eds) *Restructuring the Chinese City: changing society, economy and space.* London and New York: Routledge.

Huang, Y. (2012) Low-income housing in Chinese cities: policies and practices. *The China Quarterly*, 212, 941–64.

Huang, Y. and Clark, W. A. (2002) Housing tenure choice in transitional urban China: a multilevel analysis. *Urban Studies*, 39, 7–32.

Huang, Y. and Deng, F. F. (2006) Residential mobility in Chinese cities: a longitudinal analysis. *Housing Studies*, 21, 625–52.

Huang, Y. and Jiang, L. (2009) Housing inequality in transitional Beijing. *International Journal of Urban and Regional Research*, 33, 936–56.

Li, S.-M. (2000a) Housing consumption in urban China: a comparative study of Beijing and Guangzhou. *Environment and Planning A*, 32, 1115–34.

Li, S.-M. (2000b) The housing market and tenure decisions in Chinese cities: a multivariate analysis of the case of Guangzhou. *Housing Studies*, 15, 213–36.

Li, S.-M. (2003) Housing tenure and residential mobility in urban China: a study of commodity housing development in Beijing and Guangzhou. *Urban Affairs Review*, 38, 510–34.

Li, S.-M. (2004) *Residential Mobility and Urban Change in China: What Have We Learnt So Far?* Hong Kong: Centre for China Urban and Regional Studies, Hong Kong Baptist University.

Li, S.-M. (2009) Housing inequality in urban China: Guangzhou 1996 and 2005. *Espace populations sociétés. Space populations societies*, 3, 511–21.

Li, S.-M. and Huang, Y. (2006) Urban housing in China: market transition, housing mobility and neighbourhood change. *Housing Studies*, 21, 613–23.

Li, S.-M., Wang, D. and Law, F. Y.-T. (2005) Residential mobility in a changing housing system: Guangzhou, China, 1980–2001. *Urban Geography*, 26, 627–39.

Li, Z. and Wu, F. (2006) Socio-spatial differentiation and residential inequalities in Shanghai: a case study of three neighbourhoods. *Housing Studies*, 21, 695–717.

Li, Z. and Wu, F. (2008) Tenure-based residential segregation in post-reform Chinese cities: a case study of Shanghai. *Transactions of the Institute of British Geographers*, 33, 404–19.

Lieberson, S., Peach, C., Robinson, V. and Smith, S. (1981) An asymmetrical approach to segregation. *Ethnic Segregation in Cities*. London: Croom Helm.

Logan, J. R. and Bian, Y. (1993) Inequalities in access to community resources in a Chinese city. *Social Forces*, 72, 555–76.

Logan, J. R. and Bian, F. (1999) Family values and coresidence with married children in urban China. *Social Forces*, 77, 1253–82.

Logan, J. R., Bian, Y. and Bian, F. (1999) Housing inequality in urban China in the 1990s. *International Journal of Urban and Regional Research*, 23, 7–25.

Logan, J. R., Fang, Y. and Zhang, Z. (2010) The winners in China's urban housing reform. *Housing Studies*, 25, 101–17.

Ma, L. J. and Xiang, B. (1998) Native place, migration and the emergence of peasant enclaves in Beijing. *China Quarterly-London*, 155, September issue: 546–81.

Massey, D. S. and Denton, N. A. (1987) Trends in the residential segregation of Blacks, Hispanics, and Asians: 1970–1980. *American Sociological Review*, 52(6): 802–25.

Massey, D. S. and Denton, N. A. (1988) The dimensions of residential segregation. *Social Forces*, 67, 281–315.

Massey, D. S. and Denton, N. A. (1993) *American Apartheid: segregation and the making of the underclass*. Cambridge, MA: Harvard University Press.

NBSC, N. S. B. O. C. (2000) *Zhongguo tongji nianjian (China Statistics Yearbook, 2000)*. Beijing: China Statistics Press.

NBSC, N. S. B. O. C. (2012) *Zhongguo 2010 nian renkou pucha (China 2010 Population Census)*. Beijing: China Statistics Press.

Sato, H. (2006) Housing inequality and housing poverty in urban China in the late 1990s. *China Economic Review*, 17, 37–50.

State Council (1994) Guowuyuan Guanyu Shenhua Chengzhen Zuhfang Zhidu Gaige De Jueding (A Decision from the State Council on Deepening the Urban Housing Reform). Beijing.

State Council (1998) Guowuyuan Guanyu Jingyibu Shenhua Chengzhen Zhufang Zhidu Gaige Jiakuai Zhufang Jianshe De Tongzhi (A Notification from the State Council on Further Deepening the Reform of Urban Housing System and Accelerating Housing Construction). Beijing.

Szelenyi, I. (1983) *Urban Inequalities under State Socialism*. Oxford: Oxford University Press.

Walder, A. G. (1986) *Communist Neo-Traditionalism: work and authority in Chinese industry*. Berkeley, CA: University of California Press.

Wang, Y. P. and Murie, A. (1999) Commercial housing development in urban China. *Urban Studies*, 36, 1475–94.

Wang, Y. P. and Murie, A. (2000) Social and spatial implications of housing reform in China. *International Journal of Urban and Regional Research*, 24, 397–417.

Wang, Y. P., Wang, Y. and Bramley, G. (2005) Chinese housing reform in state-owned enterprises and its impacts on different social groups. *Urban Studies*, 42, 1859–78.

Wu, W. (2002) Migrant housing in urban China: choices and constraints. *Urban Affairs Review*, 38, 90–119.

Yang, Y., Tian, Y., Yi, C. and He, X. (2004) An analysis of intra-urban mobility and the change of urban spatial pattern – a case study of Wuhan (Da chengshi de neibu qianyi yu chengshi kongjian dongtai fenxi – yi wuhanshi weili). *Population Research (Renkou yanjiu)*, 28, 47–50.

Yeh, A. G. O., Xu, X. and Hu, H. (1995) Social space in Guangzhou City, China. *Urban Geography*, 16, 595–621.

Yi, C. and Huang, Y. (2012) Housing Consumption and Housing Ineaqulity in Chinese Cities during the First Decade of the 21st Century. *Manuscript*.

# 4 Neighborhood differentiation and inequality in Nanjing

## Implications for planning a harmonious society

*Brenda Madrazo Gonzalez*

## Introduction

It is widely known that neighborhoods are increasingly being differentiated and that there is a growing inequality in urban China (He *et al.*, 2010; Li and Huang, 2006). Thirty years ago, China was a relatively homogenous society with fairly equal housing conditions and most urban residents were exposed to rather similar urban environments. The housing reform of 1998 brought about many changes, which have significantly shaped the urban environment and the social geography of cities. Already at the turn of the century, Wang and Murie (2000) forecasted that spatial differentiation would occur according to differentiated areas related to construction periods. These newly divided cities show unprecedented level of diversity and heterogeneity in residential urban spaces (Wu, 2010b; Wu and He, 2005).

This increasing socio-spatial differentiation raises questions around inequality. In the past couple of years, China has implemented policies aimed at reducing or slowing down the growing rate of inequality. For example, limitations have been set to the number of homes that can be owned by one individual; a maximum housing area for newly built homes was limited to 90m²; or more recently, a 20 per cent income tax on home sales was announced. For these or any other policies to be effective—and in order for them to support a more equitable distribution of resources—a through understanding of the current conditions of inequality and the interdependencies occurring between neighborhoods are essential (Galster, 2001; Kearns and Parkinson, 2001). It is also imperative to identify the implications on residents' perceptions and expectations regarding the increasing differentiation. As China's leadership continues to work towards a harmonious society, a detailed examination of neighborhood differentiation between and within, together with an evaluation of levels of inequality, seems crucial for the design of spatial and social planning policies.

To this end, several scholars have made important contributions to a deeper understanding of the current urban transformation and differentiation in urban China. On one hand, socio-spatial differentiation has been studied at the sub-district level (Wu and Li, 2005) as well as at the neighborhood level with emphasis on poverty neighborhoods (He and Wu, 2007; He *et al.*, 2008; 2010; Li and Wu,

2006; Liu and Wu, 2006; Liu *et al.*, 2008; Wu, 2007; Wu and He, 2005; Wu *et al.*, 2010) and some on the residential location of the affluent (Hu and Kaplan, 2001). On the other hand, studies on housing inequality have focused on aspects of housing consumption, tenure and prices (Huang, 2004; Huang and Clark, 2002; Li,2000a, 2000b; Li, 2012; Li and Yi, 2007; Logan *et al.*, 2009). Most of these studies have used national or citywide data. To this date, with some exceptions (He, 2013), there is still a gap not only in terms of the use of contemporary data to examine the latest changes, but also in providing a comparative analysis of the extent of differentiation between and within different neighborhood types and the significance of this for inequality. In addition, little is known about residents' perceived inequality in terms of how they experience their residential space.

It is in this context that this chapter aims at creating a more comprehensive understanding of current conditions of actual and perceived inequality. By scrutinizing a multi-neighborhood household survey collected in Nanjing at the end of 2010, this study provides a deeper understanding of the current neighborhood differentiation in terms of the spatial structure and social change between and within different four neighborhood types. It is argued that even though differences between neighborhood types are quite prominent due to the spatial, institutional and temporal settings, inequality within each neighborhood type is higher and relevant to address policy-wise.

The following section provides a brief discussion on the unit of analysis, followed by an account of data and methodology. The next section provides an examination of neighborhood differentiation in terms of dwelling attributes and socio-demographic characteristics. Thereafter, inequality is measured using the Gini-coefficient and Theil index to provide a decomposition of inequality based on spatially defined subgroups. The final section concludes with recommendations for policy.

## The neighborhood as unit of analysis

In almost every part of the world neighborhoods are the core constituents of the urban fabric. Every city is composed of these residential spaces, which serve different functions for economic activities, service provision and socialization. Spatial attributes of a neighborhood vary in quantity and composition, making neighborhoods "distinctly categorized by type and/or by quality" (Galster, 2001: 2113). Physical aspects that define a neighborhood include the landscaping, streetscaping, design and materials. In addition to these physical characteristics, certain neighborhood characteristics are a reflection of the collective attributes of its residents. For example: age distribution, family composition, education levels, and occupation. Galster (2001) highlights the importance of residents, given that their aggregated attributes are assigned to the neighborhood itself. Moreover, issues of social exclusion, marginalization and segregation, all have a spatial component, which in most cases, ultimately comes down to the neighborhood level.

The term "neighborhood" was first coined by William E. Drummond in 1912 (Johnson, 2002) when planners, architects and urban policy makers were looking for a concept to improve living conditions and that could satisfy human needs. As a design solution, it provided a space for the interaction between the built environment and the residents; a micro community with a focus on housing. In China, the concept of the neighborhood was introduced by Western planners and Western-trained Chinese planners in the late 1940s (for a historical review see Lu, 2006).

Since then, the neighborhood has served as a key unit for urban development. This study takes the neighborhood as the primary unit of analysis. In particular, four neighborhood types are examined. First, *traditional-neighborhoods*: inner city neighborhoods built before 1949. Second, former *work-unit* (*danwei*): productive units mainly built during the socialist time (1949–1978), and allocated as welfare housing. Third, *commercial-neighborhoods*: began to be built in the late 1990s and sold at market prices. Fourth, *urban-villages* neighborhoods: locally developed since the 80s in the inner suburbs and urban fringe as a result of urban sprawl and land reform.

Each neighborhood type comprises a distinct set of characteristics, as each is representative of a particular time period reflecting a distinctive institutional context. Ten years into the turn of the twenty-first century and about twelve years after the housing reform, these neighborhood types co-exist in Chinese cities. Already from their spatial configuration and built environment, it is apparent that there is a growing neighborhood differentiation.

## Data and methodology

Fieldwork was carried out in the capital of Jiangsu Province, Nanjing, a second-tier coastal city. Nanjing has a historical importance, as it has been the capital of ten dynasties and the capital of the Republic of China. During the planned economy (1949–1978), it was chosen by the central government for industrial development. As a traditional industrial city, it accommodates large state-owned enterprises in heavy industry and it holds a strategic location for industrial growth in industries like petrochemical, machinery and textiles. Nowadays, it is a typical example of a Chinese city experiencing market transition and economic restructuring (He *et al.*, 2008).

A multi-neighborhood survey was conducted between October and December of 2010 by means of face-to-face home visits in the four types of neighborhoods. For each neighborhood type, there were two different neighborhoods in the sample. Traditional include Pingshijie and Diaoyutai; work-unit are Xiaoxixincun and Nanxiucun; commercial include Meihuashan and Zhonghai; and Gaojiecun and Xiangshioercun are the urban-villages. All neighborhoods are located within the urban city core of Nanjing (Figure 4.1).

The target was to gather 800 surveys in total, 100 in each neighborhood. A systematic random sampling with a fixed interval was used to select respondents. In total, 1488 addresses were visited. Of these, 678 had to be counted as nonresponse because either residents did not want to participate or there was no one at home. The response rate is of 55 per cent. In total, 826 full surveys were gathered, and after revision for completeness and consistency 804 surveys are included in

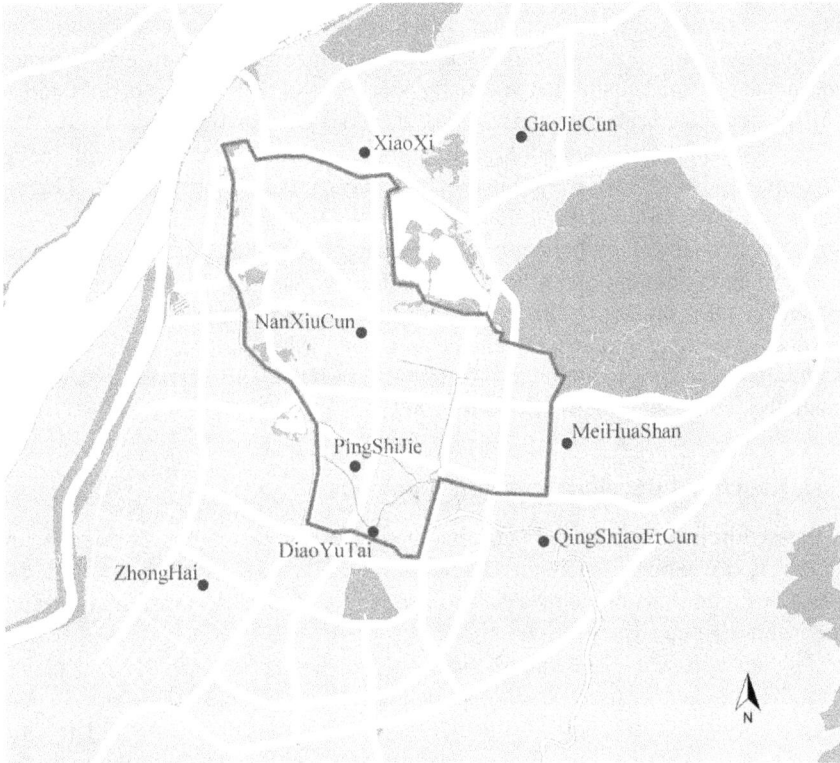

*Figure 4.1* Location of surveyed neighborhoods.

the analysis. Either the household head or the spouse completed the survey. In order to provide a more representative picture of the neighborhood, the survey gathers information not only at the individual level, but also at the household level. Socio-demographic information like age, gender, education, and hukou was collected for every household member living on the same address, resulting in a total population sample of 1937 people. The survey also gathers the respondent's current and previous housing conditions and evaluations, reasons for mobility, future expectations, and information on neighborly relations.

In order to analyze the differences between and within the neighborhoods, two commonly used measures for inequality, the Gini-coefficient and the Theil index are employed. Measurements of inequality explain the relative variation of an attribute among individuals or groups of people. The first measure was proposed by the Italian Corrado Gini and measures the distribution of an attribute, like income, over the total population sample. The coefficient varies between perfect equality measured as 0, and 1, which is perfect inequality. Since this measurement uses the mean value of the total population, a comparison of two Gini-coefficients between different groups can only tell something about the relative distribution of that attribute in comparison to the other group. This means, for example, two neighborhoods with a same Gini-coefficient of 0.3, which is already regarded as unequal, does not mean that they are equally rich or equally poor, but that their income distribution is equally distributed. Thus, this measurement lacks a comparative aspect.

To overcome this methodological problem, another tool, the Theil index proposed by Henri Theil (1967) is used in the analysis. It has the benefit of being additive across different subgroups. This means that the overall measure is the sum of inequalities within and between subgroups and, thus, a comparison between and within groups is possible. In other words, this index can be decomposed into the sum of the individual groups and the proportion of variability relative to the overall inequality can be identified. It has also been argued to be a solid analytical tool to examine inequalities attributable to between and within spatially defined subgroups (Novotný 2007).

## Neighborhood development and typology

This section incorporates the main findings of existing literature, together with fieldwork to explain the main characteristics of each neighborhood type by providing a brief historical overview of the drivers of housing transformation and their effect on how these neighborhoods look like today.

The development of neighborhoods in China has experienced several major transformations over time. Traditional-neighborhoods (Figure 4.2), which have a long history in the inner city, are the oldest type of residential area that still accommodates a significant group of the population in Chinese cities. In Nanjing, these were built during the Ming and Qing Dynasties in the fifteenth and nineteenth centuries respectively with a central courtyard. Former private housing was also built in these areas at the beginning of the twentieth century. After 1949, private property was confiscated by the state and housing got divided into smaller units for several families to share. Currently, these areas are mainly composed of rundown one- or two-story buildings, are managed by the municipal housing bureaus and are sometimes used as resettlement housing (Logan *et al.*, 1999). Given their central location, these neighborhoods have been identified as key targets for redevelopment, a socio-spatial change leading to displacement and gentrification (He, 2010; He and Wu, 2007; Li and Song, 2009; Wu, 2004a). Response from residents is very mixed and even though in some cases demolishment has occurred for several years, there is still a group of mainly elderly citizens that do not want to relocate. These neighborhoods will most likely still exist for some years as there is still resistance from the original residents to move; however, for their child it might be easier to accept compensation and redevelopment, leaving way for urban planners to demolish these areas completely. Previous research has found that these areas are generally characterized by an overrepresentation of the elderly, a high population density, low education levels, and a concentration of poverty through a mix of laid-off and migrants (He *et al.*, 2010; Liu and Wu, 2006; Wu and He, 2005).

*Figure 4.2* Traditional neighborhoods, F1&4, street view showing traditional characteristics; F2, shared semi-open kitchen; F3, view of a neighborhood street from above; F5, former private housing.

The year 1949 marked a turning point for urban development. The Chinese Communist Party (CCP) pronounced the aim of creating an egalitarian society. From then onwards national five-year plans set out the guidelines for economic and social development, consequently, having implications for the urban development. Massive construction projects were initiated by work units to ease the existing housing shortages that resulted from the Sino-Japanese war. These large-scale residential developments, the new work-unit built neighborhoods (Figure 4.3), provided residential six- to eight-story buildings with open staircases and without elevators. They resemble the company town model living facilities with a functional and economic integration of residence and production in close proximity. Apartments, canteens, dormitories, public bathhouses, nurseries and primary schools were all integrated in close proximity. Different types of work units, for example industrial, education or government, were able to provide different qualities of services and features exclusive to their residents (Lu, 2006), depending on their power and relation to the central government. Overall, this type of residence provided highly subsidized housing as part of the welfare program. It was considered a privileged form of urban housing and constituted the single

*Figure 4.3* Work-unit neighborhoods, F1 & 4, open entrance and staircase; F2–3, typical building structure; F5, neighborhood gate.

most important form of organization during the socialist period (Wu, 2010b). By the mid-1980s, work-units owned practically all of the urban public housing (Wang, 2000).

After the nationwide housing reform of 1998, sitting tenants were encouraged to buy their flats. Different schemes were created to ensure shift from rent-occupied to owned-occupied housing and the formation of the housing market (for an analysis of policies see Wang *et al.*, 2012). Overall, as these neighborhoods experienced housing privatization, and different social groups were affected (Wang *et al.*, 2005) low-income households became owners of work-unit apartments, which are generally considered low capitalized assets within the market (Huang and Clark, 2002; Wu, 2004b; Wu, 2007). Previous studies mainly focusing on manufacturing work-units, have called these areas "degraded workers villages" due to the concentration of industrial laid-off workers (He *et al.*, 2010) and given that many of these neighborhoods tend to house the urban poor that were hit by market redundancies (Wu, 2004b; 2007).

As residential development got transferred to private developers as part of the housing commodification, commercial housing neighborhoods (Figure 4.4) started to appear in the early 1990s. There is a substantial variation between neighborhoods belonging to this type. Most of the newly constructed housing after the

*Figure 4.4* Commercial neighborhoods, F1–5, landscaping, amenities and services.

reform was bought by work units and sold to employees at highly subsidized prices based on institutional factors such as employment history and occupational rank (Li, 2000b). Those built in the early period resemble work-unit housing in their physical characteristics although they differ in that they represent housing commodification, not privatization. At a later stage, the design principle of the micro-district (*xiaoqu*) was widely implemented for commercial-neighborhoods. The concept was transmitted from the Soviet Union socialist planners. This scheme gained support as it provided a unit for national community building (*shequ jianse*), a way to organize residents' lives efficiently, and the basic unit for new urban governance (Lu, 2006). These micro-districts offer variation in terms of location, amenities, landscaping, property management services, elaborated security systems and different types of building design (height, orientation, size of dwelling, number of rooms, size of bedrooms and living room). Most buildings in these areas are residential multi-story buildings and in some cases include single-family housing (villa). Developers cater to the newly rich, as in principle access to this housing now depends on income, and not institutional attachments, as it did still in the end of the 1990s. This type of neighborhood is the model for present-day planning in Chinese cities.

The last type of neighborhood examined is the "urban-village" or *chengzhoncun* (Figure 4.5) (for discussion of the concept see Chung, 2010). These neighborhoods started to emerge in the early 1990s as cities grew, and traditionally rural and collectively owned land started to be encompassed into the city. As the government reclaimed the land for urban expansion, farmers were left without their traditional means of livelihood. Therefore, farmers turned into landlords by building rooms on their housing plots and renting them out to rural migrants that moved to the

*Figure 4.5* Urban village neighborhoods, F1, street store; F2–4, diversity of housing constructions; F5, landlord's house.

city in search of employment. Planning regulations are usually not met and these
neighborhoods tend to have narrow streets to maximize housing opportunities. In
terms of height, most of the buildings are multi-storied. For example, in coastal
cities buildings can be ten to fifteen floors high, while in other cities like Nanjing,
they are just two or three floors. Urban-villages have a mixed land use where
industries are also located (Hao *et al.*, 2011). Urban officials and policy makers
tend to regard these areas as problematic and undesirable due to their gray status.
However, they offer significant affordable housing opportunities for migrants
(Wang *et al.*, 2009). Moreover, these neighborhoods tend to offer all sorts of
services from small restaurants to supermarkets and schools. These areas have
been characterized as concentrations of private rental housing (Wu, 2007) and low-
quality market rental at high prices (Liu *et al.*, 2010; Logan *et al.*, 2009).

## Current socio-spatial differentiation between and within the four neighborhood types

Using the survey data, this section examines both dwelling attributes as well as
socio-economic characteristics of the four different neighborhood types in terms

of their distribution within the neighborhood and in comparison to other neighborhood types.

### Differentiation of dwelling attributes

Among the four neighborhood types (Table 4.1) is not surprising that the largest concentration of the smallest units is located in urban-villages as these units were built with the intention of maximizing opportunities for renting one-room units to migrants. Slightly bigger units are more common in traditional-neighborhoods; but the large majority are under 60m². In work-units, most of the apartments range between 61–80m² and in this sample there were no apartments bigger than 100m². Clearly, the largest units are located in commercial housing with a majority well over 100m². Similarly, this is reflected in the number of sleeping rooms. One-bedroom units are primarily found in urban-villages and traditional areas; whereas two-bedrooms is characteristic of work units, and three-and-four-bedrooms for commercial. This does not directly reflect the size of the apartments, as traditionally, sleeping rooms used to be larger than living rooms and this relation has changed. This differentiation in terms of housing space and internal character reflects the time-institutional context in which the different neighborhoods were built and position themselves in a different niche in terms of the housing market.

Regarding facilities, in traditional housing it is common to find a partly open corridor with a few gas stoves that serves as a shared kitchen where neighbors commonly cook together, while in urban-villages it is more common for renters to have a small gas stove in their room or just outside in the corridor, reflecting a comparatively less social dynamic around food. Work-units usually have a closed

*Table 4.1* Dwelling attributes per neighborhood type

|  | Traditional | Work-unit | Commercial | Urban village |
|---|---|---|---|---|
| Housing area (m²) % |  |  |  |  |
| <= 20 | 30 | 2 | 0 | 65 |
| 21–40 | 39 | 5 | 0 | 18 |
| 41–60 | 14 | 25 | 1 | 3 |
| 61–80 | 6 | 59 | 9 | 3 |
| 81–100 | 4 | 10 | 18 | 4 |
| 101–120 | 4 | 0 | 25 | 2 |
| 121–150 | 2 | 0 | 31 | 1 |
| >= 150 | 2 | 0 | 18 | 3 |
| Number of sleeping rooms % |  |  |  |  |
| 1 | 61 | 11 | 0 | 82 |
| 2 | 25 | 74 | 38 | 10 |
| 3–4 | 12 | 16 | 62 | 7 |
| >= 5 | 2 | 0 | 1 | 1 |
| Tenure % |  |  |  |  |
| Rent | 47 | 14 | 5 | 90 |
| Own | 3 | 78 | 91 | 0 |
| Free (inherited/self-built) | 50 | 8 | 4 | 10 |

room used for cooking while commercial housing might also have an open kitchen concept. In general, units in urban-villages have no private toilet or shower, similar to traditional housing, where there are public toilets. Work-unit housing tends to have one shower and toilet per unit, while in commercial housing one or even two are most common.

In terms of tenure, traditional housing has historically been inherited from one generation to another. However, the survey results show that this has changed as half of the residents have inherited, but about the other half report to be renting. This could be explained by the ongoing redevelopment where some of the dwellings have been demolished, others emptied by the original residents and are now rented out for short term to migrants or for relocation purposes. In work-units and commercial housing the housing reform seems to have achieved its change of tenure policy as the large majority of residents own their housing (Li, 2000a). The percentage of renters in work-units and to a much smaller extent, in commercial housing, point to a clear increase for these dwellings to be rented in the private market. Many times, the owners of a work-unit move to commercial housing and rent out their work unit, or leave it to family members for free. The same situation occurs in commercial housing, where the ones that have the opportunity to buy another commercial apartment, leave their first commercial unit to a family member (parents or child). In urban-villages the tenure distribution clearly reflects the social composition of the neighborhood, where the large majority of migrants rent to a small group of original villagers, the landlords who self-built their homes.

### Differentiation in socio-demographic characteristics

An overview of all characteristics is provided in Table 4.2. On average, the household size is of three people in all neighborhoods, except in work unit where it is two. The biggest households are found in commercial housing where many times the couple brings their parents to take care of their son/daughter. Also, in traditional housing there are bigger household sizes. In some cases, this is explained by the fact that a child is registered and physically lives with their grandparents most of the week to facilitate access to schools, while parents live elsewhere. Other times, it is simply that as houses are inherited, several generations continue to live there. In work-units, one-generation household structures are common, although two or three represent the majority. Although there is a comparatively similar sized group of one-generation households in work-units and urban-villages, the distribution within the urban-village shows that overall most of the households are two or three person dwellings. This, together with the gender distribution, reflects the change in the way migrants relate to the city. Second-generation migrants are no longer young males moving alone, but families consisting of both partners and child(ren).

The distribution of different age groups is a crucial aspect to take into account to understand the different life experiences and thus, expectations of residents. Clearly, the concentration of youngest groups is in the urban-village, as half of

*Table 4.2* Socio-demographic attributes per neighborhood type

| | Traditional | Work-unit | Commercial | Urban village |
|---|---|---|---|---|
| Household size (person) % | | | | |
| 1 | 3 | 12 | 2 | 11 |
| 2 | 20 | 38 | 23 | 36 |
| 3 | 42 | 30 | 36 | 40 |
| 4 | 16 | 10 | 17 | 7 |
| 5 | 12 | 8 | 18 | 5 |
| >= 6 | 6 | 4 | 3 | 1 |
| Gender % | | | | |
| Female | 48 | 49 | 52 | 46 |
| Male | 52 | 51 | 48 | 54 |
| Age (years) % | | | | |
| 1–18 | 4 | 6 | 13 | 15 |
| 19–30 | 16 | 16 | 16 | 25 |
| 31–45 | 21 | 24 | 32 | 43 |
| 46–60 | 36 | 15 | 17 | 12 |
| >= 61 | 23 | 38 | 22 | 5 |
| Hukou % | | | | |
| Local urban | 84 | 89 | 88 | 10 |
| Other | 16 | 11 | 12 | 90 |
| Marital status %* | | | | |
| Single | 16 | 12 | 9 | 7 |
| Married | 73 | 81 | 86 | 91 |
| Divorced/widowed | 10 | 7 | 5 | 2 |
| Education %* | | | | |
| Iliterate | 7 | 3 | 2 | 4 |
| Primary | 9 | 6 | 4 | 18 |
| Highschool | 61 | 32 | 17 | 71 |
| Technical | 17 | 16 | 26 | 6 |
| University | 6 | 43 | 52 | 1 |
| Employment %* | | | | |
| Not working | 53 | 55 | 43 | 31 |
| Working | 47 | 45 | 57 | 69 |
| Occupation %** | | | | |
| Worker | 41 | 27 | 2 | 52 |
| Clerk | 30 | 25 | 58 | 9 |
| Professional | 3 | 38 | 20 | 4 |
| Entrepreneur | 0 | 1 | 12 | 0 |
| Self-employed/informal | 26 | 9 | 7 | 34 |
| Household monthly income (CN元) %*** | | | | |
| <= 1500 | 21 | 5 | 1 | 6 |
| 1501–3500 | 43 | 32 | 3 | 48 |
| 3501–5500 | 28 | 26 | 17 | 37 |
| 5501–9500 | 5 | 25 | 30 | 7 |
| 9501–10000 | 2 | 8 | 31 | 2 |
| >= 10001 | 1 | 4 | 18 | 1 |
| Length of residence % | | | | |
| Before 1949 | 17 | 1 | 0 | 2 |
| 1949–1983 | 45 | 15 | 0 | 3 |
| 1984–1997 | 16 | 29 | 3 | 10 |
| 1998–2004 | 6 | 20 | 28 | 22 |
| 2005–2010 | 16 | 35 | 69 | 63 |

*The sample only includes all household members above 18 years.
**The sample only includes all household members above 18 years old that report being employed.
***Includes main salary, bonus, subsidies, spring festival, 13th month salary of the household.

the population consists of people under thirty years old. This includes a significant number of people under eighteen, pointing at the growing number of children in these neighborhoods. Within the urban-village the largest concentration corresponds to the generation of older migrants who were born before 1980 (Fan, 2008), which most likely indicates that they have lived in the city for several years. Similarly, this age group is the largest in commercial housing indicating that relatively young people have moved to commercial housing most likely with the economic support of their parents. The largest concentration of people above sixty-one, that are the ones that have lived throughout the turbulent times of the Nanjing massacre, the Great Leap Forward or the Cultural Revolution, are in traditional and work units. In all neighborhoods, the large majority of residents older than eighteen are married. Of the single population the highest concentration is in traditional housing which point mainly to the individuals that have been relocated.

Predominantly, urban hukou is the largest group in every neighborhood type except in urban-villages where this relation is inverted. This is a clear indication that rural migrants concentrate in urban-villages but albeit the small numbers, they are also finding housing in traditional housing located right in the city center or even in some manufacturing work units. For commercial housing most of the non-local urban hukou are not rural migrants, but migrants from other cities.

Overall, in the four neighborhood types there is a relative high level of education as very few have primary school as the highest level of education achieved; although this percentage is higher in urban-villages reflecting previous urban–rural policies. Both in traditional housing and urban-villages, the majority of the population has completed their education up to high school. Although work unit shows a mix of education levels, work unit and commercial mainly house the highly educated that have completed a university degree. Education is an important factor as it has an interdependency with housing given that there is a general well-known connection between the reputation of one's university, one's job's rank, and the access to a pool of resources, being financial or in-kind.

When examining employment versus not-working (laid-off, retired, unemployed, housewife/husband) as a whole between the different neighborhood types, contrary to urban myths, urban-village is the neighborhood where the largest proportion of residents work compared to other neighborhoods. Despite the fact that most residents in the urban-villages work as service or manufacturing workers or in the informal sector, unemployment within the neighborhood still stands out as relatively high as it is expected that migrants move to the city because of work. This could be explained in different ways. First, it could be a temporal factor where the survey was undertaken relatively short before the spring festival; or it could be that the new generation of migrants move to the city without a job; or thirdly, that since both partners and child come to the city, one of them stays at home taking care of the child while they are young. In terms of unemployment, the highest rate is reported in traditional housing and work-units.

Still, the proportion is sizable in, for example, commercial housing, reflecting the grandparents that live with their son/daughter.

Even though income is a key measure for studies on differentiation and inequality, it is a complex and rather inaccurate measure in China because of all the different allowances, subsidies and in-kind modes of exchange. This item is relevant, it should always take into account its relative comparative value. Its distribution shows that the majority of the population within traditional housing earn about as much as residents in urban-villages. Nevertheless, the group under the minimum living standard is much larger in traditional housing. Households' income in work-units tend to be under the 10,000 yuan, whereas in commercial housing more households have a higher income, which can many times be much higher than the 10,000 yuan. This points to an interesting situation where high income residents do live in work-units; however, after passing certain threshold of income, most likely they move to commercial housing.

Residential mobility is contributing to the deepening of neighborhood differentiation (Huang and Deng, 2006). Research has found that neighborhood attributes are more important than dwelling attributes when it comes to preferences (Wang and Li, 2006). Not surprisingly, length of residence in both commercial housing and urban-villages show that more than 90 per cent of the residents moved in after the housing reform, with a majority of them moving after the year 2005. Conversely, traditional-neighborhoods congregate a significant group of residents that have lived the longest in the same neighborhood as their housing is inherited from generation to generation. Also, the data shows that a large group moved there after 1949, when the CCP took over and abolished private property; and that in the last five years of the first decade of the twentieth century, more people have moved in, mainly, as relocation housing. Work-units on the other hand, show that a significant group moved in during the 1980s. Still, in the five years before the data was collected, there were still a noteworthy percentage of residents moving in. This could point at a higher mobility trend, mainly in the rental market.

## Inequality between and within the four neighborhood types

### *Statistical inequality*

It has been asserted that the different neighborhood types have certain attributes in common as well as many distinctive ones. To understand the current differences between these neighborhood types in terms of inequality, using Stata, the Gini-coefficient was calculated for attributes that could indicate high inequality such as housing space, income, education, occupation, age and tenure (Figure 4.6). The two aspects that show not only the highest magnitude of inequality, but are considered to be quite unequal due to their distribution are housing area and income. The Theil index is calculated (FAO, 2006) in order to further understand the statistical degree of heterogeneity between and within the neighborhoods in terms of these two attributes (Table 4.3).

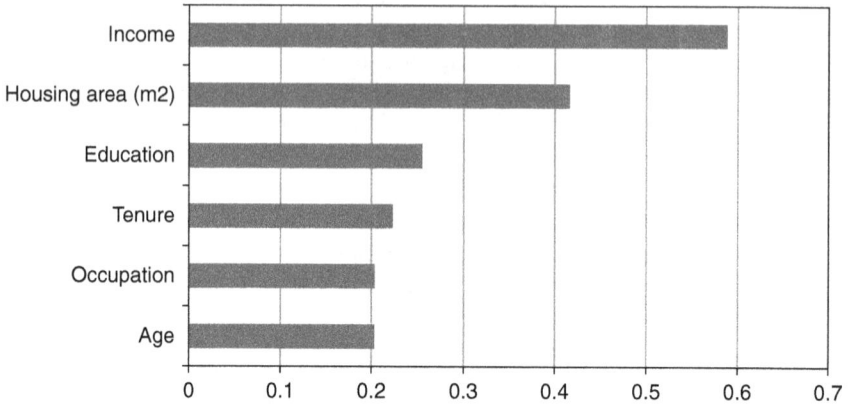

*Figure 4.6* Gini-coefficient, selected attributes of the four neighborhoods (N=804).

In terms of housing area, the overall Theil value is 0.2997. The variation is higher within than between in traditional-neighborhoods and urban-villages; whereas, the variation of m² is lower within than between in work-unit and commercial housing. This means that the variance of m² in work units and commercial housing is lower as the range of unit sizes do not vary as much. Although in principle it is true that the housing space within the average commercial-neighborhood might not vary as much; the variation within different commercial-neighborhoods can be tremendous. A similar analysis of only commercial-neighborhoods that include villas will surely give different results. In terms of the comparatively higher variance found within urban-villages, this number reflects the large differences between the housing of the two main groups: the small unit of rental accommodation and the much larger housing area of landlords. It is for this reason that the score for urban-villages is the main contributor to the overall Theil index value for housing area.

Regarding income, the absolute value of Theil is quite high at 0.8675. As already seen in the previous section; there are people with a very low income living in traditional housing whereas in commercial housing there are residents that earn much more. As seen by decomposing the value, the variation is higher within than

*Table 4.3* Theil index for housing area (m²) and household income for four neighborhood types

|  | *Housing area (m²)* | *Household income* |
|---|---|---|
| Between neighborhoods | 0.130209367 | 0.229505466 |
| Within neighborhoods |  |  |
| Traditional | 0.331657778 | 0.504918973 |
| Work-unit | 0.028242723 | 0.819361938 |
| Commercial | 0.060176548 | 0.668821364 |
| Urban village | 0.617131531 | 0.241313285 |
| Overall Theil index | 0.299729036 | 0.867521507 |

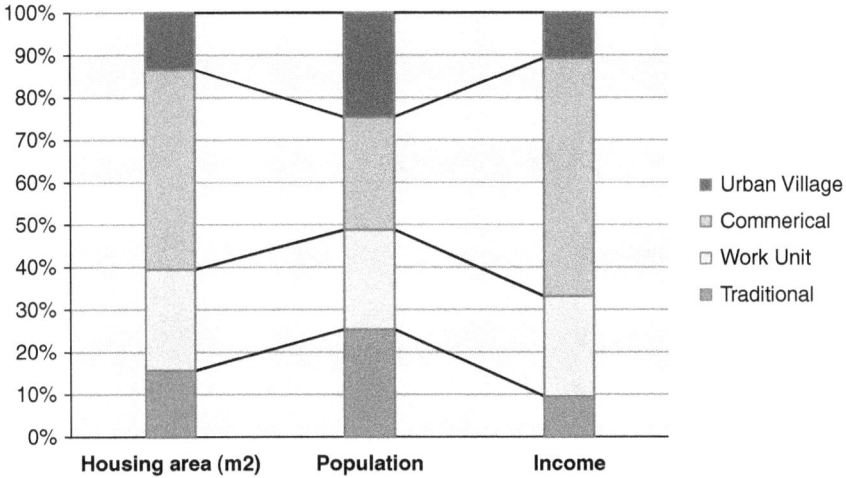

*Figure 4.7* Proportional distribution of housing area and income between four types of neighborhoods.

between the neighborhoods. This shows that in terms of income variation, all neighborhoods show between them a similar degree of inequality. However, the income variation within each neighborhood is rather high except for urban-villages. The highest inequality is shown within work-unit, followed by commercial. The once relatively equal work-unit neighborhood has turned into the most unequal in terms of income distribution after the housing reform. There is a mix of population within this type of neighborhood. On one hand, a large group of laid-off and retired population; while on the other, social-period privileged groups that were enabled to buy their housing at a subsidized price, and that up to date, their current housing still represents a rather convenient option to stay. It would be insightful to find out how many of these households only have a work-unit housing versus the number of households that in addition have an apartment in commercial housing where they live during the weekend. Work-unit neighborhood contributes the most to the overall inequality value in terms of income distribution. Figure 4.7 shows the proportional distribution of housing area and income, relative to the population size of each neighborhood. Residents of traditional and urban-village neighborhoods have a smaller share of the total housing area and income; while the population in commercial-neighborhoods has a larger proportion of both.

### Residents' perceptions

In addition to the traditional measures of inequality, it is relevant to examine residents' perceptions regarding their own evaluation of their housing conditions (Table 4.4). Responses on living status and income show that the largest concentration of more dissatisfied residents live in traditional housing, where inequality is high within the neighborhood. However, in urban-villages, where inequality is

*Table 4.4* Respondents' evaluations

|  | Traditional | Work-unit | Commercial | Urban village |
|---|---|---|---|---|
| Evaluation of housing conditions % |  |  |  |  |
| Very poor | 11 | 1 | 0 | 1 |
| Poor | 56 | 19 | 3 | 24 |
| Adequate | 27 | 53 | 35 | 68 |
| Good | 6 | 26 | 56 | 6 |
| Very good | 1 | 1 | 6 | 1 |
| Evaluation of living status % |  |  |  |  |
| Poor | 20 | 2 | 0 | 0 |
| Surviving | 49 | 23 | 0 | 25 |
| Adequate (*wenbao*) | 30 | 48 | 58 | 62 |
| Well-off (*xioakang*) | 2 | 23 | 38 | 11 |
| Wealthy | 0 | 3 | 4 | 0 |
| Evaluation of income % |  |  |  |  |
| Very poor | 10 | 1 | 1 | 2 |
| Poor | 43 | 19 | 9 | 14 |
| Neutral | 44 | 61 | 52 | 76 |
| Good | 3 | 19 | 37 | 8 |
| Very good | 0 | 0 | 2 | 1 |
| Harmonious society % |  |  |  |  |
| Not really | 25 | 51 | 7 | 18 |
| More or less | 36 | 19 | 18 | 68 |
| Yes | 39 | 29 | 75 | 14 |

also high, residents are not that dissatisfied in general. In work units, evaluations tend to be more neutral while in commercial-neighborhoods residents are the most positive.

When asked if their neighborhood constitutes a harmonious society, comparatively, residents in urban-villages are less negative than residents in traditional housing or work-units. This could well be related to a sort of lack of expectations given their institutional status, or that their system of references is very different than for the rest of the residents in cities. Interestingly, work-unit housing is where the majority of the residents are not convinced that their housing situation reflects a harmonious society. This could be for two reasons: first, their expectations are primarily reflecting communist era values like neighborhood attachment and neighborliness; second, some might still feel they are the privileged working-class group, but their housing situation does not correspond with the current options available in the city. Finally, only in commercial housing a large majority of residents feel positive. Taking into account China's recent urban history, the upgraded housing living conditions offered by new built homes is a major improvement. It is consistent then to respond positively to this new form of living.

## Conclusion

This chapter examines the intricacies of socio-spatial differentiation by looking at four different types of neighborhoods at the end of 2010 in Nanjing. The increasingly complex urban fabric present during the urban transition period has created fragmented urban experiences at the neighborhood level. This raises questions and challenges for planning a harmonious society.

Each of the four neighborhood types examined – traditional, work-unit, commercial and urban village – reflects a distinctive historical period of construction as well as unique institutional contexts. Overall, this neighborhood typology is highly differentiated as each type provides different dwelling characteristics and differentiated socio-demographic attributes. Also, each serves a distinctive function in housing diverse sectors of society.

It is thus not surprising to find that a high degree of inequality is found between them, in particular, in terms of housing area and income. However, when decomposing the relative share of inequality, it is surprising to find out that overall inequalities are higher within than between neighborhoods. For housing area this is particularly relevant for urban villages, where the majority of the residents live in small rooms and their landlords in much larger houses. In terms of income, higher variation is found in work-units and commercial neighborhoods. These significant variations within neighborhoods cannot be ignored by policy makers and planners.

A harmonious planning approach for urban China calls for and relies upon a thorough understanding of neighborhood differentiation. Moreover, further understanding of the dynamics between and within these neighborhoods is fundamental to appreciate how the neighborhoods shape residents' perceptions and expectations of their position in a more equitable society.

## Acknowledgements

This research is supported by a Toptalent grant from the Netherlands Organisation for Scientific Research (NWO). Fieldwork also benefited from the Euro-Chinese urban and regional bi-continental research scheme (ECURBS) Project funded by The European Commission under 7th Framework Programme, and the Utrecht University China and India Short Stay Fellowship.

## References

Chung, H. (2010) Building an image of villagers-in-the-city: a clarification of China's distinct urban spaces. *International Journal of Urban and Regional Research*, 34: 421–37.

Fan, C. (2008) *China on the Move: Migration, the State and the Household*. London and New York: Routledge.

FAO, Food and Agriculture Organization of the United Nations (2006) Policy impacts on inequality: Decomposition of income inequality by subgroups. EasyPol.

Galster, G. (2001) On the nature of neighborhood. *Urban Studies*, 38: 2111–24.

Hao, P., Sliuzas, R. and Geertman, S. (2011) The development and redevelopment of urban-villages in Shenzhen. *Habitat International*, 35: 214–24.

He, S. (2010) New-build gentrification in central Shanghai: demographic changes and socioeconomic implications. *Population, Space and Place*, 16: 345–61.

He, S. (2013) Evolving enclave urbanism in China and its socio-spatial implications: the case of Guangzhou. *Social and Cultural Geography*, 14: 243–75.

He, S. and Wu, F. (2007) Socio-spatial impacts of property-led redevelopment on China's urban neighborhoods. *Cities*, 24: 194–208.

He, S., Liu, Y., Wu, F. and Webster, C. (2008) Poverty incidence and concentration in different social groups in urban China: a case study of Nanjing. *Cities*, 25: 21–132.

He, S., Wu, F., Webster, C., and Liu, Y. (2010) Poverty concentration and determinants in China's urban low-income neighborhoods and social groups. *International Journal of Urban and Regional Research*, 34: 328–49.

Hu, X. and Kaplan, D. (2001) The emergence of affluence in Beijing: residential social stratification in China's capital city. *Urban Geography*, 22: 54–77.

Huang, Y. (2004) Housing markets, government behaviors and housing choice: a case study of three cities in China. *Environment and Planning A*, 36: 45–68.

Huang, Y. and Clark, W. (2002) Housing tenure choice in transitional urban China: a multi-level analysis. *Urban Studies*, 39: 7–32.

Huang, Y. and Deng, F. (2006) Residential mobility in Chinese cities: a longitudinal analysis. *Housing Studies*, 21: 625–52.

Johnson, D.L. (2002) Origin of the neighborhood unit. *Planning Perspectives*, 17: 227–45.

Kearns, A. and Parkinson, M. (2001) The significance of neighborhood. *Urban Studies*, 38: 2103–10.

Li, S. (2000a) The housing market and tenure decisions in Chinese cities: a multivariate analysis of the case of Guangzhou. *Housing Studies*, 15: 213–36.

Li, S. (2000b) Housing consumption in urban China: a comparative study of Beijing and Guangzhou. *Environment and Planning A*, 32, 1115–34.

Li, S. (2012) Housing inequalities under market deepening: the case of Guangzhou, China. *Environment and Planning A*, 44: 2852–66.

Li, S. and Huang, Y. (2006) Urban housing in China: market transition housing mobility and neighborhood change. *Housing Studies*, 21: 613–23.

Li, S. and Song, Y. (2009) Redevelopment, displacement, housing conditions, and residential satisfaction: a study of Shanghai. *Environment and Planning A*, 41: 1090–108.

Li, S. and Yi, Z. (2007) The road to homeownership under market transition. *Urban Affairs Review*, 42: 342–68.

Liu, Y. and Wu, F. (2006) Urban poverty neighborhoods: typology and spatial concentration under China's market transition a case study of Nanjing. *Geoforum*, 37: 610–26.

Liu, Y., He, S. and Wu, F. (2008) Urban pauperization under China's social exclusion: a case study of Nanjing. *Journal of Urban Affairs*, 30: 21–36.

Liu, Y., He, S., Wu, F. and Webster, C. (2010) Urban-villages under China's rapid urbanization: unregulated assets and transitional neighborhoods. *Habitat International*, 34: 135–44.

Logan, J.R., Bian, Y. and Bian, F. (1999) Housing inequality in urban China in the 1990s, *International Journal of Urban and Regional Research*, 23(1): 7–25.

Logan, J., Fang, Y. and Zhang, Z. (2009) Access to housing in urban China. *International Journal of Urban and Regional Research*, 33: 914–35.

Lu, D. (2006) Travelling urban form: the neighborhood unit in China. *Planning Perspectives*, 21: 369–92.

Novotný, J. (2007) On the measurement of regional inequality: does spatial dimension of income inequality matter? *Annals of Regional Science*, 41: 563–80.

Theil, H. (1967) *Economics and Information Theory*. Amsterdam: North-Holland.

Wang, D. and Li, S. (2006) Socio-economic differentials and stated housing preferences in Guangzhou, China. *Habitat International*, 305–26.

Wang, Y.P. (2000) Housing reform and its impacts on urban poor in China. *Housing Studies*, 15: 845–64.

Wang, Y.P. and Murie, A. (2000) Social and spatial implication of housing reform in China. *International Journal of Urban and Regional Research*, 24: 398–418.

Wang, Y.P., Wang, Y. and Bramley, G. (2005) Chinese housing reform in state-owned enterprise and its impacts on different social groups. *Urban Studies*, 42: 1859–78.

Wang, Y.P., Wang, Y. and Wu, J. (2009) Urbanization and informal development in China: urban-villages in Shenzhen. *International Journal of Urban and Regional Research*, 33: 957–73.

Wang, Y.P., Shao, L., Murie, A. and Cheng, J. (2012) The maturation of the neo-liberal housing market in urban China. *Housing Studies*, 27: 343–59.

Wu, F. (2004a) Residential relocation under market-oriented redevelopment: the process and outcomes in urban China. *Geoforum*, 35: 453–70.

Wu, F. (2004b) Urban poverty and marginalization under market transition: the case of Chinese cities. *International Journal of Urban and Regional Research*, 28: 401–23.

Wu, F. (2007) The poverty of transition: from industrial district to poor neighborhood in the City of Nanjing China. *Urban Studies*, 44: 2673–94.

Wu, F. (2010) Retreat from a totalitarian society: China's urbanism in making. In Bridge, G. and Watson, S. (eds). *A Companion to the City*. Oxford: Blackwell.

Wu, F. and He, S. (2005) Changes in traditional urban areas and impacts of urban redevelopment: a case study of three neighborhoods in Nanjing China. *Tijdschrift voor Economische en Sociale Geografie*, 96: 75–95.

Wu, F. and Li, Z. (2005) Sociospatial differentiation: processes and spaces in subdistricts of Shanghai. *Urban Geography*, 26: 137–66.

Wu, F., He, S. and Webster, C. (2010) Path dependence and the neighborhood effect: urban poverty in impoverished neighborhoods in Chinese cities. *Environment and Planning A*, 42: 134–52.

# Part II

# Housing for migrants and the urban poor

# 5 Migration and the dynamics of informal housing in China[1]

*Ya Ping Wang,[2] Huimin Du[3]
and Si-ming Li[4]*

## Introduction

Since the Second World War, various policies have been promoted by international organizations and national governments to provide housing to the urban poor. During the 1950s and 1960s, in Western Europe subsidized public housing estates were built as part of rebuilding the war-torn economies and labor stabilization (Jenkins *et al.*, 2007; Renaud, 1981; Wakely, 1988). In Latin America (Turner, 1968; Abu-Lughod and Hay, 1979) and also Southeast Asia (McGee, 1967), the post-war decades witnessed massive flows of urban-bound migrants from deprived rural areas in search of jobs and better life. Repeated subdivision of tenement houses into tiny cubicles and widespread construction of roof-top housing turned many inner-city neighborhoods into slums. Migrants who could not even afford such shelter scrambled for undevelopable marshlands and steep hillside slopes to construct squatter huts. To eradicate such urban "malaise", municipal governments in the developing "South" followed their counterparts in the industrialized "North", and undertook large-scale slum and squatter clearance; they too launched public housing projects in order to house the migrants and other urban poor.

However, with few exceptions, notably the city-states of Singapore and Hong Kong, the capacity of developing countries to supply low-cost public housing proved extremely limited. Indeed, slum and squatter clearance has been criticized for exacerbating the housing shortage of the poor. John Turner and his colleagues in the late 1960s advocated a different approach – "self-help" housing. Turner argued that squatters are not a form of social malaise, but instead they represent triumphs of "self-help" efforts. Turner's proposals have promoted individual home-ownership and self-help involvement in progressive housing provision over time. Such self-help housing is informal because of its lack of legal status and reference to official safety standards and building codes. But to Turner, the occupants of self-help housing know their needs far better than do government officials; furthermore, high regulatory standards undermine rather than guarantee more adequate housing. Self-help housing also produces better architectural solutions as it focuses on individualized household use values and not abstract market exchange values (Turner, 1968, 1986, 1988). Although other housing approaches have emerged under the neo-liberal development doctrines since the 1980s, including the enabling policies of the 1990s, and the sustainable human settlement development of the Habitat Agenda and The Millennium Development Goals (Jenkins *et al.*, 2007), the positive contributions of informal housing in low-income countries emphasized by Turner have not been seriously challenged. Nonetheless, slum and squatter clearance still happens from time to time under ferocious competition for urban land.

The post-war history of China differed significantly from other developing countries. Initially, under the central-planned socialist economy large-scale rural-to-urban migration was contained. Instead, the Rustication Program over the period 1962–1977 resulted in the sending of more than 17 million urban educated youths to the countryside (Pan, 2002). Throughout the 1960s and 1970s China's urbanization rate or the percentage of the population living in urban areas fluctuated between 16 to 18 per cent, even though industrialization proceeded apace (Chan, 1992). Dullness and lack of architectural variations might have characterized Chinese cities at that time; yet visitors to China in the 1970s and early 1980s were deeply impressed by the absence of squatting (Ma and Hanten, 1981).

China's unique experience of industrialization without corresponding urbanization came to an end with the launching of the market-oriented reforms in 1978. Migrants numbering hundreds of millions have since flocked to the country's major cities, irrespectively of the persistence of the *hukou* or household registration system. In some respects the plight of urban-bound migrants in China are much worse than those in other developing countries. This is because migrants from the rural areas, whose *hukou* still remains in the place of origin irrespective of their present place of domicile, have been deprived of access to high-status jobs, health care, social security, subsidized housing and other citizenship rights (Chan, 2009; Li *et al.*, 2010).

Until the late 1990s, the bulk of urban housing in China was public housing in the sense that it was either provided by state work units to their workers or managed by the municipal housing bureau. As such, urban housing was off limit to the migrants. Beginning from the early 1990s, there was an emerging sector of commodity housing. But clearly the great majority of migrants would not be able to afford it. While formal housing was inaccessible to the migrants, surprisingly, shantytowns remained largely absent in the Chinese urban scene. Instead of building squatter huts on the hillside, rural migrants in Chinese cities rent housing built by local villagers on former suburban farmlands. Indeed, housing in urban villages or villages encroached by urban developments has become a major source of housing for the migrants (Wang *et al.*, 2009, 2010). Of course, the lack of adequate housing is not a problem restricted to the migrants. The local urban poor also have difficulty accessing decent housing. They too have to be satisfied with housing of a more informal character, including housing in urban villages. But then what exactly is informal housing in China?

In this chapter, we focus on urban informality in China. We first define the concept of informal housing and give a general survey of informal housing in Chinese cities, in terms of physical, legal and economic characteristics. Then we shift from the physical to the social and psychological, examining in detail the changing nature of informality in urban villages based on a comparative analysis of the results from two household surveys in Guangzhou. In the conclusion section, the future of informal housing in China is considered.

## Informal housing in Chinese cities

Since Turner's study of slums and squatter settlements in Latin American cities, the term "informal housing" has been used to represent a wide range of shelters. But informal housing is quite a loose concept; there has not been any consensus on what constitutes "informal housing". In practice, the meaning of informal housing could be quite different in different cities and countries. Also, housing, including informal housing, is a physical asset as well as a social and psychological concept and is produced and shaped by specific political, societal and economic contexts. As such, informal housing – which covers a variety of settlement types, such as, among others, slum, shanty, ghetto, squatter settlement, self-help housing and spontaneous community – is more of a relative than an absolute concept (Gilbert, 2007). Perhaps it is useful to think of a spectrum in which the degree of housing informality can be viewed from many different angles. A way to delineate the degree of housing informality is given in Table 5.1, which measures housing informality with respect to building style, the way of construction, uses/users, exchange market, ownership, etc. Moreover, housing is more than a real property or shelter. A house is a place where its occupants would call it home, a place where one can fall back to under social and emotional crisis. It is also a place where social bonding within a family is developed and sustained, and where intense socialization takes place. Beyond the house there is the neighborhood, which, for many people, especially residents of squatter areas, slums and other informal settlements, is a direct extension of the home: cooking is done outside the dwelling; children play on dirty fields; men and women chitchat constantly in the courtyard. Therefore, the concept of housing informality also connotes social (such as social relations, social networks and social capital) and psychological (such as housing satisfaction and attachment to the neighborhood as well as stay-leave intentions) meanings.

In China, government officials are often proud to show foreign visitors that there is no informal housing in Chinese cities. Indeed overseas visitors would be impressed by the ultra-modern landscapes they see: the skyscrapers of the Pudong New District of Shanghai; the iconic Olympic Stadium and Opera House in Beijing; the proliferation of university towns and luxurious residential estates in cities all over the country. Yet, in reality, there are many poor areas, which are often hidden from the sight of tourists. For instance, tens of millions of migrant workers live in construction sites; also equally large numbers of young migrant workers live in factory dormitories where up to twelve people share a single room. Furthermore, the majority of migrants and other urban poor in Chinese cities could be found in the remaining traditional housing areas of the city centers and, of course, urban villages. These different types of settlement exhibit varying degree of informality. Below we document a number of such poor areas.

Table 5.1 Conceptualization of formal versus informal housing

| | Formal housing | Informal housing | |
| --- | --- | --- | --- |
| | Commercial and public housing | Self-built/self-help housing | Slum and squatter housing |
| Way of construction | Involve developers, architects, and building companies; use of modern technologies | Use of small contractors, helpers; simple design following neighbors' examples | Self-help approach; put up simple structures initially and improve them over time |
| Materials of construction | Steel, cement, bricks, and other modern construction materials | Bricks, cement or plaster, timber, some with small amount of steel | Bricks, cardboard, wood board, waste steel or plastic sheets, etc. |
| Style of buildings | Cottages or town houses, luxury apartments and flats in tenement or tower block buildings in properly planned estates often fenced and gated | Individual family buildings of various size and style, ranging from one to several stories, in village style setting with clear street patterns | Normally single story structures crowded together; small irregular passages between them |
| Land title and ownership | Clearly defined land titles in either state, institutional or private ownership | Ambiguity or customary land ownership, often related to traditional land entitlements | Invaded land initially owned by the state or other institutions; without legal title |
| Source of funding and finance | Complicated housing finance arrangement involving Bank and other financial institutions | Family savings or loans from relatives, friends, occasionally banks | Limited investment, mainly using waste materials saved and picked up from nearby areas |
| Management and administrative control | Integration with formal urban administrative system; professional estate management arrangement | Traditional and less formal settlement management; limited administrative control | No formal management arrangement |
| Linkage with traditional housing | No linkage | Improved or extended traditional village housing or redevelopment housing | Running down traditional housing areas or newly emerged squatters as a response to urbanization and urban poverty |
| Linkage with sectors of economy | Residents engaged in formal market economy or state sectors | Residents engaged in various economic sectors including small services and businesses | Residents engaged in informal economy, such as street trading, short labor, waste collection, etc. |
| Main users | Urban rich and middle classes including officials, managers and professionals | Landlords, middle- to low-income workers, working-class migrants | Unemployed, urban poor, new migrants, etc. |

Source: Authors.

## Poor traditional housing in city centers

Extensive urban redevelopment programs have resulted in large-scale eradication of poor housing districts in the city center. Most original residents have been relocated to resettlement housing in the outskirts. However, in almost every large city in China there remain pockets of old housing areas comprising run-down and extensively subdivided courtyard houses and tenement flats as well as makeshift structures, which are termed *penghuqu* (棚户區). Moreover, workers' residences in many work-unit compounds are also in a state of dilapidation these days.

In Chongqing, for example, property developers tended to bypass the poor traditional housing areas on steep slopes. Jiaochangkou and Shibanpo were two such areas, which were less than a ten-minute walk from the central square, Jiefangbei or the Statute of Liberation. Because of their central location, these areas were very active in informal economic activities with small shops and street markets. Minor streets in these areas were in fact stairs; some of them were very narrow and it would be impossible to move large furniture through the narrow staircases. Timbers and bamboo were the main construction material. The infrastructures in the areas were very poor, with water pipes running along the street and sewage flowing in open or covered ditches. Most families did not have internal kitchens and toilets; and cooked their food on stoves outside the house. Residents of these areas were a mix of the original urban families and rural migrants. The unemployment rate was higher than the city average. Most migrants living there were either small traders selling farm products on the street or "*Bangbang Jun* (棒棒軍)"; the latter refer to laborers who helped others to carry goods in river ports, railway and bus stations and shops in the city. They were extremely useful in a hilly city where other means of transport was difficult to function.

## Housing in urban villages

The most prominent informal housing areas in Chinese cities are the urban villages – *chengzhongcun* – which are located on the (former) urban–rural fringe. Because of urban expansion, land farmed by the villagers has been gradually taken over for infrastructure and property development, and these villages physically become parts of the urban built-up areas. However, due to the *hukou* system, these villages continue to maintain their rural organization, falling outside the urban management system and not subject to proper planning controls. Deprived of their means of livelihood, more specifically the farmlands, the villagers built residential structures, often on top of one another, on land plots originally designated for their own accommodation as rental properties to generate incomes. The hygienic conditions of urban villages generally are very poor, and, the narrow alleys in these villages substantially heighten fire hazards, as fire engines would not be able to get through.

In cities in the prosperous Pearl River Delta and Yangtze Delta, almost all villages located within commuting distances from urban centers there have been turned into urban villages. Traditional family houses have either been extended or demolished and replaced with high-rise buildings. Shenzhen and Dongguan where the migrant population is many times the population with the proper *hukou* represent two extreme cases. When the Shenzhen Special Economic Zone (SEZ) was set up in 1980, the government took a piecemeal approach when acquiring land for development from local villages. As urban development intensified and more land was taken out of agricultural production, all villages became urban villages of some sort. The traditional village layout in Shenzhen was simple. Each family occupied a small courtyard, which contained one or several simple one- to two-story houses built of bricks and timber. The courtyards were often lined up in rows with streets between them. Larger and richer families would have more buildings and yards. When the city grew and the demand for rental housing increased, unauthorized building activities ran out of control in many villages. New houses were constructed with modern materials such as steel and concrete. In the 1980s and the early 1990s, most buildings constructed were below five stories. From the late 1990s onwards, 80 per cent of new buildings were between six and nine stories; 5 per cent were over ten stories, and some even reached twenty stories (Shenzhen City Urban Village Redevelopment Planning Working Group, 2004). In order to maximize floor space, only very narrow gaps were left between buildings. This practice resulted in extremely high density and the so-called "kissing buildings".

A Shenzhen government report showed that in 2004 urban villages occupied a total land area of 9,204 hectares. There were altogether 307,000 privately owned dwellings, of which 44 per cent were constructed after 1999. The average size of construction floor space per building was 343 square meters. Inside the part of the city designated as SEZ, it was 532 square meters (Shenzhen City Urban Village Redevelopment Planning Working Group, 2004). In Futian District, there were 15 urban villages; together they occupied 390 hectares of land and housed 572,100 migrants, in addition to 19,300 local villagers (China Academy of Urban Planning and Design, Shenzhen Branch, 2004).

In other cities, the scale of urban village development is not as large. Still, in the inland city of Xi'an, for example, among the 624 administrative villages located inside the six urban districts and four development zones, 286 had less than 0.3 mu of land per capita in 2010 and were officially classified as urban villages. These urban villages were homes to 370,000 rural residents. Xi'an also includes three suburban districts and counties, where another 40 villages with a combined population of 90,000 were classified as urban villages (He, 2010). Similar to urban villages everywhere, Xi'an's urban villages were the prime locations for low-cost housing and small businesses. Compared with the coastal areas, houses in urban villages in Xi'an and other inland cities are more informal. Very few houses remain with the original courtyard layout and style. Most houses have been extended both horizontally and vertically; however, buildings over five stories are rare. Some houses have been extended to include part of the street. As a result, street light or power line poles could be found like pillars inside the rooms. Because most space has been covered up, some rooms on the ground floor deep inside the courtyard may not even have enough oxygen for breathing, not to mention the lack of natural light.

# Changing social and psychological informality

In this section we examine the social and psychological connotations of housing/ residential informality and living in urban villages in China and the extent to which the social and psychological well-being of migrants in urban villages have changed in recent times, based on two household surveys of temporary migrants in urban villages in Guangzhou conducted respectively in 2005 and 2010. The same 12 urban villages in 3 suburban areas (with 25 respondents in each urban village) were investigated in the two surveys. Comparing the results of the two surveys allows us to provide answers to the following time-related questions: whether living conditions in urban villages are improving or deteriorating; whether there exist demographic and economic changes in urban villages; whether migrants' informal social relations and networks experience major restructuring; and whether there are changes in migrants' relationships with the host village and city.

## *Living conditions and demographic features of migrants*

Table 5.2 compares the housing conditions of urban villages in Guangzhou in 2005 and 2010. It is clear that the housing conditions improved considerably through time. The living space per household member increased from 17 to 25 square meters, but the markedly higher standard deviations indicated much greater differentiation. In terms of facilities, there had been a notably higher rate of access to water, electricity and private toilets since 2005. The majority had their private kitchens, but the usage of gas was extremely low. More than half had a television in 2010, and nearly 40 per cent had a (presumably mobile) telephone. The most striking change involved internet usage. In 2005 only 4 per cent of households had private internet; the figure increased to 27 per cent in 2010.

When compared with housing conditions in the slums in other places (UN-Habitat, 2003), housing conditions in urban villages in Guangzhou are quite

*Table 5.2* Housing conditions in urban villages in Guangzhou

|  | | 2005 | 2010 |
|---|---|---|---|
| No. of respondents | | 300 | 299 |
| Living space per household member (square meter/per person) | (mean) | 16.8 | 24.7 |
| | (SD) | 10.4 | 23.6 |
| Proportion of households with more than two persons per room (%) | | 18 | 27 |
| Private kitchen (%) | | 62 | 78 |
| Private toilet (%) | | 86 | 82 |
| Private water and electricity (%) | | 85 | 84 |
| Private gas (%) | | 4 | 17 |
| Private telephone (%) | | 24 | 39 |
| Private television (%) | | 49 | 63 |
| Private internet (%) | | 4 | 27 |

Source: Survey data.

acceptable. Basic services like access to water, electricity, and sanitation facilities are widely available. Surfaced roads, waste collection systems, rainwater drainage, street lighting and even CCTV are gradually being provided in many places, although waste water, trash and garbage are still widespread across the village. High density of building is not necessarily associated with overcrowding within the dwelling; residents in the urban villages have a relatively large space per person. Yet, comparing 2005 and 2010, the proportion of households sharing a dwelling increased from 9 to 22 per cent. And the share of residences accommodating more than two persons per room increased from 18 to 27 per cent. Probably this was due to increase in rent.

Urban village is largely a rural migrant settlement. Rural migrants comprised as large as 80 per cent in each survey. In both surveys the percentage with junior secondary education ranked first at over 40 per cent, and senior secondary ranked second. Surprisingly, migrants in urban villages in 2010, compared with 2005, had lower education levels in general. Self-employment remained the largest occupation with shares of 30 to 40 per cent; the proportion of either physical laborers or skilled workers decreased by around 10 per cent. The average household size of the migrant population was similar in 2005 (2.4 people per household) and 2010 (2.3 people per household). But in respect to household composition there were an increase in singles and couples without children and a decrease in couples with children. Reflecting the general increase in income levels in China, compared with the 2005 sample, the 2010 sample showed an increase of 79 per cent from RMB 1,779 to RMB 3,178 in monthly household income. At the same time income inequality worsened. The Gini coefficient of household income rose from 0.31 to 0.35. Housing cost increased dramatically. The average rent paid almost doubled and the average rent per square meter increased by 109 per cent from RMB 11.7 to RMB 24.5. The ratio of rent to household income increased slightly from 20 to 22 per cent.

### Native place ties and local neighborhood networks

Inhabitants of informal settlements "tend to function as much as possible outside the boundaries of the state and modern bureaucratic institutions, basing their relationships on reciprocity, trust, and negotiation rather than on the modern notions of individual self-interest, fixed rules and contracts" (Bayat, 2000: 548–49). Bayat (2000: 549) explains that it is not because these people are not or anti-modern, but because "modernity is a costly affair" and "the conditions of their existence compel them to seek an informal mode of life." In their quest for an informal life, temporary migrants in urban villages resort to the native place ties as well as local neighborhood networks in the destination place. The native place ties, linked with economic specialization, were significant in migrant enclaves like *Zhejiangcun* in Beijing (Solinger, 1999; Xiang, 2000; Zhang, 2001). Urban village is not only a living space but also a place where migrants learn to make a living. The neighborhood-based contacts and networks help new migrants to learn about job opportunities, rental information and adjust to the new environment.

*Table 5.3* Changes in native-place networks

|  |  | 2005 | 2010 |
|---|---|---|---|
|  |  | (%) | |
| How to get current job | relatives and friends | 30 | 16 |
|  | *tongxiang* | 15 | 8 |
|  | self-employed | 29 | 50 |
| How to obtain housing information | relatives and friends | 50 | 18 |
|  | *tongxiang* | 38 | 8 |
|  | advertisement | 8 | 42 |
| How to obtain information about GZ | relatives and friends | 77 | 65 |
|  | *tongxiang* | 78 | 42 |
|  | media | 12 | 21 |
| Introduce and help relatives and friends migrate to GZ |  | 71 | 55 |
| Ask for help when in trouble | relatives and friends | 22 | 8 |
|  | *tongxiang* | 14 | 5 |

Source: Survey data.

However, under rapid social change, in urban villages in Guangzhou these informal social supports appear to be decaying.

First, the traditional kinship-based and place-based social networks are weakening. This can be seen at the level of individual urban life (see Table 5.3). In 2005, the majority of migrants obtained information about Guangzhou before migration from relatives, friends and *tongxiang* or people from the same home village. In 2010, the importance of relatives and friends and *tongxiang* as source of information decreased substantially. At the same time the media gained importance: in 2005, 12 per cent of the sampled migrants obtained information about Guangzhou from the media; in 2010 the figure increased to 21 per cent. Also, proportionately fewer migrants introduced and helped relatives and friends to migrate to Guangzhou. The most striking change involved the source of housing information. The share of "relatives, friends and *tongxiang*" as a source of information decreased by 30 percentage points or more. In contrast, advertisement became the most important information source. Equally, the effects of relatives, friends, and *tongxiang* in job attainment were weaker. When migrants in urban villages got in trouble, they became less likely to ask relatives, friends, or *tongxiang* for help.

Second, the local neighborhood ties are decaying (see Table 5.4). The decline in out-door recreation activities is obvious. In 2010, 60 per cent or more had never been to places of entertainment or sports centers; nearly 30 per cent had never gone to restaurants; 22 per cent had never been to a park; and another 14 per cent had never been to a shopping mall. The comparable figures for 2005 were: 26, 13, 5 and 2 per cent respectively. With regard to neighborly relations, the ratings on friendliness, care-giving, trust and familiarity decreased without exception, although most ratings were still positive except care-giving. The proportion of residents never visiting neighbors increased from 4 to 22 per cent. Migrants' interaction with locals decreased as well: 28 per cent had never helped

*Table 5.4* Changes in neighborhood networks

|  |  | 2005 | 2010 |
| --- | --- | --- | --- |
| Interaction with locals (%) | never communicate with locals | 2 | 11 |
|  | never help each other with locals | 9 | 28 |
|  | never visit neighbors | 4 | 22 |
| Neighborly relation (0–100) | friendliness | 71 | 69 |
|  | caregiving | 66 | 56 |
|  | trust | 69 | 63 |
|  | familiarity | 68 | 60 |
| Out-door recreation activities (%) | never go to shopping malls | 2 | 14 |
|  | never go to parks | 5 | 22 |
|  | never go to sports centers | 32 | 64 |
|  | never go to restaurants | 13 | 29 |
|  | never go to places of entertainment | 26 | 60 |

Source: Survey data.

each other with locals and 11 per cent never communicated with locals. In general, migrants' social life in urban villages has become even more isolated and less intimate.

It is worth noting that when we look beyond the local social networks, we may find the continuity of traditional social ties. Migrants can maintain close social ties across geographical areas because of improved access to information and communications technologies (ICTs). The increased proportion of households having (mobile) telephones and access to the internet may indicate that they communicate increasingly by phone and internet with people beyond the immediate neighbors.

*Migrants' relationships with the host place*

The surveys have provided overwhelming evidence that more migrants in urban villages are living in improved housing conditions than in the past. However, in 2010 proportionally fewer migrants were satisfied with the residence and with the neighborhood (see Table 5.5). Why did the improved living conditions fail to satisfy more dwellers? The major reason could be the massive increase in rent and home prices. Notably, migrant residents in urban villages in Guangzhou have become more pessimistic about housing prospects. In 2005 about half were confident to find a satisfactory residence in the city and more than 60 per cent were confident to improve their living condition. In 2010 the percentages decreased by more than 30 percentage points. Commodity housing purchase is far from reach because of the soaring housing price since 2005. In 2005, 42 per cent of temporary migrants had an intention to purchase a house in Guangzhou; the figure decreased to only 9 per cent in 2010. Besides, the majority of temporary migrants have come to Guangzhou for employment and money-making at the sacrifice of living condition. Compared with the housing conditions in their home places, proportionally more migrants reported being worse-off and fewer reported being better-off.

Equally, fewer migrants had a positive sentiment towards the city; about half showed an apathetic attitude, an increase of 19 percentage points, compared to

*Table 5.5* Residential satisfaction, housing prospect and stay-leave intention

|  |  |  | 2005 | 2010 |
|---|---|---|---|---|
|  |  |  | (%) | |
| Residential satisfaction | satisfied with residence |  | 31 | 26 |
|  | satisfied with neighborhood |  | 26 | 17 |
|  | housing conditions compared with the home place | (better) | 34 | 13 |
|  |  | (worse) | 51 | 74 |
| Housing prospect | have NO confidence to find satisfactory residence |  | 49 | 63 |
|  | have NO confidence to improve living condition |  | 12 | 30 |
| Stay-leave intention | to stay in the residence | (yes) | 31 | 55 |
|  |  | (no) | 7 | 10 |
|  | to stay in the neighborhood | (yes) | 29 | 41 |
|  |  | (no) | 8 | 23 |
|  | to stay in GZ | (yes) | 22 | 34 |
|  |  | (no) | 31 | 28 |
| City sentiment | NOT bring families to GZ |  | 37 | 71 |
|  | like GZ |  | 62 | 42 |
|  | indifferent to GZ |  | 30 | 49 |

Source: Survey data.

2005. In terms of place attachment, the 2010 sample showed that 42 per cent had no neighborhood attachment and 41 per cent had no city attachment; in contrast, only 16 per cent had neighborhood attachment and 15 per cent had city attachment. Nonetheless, more migrants were willing to stay in their residence, the neighborhood and the city: the proportion of stay intention increased by 24, 12, and 12 percentage points respectively. However, of the 2005 survey, only 37 per cent had no intention to bring their families to Guangzhou. In 2010, the figure rose to 71 per cent. It may be related to their precarious housing situation in the city. In fact, housing is the most overriding concern (53.6 per cent) of the temporary migrants. After housing, employment (45.1 per cent) is next in difficulty, followed by medical care (40.5 per cent).

In sum, migrants' sense of place in 2010 was characterized by moderate housing satisfaction and neighborhood satisfaction, weak neighborhood attachment and city attachment, and apathy towards the city. Yet the stay group constituted the largest proportion; in comparison in 2005 the uncertain group was the largest. Arguably, migrants' relationships with the host place have become more instrumental and dependent: people lack a positive emotional connection with the place; their continuing residence in the city to a large extent is compelled by the conditions of need and limited choice.

## The future of migration and informal housing

Chinese urban villages and *penghuqu*, as the main destinations for migrants and urban poor, share many features of the shanty towns in other developing countries. Unlike the latter, however, housing in the Chinese urban villages are built by local villagers on their own land and rented out to the migrant workers. There is no land invasion and the shelters provided are of comparatively better quality than those found in the typical shanty town. Urban villages and *penghuqu* are not ideal settlements from a position of outsider. Zhu (2004) argues that urban villages represent a form of market failure, resulting from the logic of the tragedy of commons in a situation under which the pro-growth local government fails to act as a disinterested regulatory agent. Municipal governments generally see urban villages as an eyesore, and there have been repeated attempts to eradicate such settlements.

But there are also scholars who contend that urban villages have an indispensable role to play during this period of rapid urbanization (see, for example, Wang *et al.*, 2009, 2010). In particular, their presence benefits two groups of relatively poor people, namely, the tenants and local villagers. Not only do the lowly paid rural migrants but also some recent university graduates have to seek accommodation in urban villages. Other tenants include young adults who would like to find an alternative to their parents' cramped apartment. Without this cheaper housing option, these people would find it very difficult to survive in the city. In addition, economic activities in these villages such as food markets and small shops provide a means of living to both the migrant-tenants and the original residents. Of course, the latter, whose farmlands have been requisitioned by the local authority, also collect rental incomes from the properties they built. In short, urban villages have changed the simple rural–urban division of the Chinese society. They provide the space and time for the rural people (both locals and migrants) to adapt to the new way of life under rapidly urbanization, a point that is usually ignored by neo-liberal economic doctrines.

The emergence of urban villages is not due to one or two persons' preference or choice; it is the consequence of the unequal development in the Chinese society and the uneven process of urbanization. Older urban villages may have been redeveloped and absorbed into the main urban fabrics; however, at the same time new ones further away from the city center are created. They continue to provide affordable housing to the migrants and the poor. Currently, China's urbanization rate is still slightly higher than 50 per cent; massive rural-to-urban migration will persist for quite some time to come. Similar to most developing countries, it is unlikely that municipal governments in China are able to provide enough public and affordable housing to satisfy the needs of the migrants and other urban poor. Worse still, Chinese local authorities often disregard the migrants in formulating social and urban development plans, pretending that one day the "temporary residents" will leave when their labor is no long required.

Importantly, informality should not be simply seen as social disorganization; it can be a socio-spatial mechanism and an organizing urban logic (Roy and Alsayyad, 2004). "Urban informality does not simply consist of the activities of the poor, or a particular status of labor, or marginality. Rather, it is an organizing logic which emerges under a paradigm of liberalization" (Alsayyad, 2004: 26). Temporary migrants in urban villages in China, like those in urban subaltern in Global South

(Bayat, 2000), are compelled to seek an informal mode of life by the conditions of their existence or the necessity to survive and achieve a dignified life. In this chapter, we have examined different aspects of informality of urban villages and other substandard settlements in Chinese cities. Our findings show that the living conditions in urban villages, in particular, have improved considerably through time, and they are quite acceptable when compared with informal settlements in the Third World cities. But the demographic composition of urban villages has not changed much.

Beyond the physical characteristics of urban villages, an "atomized" migrant society is developing; temporary migrants are being more individualized in their informal life in urban villages. On one hand, the weakening of traditional kinship-based and place-based social networks is apparent: migrants become more isolated from the support of kinship, friendship and *tongxiang* in times of need or trouble. On the other, the decaying of local neighborhood networks is visible. The 2005 survey suggested that physical closeness and social similarity do not necessarily make intense neighboring; the situation became clearer in 2010. In contrast, elements of market culture like advertisement and media have more important impacts on migrants' lives. The fact that the proportion of households without tenancy agreement decreased from 76 to 58 per cent indicates the development of the modern notion of contracts. Migrants' relationships with the host place become more instrumental and dependent. Although the housing prospects have become less promising, nonetheless proportionately more migrant residents in urban villages exhibit an intention to stay in the residence, the neighborhood and the city.

It is often assumed that informal housing of different kinds is the poor's first step in climbing the urban housing ladder. In reality, for many, they will probably remain there forever. In other words, informal housing is more than a transitional space. Recent huge home price inflations in Chinese cities have rendered commodity housing unaffordable even to lowly paid general workers with local *hukou* as well as young professionals. The situation for temporary migrants is even more precarious as they are as a rule excluded from public housing. To the urban poor, informal housing in urban villages and elsewhere remains their only choice. Moreover, the informal economy in urban villages, which provides not only a means of living but also relatively affordable daily necessities such as food items to their residents, is an important part of urban life in cities. Arguably, urban villages will stay for quite some time in the foreseeable future. Perhaps it may be noted that even in Hong Kong, a high-income city-state known for its massive public housing programs, extensive illegal roof-top housing and scattered squatting remain part of the urban scene. Also, rural villages in the New Territories, the suburban area of Hong Kong, have experienced urban-village transformation very similar to that in cities in mainland China.

Under the current land tenure system in China, municipal governments are given the sole authority to requisition rural land, which is often conducted by force, and collect the revenues from subsequent sale of land leases. In fact, land leasing or land sales proceeds have become the single-most important source of income for municipal government (Lin, 2009). One after another, urban villages and other informal settlements have been cleared to give way to luxurious high-rise commodity housing estates. This is especially the case in cities where most agricultural land has already been developed, so that the local authority has to look to the urban villages to refurbish its land bank. But urban village clearance results in the uprooting of thousands of inhabitants, and the demolition of the very dynamic informal housing market also destroys the informal economic activities that go along with it. To the local villagers, forceful rehousing in high-rise flats effectively implies the termination of century-honored village life, which would be valued much more than the meager compensations the villagers receive. It is no wonder that village redevelopment is often resisted by the original villagers.

To the migrant-tenants, the psychological costs associated with urban village clearance may not be as high, although a few would have stayed in the village for quite some time and, as such, have developed their daily routines and social networks there. When asked by researchers where they will go when their rental housing is demolished, the answer is often very simple: "go to another village." But relocating to a new and more outlying urban village in search of affordable housing is by no means a pleasant experience. Worsened inaccessibility will cause geographical and social isolation, and further jeopardize job opportunities. Clearly, forceful removal of informal housing and urban villages will further marginalize the poor and the lowly paid migrant workers.

## Notes

1   This chapter builds and expands on an early Chinese version, which has been accepted by a journal in China (*Urban and Rural Planning*). The authors would like to acknowledge the financial support of the Hong Kong Research Grant Council (Grant Nos. HKBU2420P7 and HKBU243209) for the conduct of the 2005 and 2010 Guangzhou surveys.
2   Ya Ping Wang, Professor, Chair in Global City Futures, School of Social and Political Sciences, University of Glasgow, 25 Bute Gardens, Glasgow G12 8RS, UK. Email: yaping.wang@glasgow.ac.uk
3   Humin Du, PhD candidate, Department of Geography, Hong Kong Baptist University, Hong Kong. Email: helenduhuimin@gmail.com
4   Si-ming Li, Chair Professor in the Department of Geography, and Director of the David C. Lam Institute for East-West Studies, Hong Kong Baptist University, Hong Kong. Email: lisiming@hkbu.edu.hk
5   1 mu = 1/15 hectare.

## References

Abu-Lughod, J. L. and Hay, R. (eds) (1979) *Third World Urbanization*, New York: Methuen.
Alsayyad, N. (2004) 'Urban informality as a "new" way of life', in Roy, A. and Alsayyad, N. (eds) *Urban Informality: Transnational Perspectives from the Middle East, Latin America and South Asia*, Lanham: Lexington Books.

Bayat, A. (2000) 'From "dangerous classes" to "quiet rebels" politics of the urban subaltern in the Global South', *International Sociology*, 15 (3): 533–57.

Chan, K. W. (1992) 'Economic growth strategy and urbanization policies in China, 1949–1982', *International Journal of Urban and Regional Research*, 16 (2): 275–305.

Chan, K. W. (2009) 'The Chinese *hukou* system at 50', *Eurasian Geography and Economics*, 50 (2): 197–221.

China Academy of Urban Planning and Design, Shenzhen Branch (2004) Shenzhenshi futianqui chengzhongcun gaizao zhanlue guihua [Shenzhen City Futian District renewal strategy and planning of 'Village in Urban Area'] (mimeo in Chinese).

Gilbert, A. (2007) 'The return of the slum: does language matter?', *International Journal of Urban and Regional Research*, 31 (4): 697–713.

He, D. F. (Director of Xi'an Municipal Urban Village Redevelopment Office) (2010) Operational methods and some experiences of urban village redevelopment in Xi'an. Speech at the National Forum of Urban Village Redevelopment held in Zhengzhou (unpublished document in Chinese).

Jenkins, P., Smith, H. and Wang, Y. P. (2007) *Planning and Housing in the Rapidly Urbanising World*, London; New York: Routledge.

Li, L., Li, S. M. and Chen, Y. (2010) 'Better city, better life, but for whom?: the *hukou* and resident card system and the consequential citizenship stratification in Shanghai', *City, Culture and Society*, 1 (3): 145–54.

Lin, G. C. S. (2009) *Developing China: land, politics and social conditions*, London; New York: Routledge.

Ma, L. J. C. and Hanten, E. W. (eds) (1981) *Urban Development in Modern China*, Boulder, CO: Westview Press.

McGee, T. G. (1967) *The Southeast Asian City: a social geography of the primate cities of Southeast Asia*, London: Bell.

Pan, Y. (2002) 'An examination of the goals of the rustication program in the People's Republic of China', *Journal of Contemporary China*, 11 (31): 361–79.

Renaud, B. (1981) *National Urbanization Policy in Developing Countries*, New York: Oxford University Press.

Roy, A. and Alsayyad, N. (eds) (2004) *Urban Informality: transnational perspectives from the Middle East, Latin America and South Asia*, Lanham: Lexington Books.

Shenzhen City Urban Village Redevelopment Planning Working Group (2004) Shenzhenshi chengzhongcun gai zao zongtiguihua dagang, chuzuwu chubu diaocha baogao [Shenzhen City Urban Village Improvement Overall Planning Outline, Initial Investigation Report on Private Housing]. Unpublished report.

Solinger, D. J. (1999) *Contesting Citizenship in Urban China: peasant migrants, the state, and the logic of the market*, Berkeley, CA: University of California Press.

Turner, J. F. C. (1968) 'Housing priorities, settlement patterns, and urban development in modernizing countries', *Journal of the American Planning Association*, 34 (6): 354–63.

Turner, J. F. C. (1986) 'Future directions in housing policies', *Habitat International*, 10 (3): 7–25.

Turner, J. F. C. (1988) 'Introduction', and 'Conclusions', in Turner, B. (ed). *Building Community: a third world case book*, London: Building Community Books.

UN-Habitat (2003) *The Challenge of Slums: global report on human settlements*, London: Earthscan Publication Limited.

Wakely, P. (1988) 'The development of housing through the withdrawal from construction: changes in Third World housing policies and programmes', *Habitat International*, 12 (3): 121–31.

Wang, Y. P., Wang, Y. and Wu, J. (2009) 'Urbanization and informal development in China: urban villages in Shenzhen', *International Journal of Urban and Regional Research*, 33 (4): 957–73.

Wang, Y. P., Wang, Y. and Wu, J. (2010) 'Housing migrant workers in rapidly urbanizing regions: a study of the Chinese model in Shenzhen', *Housing Studies*, 25 (1): 83–100.

Xiang, B. (2000) *Transcending Boundaries: Zhejiangcun: the story of a migrant village in Beijing*, Beijing: Sanlian (in Chinese).

Zhang, L. (2001) *Strangers in the City: reconfiguration of space, power, and social networks within China's floating population*, Stanford, CA: Stanford University.

Zhu, J. (2004) 'Local developmental state and order in China's urban development during transition', *International Journal of Urban and Regional Research*, 28 (2): 424–47.

# 6 Housing access, sense of attachment, and settlement intention of rural migrants in Chinese cities

Findings from a twelve-city migrant survey

*Zhilin Liu and Yujun Wang*

## Introduction

China is currently celebrating thirty years of economic success and expecting accelerated urbanization within the next two decades. Yet many have doubted the long-term sustainability of China's urbanization due to continuous discrimination and marginalization of rural migrants from mainstream urban societies. On the one hand, rural-to-urban migration continues with its massive pace and scale and is considered a fundamental force of China's economic miracle. According to the Sixth Population Census, the number of migrants living in a different municipality from their place of official household registration (*hukou*) had reached 221.4 million by 2010, accounting for 16.53 per cent of the total population (1.34 billion) in Mainland China (National Bureau of Statistics of China, 2011).

On the other hand, rural-to-urban migrants constitute the largest group of China's new urban poor (Wang, 2004; Wu, 2004) who continue to face stark discrimination in urban labor and housing markets because they do not have the official local residency (*hukou*) (Yang and Guo, 1996; Fan, 2001; Sun and Fan, 2011; Wang *et al.*, 2010; Wu, 2002, 2004). A large number of rural migrants have to live in informal housing settlements such as urban villages that are marginalized spatially and socially from mainstream urban societies (He *et al.*, 2010; Wang *et al.*, 2010; Wu, 2007; Zheng *et al.*, 2009). Meanwhile, until recently, a group of "undocumented" migrants internally within the country (Wu, 2012), had been excluded from most government-sponsored welfare programs including affordable housing, health care insurance, and social security, and their children excluded from public schools (Xu *et al.*, 2011; Tao and Xu, 2007).

In recent years, integration of rural migrants into the mainstream urban society has gained priority in policy agenda. In the Twelfth Five-Year Plan (2011–2015), the central government declared that "the primary task of promoting urbanization is to gradually transform rural migrants to urban residents" through reforming the *hukou* system and expanding the coverage of public services including affordable housing and basic safety-net welfare. However, the rate of settlement intention among migrants is not as strong as usually suspected in public debates. From a 2006 survey, Zhu and Chen (2010) found that, in Fujian Province, only 57.5 per cent of migrants in Fujian Province intended to make permanent migration to cities, with 35.8 per cent willing to settle down in current destination city and 21.7 per cent planning to move to other cities. Fan (2011) found that only 38.2 per cent of migrant workers in Beijing were willing to permanently stay in Beijing whereas 45.2 per cent plan to leave sometime in the future. Nevertheless, in spite of a growing body of literature on integration and settlement of rural migrants in Chinese cities (e.g. Zhu, 2007; Zhu and Chen, 2010; Fan, 2011; Hu *et al.*, 2011; Wang and Fan, 2012), empirical evidence has been limited regarding the extent to which housing experiences and sense of attachment may play a role in determining a rural migrant's intention to make permanent settlement in cities.

In light of this literature gap, this chapter takes advantage of data derived from a twelve-city migrant survey conducted in 2009, and investigates the extent to which housing access, along with other variables including social networks and social interaction, migration experiences, and socio-demographic variables, may contribute to stronger sense of attachment of rural migrants toward urban societies and eventually their intention to make permanent migration from villages to cities. The rest of this chapter includes the following sections. Next, we review relevant literatures on migration and settlement, arguing that housing experiences should been be accounted for in explaining migrant settlement intention. After introducing data sources and model specification, we present findings from descriptive statistics and regression models using data derived from a twelve-city migrant survey, and a discussion of research findings is presented in the conclusion section.

## Literature review

Numerous studies have revealed that rural migrants experience tremendous discrimination and marginalization in the Chinese urban society as "second-tier citizens" without local *hukou*. These experiences arguably have had consequences not only on migrants' subjective well-being (Nielson *et al.*, 2009; Zhang *et al.*, 2009), but also on how migrants view cities as possible permanent homes and whether they are willing to make permanent stay as opposed to return to rural villages. Although the intention and outcomes of permanent settlement of migrants appeared to have increased over recent years (Zhu and Chen, 2010), many institutional, social, and individual factors continue to impede such intention.

Early studies on migrant settlement tended to emphasize the role of *hukou* status as an institutional barrier preventing stronger urban integration and settlement intention. This explanation, as argued by Zhu (2007), is not sufficient. Not having local *hukou* may reduce settlement intention because it largely contributes to the discriminated nature of employment, housing, and other life experiences of rural migrants in Chinese cities. Migrant workers are often segregated into certain low-class sections of the labor market, such as service, manufacturing, and construction sectors, which are usually low-skilled, low-paid, and unstable jobs (Yang and Guo, 1996; Fan, 2001; Sun and Fan, 2011). Due to the unstable prospects of employment, a temporary form of migration thus becomes a family strategy to maximize economic opportunities while diversifying risks (Zhu, 2007), creating the phenomena of split households and circular migration (Fan, 2011).

Migration studies in the international literature mostly concern international migration, which pays great attention to the distinct patterns of permanent settlement vs. temporary and circular migration (e.g. Massey and Akresh, 2006). Whereas existing studies may differ in research focus, empirical evidences are not yet conclusive regarding determinants of settlement intention and outcomes. Among widely accepted factors, migration experience, i.e. duration of residence in the destination, is usually found to contribute positively to settlement (Khraif, 1992; Massey and Akresh, 2006). Stronger social networks and social interaction at the destination also encourage intention of permanent settlement rather than returning to the origin country or city (Reyes, 2001; Korinek *et al.*, 2005). A series of socio-demographic factors are also found important, but scholars have debated whether income (economic opportunities) and education (human capital) encourage or discourage settlement (e.g. Massey, 1987; Jasso and Rosenzweig, 1988) and the possible selectivity problem in the process (Massey and Akresh, 2006: 955).

Studies on rural migrants in China also have highlighted the above variables as factors conductive to settlement intention. As well summarized by Fan (2011), scholars typically found younger migrants with more education to have stronger intention to settle down in cities. Whereas findings about the role of marital status are mixed, Fan (2011) revealed that it is household arrangements that really affect a migrant's long-term plan to settle down or return. Zhu (2010) further found the positive effects of stable job contract and family income on migrants' settlement intention, proving the role of a more stable prospect of employment and economic opportunities in migrants' settlement decision.

While most studies have focused on socio-demographic variables and migration experiences as factors of settlement intention, far less attention is given to the role of housing experiences – and consequently, sense of attachment to the place – that may motivate rural migrants to settle down in cities. As widely documented in the literature, rural migrants in China experience particularly acute marginalization in the urban housing system, resulting from the double constraints of both migrants' incapability to compete in China's emerging urban housing market as well as the *hukou*-based institutional barrier that limits migrants' access to urban housing (Wu, 2004). Recent housing reforms in Chinese cities, though offering more freedom and choices for residents (Li, 2000; Huang, 2004; Li and Yi, 2007), have been limited to housing for "urban residents" and largely neglected the needs of migrants despite their large contribution to urban economic development (Wang, 2003; Wang *et al.*, 2010). Rural migrants in urban China often find themselves not able to afford market-price commodity housing with clearly defined property structure – because they are often in the low-income strata, and not eligible for government-funded affordable housing program – which are only available to legally registered urban residents. The newly launched Public Rental Housing Program (*gonggong zulin zhufang*) began to include non-*hukou* migrant workers as its intended beneficiaries. Nonetheless, implementation of this program has been limited and often aimed only toward more educated, professional migrants while continuously excluding rural migrants (Huang, 2012). With limited access to the above types of formal housing, most rural migrants resort to dorms provided by employers, or informal housing in migrant enclaves such as urban villages (He *et al.*, 2010; Wu, 2002; Zheng *et al.*, 2009).

Access to formal housing may affect a rural migrant's settlement intention in three ways. First, compared to dorms and informal settlements that often indicate minimal living space and inadequate facilities, formal housing tends to offer better housing quality, which may increase a rural migrant's satisfaction with one's own condition and prospect in cities. Second, living in formal housing provides more opportunities for interaction with local people in daily-life experiences and thus may foster stronger social integration, even though the chance to experience discrimination also may be higher. Third, with better housing conditions and more social integration, rural migrants are likely to develop stronger sense of attachment toward the place where they live and work, thus motivating stronger settlement intention. Thus, the empirical analysis of this chapter investigates the extent to which access to formal housing may predict stronger sense of attachment, which, in turn, encourages migrant settlement intention.

## Research design

### *Data sources*

Data for this analysis was derived from a large-scale migrant survey conducted in twelve cities in 2009 that was funded by Natural Science Foundation of China and jointly implemented by scholars from various universities and research institutes in China. The survey seeks to collect information of migrants' life experiences in the city and in their hometowns. Respondents for the survey were limited to migrants who currently worked in the survey city but did not have local urban *hukou*, including migrants from other municipalities and those who were born in the survey city but only had rural *hukou*.

Sampling for the survey followed a multi-stage, stratified process. First, twelve cities were selected from four major urbanized regions in China—the Yangtze Delta, the Pearl River Delta, the Bo-Hai Rim, and the Chengdu–Chongqing Region (see Figure 6.1 for location of twelve sample cities). In each region, three cities were selected including one large city, one medium-size city, and one small city to seek representativeness of various types of destinations of rural–urban migrations. In each city, five sub-districts (*jiedao*) were selected, and in each sub-district, 40 migrant workers were selected to participate in the survey, which comprised 200 total respondents in each city. A combination of random sampling (whenever possible), convenience sampling and quota sampling (when a sampling frame is not accessible) was adopted in order to ensure representativeness as much as possible. The survey was performed in face-to-face structured interviews to ensure higher response rates and accuracy, with each interview lasting approximately 2–2.5 hours. The entire survey yielded a total of 2,394 valid samples, but

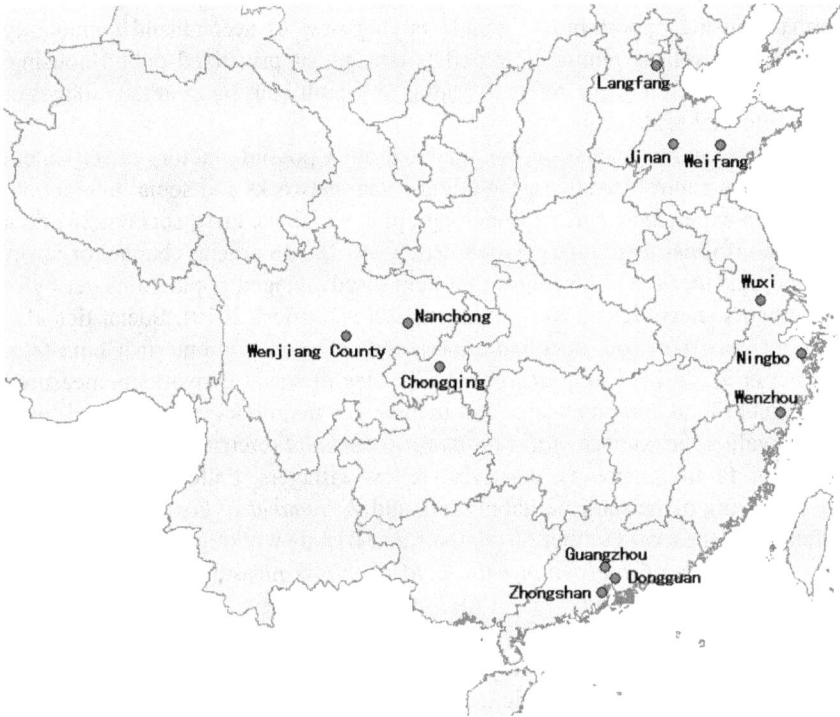

*Figure 6.1* Location of twelve sample cities.

this paper only focuses on rural migrants, i.e. migrants with agricultural *hukou*, which includes a total of 1,953 samples.

## Research questions and variable specification

We specifically seek to answer two related research questions. First, to what extent housing access may determine a rural migrant's sense of attachment toward the neighborhood and the destination city. Second, to what extent such sense of attachment, along with other factors, may predict a rural migrant's settlement intention? In the survey, there were two questions specifically asking sense of attachment: "do you feel attached to the neighborhood where you live" and "do you feel attached to the city where you live now." The answer "yes, feels like home" was coded as 1 (i.e. feel attached), whereas the answers including "feels indifferent" and "does not feel at home at all" were coded as 0. The questionnaire also asked migrants with rural *hukou* "whether they intend to permanently settle in cities or return to home villages in the long run." The answer "move back to village" was coded 0 (i.e. no intention), while the answers "will settle in city if there is an opportunity" and "both choices are fine" were coded as 1 (i.e. settlement intention). Regarding *housing access*, three sources of housing were identified: employer-provided dorms, formal housing, and informal housing (reference category). For migrants, formal housing opportunities include buying new or secondhand commodity housing, as well as renting commodity housing or privatized public housing, whereas informal housing refers to renting self-built housing in urban villages or other informal settlements.

From the above discussion, we included other possible factors of settlement intention as control variables, including social networks and social interaction, migration experience, and socio-demographic variables. First, social network, a form of informal institutions (Granovetter, 1975), is a crucial channel of information, resources, and leverages that help disadvantaged populations get by in the urban society (Kleit, 2001; Pinkster, 2009; Curley, 2010). Social ties also play an important role in urban experiences of rural migrants in China (e.g. Palmer *et al.*, 2011; Liu *et al.*, 2013). The size of social networks is measured at neighborhood and city scales and included in the model in the natural logarithms value: *the number of ties in the neighborhood* referring to the number of extended family members, relatives, fellow villagers, colleagues, and other friends living in the same neighborhood, and *the number of ties at the city scale* referring to the total number of relatives and friends working in the destination city. *Frequency of interaction with local people* is measured on a 1–5 Likert scale, with 1 indicating "very little" and 5 indicating "very often", and is assumed to have enabling effects on rural migrants' intention to permanently stay in the city. On the contrary, *past experience of discrimination by local people* may reduce such intention.

Second, migration experience was measured by the number of years living in the city, which has been found to contribute positively to settlement intention in the literature (Massey and Akresh, 2006). The longer a rural migrant lives in the same city, the more adapted they are to urban life and thus develop stronger sense of attachment as well as settlement intention. *Duration of residence in the same neighborhood*, however, may contribute to neighborhood attachment (as shown in Wu, 2012) but not necessarily cultivate city-scale attachment and settlement intention. In addition, various empirical studies have found a series of socio-demographic variables to be factors of neighborhood attachment (e.g. Austin and Baba, 1990; Massey and Akresh, 2006; Wu, 2012) and settlement intention (e.g. Zhu and Chen, 2010; Fan, 2011). Thus we included type of migration, marital status, age cohort, occupation, type of employers, years of schooling, and income (measured by the natural logarithm of per capita household income from non-agricultural work). Occupation was recoded as a dummy variable with '1' referring to medium- to high-skilled jobs, with '0' referring to low-skilled positions. Type of *danwei* was also a dummy variable measuring if a rural migrant works in the public sector (coded as 1, and 0 if otherwise). Age cohort refers to whether a rural migrant was born before or after 1980, the latter of which indicates the so-called "second-generation migrants." Finally, *cross-province migration*, also a dummy variable, measures if a rural migrant originally comes from other provinces, with reference category indicating within-province migration. See Table 6.1 for descriptive statistics of key variables.

## Findings from descriptive statistics

This section presents preliminary findings from descriptive statistics to explore relationships of sense of attachment and settlement intention with key independent variables. As shown in Table 6.1, less than 55 per cent of respondents expressed willingness to settle in cities (be it the destination city or other cities) as opposed to return to home villages. 57.94 per cent and 61.79 per cent of rural migrants reported to feel attached to the neighborhood and to the destination, respectively. Yet, housing opportunities are limited: only 12.74 per cent of rural migrants in the sample live in a unit from the formal housing market, whereas nearly a half of rural respondents (48.50 per cent) rent an informal housing unit.

*Table 6.1* Descriptive statistics of key variables

| Variable names | | Frequency | Percentage |
| --- | --- | --- | --- |
| Willingness to settle in the | Yes | 1,058 | 54.68 |
| destination city | No | 877 | 45.32 |
| Feel attached to the neighborhood | Yes | 1,128 | 57.94 |
| | No | 819 | 42.06 |
| Feel attached to the destination city | Yes | 1,203 | 61.79 |
| | No | 744 | 38.21 |
| Experience of discrimination | Yes | 386 | 19.94 |
| | No | 1,550 | 80.06 |
| Sources of current housing | Formal housing | 229 | 12.74 |
| | Informal housing | 872 | 48.50 |
| | Dorms | 697 | 38.77 |
| Type of migration | Within-province | 1,158 | 59.29 |
| | Cross-province | 795 | 40.71 |
| Gender | Female | 851 | 43.57 |
| | Male | 1,102 | 56.43 |
| Marital status | Not married | 709 | 36.32 |
| | Married | 1,243 | 63.68 |
| Generation of migrants | First gen. migrant | 1,032 | 52.82 |
| | New gen. migrant | 921 | 47.18 |
| Occupation | Low skill | 1,690 | 88.95 |
| | Skilled | 210 | 11.05 |
| Type of *danwei* | Other types[a] | 1,814 | 95.27 |
| | public sector | 90 | 4.73 |
| Age | | Avg 31.85 (10.17)[b] | |
| Number of ties in the neighborhood | | Avg 11.22 (16.14) [b] | |
| Number of ties working in the city | | Avg 12.02 (19.10)[b] | |
| Frequency of interaction with local people | | Avg 2.83 (1.42)[b] | |
| Duration of residence in the neighborhood (months) | | Avg 27.29 (31.56)[b] | |
| Duration of residence in the city (years) | | Avg. 5.68 (5.09)[b] | |
| Years of schooling | | Avg. 8.39 (3.28)[b] | |
| Household income (1,000 yuan)[c] | | Avg. 21.55 (32.97)[b] | |

Notes: [a] Other types including joint venture, private firms, self-employed and others.
[b] Mean value of the sample (standard deviation in the parenthesis).
[c] Per capita household income from non-agricultural work.

Source: 2009 Twelve-city migrant survey.

Bivariate analysis shows that access to formal housing is associated with better integration of rural migrants in the urban society, and thus stronger sense of belongings toward the destination city where they now work and live. As reported in Table 6.2, neighborhood attachment is the strongest among rural migrants living in formal housing, with 71.18 per cent reporting to "feel at home" in the neighborhood. Only 57.63 per cent of respondents living in informal housing and 52.95 per cent of "dorms" dwellers reported to feel the same. The percentage of feeling attached to the destination city also is the highest (74.24 per cent) among rural migrants with access to formal housing. Although a slightly higher percentage of rural migrants living in informal housing than dorm dwellers reported to "feel at home" in the neighborhood and in the city, the settlement intention of migrants with informal housing is the lowest among all rural migrant respondents.

Bivariate correlation analysis, reported in Table 6.3, shows that the sense of attachment possessed by rural migrants have strong and positive correlations with most independent variables with two exceptions. First, exposure to discrimination by local people has negative correlation with both attachment to the neighborhood and attachment to the destination city (see Table 6.3). Second, the number of ties in the neighborhood correlates with neighborhood attachment but not with attachment to the city. In addition, settlement intention correlates with fewer variables, except frequency of interaction with local people and access to formal housing, both of which show positive correlations. Settlement intention also significantly correlates with sense of attachment to the city, but not with attachment to the neighborhood.

## Findings from regression analysis

We employed logistic regression models to further test the extent to which access to formal housing may predict stronger sense of attachment and stronger intention of settlement, when controlling for social networks and social interaction, duration of residence, and socio-demographic variables. We hypothesize that, as formal housing normally provides better housing conditions, better subjective well-being, and stronger urban identity, access to formal housing may help cultivate a stronger degree of place-based sense of belonging and thus increase the intention to settle down in cities. We also hypothesize that a rural migrant who feels attached to the neighborhood and the destination city is more likely to have stronger settlement intention.

### Model results for sense of attachment

Regression results were similar in both models for sense of attachment as reported in Table 6.4. First of all, as predicted and indicated from bivariate analysis, access to formal housing significantly predicts stronger sense of attachment of rural migrants toward both the neighborhood and the destination city. Holding other variables constant, being able to live in formal housing increases

Table 6.2 Sense of attachment and intention of settlement by sources of housing

| | Attachment to the neighborhood | | | Attachment to the city | | | Settlement intention | |
|---|---|---|---|---|---|---|---|---|
| | Not home at all | No difference | Feel at home | Not home at all | No difference | Feel at home | No | Yes |
| Dorms | 43 | 284 | 368 | 62 | 224 | 409 | 304 | 388 |
| | 6.19% | 40.86% | 52.95% | 8.92% | 32.23% | 58.85% | 43.93% | 56.07% |
| Informal housing | 66 | 303 | 502 | 94 | 254 | 523 | 446 | 423 |
| | 7.58% | 34.79% | 57.63% | 10.79% | 29.16% | 60.05% | 51.32% | 48.68% |
| Formal housing | 19 | 47 | 163 | 25 | 34 | 170 | 70 | 151 |
| | 8.3% | 20.52% | 71.18% | 10.92% | 14.85% | 74.24% | 31.67% | 68.33% |
| Total valid sample | 128 | 634 | 1,033 | 181 | 512 | 1,102 | 820 | 962 |
| | 7.13% | 35.32% | 57.55% | 10.08% | 28.52% | 61.39% | 46.02% | 53.98% |
| Pearson Chi-Square (p-value) | 31.81 (0.000)*** | | | 27.15 (0.000)*** | | | 29.36 (0.000)*** | |

Source: 2009 twelve-city migrant survey.

*Table 6.3* Bivariate correlation coefficients of key variables

| | Settlement intention | Feel attached to the neighborhood | Feel attached to the destination city |
|---|---|---|---|
| Feel attached to the neighborhood | 0.037 | – | |
| Feel attached to the destination city | 0.102*** | 0.559*** | – |
| Living in formal housing | 0.108*** | 0.105*** | 0.101*** |
| Duration of residence in current neighborhood (months) | −0.010 | 0.124*** | 0.108*** |
| Number of ties in the neighborhood (logged) | −0.003 | 0.055* | 0.001 |
| Duration of residence in current city | −0.038 | 0.088*** | 0.086*** |
| Number of ties in the destination city (logged) | −0.022 | 0.090*** | 0.115*** |
| Experience of discrimination by local people | −0.016 | −0.088*** | −0.112*** |
| Frequency of interaction with local people | 0.156*** | 0.098*** | 0.171*** |

Notes: $*p<0.05$; $**p<0.01$; $***p<0.001$.

Source: 2009 twelve-city migrant survey.

the odds of feeling attached to the neighborhood by 68.7 per cent than living in informal housing settlements (reference category) on a .01 significant level (Table 6.4). Access to formal housing also increases the odds of attachment to the destination city by 54.7 per cent ($p<.05$).

Second, the size of social networks also helps cultivate place-based sense of belongings. All else equal, knowing more people in the neighborhood predicts a higher likelihood to feel attached to the neighborhood, but does not necessarily enhance the attachment to the city. Vice versa, knowing more people in the city predicts a higher likelihood to feel attached to the city, but is not significantly related to neighborhood attachment. On the other hand, more frequent interaction with local people, an indication of the strength of social engagement to the urban society, predicts a significantly higher likelihood of attachment.

Not surprisingly, having experienced discrimination by local people significantly reduces a rural migrant's sense of belonging at both neighborhood and city scales, even when other variables are controlled for. Regarding duration of residence, the longer a rural migrant lives in the same neighborhood, the more likely he or she would feel attached to the neighborhood and to the destination city. As shown in the literature, longer duration of residence may enhance acquaintance with the place and thus enhancing the sense of attachment to the place (Wu, 2012). For rural migrants who remain "floating" and "temporary" in cities, longer duration of residence in one neighborhood may offer some sense of stability compared to the typical experiences of short-term leases and even forced relocation. Interestingly, coefficients of year of living in the destination city are not significant in both models, although correlations are found significant in bivariate

*Table 6.4* Logistic regression results for sense of attachment of rural migrants

| | Attachment to the neighborhood | | Attachment to the destination city | |
|---|---|---|---|---|
| | B | SE | B | SE |
| *Sources of current housing (ref: informal housing)* | | | | |
| Dorms | −0.224 | 0.137 | −0.204 | 0.139 |
| Formal housing | 0.523** | 0.199 | 0.436* | 0.206 |
| *Social networks and social interaction* | | | | |
| Number of ties in neighborhood (logged) | 0.204** | 0.066 | 0.005 | 0.066 |
| Number of ties in destination city (logged) | 0.041 | 0.030 | 0.073* | 0.030 |
| Frequency of interaction with local people | 0.117** | 0.043 | 0.221*** | 0.044 |
| Experience of discrimination | −0.560*** | 0.145 | −0.495*** | 0.146 |
| *Duration of residence* | | | | |
| Duration of residence in neighborhood (month) | 0.006* | 0.002 | 0.006* | 0.002 |
| Duration of residence in destination city (year) | −0.015 | 0.014 | −0.007 | 0.015 |
| *Socio-demographics* | | | | |
| Gender (male=1) | −0.464*** | 0.117 | −0.289* | 0.119 |
| Marital status (Married=1) | 0.423** | 0.158 | 0.054 | 0.162 |
| New-generation migrants (Born after 1980) | −0.373* | 0.162 | −0.330* | 0.165 |
| Year of schooling | −0.003 | 0.021 | 0.005 | 0.021 |
| Per capita income (logged) | −0.015 | 0.080 | −0.006 | 0.082 |
| Cross-provincial migration | 0.285* | 0.121 | 0.358** | 0.124 |
| *Constant* | −0.077 | 0.800 | 0.055 | 0.816 |
| McFadden's R square | 0.067 | | 0.059 | |
| McFadden's Adj R square | 0.051 | | 0.043 | |
| Cox-Snell R square | 0.086 | | 0.073 | |
| Nagelkerke R square | 0.116 | | 0.101 | |
| N | 1442 | | 1442 | |

Notes: *$p<0.05$; **$p<0.01$; ***$p<0.001$.

Source: 2009 twelve-city migrant survey.

analysis (see Table 6.3), indicating a more complicated relationship between migration experience and attachment.

Finally, model results show significant explanatory power of several socio-demographic variables in predicting sense of attachment. Male migrants are less likely than female migrants to feel attached to the neighborhood, which may be a result of the gender-based role that renders more engagement of females within the neighborhood (see Table 6.4). Being unmarried and born after 1980 predicts a lower likelihood of neighborhood attachment, possibly due to different life styles of migrants in different life-cycle stages in that young and unmarried migrants are less likely to be involved in neighborhood-based networks and activities. Younger-generation migrants also are less likely to feel attached to the destination city, though being married does not significantly predict one's sense of attachment to the city. Furthermore, higher-income, more-educated migrants are not necessarily more likely to develop stronger sense of attachment to the neighborhood or the city.

*Model results for settlement intention*

To examine the determinants of settlement intention, we first ran the base model with only housing access, social networks and social interaction, duration of residence, and socio-demographic variables, and then further included two attachment variables in the full model (see Table 6.5 for model results). Controlling for all other variables, attachment to the destination city – but not attachment to the neighborhood – remains significant in predicting settlement intention of rural migrants. All else equal, feeling attached to the destination city increases the odds of a rural migrant's willingness to settle down in cities by 52.5 per cent (odds ratio = 1.525). Compared to informal settlements, living in dorms reduces a rural migrant's settlement intention by 30.3 per cent (odds ratio = 0.697, $p < 0.05$ in the full model), when other variables held constant (see Table 6.5). The coefficient is consistent in the base and full model. On the other hand, access to formal housing significantly improves a rural migrant's

*Table 6.5* Logistic regression results for settlement intention of rural migrants

|  | Base model | | Full model | |
| --- | --- | --- | --- | --- |
|  | *B* | *SE* | *B* | *SE* |
| *Sources of current housing (ref: informal housing)* | | | | |
| Dorms | −0.362** | 0.127 | −0.361** | 0.128 |
| Formal housing | 0.630*** | 0.174 | 0.615*** | 0.175 |
| *Social networks and social interaction* | | | | |
| Number of ties in destination city (logged) | −0.040 | 0.027 | −0.046 | 0.027 |
| Frequency interaction with local people | 0.132*** | 0.039 | 0.111** | 0.040 |
| Experience of discrimination by local people | 0.105 | 0.133 | 0.150 | 0.134 |
| *Duration of residence (migration experience)* | | | | |
| Duration of residence in destination city (year) | 0.017 | 0.012 | 0.015 | 0.012 |
| *Socio-demographics* | | | | |
| Gender (Male = 1) | −0.145 | 0.109 | −0.124 | 0.109 |
| Marital status (Married = 1) | −0.650*** | 0.150 | −0.657*** | 0.152 |
| New-generation migrants (Born after 1980) | 0.246 | 0.149 | 0.264 | 0.150 |
| Year of schooling | 0.090*** | 0.020 | 0.089*** | 0.020 |
| Per capita income (logged) | 0.003 | 0.076 | 0.006 | 0.077 |
| Cross-province migration | 0.365*** | 0.111 | 0.337** | 0.112 |
| Occupation (Skilled = 1) | 0.353*** | 0.181 | 0.379* | 0.181 |
| Type of *danwei* (Public sector = 1) | 0.277 | 0.257 | 0.279 | 0.258 |
| *Sense of attachment* | | | | |
| Feel attached to the neighborhood | | | −0.093 | 0.130 |
| Feel attached to the destination city | | | 0.422** | 0.132 |
| *Constant* | −0.799 | 0.744 | −0.975 | 0.751 |
| McFadden's $R^2$ | 0.078 | | 0.083 | |
| McFadden's Adj $R^2$ | 0.065 | | 0.068 | |
| Cox-Snell R square | 0.102 | | 0.108 | |
| Nagelkerke R square | 0.137 | | 0.144 | |
| N | 1652 | | 1650 | |

Notes: *$p < 0.05$; **$p < 0.01$; ***$p < 0.001$.

Source: 2009 twelve-city migrant survey.

settlement intention by nearly 85 per cent, compared to living in informal settlements (odds ratio =1.850).

Duration of residence in the destination city does have significant explanatory power for either sense of attachment to the city or settlement intention of rural migrants. One possible reason is that we only consider migration experience in current city rather than measuring the total number of years since leaving villages, which may be a better indication of migration experience. Although the discrimination experience variable does not have significant explanatory power on settlement intention, from early analysis we know that exposure to discrimination significantly reduces rural migrants' sense of attachment and thus indirectly affect their willingness to settle down in cities. Meanwhile, knowing more people does not significantly increase a rural migrant's settlement intention; rather, more social engagement – measured by interaction frequency with local people – helps enhance such intention.

With respect to socio-demographic variables, more-educated, unmarried, cross-province migrants are significantly more likely to have settlement intention. All else equal, each additional year of schooling increases the odds of willingness to settle by 9.3 per cent (odd ratio = 1.093, see Table 6.5). A married migrant is only 51.8 per cent likely to have settlement intention compared to an unmarried migrant, holding other variables constant. Similar to findings from Zhu and Chen (2010), the odds of settlement intention are higher among cross-province migrants than within-province migrants. Yet contrary to the public opinion but resonating findings from Fan (2011), we find no significant relationship between age cohort with settlement intention: the so-called "new-generation" rural migrants may be more willing to settle down in cities but the difference is not significant in our models. In addition, having a better job also significantly enhances settlement intention: rural migrants with medium- to high-skilled jobs are 46.0 per cent more likely than those with low-skilled jobs to have the intention of permanent migration.

## Conclusions and discussion

For the new Chinese leadership, promoting the so-called "people-oriented" urbanization is key to the country's long-term development, and promoting full integration of the large number of rural migrants into the urban society key to the urbanization goal. Whereas social security, job training, and labor protection continue to assume top priority, never before has housing gained so much attention in national policy agenda. Provision of decent housing and basic safety-net welfare are seen as crucial components in the policy package to promote urban integration and stimulate settlement intention of rural migrants. Yet contrary to the heated public debate, empirical evidence has been limited regarding the relationship between housing and settlement of rural migrants in Chinese cities.

Built upon a growing body of literature on rural-to-urban migration in China, in this chapter we sought to demonstrate the important role that housing plays in migrants' decision to settle down in cities or to move back to the countryside. Data derived from a twelve-city survey indeed revealed that, although a large proportion of rural migrants prefer returning to villages instead of staying in cities, those who are able to access the formal housing system have significantly stronger settlement intention, even when other variables are controlled for. The enabling role of access to formal housing is also reflected to its positive contribution to the sense of attachment that rural migrants develop toward the neighborhood and the destination city, another important and significant factor of settlement intention found in the analysis.

Results from the empirical analysis also resonate findings from existing studies regarding determinants of settlement intention. Besides housing opportunities, other aspects of daily-life urban experiences also are found contributory to both attachment and settlement intention of rural migrants. Knowing more people and, more importantly, keeping more frequent interaction with local people both reflect better social integration in daily life and contribute positively to sense of attachment and settlement intention. In addition, cross-province migrants who are married, more-educated and with better jobs are more likely to express settlement intention. Empirical analysis also revealed several interesting and unexpected findings. First, although rural migrants may have lower sense of attachment if they have experienced discrimination by local people, they nevertheless express no significantly different intention of settlement. Second, longer duration of residence in the destination city does not have a significant relationship with the odds of intention to settle down in cities. Finally, settlement intention is not significantly higher among the so-called "new generation" of rural migrants than migrants born before 1980, although the regression coefficient is positive. In fact, new-generation migrants in our survey expressed lower sense of attachment both toward the neighborhood and toward the destination city.

A caveat to this study is that, while we found statistical significance of the relationship between housing access and settlement intention, the process in which rural migrants make settlement decisions involves complicated dynamics. Both objective circumstances, such as socio-demographic characteristics, migration history, and life experiences in cities, as well as subjective feelings, such as life satisfaction and sense of attachment, may affect a migrant's decision to settle down. Because of the cross-sectional nature of our data, it is difficult to claim exactly the causal and interactive mechanisms of the multi-faceted urban experiences of rural migrants in China. Furthermore, stronger settlement intention does not mean actual settlement behavior or outcomes, which are subject to even more complex conditions. More analysis thus is valuable, if longitudinal data are made available, to move beyond intention to explore actual outcomes of integration and settlement of migrants in Chinese cities.

## References

Austin, D. M. and Baba, Y. (1990) "Social determinants of neighborhood attachment", *Sociological Spectrum*, 10: 59–78.
Curley, A. M. (2010) "Relocating the poor: Social capital and neighborhood resources", *Journal of Urban Affairs*, 32 (1): 79–103.

Fan, C. C. (2001) "Migration and labor market returns in urban China: Results from a recent survey in Guangzhou", *Environment and Planning A*, 33 (3): 479–508.

Fan, C. C. (2011) "Settlement intention and split households: Findings from a survey of migrants in Beijing's urban villages", *China Review – an Interdisciplinary Journal on Greater China*, 11 (2): 11–41.

Granovetter, M. (1995) *Getting a Job: A study of contacts and careers*. Chicago: University of Chicago Press.

He, S., Liu, Y., Wu, F. and Webster, C. (2010) "Social groups and housing differentiation in China's urban villages: An institutional interpretation", *Housing Studies*, 25 (5): 671–91.

Hu, F., Xu, Z. and Chen, Y. (2011) "Circular migration, or permanent stay? Evidence from China's rural–urban migration", *China Economic Review*, 22 (1): 64–74.

Huang, Y. (2004) "The road to homeownership: A longitudinal analysis of tenure transition in urban China", *International Journal of Comparative Sociology*, 28 (4): 774–95.

Huang, Y. (2012) "Low-income housing in Chinese cities: Policies and practices", *The China Quarterly*, 212: 941–64.

Jasso, G. and Rosenzweig, M.R. (1988) "How well do US immigrants do? Vintage effects, emigration selectivity, and occupational mobility", *Research in Population Economics*, 6: 229–53.

Khraif, R. M. (1992) "Permanent versus temporary rural migrants in Riyadh, Saudi Arabia: A logit analysis of their intentions of future mobility", *GeoJournal*, 26 (3): 363–70.

Kleit, R. G. (2001) "The role of neighborhood social networks in scattered-site public housing residents' search for jobs", *Housing Policy Debate*, 12 (3): 541–73.

Korinek, K., Entwisle, B. and Jampaklay, A. (2005) "Through thick and thin: Layers of social ties and urban settlement among Thai migrants", *American Sociological Review*, 70 (5): 779–800.

Li, S. M. (2000) "Housing consumption in urban China: A comparative study of Beijing and Guangzhou", *Environment and Planning A*, 32 (6): 1115–34.

Li, S. M. and Yi, Z. (2007) "The road to homeownership under market transition: Beijing 1980–2001", *Urban Affairs Review*, 42: 342–68.

Liu, Z., Wang, Y. and Tao, R. (2013) "Social capital and migrant housing experiences in urban China: A structural equation modeling analysis", *Housing Studies*, 28 (8): 1155–74.

Massey, D. S. (1987) "Understanding Mexican migration to the United States", *American Journal of Sociology*, 92: 1372–403.

Massey, D. S. and Akresh, I. R. (2006) "Immigrant intentions and mobility in a global economy: The attitudes and behavior of recently arrived US immigrants", *Social Science Quarterly*, 87 (5): 954–71.

National Bureau of Statistics of China (2011) *First Communique of Main Data Results from the 2010 Sixth National Population Census* (Released 28 April 2011). Online. Available HTTP: <http://www.stats.gov.cn/tjgb/rkpcgb/qgrkpcgb/t20110428_402722232.htm> (Accessed 23 May 2011).

Nielsen, I., Smyth, R. and Zhai, Q. (2009) "Subjective well-being of China's off-farm migrants", *Journal of Happiness Studies*, 11 (3): 315–33.

Palmer, N. A., Perkins, D. D. and Xu, Q. (2011) "Social capital and community participation among migrant workers in China", *Journal of Community Psychology*, 39 (1): 89–105.

Pinkster, F. (2009) "Neighborhood-based networks, social resources, and labor market participation in two Dutch neighborhoods", *Journal of Urban Affairs*, 31 (2): 213–31.

Reyes, B.I. (2001) "Immigrant trip duration: The case of immigrants from Western Mexico", *International Migration Review*, 35 (4): 1185–204.

Sun, M. and Fan, C. C. (2011) "China's permanent and temporary migrants: Differentials and changes, 1990–2000", *The Professional Geographer*, 63 (1): 92–112.

Tao, R. and Xu, Z. (2007) "Urbanization, rural land system, and social security for migrants in China", *Journal of Development Studies*, 43 (7): 1301–20.

Wang, W. W. and Fan, C. C. (2012) "Migrant workers' integration in urban China: Experiences in employment, social adaptation, and self-identity", *Eurasian Geography and Economics*, 53 (6): 731–49.

Wang, Y. P. (2003) "Living conditions of migrants in inland Chinese cities", *The Journal of Comparative Asian Development*, 2: 47–69.

Wang, Y. P. (2004) *Urban Poverty, Housing and Social Change in China*. London and New York: Routledge.

Wang, Y. P., Wang, Y. and Wu, J. (2010) "Housing migrant workers in rapidly urbanizing regions: A study of the Chinese model in Shenzhen", *Housing Studies*, 25 (1): 83–100.

Wu, F. L. (2004) "Urban poverty and marginalization under market transition: The case of Chinese cities", *International Journal of Urban and Regional Research*, 28 (2): 401–23.

Wu, F. L. (2007) "The poverty of transition: From industrial district to poor neighborhood in the city of Nanjing, China", *Urban Studies*, 44 (13): 2673–94.

Wu, F. L. (2012) "Neighborhood attachment, social participation, and willingness to stay in China's low-income communities", *Urban Affairs Review*, 48 (4): 547–70.

Wu, W. (2002) "Migrant housing in urban China – Choices and constraints", *Urban Affairs Review*, 38 (1): 90–119.

Wu, W. (2004) "Sources of migrant housing disadvantage in urban China", *Environment and Planning A*, 36 (7): 1285–304.

Xu, Q., Guan, X. and Yao, F. (2011) "Welfare program participation among rural-to-urban migrant workers in China", *International Journal of Social Welfare*, 20 (1): 10–21.

Yang, Q. H. and Guo, F. (1996) "Occupational attainments of rural to urban temporary economic migrants in China: 1985–1990", *International Migration Review*, 30 (3): 771–87.

Zhang, J., Li, X., Fang, X. and Xiong, Q. (2009) "Discrimination experience and quality of life among rural-to-urban migrants in China: The mediation effect of expectation–reality discrepancy", *Quality of Life Research*, 18 (3): 291–300.

Zheng, S., Long, F., Fan, C. C. and Gu, Y. (2009) "Urban villages in China: A 2008 survey of migrant settlements in Beijing", *Eurasian Geography and Economics*, 50 (4): 425–46.

Zhu, Y. (2007) "China's floating population and their settlement intention in the cities: Beyond the *hukou* reform", *Habitat International*, 31: 65–76.

Zhu, Y. and Chen, W. (2010) "The settlement intention of China's floating population in the cities: Recent changes and multifaceted individual-level determinants", *Population, Space and Place*, 16 (4): 253–67.

# 7 Effectiveness, efficiency and equity

## An empirical evaluation of the cheap rental housing program in Beijing, China

*Chengdong Yi and Youqin Huang*

## Introduction

Chinese cities have experienced an unprecedented housing boom in recent decades, with massive investment in new private housing – "commodity housing" (shang pin fang). Consequently, housing consumption has increased significantly in Chinese cities; the rate of homeownership skyrocketed from 20 per cent in the 1980s to 70 per cent in 2010, and per capita residential floor space increased from 4 m² to 29 m² during the same period (NBSC, 2011; Huang and Clark, 2002). Yet this unprecedented housing improvement is not necessarily shared by all social groups. Housing poverty and residential crowding remain acute especially among low-income households. In 2005, 7.4 per cent of urban households experienced severe crowding with per capita living space less than 8 m² (Ni and Yi, 2009). Meanwhile, housing price has been rising rapidly, with the national average price of "commodity housing" more than doubled (Figure 7.1). The lack of decent and affordable housing especially among low-income households has become an increasingly acute problem and is threatening social and political stability in China.

To achieve the goal of "decent housing for all," the Chinese government has been establishing a system of low-income housing in the last decade. In a watershed document in 1998 (No. 23), State Council ended public housing provision, but aimed to establish a multi-level housing provision system with "cheap rental housing" (lian zu fang, hereafter CRH) for the lowest-income households, and "economic and comfortable housing" (jingji shiyong fang, hereafter ECH) for low- and middle-income households, the latter of which was redefined as low-income housing in 2007. CRH refers to housing subsidies in the rental sector, which can be provided in different forms: 1) "public housing with controlled rents" (shiwu peizu, hereafter "public housing") – public housing provided by the government or work units with government controlled rents; 2) "rent subsidies" (zujin butie) – monetary subsidies to low-income households who rent private housing on the market. ECH is ownership-oriented housing provided by developers on free land allocated by local municipal governments, sold to qualified households with government controlled prices and partial property rights.[1] Yet since it has been defined as low-income housing, the provision of ECH has declined significantly (Huang, 2012). Thus CRH has been the main type of low-income

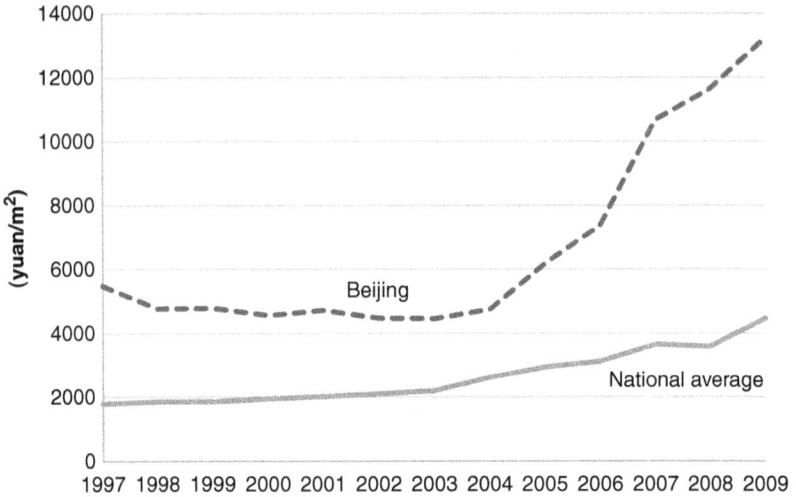

*Figure 7.1* Commodity housing price in China and Beijing over time.
Source: National Bureau of Statistics of China, 1998–2010.

housing in China till 2010 when the government started a new type of subsidized housing – "public rental housing" (gongfong zulin fang).[2]

Yet, since 1998 when CRH was officially established, housing marketization has been accelerated, and most municipal governments lacked commitment to CRH due to emphasis on economic goals (Huang, 2012). Faced with increasing discontent due to the lack of housing affordability, the central government has refocused on low-income housing since 2007 with ambitious goals and massive investment (Huang, 2012). For example, State Council (2007) required that households that receive Minimum Standard of Living Assistance (MSLA, or "di bao") and meet the criteria of housing difficulty should be 100 per cent covered by the CRH system in large and medium cities by the end of 2007 and in all county-level cities by the end of 2008 – the so-called "ying bao jin bao."[3] By the end of 2010, the coverage of CRH should be extended to all urban low-income households. Meanwhile, the central government has pumped 10.6 billion yuan in 2007 and 37.5 billion in 2008 in subsidized housing, and required local governments to develop 5.84 million units of subsidized housing in 2010 and another 36 million units during 2011–2015 (State Council 2011, No.1; Huang, 2012). In the macro context of neoliberalism, China has entered an era of state intervention in low-income housing.

As the national capital, Beijing demonstrates the characteristics of other Chinese cities; yet, it has its own uniqueness. On the one hand, Beijing follows closely and implements low-income housing policies issued by the central government. On the other hand, Beijing Municipal Government (BMG) is severely constrained in low-income housing as it does not have control over a massive stock of subsidized housing and land in the city that are under the jurisdiction of powerful work units at the central government level, such as ministries, large public institutions, and state owned enterprises (SOEs). After 1998 when the provision of public housing was officially ended, these powerful work units can still request free land from BMG or use previously allocated land to develop ECH for their employees. This led to a much smaller share of urban land that is directly under the jurisdiction of BMG, and even a smaller share is for low-income housing development.

As the political, economic and culture center, Beijing is a strong magnet to both population and industries. With the rapid industrialization and urbanization, Beijing has grown rapidly in recent decades, with 19.6 million population in 2010 (BSB, 2011). There have also been massive urban renewals and shantytown rebuilding in Beijing, creating massive displacement of the urban poor. The influx of migrants and large scale of resettlement have created a large demand for affordable housing. Meanwhile, housing price in Beijing is much higher than the national average, and the average price for commodity housing increased 2.6 times from 5,062 yuan/m² in 2001 to 13,224 yuan/m² in 2009 (NSBC, 2010) (Figure 7.1). The Price-Income Ratio in Beijing was 9.3 in 2007, much higher than the affordable range of 3-5 according to UN-HABITAT (Man *et al.*, 2011). This makes low housing affordability and poor housing condition, especially among low- and middle-income households, even more acute in Beijing than other cities (Yang *et al.*, 2010). In 2005, about 19 per cent of urban households experienced housing crowding with per capita living space less than 8 m² (Ni and Yi, 2009).

BMG has been establishing a low-income housing system centered on CRH since 1998. This chapter aims to evaluate the CRH program in Beijing and assess its effectiveness in policy implementation, efficiency in subsidy provision, and equity in subsidy distribution. After a literature review, we will examine CRH policy in Beijing, and then we will use the CRH Application and Verification Information System to evaluate the CRH program.

## Research context and literature review

While mean-tested housing policy is common in the West (Bridge *et al.*, 2003), low-income housing policy is relatively a new phenomenon in China, let alone policy evaluation. Many research shows that policy evaluation is essential to improve housing policies and programs, and both the government in the UK and US require independent policy and program evaluation (Cabinet Office 2003; Renger *et al.*, 2003).

Housing policies and programs are often evaluated in the following dimensions. First, the effect of housing policy/program on the housing market, such as housing price, property value, and housing supply. In general there is a very low price elasticity of supply due to a fairly low-income elasticity of demand by low-income households and responsiveness of the market on the supply-side through vacancy adjustment (Barnett and Lowry, 1979; Mills and Sullivan, 1981; Rydell, 1982; Malpezzi and Maclennan, 2001). There is also a "crowding out" effect with subsidized housing units replacing private housing units such that low-income housing programs do not necessarily increase housing supply (Swan, 1973; Murray 1983,

1999; Malpezzi and Vandell, 2002). In contrast to the common fear, low-income housing does not seems to have a negative effect on property value of nearby housing (Schafer, 1972; DeSalvo, 1974; Goetz *et al.*, 1996; Green *et al.*, 2001). Different types of low-income housing may have different effects on different types of neighborhoods, and in some circumstances there is positive impact on property value (Santiago *et al.*, 2001).

The second line of evaluation focuses on low-income households' residential satisfaction and socio-economic wellbeing in different low-income housing programs, such as satisfaction on the physical and spatial qualities of housing, its architectural desirability (Liu, 2003; Ornstein, 2005; Fatoye and Odusami, 2009), accessibility (Apparicio and Seguin, 2006), and the efficiency of housing management and administration (Valenca, 2007; Sengupta and Sharma, 2008; Hsieh, 2009). In general, low-income households living in ownership-oriented housing, single family houses, and better housing and neighborhoods are more satisfied (Rent and Rent, 1978; Rohe and Stegman 1994a, b).

The third line of evaluation focuses on effectiveness, efficiency and equity of housing policies and programs. Effectiveness refers to the degree of a policy target that has been achieved, while efficiency refers whether the policy is implemented with low cost. Headey (1978) uses both "horizontal equity" – equal treatment of people in equal positions – and "vertical equity" – unequal treatment of people in unequal positions and more subsidies to those in worse condition – to assess public policy such as housing policy. The lack of effectiveness, efficiency and equity in public housing is common in both developed and developing countries (Malpezzi, 1999). It is estimated that only one-third of low-income rental households eligible to receive housing assistance actually do so in the US while low-income homeowners receive less subsidies than middle- and high-income homeowners (US General Accounting Office, 2001; Olsen, 2003). Yet, Quigley (2000) argued American housing policy had moved from project- to tenant-based housing subsidies, and thus had improved its efficiency and effectiveness. It has been a common wisdom that demand-side, income-related housing subsidy programs are generally more effective in getting decent and affordable housing to the needy than public housing and other supply-side programs (Olsen, 2003). While many housing policies have been successful in their own terms, many housing problems identified at the beginning of the policy period have not been addressed effectively because of the nature of the policy making process (Stephens, 2005). In most developing countries public housing programs have failed to provide decent, affordable and adequate housing to the target population (Mukhija, 2004). Chiu (2002) argues that the ownership-oriented housing assistance in Hong Kong has intensified the vertical and horizontal inequity, while Bramley *et al.* (2002) found huge regional differences in the efficiency and effectiveness of low-income home ownership program in England.

Despite decades of providing public housing to the mass, low-income housing policy is relatively a new concept in China, and the Chinese government has been experimenting with housing policy since the late 1990s. Huang (2012) argues that the low-income housing program in China has so far failed to provide adequate housing to the poor mainly because of the central government's lack of a clear mission for low-income housing, local governments' lack of commitment, and the exclusion of massive migrants. Many low-income households with housing difficulties are not covered by low-income housing programs and they have benefited little from housing reform (Zhang, 1998; Lai, 1998; Lee, 2000). Wang (2000) argues that acute housing problems among low-income households are results of social welfare reforms that ignore interests of low-income households.

There is a small body of literature in Chinese, which focuses on descriptive analysis of housing policies, problems of low-income housing, and policy recommendations (e.g. Tian, 1998; Yao, 2003; Jia 2005; Ye *et al.*, 2006; DRC, 2007). Compared to other countries, Xiong *et al.* (2009) argued that the coverage of CRH in China is not adequate and there is severe financial shortage for CRH. There has been very limited research on CRH in specific cities such as Beijing. Shao (2002) argues that CRH in Beijing has problems such as small coverage, complicated application process, the lack of appropriate housing, poor exist mechanism, and the lack of matching infrastructure. Problems in ECH have been well documented, such as high income price ratio, mismatch in supply and demand, unclear target group, problems in allocation, and rent-seeking behavior among homeowners (Qian, 2003; Lin, 2007; Che and Guo, 2009; Li, 2009).

In sum, there has been very limited research on housing policy evaluation in China. Most existing research focuses on conceptual analysis of housing policy in China, with few empirical analyses due to the lack of systematic data. This chapter aims to fill the literature gap by conducting an empirical evaluation of the CRH system in Beijing.

## The evolution of cheap rental housing policy in Beijing

Following the call of the central government, Beijing Municipal Government has been establishing a CRH system since 1999 (BMG, 1999). Yet, with accelerated housing marketization, BMG did not do much in the following years till 2007 when the central government was determined to improve housing condition of low-income households (State Council, 2007). BMG responded with a series of policies to formalize various aspects of CRH in the following years, including the "Management Method for Cheap Rental Housing in Beijing," which defined the target population, housing source, verification and allocation, and management of CRH (BMG, 2007a; BBHURD, 2010b; BHIO, 2010b, 2011). It also set up clear targets for low-income housing. For example, in 2009, Beijing Bureau of Housing and Urban–Rural Development aimed to complete two million m² subsidized housing, and raised the concept of "two 50 per cent" in 2010, meaning land for subsidized housing (including CRH) should be more than 50 per cent of all land for housing development, and the number of units for subsidized housing should be more than 50 per cent of total new housing development (BBHURD, 2010a). The government aimed to build 4000 units of CRH in 2010, and basically solve housing difficulties of qualified households who passed the verification by the end of 2009 (BHIO, 2010a). This reenergized commitment to CRH by the local government is a result of the political pressure and financial support from the central government (Huang, 2012).

Since the government has been "muddling through" its low-income housing policy, the specific contents such as the target population, methods and standards of housing subsidy, and management of CRH have changed over time.

### Target population and entry criteria

In Beijing, the target population for CRH has expanded over time from the lowest-income households to low-income households with housing difficulties (Table 7.1). In 2001, BMG clearly identified that households who meet the criteria of the lowest-income and housing difficulties could apply for CRH. The lowest-income households referred to urban "di bao" households whose per capita income was lower than the minimum standard of living (300 yuan/month) and who have received Minimum Standard of Living Assistance for more than one year (BLHMB, 2001). "Housing difficulties" is defined as per capita living space no more than 7.5 m². In addition, "special groups" such as people who are disabled or being resettled, having major illnesses, old State Owned Enterprise (SOE) employees with housing difficulties, and SOE Model Workers with housing difficulties are also qualified for CRH. Since 2005, the target has expanded to low-income households with per capita living space no more than 7.5 m², with the income standard rising gradually over time (580 yuan in 2005, 697 yuan in 2009, 960 yuan in 2010) (BBHURD, 2005a, 2005b; BBHURD, 2010b). Household asset was added as another entry criterion in 2007.[4] In addition, applicants for CRH must hold local

*Table 7.1* Targets and entry criteria for Cheap Rental Housing in Beijing

| Year | Target | Entry criteria (meet all) |
|---|---|---|
| 2001–2005 | Lowest-income households with housing difficulties | 1: "Di bao" households with per capita income <= 300 yuan/month;<br>2: Per capita living space <= 7.5 m² |
| 2006–2009 | Low-income households with housing difficulties | 1: Per capita income <= 580 yuan/month, including di bao households;<br>2: Per capita living space <= 7.5 m²<br>3: Household assets was added in 2007<br>  One-person households: <= 150 K yuan<br>  Two-person households: <= 230 K yuan<br>  Three-person households: <= 300 K yuan<br>  Four-person households: <= 380 K yuan<br>  Five+ person households: <= 400 K yuan |
| 2009–July 2010 | Low-income households with housing difficulties | 1: Per capita income <= 697 yuan/month<br>2: Per capita living space <= 7.5 m²<br>3: Household assets same as above |
| August 2010 | Low-income households with housing difficulties | 1: Per capita income <= 960 yuan/month<br>2: Per capita living space <= 7.5 m²<br>3: Household assets same as above |

Source: Various policy documents.

non-agricultural household registration (hukou), and live in Beijing (BBHURD, 2007a), which excludes low-income migrants from accessing CRH.

## Methods and standards of housing subsidies

CRH in Beijing is allocated mainly through the demand-side subsidies – "rent subsidy," supplemented by the supply-side subsidies – "public housing" (BBHURD, 2007a). This is consistent with the trend in the West. The principal in Beijing is that "di bao" households and special groups should be provided "public housing," while the other low-income households should receive "rent subsidy."

The principle for CRH is to guarantee low-income households' basic housing needs, and the level of subsidy is determined by the budget and households' housing condition. The amount of "rent subsidies" is determined by factors such as household size, per capita subsidized housing standard, monthly rent subsidy standard per square meter, and household income; and the maximum and minimum rent subsidies are pre-determined. For example, in 2007, the rent subsidy standard was 40 yuan/$m^2$/month in eight urban districts, and the minimum and maximum rent subsidy was 550 and 1500 yuan/month, respectively (BBHURD, 2007c). The subsidy standard for "public housing" is per capita living space 10 $m^2$. Depending on household structure, gender, age and household size, different types of apartments will be allocated. Rents are government regulated, and in 2005, the rent standard for "public housing" was 5 per cent of household income of the lowest-income households (BCDR, 2005).

## Verification, monitoring and management

Due to the lack of credible income information in China, Beijing municipal government adopts a system of "three levels of verification, and two levels of public display" (BBHURD, 2007a), a rather complicated and lengthy process. Applicants for CRH need to submit their applications to the Street Office (jie dao) for preliminary verification, the District Government for second verification, and Beijing Housing Indemnity Office for final verification. The preliminary verification results are required to be displayed in public at the applicants' hukou registration place, current residence, and work place, and the second verification result by the District Government is required to be displayed on the district government website or other required spaces. Public display is used to discourage cheating in application. Meanwhile, the beneficiaries of CRH are required to submit information about their housing, income, household size, and assets annually to the district level housing indemnity office, while the latter need to check their information regularly to ensure accuracy.

In summary, the Beijing Municipal Government has taken a long way in establishing a system of CRH for low-income households amidst of housing reform and market transition. It is clear that policy-wise the BMG has strengthened its commitment in recent years with a larger target population and more detailed regulations on CRH. Now the question is whether and how are these policies being implemented. Is the CRH system in Beijing effective in policy implementation, efficient in subsidy provision, and equitable in subsidy allocation?

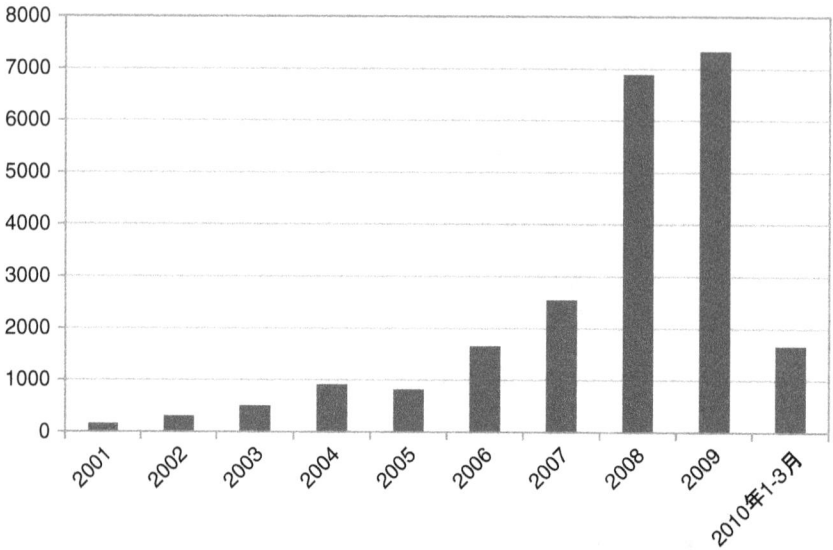

*Figure 7.2* Number of verified applicants for Cheap Rental Housing in Beijing.

## An empirical analysis

The following empirical study utilizes mainly the CRH Application Verification Information System dataset, which is complied by Beijing Housing Indemnity Office (BHIO). It includes the profiles of applicants for CRH who have passed the verification system – verified applicants. Qualitative data such as reports by BHIO, and interviews of BHIO staff and CRH applicants are also used.

The number of verified CRH applicants was very small in the first a few years of the twenty-first century (only 156 in 2001 and 821 in 2005) (Figure 7.2). But it has been increasing rapidly especially since 2007 when the government refocused on low-income housing, and established the ambitious goal of "ying bao jin bao" (BMG, 2007b, c). The number of verified applicants reached 6,893 in 2008 and 7,336 in 2009. By March of 2010, the cumulative number of verified applicants for CRH in Beijing reached 22,788 households.

Verified applicants for CRH come mostly from the urban core, with about 49 per cent from the old urban districts, 38 per cent from the new urban districts, and only 13 per cent from the far suburbs (Table 7.2).[5] The main reason for the urban concentration of CRH applicants is that urban households with per capita living space less than 10 m[2] and the lowest-income urban households mostly live in the inner city due to the prevalence of old dilapidated bungalows in the inner city. Most of CRH applicants are in their 40s and over 50, and the most common household structure is three-person households due to the one-child policy. Not surprisingly, "di bao" households account for more than 60 per cent of CRH applicants. It is clear that households with low income and assets are given priority

*Table 7.2* Characteristics of verified applicants for Cheap Rental Housing

| | N | % | | % |
|---|---|---|---|---|
| Total | 22788 | 100 | *Age* | |
| *Old urban districts* | *11146* | *48.9* | < = 30 | 5.8 |
| Xicheng | 6063 | 26.6 | 31 – 40 | 15.9 |
| Dongcheng | 5083 | 22.3 | 41 – 50 | 48.8 |
| *New urban districts* | *8707* | *38.2* | 51– 60 | 21.2 |
| Chaoyang | 2787 | 12.2 | 61 + | 8.3 |
| Fengtai | 2266 | 9.9 | | |
| Shijingshan | 2247 | 9.9 | *Household type* | |
| Haidian | 1407 | 6.2 | Missing | 0.1 |
| *Far suburbs* | *2935* | *13.0* | Di bao households | 62.8 |
| Fangshan | 320 | 1.4 | Low-income households | 35.1 |
| Tongzhou | 743 | 3.3 | Other special groups | 2.0 |
| Shunyi | 84 | 0.4 | | |
| Changping | 165 | 0.7 | *Household size* | |
| Daxing | 76 | 0.3 | 3-person | 38.8 |
| Mentougou | 929 | 4.1 | | |
| Huairou | 136 | 0.6 | *Annual household income (1,000 yuan)* | |
| Pinggu | 18 | 0.1 | 0 | 48.6 |
| Miyun | 309 | 1.4 | 0<X<= 5 | 11.5 |
| Yanqing | 155 | 0.7 | 5<X<= 10 | 14.6 |
| | | | 10<X<= 15 | 14.1 |
| | | | 15<X<= 20 | 8.8 |
| | | | 20 + | 2.4 |
| | | | *Household assets (1,000 yuan)* | |
| | | | 0 | 82.3 |
| | | | 0<X<= 50 | 11 |
| | | | 50<X<= 100 | 3.2 |
| | | | 100<X<= 150 | 2.0 |
| | | | 150 + | 1.5 |

to pass the verification. More than 60 per cent of verified applicants have annual household income less than 5,000 yuan, and 98 per cent have less than 20,000 yuan, while 82 per cent of applicants have no assets at all.

### *Effectiveness of the CRH program*

Effectiveness refers to how well a policy target has been achieved in actual implementation. Where there are many different policy targets, we focus on policy coverage. The government set up the goal of "ying bao jin bao" in 2007, which means that ultimately all low-income households who need housing assistance should be covered by the CRH system, and the most vulnerable group – "di bao" households with housing difficulties should be 100 per cent covered first. Yet, in reality, there is a lack of effectiveness in policy coverage. There are huge gaps between who *should* be covered, who are *qualified* to be covered, and who are *actually* covered by CRH, and the coverage of CRH is extremely low in Beijing.

In 2005, there were 4.41 million urban households in Beijing (BMPSB, 2007). Adopting the 20 per cent of total urban households as low-income households, an income division method by National Statistical Bureau of China, there were 880,000 low-income households who *should* be covered by CRH under the goal of "ying bao jin bao" (100 per cent). Yet, only low-income households with local non-agricultural registration are qualified for CRH in Beijing. According to Beijing Bureau of Public Security, there were 642,000 low-income households with local non-agricultural registration (20 per cent of 3.21 million urban households with non-agricultural registration), which accounted for 73 per cent of all low-income households (Figure 7.3). Furthermore, only those who meet the entry criteria can potentially apply for CRH. In 2005, there were 38,300 "di bao" households with per capita living space no more than 7.5 m², and 44,500 other low-income households with per capita monthly income between 310 and 580 yuan and per capita living space no more than 7.5 m², both of which should be covered by CRH. Yet they together accounted for only 9.4 per cent of all low-income households in Beijing, who are actually *qualified* to apply for CRH. This shows that the qualifying criteria for CRH are extremely strict, which excludes the majority of low-income households from accessing CRH.

Among those who are qualified for CRH, not every household has applied, or received housing subsidies. By the end of March of 2010, 22,630 households were covered by CRH, which accounted for only 2.6 per cent of all urban low-income households, and 27.3 per cent of qualified applicants. Among those covered by CRH, there were 14,320 "di bao" households, which accounted for only 37.4 per cent of all "di bao" households in 2005. Thus even among the most vulnerable "di bao" households, the coverage is way below 100 per cent. In other words, whatever the target group is, be it urban low-income households, qualified low-income applicants, or "di bao" households, the goal of "ying bao jin bao" has far from been

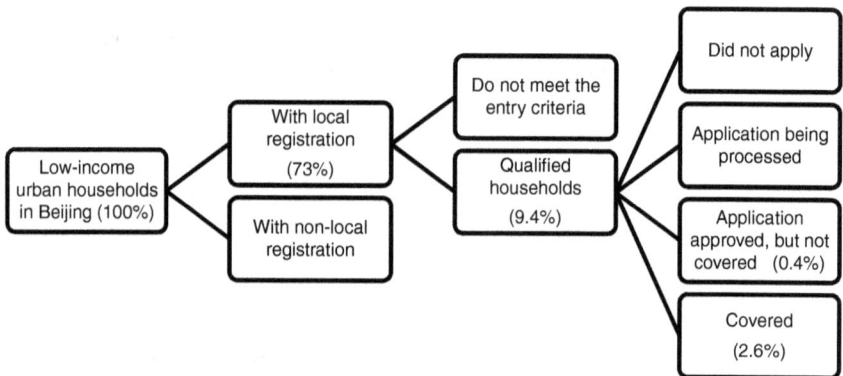

*Figure 7.3* Extremely low coverage of Cheap Rental Housing in Beijing.

achieved in Beijing. This extremely low coverage demonstrates the lack of effectiveness in CRH.

There are many factors that may contribute to the failure of "ying bao jin bao" and the low coverage of CRH. On the one hand, the lack of commitment and efficiency from the government contributes to the low coverage. As discussed earlier, low-income housing has not been a priority for the government during housing marketization. While low-income housing has been re-emphasized since 2007, local governments continue to focus on economic goals with limited financial and land commitments to low-income housing (Huang, 2012). The overly strict entry criteria, the lengthy and complicated application and verification process, and slow distribution of CRH to qualified households further contribute to the low coverage. On the other hand, many qualified households surprisingly choose not to apply for CRH. For example, by 2006, only 15 per cent of "di bao" households have applied for subsidies. According to BBHURD (2007b), there are various reasons why most "di bao" households do not apply for CRH. As discussed earlier, many low-income households live in old neighborhoods in inner cities where services and infrastructure are generally better than suburbs where most public housing is located. Compared to medical service and children's education, improving housing condition is not necessarily the priority for many lowest-income households. They may prefer to live in current housing to access better medical services and education in inner cities, and to avoid potentially higher living cost in suburbs considering transportation, shopping, children's schooling, and medical services. In addition, many old neighborhoods in inner cities may be gentrified in the future, and residents may receive massive resettlement compensation. Thus despite poor housing condition, many low-income households do not want to move away from inner cities to public housing elsewhere for fear of losing potentially large financial compensation in the case of gentrification. Furthermore, rent subsidies are often too low for them to rent decent housing on the market, thus many do not even bother to apply.

### Efficiency in subsidy provision

Due to the lack of data on overall cost of the CRH program, we focus on subsidy method to evaluate efficiency in subsidy provision. There is a high degree of efficiency in subsidy provision as the majority of subsidies are provided through monetary "rent subsidies." Between 2001 and April 1st, 2010, 25.6 per cent of all CRH beneficiaries in Beijing accessed "public housing," and 74.4 per cent received "rent subsidies" (Table 7.3). Because "rent subsidy" does not require a massive lump sum investment, it is possible to subsidize more needy households with limited funding and within a short span of time. It can also avoid the spatial concentration of low-income households and related social problems. Thus it is more efficient than "public housing" in both financial and social cost. But low-income households may not have access to affordable and appropriate housing. This is especially the case in Beijing where developers have been providing mainly upscale housing for the elite and there is a shortage of small, affordable housing

*Table 7.3* Types and amount of housing subsidy for Cheap Rental Housing

|  | Public housing (%) | Rent subsidy (%) | Total (%) | Average rent subsidy per person per m² of living space (yuan) |
|---|---|---|---|---|
| *Total* | 25.6 | 74.4 | 100 | 40.3 |
| *Household type* |  |  |  |  |
| Di bao households and special groups | 87.0 | 13.0 | 100 |  |
| Other low-income households | 5.4 | 94.6 | 100 |  |
| *Old urban districts* | 17.6 | 82.4 | 100 | 42.9 |
| Dongcheng | 21.5 | 78.5 | 100 | 45.2 |
| Xicheng | 17.4 | 82.6 | 100 | 43.8 |
| Chongwen | 28.1 | 71.9 | 100 | 41.4 |
| Xuanwu | 7.8 | 92.2 | 100 | 38.3 |
| *New urban districts* | 36.4 | 63.6 | 100 | 43.4 |
| Chaoyang | 40.3 | 59.7 | 100 | 43.4 |
| Fengtai | 25.2 | 74.8 | 100 | 43.9 |
| Shijingshan | 49.9 | 50.1 | 100 | 42.3 |
| Haidian | 25.2 | 74.8 | 100 | 44.1 |
| *Far suburbs* | 24.1 | 75.9 | 100 | 17.5 |
| Mentougou | 42.9 | 57.1 | 100 | 19.9 |
| Fangshan | 0 | 100 | 100 | 12.2 |
| Tongzhou | 39.8 | 60.2 | 100 | 19.8 |
| Shunyi | 1.2 | 98.8 | 100 | 14.1 |
| Changping | 0.6 | 99.4 | 100 | 19.8 |
| Daxing | 11.8 | 88.2 | 100 | 16.9 |
| Huairou | 0.7 | 99.3 | 100 | 15.8 |
| Pinggu | 0 | 100 | 100 | 15.0 |
| Miyun | 0 | 100 | 100 | 17.3 |
| Yanqing | 100 | 100 | 0 | 10.0 |

units on the market. In comparison, "public housing" guarantees the beneficiaries to have access to housing, but it is more costly (financially and administratively) due to the initial housing construction and the following housing management. It also tends to result in the spatial concentration of low-income households.

Yet, there are large variations across social groups and space. For example, "di bao" households and other "special groups" such as those who are disabled or have major diseases are much more likely to access "public housing" (87 per cent) than other low-income households. While "public housing" is more costly in initial investment and following management, this high rate of "public housing" among the most voluntary groups is in fact a policy design to ensure their access to housing. In addition, households in old urban districts are much more likely to access "rent subsidy" (82.4 per cent), and those in new urban districts are more likely to receive "public housing" (36.4 per cent). One main reason for this spatial difference is that there is more "public housing" in new urban districts than in the inner city.

On average, beneficiaries receive about 40 yuan per person per m² of living space per month. Yet, subsidies are much higher in urban districts than far suburbs. As market rents are much higher in urban districts than far suburbs, the differentiated subsidy level is an efficient way to provide subsidies in differenti-ated local housing markets.

### Equity in the allocation of CRH

Equity has been a main concern in the allocation of low-income housing (Headey, 1978). The overall system of housing subsidy in Chinese cities generally lacks equity as the government focused on middle-income households and ownership-oriented subsidies such as ECH at least before 2007 while many low-income households are not subsidized or receive fewer subsidies than high-income households (Huang, 2012). Furthermore, despite their economic contribution, massive low-income migrants in Beijing are excluded from accessing subsidized housing including CRH, which embodies the most significant inequity. There are 7.05 million migrants in Beijing, accounting for 35.9 per cent of its usual resi-dents (Beijing 6th Census Leading Group Office, 2011). Many migrants have been living and working for years in cities, and living in extremely poor housing condition; yet they are not entitled to housing subsidies. Recently, the Beijing government has allowed migrants working in industrial parks to apply for "public rental housing." While this is one step towards the right direction, few migrant have enjoyed housing subsidies. Thus the profound inequity between migrants and local residents remains.

Yet, among the beneficiaries of CRH in Beijing, equity seems to be less a concern as CRH has achieved equity in many, although not all, aspects. For exam-ple, both the policy design and actual implementation of subsidy methods embodies vertical equity, as applicants in more difficult situations are given priority accessing "public housing" instead of "rent subsidy." According to BBHURD (2009a), households who meet the entry criteria for CRH and "di bao" households and other special groups can apply for "public housing." Table 7.3 shows that the majority of "di bao" households and special groups have access to "public housing," while other low-income households are more likely to receive "rent subsidies."

While the policy design for the subsidy standard for "public housing" embod-ies vertical equality, the implementation does not. The subsidy standard for "public housing" depends on factors such as household size, household structure, gender and age composition. In general, the subsidy standards are one-room bungalows for one-person households, one-bedroom apartments for couples and single-parent families with same sexes, two-bedroom apartments for single-parent families with different sexes and three-person households, and three-bedroom apartments for households with four or more people (BBHURD, 2007a) (Table 7.4). The policy design shows larger households in need of more housing should receive larger units of public housing – vertical equity. However, the actual allocation of public housing shows that while smaller households receive more subsidies than the standard, larger households receive much less subsidies than the standard, which demonstrates the lack of vertical equity. For example, among households who are qualified for three-bedroom apartments, only a small proportion of them actually accessed three-bedroom apartments (5.8 per cent of

*Table 7.4* Gaps between policy and practice on low-income housing allocation

| Household size (person) | Household structure | Subsidy standard according to housing policy | Actual public housing allocation |
|---|---|---|---|
| 1 | Single (including divorced and widowed) | One room bungalows | 97.4% with one-room bungalows, 2.5% with two-room and 0.1% with three-room bungalows |
| 2 | Couple, single parent households with same sex | One-bedroom apartments | Couple: 98.6% with single-room, 1.2% with two-room and 0.2% with three-room bungalows; Same sex single parent households: 97.7% with single-room, and 2.3% with two-room bungalows |
|   | Single parent households with different sexes (children > = 10 years old) | Two-bedroom apartments or two room bungalows | 86.3% with two-room, 13.7% with one-room apartments |
| 3 | Couples with children, or couples with parents from one side of the family |  | 92.0% with two-room, 7.5% with one-room and 0.5% with three-room apartments |
|   | Three-generation family |  | 57.4% with two-room, 2.9% with one-room and 39.7% with three-room apartments |
| 4 | Two couples, or couples with two single children with same sexes | Three-bedroom apartments | 10.0% with one-room, 84.2% with two-room, 5.8% with three-room apartments |
|   | Couple with two single children with different sexes (children > = 10 years old) |  | 22.3% with two-room, 76.7% with three-room apartments |
|   | Couple, children and parents from one side of the family |  | 57.4% with two-room, 2.9% with one-room and 39.7% with three-room apartments |
| 5 | Three-bedroom apartment, or adjust according to household structure |  | 73.7% with three-room, 26.3% with two-room apartments |

two couples or couples with two single children with same sexes, and 39.7 per cent of couples or children and parents from one side of the family), while most accessed smaller units. This inequity in allocation may be a result of the mismatch between available types of dwellings and households structure.

In contrast, the allocation of "rent subsidy" in Beijing embodies both vertical and horizontal equity. The amount of rent subsidy is calculated using specific formula, which includes factors such as the subsidy standard for the specific district/county in the amount of per capita living space, the floor space of existing housing, rent subsidy standard, household size and household income.[6] Thus households with same housing condition, income level and neighborhood would receive the same amount of rent subsidies, and those with lower income and worse housing condition would receive more subsidies. Despite equity in "rent subsidy," rent subsidy in Beijing is much lower than that in other large cities (DRC, 2010). In 2009, the actual rent subsidy standard in urban districts in Beijing was only about 30 yuan/month/m$^2$, which accounted for about 60 per cent of the average market rents. With rapidly rising market rents in Beijing, it is difficult for households to rent decent housing meeting the per capita housing subsidy standard in floor space with their rent subsidies.

## Conclusion and discussion

As the Chinese government refocuses on low-income housing in recent years, we evaluate the effectiveness, efficiency and equity of the CRH program in Beijing. While Beijing has come a long way establishing the system of CRH, there is a severe lack of effectiveness in CRH, demonstrated by its extremely low coverage. With less than 3 per cent of all urban low-income households, 27 per cent of qualified low-income households, and 37 per cent of "di bao" households covered by CRH, it is obvious Beijing has not achieved the goal of "ying bao jin bao." Yet, there is generally a high degree of efficiency in subsidy provision, with the majority of households receiving "rent subsidy" instead of "public housing." While there is significant inequity in the overall low-income housing system, inequity seems to be less problematic within the system of CRH. The policy design for subsidy allocation embodies both vertical and horizontal equity; yet the actual allocation achieves equity in some aspects but not others.

The lack of effectiveness and to a less degree equity in CRH shows that the Beijing Municipal Government needs to significantly improve CRH to achieve the goal of "ying bao jin bao." First of all, the government needs to commit much more resources (capital, land for CRH development, and personnel to manage CRH) to at least cover all "di bao" households and qualified low-income households. In fact, the BMG has stepped up its commitment since 2010. For example, in 2011, BMG planned to build or purchase 200,000 units of subsidized housing, half of which is for subsidized housing, and the other half is for resettlement (BBHURD, 2011). BMG also aimed to build at least 60,000 units of "public rental housing," and allocate at least 20,000 "public rental housing" by the end of 2011. Qualified households for CRH have priority in accessing "public rental housing," and enjoy rents comparable to CRH (BBHURD, 2009, No. 525). BMG also aims to provide rent subsidy to 20,000 households. The goal is to cover all CRH applicants who have passed the verification.

Second, the entry criteria for CRH are too strict and need to be relaxed and adjusted over time. The current target population for CRH is low-income urban households with local non-agricultural registration who meet the income, asset and housing criteria. It excludes low-income households without local registration and those who do not meet all criteria on income, housing and asset. Furthermore, the income criterion is mainly related to the minimum wage, which is lower than the lowest 20 per cent of income group defined by the National Statistical Bureau of China.[7] It also ignores factors such as CPI and market rents on housing affordability of low-income households. While the income criterion has been increased significantly in recent years, CPI and housing price are rising even faster. Thus the entry criteria needs to be further adjusted over time to reflect low-income households' housing difficulty.

Third, the subsidy method and subsidy standard for CRH need to be adjusted. Even though "public housing" is a supplementary method, it is essential to "di bao" households and other special groups. So far the focus of low-income housing in Beijing is to provide housing to low-income households, while their employment, transportation and social integration are often ignored. Thus many districts/counties developed low-income housing at remote locations to reduce financial investment; yet it created spatial mismatch with prevalent problems in employment and accessibility among beneficiaries. Thus, low-income housing development needs to be more coordinated with transportation, employment and other services. Recently, the government initiated the concept of "pei tao jian she" (or inclusionary housing), requiring developers to provide subsidized housing, including CRH, in proportion in their private housing development (State Council, 2007; MOHURD, 2007, 2010). This in theory should alleviate the spatial marginalization of public housing and create mixed income neighborhoods, although the real impact is yet to be seen. In addition, market rents in Beijing have been rising rapidly, while "rent subsidy" adjustment tends to lag behind, which reduces the actual size of dwellings households can afford to rent. In comparison, those with "public housing" enjoy lower than market rent decided by the government and its adjustment has been very slow. Thus there is an increasingly significant inequality between those accessing "public housing" and those receiving "rent subsidy", with the former receiving higher subsidies than the latter.

Fourth, as mentioned earlier, the most significant inequity is the exclusion of migrants from housing subsidies including CRH. We argue that migrants should have housing rights in cities, and the government should set up a threshold to include at least some low-income migrants into the CRH system. It is encouraging that recently qualified migrants are allowed to access "public rental housing." Yet more profound reforms in the household registration and changes in low-income housing policy are needed to ensure equity.

## Notes

1   State Council 1998. Developers are allowed to have only 3 per cent profit margin, and the average price for ECH has been roughly 50–60 per cent of the average price for all housing during 1998–2006. Homeowners of ECH only have the right of occupancy and use-right, and they are not allowed to sell their homes on the market for profit within the first five years unless they pay the gap between discounted and market prices.

2   "Public rental housing" is the latest type of subsidized housing, promoted by the government since 2010 to meet the housing needs of lower-middle income households,

especially new employees and qualified migrants (MOHURD, 2010). It may be owned by the government or private investors, but rents are regulated by the government. Thus it is different from "public housing with controlled rents."

3   "Di Bao" households refer to households who are qualified to receive Minimum Standard of Living Assistance, a monthly allowance from the government to ensure their basic standard of living.

4   Household assets include housing, the net worth of cars, cash, bonds, investment (including stocks), bank deposits and loans to others.

5   Dongcheng and Xicheng district here include previously Dongcheng, Xicheng, Xuanwu, and Congwen district. The four old urban districts were combined into two districts in 2010.

6   Rent subsidies in eight urban districts are calculated differently for "di bao" households and other low-income households. For "di bao" households: monthly rent subsidy = subsidy standard/month/m$^2$ * (per capita subsidy standard in the amount of floor space – per capita living space with current dwelling) * household size. For other low-income households, monthly rent subsidy = subsidy standard/month/m$^2$ * (per capita subsidy standard in the amount of floor space – per capita living space with current dwelling) * household size – (per capita monthly income – the minimum standard of living in Beijing) * household size. In far suburbs, local district/county government can set up their own subsidy standards.

7   In 2009, the low-income standard in Beijing was adjusted from 960 yuan per capita per month to 1520 yuan. Using the 20 per cent method by NBSC, the average income for low-income households was 11,729 yuan with a range of 4,569–16,181 yuan, which is much higher than the standard in Beijing.

# References

Apparicio, P. and Seguin, A. (2006) 'Measuring the accessibility of services and facilities for residents of public housing in Montreal', *Urban Studies*, 43(1), 187–211.

Barnett, C. L. and Lowry, I. S. (1979) How housing allowances affect housing prices. Rand Corporation, Report R-2452-HUD, September.

Beijing Bureau of Housing and Urban–Rural Development (BBHURD) (2005a) A notice of expanding the coverage of Cheap Rental Housing of Beijing (Guanyu kuoda Beijing shi lianzu zhufang fugai mian youguan wenti de tongzhi), No. 966.

——(2005b) Planning of housing construction of Beijing during 2006–2010 (Beijing shi zhufang jianshe guihua (2006–2010)).

——(2007a) Method of application, verification and allocation of Cheap Rental Housing of Beijing (Beijing shi chengshi lianzu zhufang shenqing shenhe ji peizu guanli banfa), No. 1213.

——(2007b) The report of Cheap Rental Housing of Beijing (Beijing lianzu zhufang baogao), restricted data.

——(2007c) A notice about adjusting rent subsidies for Cheap Rental Housing in Beijing (Guanyu tiaozheng Beijing shi lianzu zhufang zufang butie biaozhun youguan wenti de tongzhi).

——(2009a) A notice about several issues related to the management of public housing with controlled rents in Cheap Rental Housing (Guanyu lianzu zhufang shiwu peizu guanli ruogan wenti de tongzhi), No. 536.

——(2009b) A notice on the implementation of the document No. 131 in 2008 by State Council to promote the healthy development of real estate market in Beijing (Guanyu guanche guobanfa [2008] 131 hao wenjian jingshen cujin benshi fangdichan shichang jiankang fazhan de shishi yijian), No. 43.

——(2010a) A notice on the implementation of the document No. 4 in 2010 by State Council to promote the stable and healthy development of real estate market in Beijing (Guanyu guanche guobanfa [2010] 4 hao wenjian jingshen cujin benshi fangdichan shichang pingwen jiankang fazhan de shishi yijian), No. 72.

——(2010b) A notice of adjusting the income entry standard of Cheap Rental Housing of Beijing and related issues (Guanyu tiaozheng benshi lianzu zhufang jiating shouru zhunru biaozhun youguan wenti de tongzhi), No. 434.

——(2011) Plan of construction and acquisition of affordable housing in 2011 (2011 nian quanshi baozhang xing zhufang jianshe shougou jihua), Online available at http:// zhengwu.beijing.gov.cn/bmfu/bmts/t1175192.htm.

Beijing 6th census Leading Group Office (2011) A report on main statistics from 2010 the 6th census in Beijing (Beijingshi diliuci quanguo renkou pucha zhuyao shuju gongbao), Online available at http://www.bjstats.gov.cn/sjjd/jjxs/201105/t20110505_201436.htm.

Beijing Commission of Development and Reform (BCDR) (2005) A notice about redistributing the rent management method for urban Cheap Rental Housing from State Commission of Development and Reform and Ministry of Housing and Urban–Rural Development (Guanyu zhuanfa guojia fazhan gaigewei, jianshbu yinfa chengzhen lianzu zhufang zujing guanli de baifa de tongzhi).

Beijing Housing Indemnity Office (BHIO) (2010a) An implementation plan of making a transparent project of Cheap Rental Housing of Beijing (Beijing shi baozhang xing zhufang quancheng yangguang gongcheng shishi fang'an), No. 14.

——(2010b) Suggestions on further strengthening the development and management of Cheap Rental Housing in Beijing, No. 36.

—— (2011). A compilation of Housing Indemnity Policy in Beijing (Zhufang baozhang zhengce huibian), restricted data.

Beijing Land and Housing Management Bureau (BLHMB) (2001) Implementation advice of trial management of Cheap Rental Housing of Beijing (Beijingshi lianzu zhufang zijin guanli shishi banfa), No. 1005.

Beijing Municipal Government (BMG) (1999) The implementation of further deepening the urban housing reform and speeding up housing construction (Beijing shi jinyibu shenhua chengzhenzhufang zhidu gaige jiakuai zhufang jianshe shishi fang'an), No. 21.

——(2001) A notice of trial method of Cheap Rental Housing Management of Beijing (Guanyu beijing shi lianzu zhufang guanli shixing banfa), No. 62.

——(2007a) Implementation suggestions from Beijing Municipal Government about implementing "suggestions from State Council on Solving Housing Difficulty of Urban Low-income Households", No. 22.

——(2007b) Method of Cheap Rental Housing Management of Beijing (Beijing shi lianzu zhufang guanli shixing banfa), No. 26.

——(2007c) Notice of implementation of the document of State Council to solve the housing difficulty of urban low income families (Guanyu guanche luoshi guowuyuan guanyu jiejue chengshi dishouru jiating zhufang kunnan de ruogan yijian de shishi yijian), No. 22.

Beijing Municipal 1% Population Survey Bureau (BMPSB) (2007) *Beijing's 1% Population Survey in 2005*. Beijing: China Statistics Press.

Beijing Municipal Public Security Bureau (2009) A notice of provisional measures of qualification of low income families in Beijing, No. 443.

Beijing Statistics Bureau (BSB) (2011) Report of main statistics from the 6th population census in Beijing (Beijing shi di liuci renkou pucha zhuyao shuju gongbao). Beijing: China Statistics Press.

Bramley, G., Morgan, J., Cousins, L. and Dunmore, K. (2002) *Evaluation of the Low Cost Home Ownership Program*, London: Office of the Deputy Prime Minister.

Bridge, C., Flatau, P., Whelan, S., Wood, G. and Yates, J. (2003) Housing assistance and non-shelter outcomes, final report. Melbourne, AHURI: WA Research Centre and Sydney Research Centre.

Cabinet Office (2003). The magenta book: guidance notes for policy evaluation and analysis. London: Government Chief Social Researcher's Office, Prime Minister's Strategy Unit.

Che, S. and Guo, L. (2009) 'Evaluation of economic and comfortable housing in Beijing (Beijing shi jingji shiyong fang zhengce pinggu)'. *Journal the Cadre Institute of Economics and Mangement (Beijing jingji guanli ganbu xueyuan xuebao)*, 24(4): 3–10.

Chiu, R. L. H. (2002) 'Social equity in housing in the Hong Kong special administrative region: A social sustainability perspective', *Sustainable Development*, 10(3): 155–162.

DeSalvo, J. S. (1974) 'Neighborhood upgrading effects of middle income housing projects in New York City', *Journal of Urban Economics*, 1(3): 269–77.

Development Research Center (DRC) (2010) The research report of the policies to improve the housing security system in Beijing.

Fatoye, E. O. and Odusami, K. T. (2009) Occupants' Satisfaction Approach to Housing Performance Evaluation: The case of Nigeria. Paper Presented at the RICS COBRA Research Conference held at the University of Cape Town, 10–11th September, 2009. Downloaded from www.rics.org/cobra on 22nd February 2010.

Green, R. K. and Malpezzi, S. (2001) *A Primer on US Housing Markets and Policies*. The Urban Institute Press for the American Real Estate and Urban Economics Association. Washington, DC: The Urban Institute.

Goetz, E. G., Lam, H. K. and Heitlinger, A. (1996) *There Goes the Neighborhood? The Impact of Subsidized Multifamily Housing on Urban Neighborhoods*. Minneapolis: University of Minnesota Center for Urban and Regional Affairs.

Headey, B. (1978) *Housing Policy in the Developed Economy: the United Kingdom, Sweden and the United States*. London: Croom Helm.

Hsieh, H.R. (2009) 'Issues and proposed improvements regarding condominium management in Taiwan', *Habitat International*, 33: 73–80.

Huang, Y. (2012) 'Low-income housing in Chinese cities: policies and practices', *China Quarterly*, 212: 941–64.

Huang, Y. and Clark, W. A. V. (2002) 'Housing tenure choice in transitional urban China: a multilevel analysis', *Urban Studies*, 39(1): 7–32.

Jia, S. (2005) *A Study of Patterns of Urban Housing Security* (Chenzhen zhufang baozhang moshi yanjiu). Beijing: Economic Sciences Press.

Lai, O.K. (1998) 'Governance and the housing question in a transitional economy, the political economy of housing policy in China reconsidered', *Habitat International*, 22(3): 231–43.

Lee, J. (2000) 'From welfare housing to home-ownership: the dilemma of China's housing reform', *Housing Studies*, 15: 61–7.

Li, P. (2009) 'The evolution of and regional variation in economic and comfortable housing policy design in China' (Zhongguo jingji shiyong fang zhengce zhiding de yanbian yu quji chayi), *Urban and Regional Planning and Studies (Chengshi yu quyu guihua yanjiu)*, 2(2): 68–86.

Lin, G. (2007) 'An economic analysis of the economic and comfortable housing policy' (Jingji shiyong zhufang zhengce de jingjixue fenxi), *Beijing Social Sciences (Beijing shehui kexue)*, 2: 78–82.

Liu, A. M. (2003) There is Quality After all: Residential Post Occupancy Evaluation in Housing Projects in Hong Kong. Paper for the CIBTG International Conference, October, Hong Kong.

Malpezzi, S. (1999) 'Economic analysis of housing markets in developing and transition economies', in P. C. Cheshire and E. S. Mills (eds), *Handbook of Regional and Urban Economics*, Vol. 3, Chapter 44, 1791–864.

Malpezzi, S. and Maclennan, D. (2001) 'The long run price elasticity of supply of new construction in the United States and the United Kingdom', *Journal of Housing Economics*, 10(3): 278–306.

Malpezzi, S. and Vandell, K. (2002) 'Does the low-income housing tax credit increase the supply of housing?' *Journal of Housing Economics*, 11(4): 360–80.

Man, J. Y., Zheng, S. and Ren, R. (2011) 'Housing policy and housing markets: trends, patterns and affordability', in J. Y. Man (ed.) *China's Housing Reform and Outcomes*, Cambridge: MA: Lincoln Institute of Land Policy, 1–18.

Mills, E. S. and Sullivan, A. (1981) 'Market effects', in Bradbury, K. L. and Downs, A. (eds) *Do Housing Allowances Work?* Washington, DC: The Brookings Institution.

MOHURD (1999) Management method on Urban Cheap Rental Housing (Chengzhen lianzu zhufang guanli banfa), No. 70.

——(2007) Management regulation on ECH (Jingji shiyong zhufang guanli baifa), No. 258

——(2010) Suggestions on accelerating the development of public rental housing (No. 87. Guangyu jiakuai fazhan gonggong zulin zhufang de zhidao yijian). http://www.mohurd. gov.cn/zcfg/jswj/zfbzwj/201006/t20100612_201308.htm.

Mukhija, V. (2004) 'The contradictions in enabling private developer of affordable housing: a cautionary case from India', *Urban Studies*, 4(11): 2231–44.

Murray, M. P. (1983) 'Subsidized and unsubsidized housing starts: 1961–1977', *Review of Economics and Statistics*, 65(4): 590–97.

——(1999) 'Subsidized and unsubsidized housing stocks 1935–1987: crowding out and cointegration', *Journal of Real Estate Finance and Economics*, 18(1): 107–24.

National Bureau of Statistics of China (NBSC) (2011) *China Statistical Yearbook 2010*, Beijing: China Statistics Press.

Ni, N. and Yi, C. (2009) 'An analysis on the changes of housing conditions of urban families during 2000–2005', *Management Observation (Guanli guancha)*, 8: 52–3.

Olsen, E. O. (2003) 'Housing programs for low-income households', in R. Moffitt (ed.) *Means-Tested Transfer Programs in the United States*, Chicago: University of Chicago Press.

Ornstein, S. H. (2005) *Post Occupancy Evaluation in Brazil, Evaluating Quality in Educational Facilities*, Sao Paulo: School of Architecture and Urbanism, University of Sao Paulo, Brazil.

Qian, Y. (2003) 'An analysis of low-income housing policy in China: economic and comfortable housing and Cheap Rental Housing', *Zhongguo fangdichan (China Real Estate)*, 8, 57–60.

Quigley, J. M. (2000) *A Decent Home: Housing Policy in Perspective*, Brookings-Wharton Papers on Urban Affairs.

Rent, G. S. and Rent, C. S. (1978) 'Low-income housing factors related to residential satisfaction', *Environment and Behavior*, 10(4): 459–88.

Renger, R., Parssons, O. and Cimetta, A. (2003) 'Evaluating housing revitalization projects: critical lessons for all evaluators', *American Journal of Evaluation*, 24(1): 51–64.

Research Teams of DRC of State Council (2007) 'The judgments of China housing market and perspective of housing policy', *Reform (Gaige)*, 12: 5–12.

Rohe, W. M., and Stegman, M. A. (1994a) 'The effects of homeownership: on the self-esteem, perceived control and life satisfaction of low-income people', *Journal of the American Planning Association*, 60(2): 173–84.

——(1994b) 'The impact of home ownership on the social and political involvement of low-income people', *Urban Affairs Review*, 30(1): 152–72.

Rydell, C. P. (1982) *Price Elasticity of Housing Supply*, Rand Corporation, R-2846-HUD, September.

Santiago, A. M., Galster, G. C. and Tatian, P. (2001) 'Assessing the property value impacts of the dispersed housing subsidy program in Denver', *Journal of Policy Analysis and Management*, 20(1): 65–88.

Schafer, R. (1972) 'The effect of BMIR Housing on property values', *Land Economics*, 48(3): 282.

Sengupta, U. and Sharma, S. (2008) 'No longer Sukumbasis: challenges in Grassroots-led squatter resettlement programme in Kathmandu with special reference to Kirtipur Housing Project', *Habitat International*, 33: 34–44.

Shao, D. (2002) 'The effects and development trend of Cheap Rental Housing Policy of Beijing', *Capital Economy (Shoudu jingji)*, No. 11.

State Council (1998) Notice of further deepening the urban housing reform and speeding up housing construction (Guanyu jinyibu shenhua chengzhenzhufang zhidu gaige jiakuai zhufang jianshe de tongzhi), No. 23.

—— (2007) Suggestions from State Council about solving housing difficulties of urban low-income households (Guowuyuan guanyu jianjue chengshi di shouru zhufang kunnan de ruogan yijian), No. 24.

——(2011) The work report of central government (Zhongyang zhengfu gongzuo baogao).

Stephens, M., Whitehead, C. and Munro, M. (2005) *Lessons from the Past, Challenges for the Future for Housing Policy*. London: Office of the Deputy Prime Minister.

Swan, C. (1973) 'Housing subsidies and housing starts', AREUEA Journal 1 (Fall), 119–140.

Tian, D. (1998) *International Experiences and China's Realistic Options of Housing Policy*, Beijing: Tsinghua University Press.

US General Accounting Office (2001) Department of Housing and Urban Development: Status of Achieving Key Outcomes and Addressing Major Management Challenges, GAO-01-833, July 6. http://www.gao.gov/new.items/gpra/gpra.htm

Valenca, M. M. (2007) 'Poor politics–poor housing policy under the Collor Government in Brazil (1990–1992)', *Environment and Urbanization*, 19(2): 391–408.

Wang, Y. (2000) 'Housing reform and its impacts on the urban poor in China', *Housing Studies*, 15(6): 845–64.

Yang, Z., Yi, C. and Zhang, H. (2010) 'Evaluation of the housing affordability in Beijing with the Residual Income Approach' (Jiyu shenyu shouru fa de Bejing juming zhufang kezhifu nengli fenxi), *Urban Studies (Chengshi fazhan yanjiu)*, 10: 36–40.

Yao, L. (2003) *A Study on the Patterns of Public Housing Policies in China*, Shanghai: Shanghai University of Finance and Economics Press.

Ye, J., Wu, D. and Wu, J. (2006) 'A study on the Chinese housing policy during social transition: practice and development', *Housing Finance International*, 20(3): 50–58.

Xiong, G., Zhu, Q. and Yang, D. (2009) 'Study on international experience and China's affordable housing construction' (Gguoji jingyan yu woguo lianzufang jianshe), *International City Planning (Guoji chengshi guiha)*, 24 (1): 37–42.

Zhang, X. Q. (1998) *Privatisation: a study of housing policy in urban China*. New York: Nova Science Publishers.

# Part III
# Housing for the middle class and the rich

# 8    The gated communities of châteaux in China

## Back to feudalism?

*Guillaume Giroir*

## Introduction

For over twenty years, the areas of luxury villas have proliferated around the Chinese cities. For the last ten years they have been the subject of several studies (G. Giroir, Huang Youqin, Pow Choon-Piew, L. Tomba, Fulong Wu). Some research has focused on case studies (e.g. Fontainebleau Villas: G. Giroir, 2006) or examples of different themes (e.g. hyper-luxury gated communities in China: G. Giroir, 2012, 2013). In 2004, journalists from around the world discovered with amazement the château Zhang-Laffitte, a copy of the eponymous French château on the outskirts of Beijing. Since then, other examples of châteaux were born in China. But so far, no research has described as such, across the whole of China, the combination of the two forms of architecture, gated communities composed of châteaux. The objective of this study is to fill this gap.

This type of gated community is clearly a unique territorial phenomenon. Inevitably, it raises many questions in a China still officially communist and historically built on anti-feudalism. Do the gated communities of châteaux say something about China beyond their architectural form and marketing function? Can they give rise to a non-commercial interpretation? If this is the case, what do the gated communities of châteaux let us know about the profound nature of Chinese society? These questions will be developed of three distinct and inter-related sections.

In a first part, we will try to define and delineate the gated communities of châteaux as a scientific object in its own right. A second part will propose a typology of architectural forms observed on the basis of a discussion on several criteria. The final section will address the question of the relationship between this new architectural form and the current political system of China.

## 1.  The phenomenon of the gated communities of châteaux in China: methodological difficulties of identification

The analysis of gated communities of châteaux faces a series of theoretical and practical difficulties. The first of these is to identify the concept of a château.

## *1.1 The concept of a château*

In general, at what point can one speak of "châteaux"? What is the boundary between a large villa and a château, or a mansion and a château? What are the distinctive architectural features of châteaux? Basically, what is a château? In reality, it is difficult to give an absolute definition of the concept of the château, so great is the diversity of their architectural forms. Schematically, a château is four main types of buildings:

1) A feudal fortress defended by walls, ditches and ramparts, mostly in rural areas.
2) A palace, a residence of an emperor, a king or a lord, in urban areas, most often without fortifications. More generally, extensive construction of prestige, with towers and turrets, surrounded by a park with gardens, ponds, etc. (cf. Palais du Louvre, Palais du Luxembourg, Buckingham Palace ...). Refers also to the imposing residences of the great families of most Italian cities: Palazzo Pitti (Florence), Palazzo Grassi (Venice), Palazzo Farnese (Rome).
3) A manor (or country house): This is usually a small château little or not fortified, that belongs to a vassal (or country gentleman), which directly manages the operation of its land. In France, we find many in the Perche and the Pays d'Auge (walls with mud and timber). One can associate the mansions, spacious home often in the middle of a park (in English, mansion).
4) A noble's house whose domain is a vineyard in Bordeaux.

The château is a particular architectural form developed from the Middle Ages in Europe, in Middle East and in Asia. Present in other continents, it is still in Europe that this model has led to architectural forms the most numerous and varied. In fact, European-style châteaux were the most imitated around the world. In Europe, the major phase of châteaux building was between the tenth and nineteenth centuries. Within this long period, several generations of châteaux can be distinguished, including the Middle Ages, the Renaissance, the seventeenth, eighteenth and nineteenth centuries. The French-style château was perhaps one of the most emblematic archetypes of the château. In fact, France is the second country in the world by the density of châteaux/inhabitants (behind the Czech Republic). Overall, France is the land of châteaux par excellence. Some French regions have hundreds or even thousands of châteaux:[1] for example, about 300 châteaux in the Loire Valley (Renaissance style); 300 in the Paris area; 400 châteaux in Sologne (nineteenth century); 150 manor houses and châteaux in Normandy; 1,001 (or 1,500 according to J. Secret, 1950) châteaux, manors and country houses in Perigord[2] ... Outside of France, Scotland has about 400 châteaux.

To summarize, the notion of the château is not entirely clear; hence, for instance, the large variations between the estimations of the total number of châteaux in France. However, the main criterion for defining the gated communities of châteaux is based on the architectural style. According to this definition, there are only a handful of gated communities of châteaux in China.

## 1.2 Practical difficulties in identifying the gated communities of châteaux in China

But once the notion of the château is clarified, how do you know where are the gated communities of châteaux in China? To the difficulties inherent in identifying a clear and indisputable château, in addition there are specific challenges to their identification in China. In China, the gated communities consisting of luxury villas have become quite common in more or less distant suburbs of major cities in China. It is not unusual to see impressive villas of several thousand m² without being able to talk about them as real châteaux. Despite their big surface, these mega-villas lack the architectural features that define the châteaux.

The first question about the gated communities of châteaux in China is: how to identify them? This seemingly simple question deserves a detailed answer as there are many obstacles to locate this type of upscale residential enclave. The identification of this particular class of gated communities faces many methodological and practical difficulties. There is no comprehensive list, incorporating all gated communities composed of châteaux for all of China. Such research must therefore remain an empirical work, both thorough and inevitably incomplete. One of the only ways to try to make such a selection is to consider the toponym of those residential areas. This method still requires validation in each case. Indeed, the relationship between place names and architectural style is far from simple, and it shows on the contrary a large array of combinations, and so many false evidence, or traps.

First, the term "château" has some semantic variants. We thus find the term "palais" in some enclaves, such as the Palais de Fortune (Beijing), or "mansion." In addition, in some cases, there is correspondence between the Western name and Chinese name, as in the Palais de Fortune, translated into Chinese by Caifu Gongguan (*caifu* means "wealth" and *gongguan* "palace, imperial residence"). But this is far from always the case. Sometimes the allusion to the aristocratic world is not marked or even absent. The name Fontainebleau Villas (Shanghai) is translated into Chinese by Fengdan bailou bieshu, literally "Villas of the red *Liquidambar formosana* and the white dew." We are far from the French château that is supposed to imitate. Sometimes, the reference to the aristocratic world may be present in the Chinese place name but not match the English name of the enclave: thus, the complex of châteaux Emperor Zillah said Junting in Chinese, which literally means "great hall of the king or the emperor."

In the case of Favorview Palace (Huijing Xincheng, Guangzhou), the place name is doubly misleading. Not only it is not a palace but tall buildings, but the English word "palace" does not correspond at all to the Chinese word used as "Xincheng" ("new town"). Therefore, some housing developments named "châteaux" or "palaces" are not; conversely, some gated communities of châteaux do not include the term "château" or "palace." In addition, what is called "châteaux" is sometimes more loosely inspired by large villas in the architecture of châteaux (see below pseudo-châteaux). Some gated communities called "manor" (Huxi Manor, Wuxi, Green Sea Manor, Beijing) consist of luxury villas with no possible comparison with châteaux.

More generally, if the architectural category of "châteaux" includes various architectural forms in the West, this is even more so in China dominated by approximate copies of European châteaux. Add to this the fact that even in gated communities of true châteaux, those châteaux have a size most often reduced. In most cases, it's rather mini-châteaux. The concentration of this type of construction in a kind of enclosed subdivision of villas alone explains their relatively small size.

In addition, sometimes the term "château" is not at all châteaux or similar types of construction but high-rise luxury buildings. This is the case, for example, of Château Pinnacle in Shanghai, a luxury residential development comprising 30 floors of apartments from 209 to 618 m$^2$. These towers called "châteaux" can also correspond to high-rise luxury hotels as in the Oak Château Beijing Chaoyang District, Château de Luze Hotel (Beijing), or Château Star River Hotel Panyu (Guangzhou). In other cases, as in the hotel Château HOMA Yuzi Paradise (Guilin), the use of the term of the château is even more incongruous. Indeed, in a large park of 535 hectares dotted with more than 200 sculptures, the first site of contemporary art in China, the hotel HOMA (for Hotel of Modern Art) sits, a futuristic building with green roofs and windows with smoked glass. In these cases, the addition of the term "château" is only one way to serve the luxury of the hotel[3] without the architecture of the building having anything to do with a château.

Conversely, some gated communities of châteaux do not appear explicitly as such through their name. The Emperor Zillah, Sandalwood have no reference to châteaux, even though they are iconic examples of the gated communities of châteaux. This is also true in the case of Splendor Longfor Summer Palace (in Chinese: Longhu Yiheyuan zhu). The allusion to the Summer Palace, i.e. the famous imperial garden in Beijing, does not refer to an architectural built form.

Another aspect helps to make it difficult to identify the gated communities of châteaux in China, namely the heterogeneity of architectural constructions on the scale of the gated communities themselves. Thus, contrary to what one might think, all residential units of Fontainebleau Villas are far from being reduced to replicas of the château of Fontainebleau, and they also include for instance various forms of architecture as Dutch large timbered farms. Also the term "château" does not mean that it is exclusively a French château. Often, there is a mix of architectural styles, with the association of French style to other European styles (Italian, English).

## 2. The gated communities of châteaux in China: a typology

The gated communities of châteaux, despite their small number, are nonetheless characterized by a certain diversity. Factors for this heterogeneity are many. One of the major criteria of differentiation lies in the size of the residential enclave: the number of châteaux from a few tens (e.g. Emperor Zillah) to more than 200 (250 at the Palais de Fortune). The location may be within the city (e.g. Le Château) or the suburban areas (e.g. Fontainebleau Villas). The gated communities of châteaux are also distinguished by their architectural style. Some of them are clearly inspired by the French châteaux, while others claim a European connection without elaborating.

The term "neo-feudalism" is defined here as a set of architectural features typical of the former European Ancien Regime, but without the current political context in which these forms take place can be defined as feudal.

### 2.1 The pseudo neo-feudalism: the villas-châteaux

In architectural terms, various gated communities of châteaux do not really correspond to clusters of buildings like châteaux. The term "château" here works primarily as an advertising argument. The residential enclaves themselves consist only of impressive luxury villas, although sometimes they show an intermediate form between châteaux and villas. However, these gated communities are nonetheless sometimes residential areas strongly influenced by feudal references.

The most emblematic case is represented by Château Regalia, a suburb of Beijing, with the Château Regalia reflecting the ambiguity of the architectural identity of some gated communities. This enclave seems to be similar to a gated community of French châteaux. The name itself contains the word "château." The types of villas are known as "Duke," "Count," claiming a clear connection to the world of the nobility. But the architecture of the villas is in Mediterranean style. No reference is made to the French identity in particular. The club house is meant to be an imitation of the palace of the Alhambra (Spain). Above all, nothing in the style of the villas will recall the architecture of châteaux, whether French or not. We can talk in this regard of a pseudo-gated community of French châteaux.

Another example is Le Château in the western suburbs of Shanghai. This complex launched in 2001 is located in the Hongqiao Development Zone. Despite the geographical name and the ubiquity of the term "château" in the advertising site, it is certainly luxury villas, but not real châteaux. The 60 "châteaux" in French can be divided into "House of Beaune," "House of Cannes," and "House of Lyon." The Chambord Villas (Qingpu district, Shanghai) are another case in point. The name explicitly claims an imitation, or at least an inspiration to the famous château of the Loire Valley (France). In fact, the architectural form owes nothing to the French royal heritage site.

### 2.2 The gated communities of European-style châteaux: allogeneic neo-feudalism

In most gated communities of châteaux in China, foreign inspiration is clearly claimed. The name of the residential complex, the architectural form, advertising define a non-Chinese feudal legacy, an allogeneic neo-feudalism. Several examples can be cited: Beijing (Palais de Fortune...) or Shanghai (Emperor Zillah, Sandalwood, Fontainebleau Villas ...).

The gated communities of French-style châteaux are the most represented. Some have already been described as the Fontainebleau Villas (G. Giroir, 2006). Others are more recent. One of the most outstanding examples is formed by the Palais de Fortune (Beijing), a program of 30 hectares sold in 2005 that consists of 172 (250 in the future) mini-nineteenth-century French châteaux along the Wenyu river (Figures 8.1 and 8.2).

*Figure 8.1* Entrance to the Palais de Fortune (Caifu Gongguan). G. Giroir, June 2011.

*Figure 8.2* Domes of châteaux beyond the walls of the Palais de Fortune. G. Giroir, June 2011.

The advertising slogan says "Mansion for Fortune Top 500 CEOs." The elements belonging to a noble rhetoric are multiple: grids with black and gold metal lilies, emblazoned with golden crowns above the portal, neo-classical colonnades, terraces overlying the front building, main door complex inspired by Versailles... The promoter, Wang Zhe, president of Fortune Real Estate, after a visit to France, wanted to build a concentrate of the "wonderful style" of Versailles, the "majesty" of the Louvre and the "nobility" of Château Laffitte.[4] The mini-châteaux have an area of at least 1,500 m², but one of them is 3,000 m². Their price varies from 43 to 63 million yuan.

The residential enclave Emperor Zillah is located in Pudong, the area of luxury villas Dongjiao, 800 m from the Tomson Golf, south of the river Zhangjia (Figures 8.3 and 8.4). Its real name, "Stately Home. Zillah Emperor," emphasizes the proximity of Dongjiao State Guest Hotel to the West. These are 25 real châteaux and manors from 1,300 m² to 2,000 m². Several styles coexist: "early classical revival," "Adam," "English Georgian," "Mediterranean," "French chateauesque," "Beaus Arts" (sic), "English Tudor." But the French and English style dominate. On French châteaux, advertising states: "Nostalgic feeling – the style of French château." For English country houses, it says, "The world's most noble-English Tudor."

Sandalwood (in Chinese Tangong, "Palace of Sandalwood") is another example. This is a set of 18 mini-palaces situated in Shanghai's Changning District. Opened in December 2005, this is the first complex of hyper-luxury "villas" located within the dense area of Shanghai. It is located close to the Xijiao Hotel

*Figure 8.3* The gated community of châteaux Junting, Shanghai. G. Giroir, June 2011.

*Figure 8.4* Advertising for a French-style château in Junting. G. Giroir, June 2011.

for State guests to receive foreign executives. The architecture was designed by an American firm: WATG (USA), Hirsch Bedner Associates, Wilson Associates. The investor and developer are local: Shanghai Xijiao Ditingyuan fangdichan kaifa youxian gongsi (Ditingyuan Shanghai Xijiao Company). A number of items refer to the aristocratic world. The style is aristocratic, based on the values of grandeur, nobility, exclusivity, of timelessness and permanence. Sandalwood thus represents a set of 18 small palaces and mansions, focusing on classic European styles. The main countries represented are: France (Fontainebleau, Riviera...), UK (imperial, English park, Georgian), Italy (Florence, Tuscany). The gardens themselves, designed by the company Collin Belt (Hong Kong), are classic. The rate of green space of Sandalwood Villas is 40 per cent. The name itself refers to the feudalism. Sandalwood (*pterocarpus Santallinus*) is regarded in China as the most noble. It is grown in parts of Guangdong and Guangxi provinces. Since the Ming dynasty, it became customary to make the furniture of the imperial palaces of sandalwood. Extremely slow growth, hardness, density, and very dark colour symbolize the nobility, the rarity and magnificence. It is also used to make musical instruments like the *erhu*. Sandalwood also has a religious value. The smoke would have the power to cast out evil spirits; chips are burned in temples during religious ceremonies.

One of the websites to sell the villas is explicit. To quote the site www.villa. focus.cn "*Tudi xique putongren maibuqi, hao zhai sheshi lingren zeshe...*" ("Because of the limitation of land imposed by the government, ordinary people can not buy such houses; however, the hyper-luxury leaves you speechless"). In fact, selling prices show very high levels of between 60 million yuan to 98 million yuan (2009). The villas are located in a site of 47,384 m² including 31,200 m² of living space for all villas. Each palace has a living area of between 1,500 and 1,800 m² (surface area), 2,500 m² with the garden. Each has an indoor pool and, more rarely, a private theater.

### 2.3 The gated communities of imperial-style châteaux or the endogenous neo-feudalism

Some gated communities of châteaux, while showing the architectural similarities with those belonging to an imported neo-feudalism, are more an expression of the Chinese society and history. This anchoring in an endogenous neo-feudalism manifests itself through various forms reminiscent of imperial China. The most representative example is probably Longfor Summer Palace Splendor (Longhu Yiheyuan zhu) (Figures 8.5 and 8.6).

Analysis of the advertising of the marketing site of this residential complex reveals its uniqueness. The elements of continuity with the imperial period are found in all areas. Here, it's not about villas, but "little palaces," "houses of the king," The architecture of this hyper-luxurious gated community is directly inspired by the Summer Palace through its doors, roofs and windows. The hyper-luxury here is spectacular: the 91 palaces each have a garage for 11 cars, a personal museum of 500 m², a private club and three presidential suites. Their living area is between 1,000 and 3,600 m², developed over four floors, two above the ground,

*Figure 8.5* The gated community of châteaux Longhu Yiheyuan zhu (Longfor Splendor Summer Palace). G. Giroir, June 2011.

*Figure 8.6* Longhu Yiheyuan zhu (Longfor Splendor Summer Palace). G. Giroir, June 2011.

they are integrated into a vast complex of 97,809 m². The use of limestone facade imported from France and Portugal was intended to add to the feeling of grandeur. The gardens were designed on the principle of construction of the imperial gardens (*chuan zhen huangjia yuanlin jianzhi*).

The location of these palaces is closely related to the high places of imperial power in China. They are located at the intersection of three famous imperial gardens (*san dahuangjia yuanlin zhongxin weizhi*) created by the Qing emperors, Kangxi, Yongzheng and Qianlong. Indeed, they are just 50 meters to the east of the Summer Palace (Yiheyuan), south of Yuanmingyuan and Western Guchang Chunyuan. In a paradoxical but highly symbolic continuity between imperial China and Communist China, hyper-luxurious character is also due to their close proximity to the campus of the Central Party School (*Dangxiao*) which trains executives in the PRC. The centrality of this unique residential enclave is reinforced by the major universities (Qinghua, Beida) whose vast campus occupy part of the district of Haidian, northwest of Beijing.

Continuity with imperial China is also expressed through an explicit historical perspective. It is written that "the dream of the imperial family continues" (*zai xuchuan shijiazu zhi mengxiang*). "The Last Emperor is set in this glorious place, with the palace Longfor, glory continues." In a very Chinese formulation, a unique historical perspective is added: "Hidden 300 years, 60 years of fermentation (*yunniang*), and finally a great celebration of the Chinese family." In other words, Longfor remained hidden for 300 years since the creation of the Summer Palace by Emperor Qianlong in 1750. Then, between 1949 and 2009, occurred the maturation phase, here the chronology is cleverly transformed as needed to promote these hyper-luxurious architectural forms. The Maoist period is not mentioned as such, the period of opening and reform neither. It is as if, like a great wine to keep, the project Longfor embodied the quintessence, the outcome but also the overcoming of the imperial legacy. The brochure states: "300 years after we were offered a special land (*tegong tudi*)." One can even understand that these 300 years of evolution since the foundation of the Summer Palace have given birth to an architecture still above its model. It is stated that the developers have spent 12 years to choose the ideal site according to the principles of *fengshui*, but also the "wisdom" (*zhihui*). The site has an exceptional *fengshui* thanks to the concentration of imperial famous places but also to natural elements such as the Yanshan Mountains to the north and the various lakes (e.g. Kunming Lake of Summer Palace) and parks.

## 3. The gated communities of châteaux, a symptom of a return to feudalism in China?

The attempt of a typology above shows that the phenomenon of gated communities of châteaux in China is far from anecdotal. If these gated communities are rare, the number of châteaux, their architectural diversity, the extravagance of their level of luxury and prices reflect their relative importance and their significance in the urban space.

But how to interpret these gated communities of châteaux? Obviously, it would be very interesting and useful to know who lives in these luxurious properties. This information would help to the interpretation. Unfortunately, sociological research on the residents of the most luxurious gated communities, has never been truly undertaken, for obvious reasons of confidentiality, not only in China. This scientific task seems to be even more difficult for the gated communities of châteaux. It is a undeniable limit to a complete analysis. However, even without this kind of information, the existence of this type of residential enclave, unthinkable in the Maoist period, makes sense in today's China. The gated communities of châteaux take place in a context where the social inequalities is becoming a very sensitive issue. All the more, these enclaves of châteaux are not isolated phenomena, they are part of a social, economic and political context, that of China today. This finding should be taken into account when trying to interpret this urban enclave.

### 3.1 The commercial interpretations and their limits

One type of possible reading of the phenomenon of gated communities of châteaux in China focuses on the mechanisms of market economy.[5] This is the most obvious approach. The nouveaux riches are committed to each other in a race to ostentation, all strive to live in ever more luxurious homes. In this regard, the "château" is the great architectural form and unsurpassable in terms of luxury residential. In addition, the market for hyper-luxury gated communities in China is highly competitive. Developers must constantly think about new architectural forms in an attempt to satisfy customers eager for novelties and new distinction. Subdivisions of châteaux are a means to differentiate themselves from the rest of the market. It is a classic branding advertising strategy. The results of this strategy show a strong ambivalence. On the one hand, the enclaves of châteaux are manifestations of the emergence of the luxury that embodies the values of elegance and classicism in society. On the other hand, the gated communities of châteaux can also be interpreted negatively, as the triumph of bad taste and kitsch typical of the nouveaux riches. They can be seen as kinds of theme parks, or one of many manifestations of the disneylandization of the world.[6]

Such interpretations do offer the keys to useful and relevant interpretation of the phenomenon of gated communities of châteaux, but they are unable to account for all aspects. First, they seem mainly suited to the interpretation of gated communities for the middle class. They do not take into account the specificity of hyper-luxury gated communities in China. They describe this type of gated communities without placing them in the political, ideological and historical context of China. The centrality given only to the market logic in the interpretation leads to a trivialization of the phenomenon and ignores the relationship between the architectural form and the Chinese society as a whole. This lack of contextualization does not bring out the anomaly of such residential enclaves in a still officially communist regime and the strange continuity that can be detected between the post-Mao China and imperial China. But in fact, the residential enclaves of châteaux in China raise questions that go well beyond the purely architectural and commercial areas.

### 3.2  For an historical and political interpretation: back to feudalism?

If it does not take a reductive interpretation, that is to say exclusively commercial of this phenomenon, many questions arise. Is it common for elites of a communist country to live in châteaux, the undisputed symbol of feudalism? Living in a château in a country still officially communist like China may be ideologically neutral and banal?

It is not about to get into a debate on the complex historical nature of the political, social and economic system of China's pre-Communist era. We know the discussion and controversy going back to Marx itself on the "Chinese feudalism," the "Asiatic mode of production,"[7] or "Oriental despotism" (K. Wittfogel, 1957).[8] Various researchers, Chinese and Western, emphasized the similarities but also profound differences between European feudalism and the historical Chinese feudalism. Thus, Huang Minlan, based on the definition of European feudalism according to historian Marc Bloch pointed out that the feudalism involves the division of power into fiefdoms, while the concentration of power in China in the hands of the emperor and bureaucracy must lead to use the term despotism.[9] He says: "Despotism exists only in Eastern society, where there is no feudalism." He cites He Huaihong who talks about "despotic feudalism." Feudalism in China owns particular characteristics; for convenience, we adopt here the term "feudalism" but this term may refer either to the "Chinese or Eastern feudalism" or "Oriental despotism." Nevertheless, the châteaux, as forms of feudal architecture, are not a priori accordance with the communist ideology.

In fact, the anti-feudalism finds its origins in the history of the Chinese Communist Party. From the beginning of the twentieth century, the Chinese revolutionary movement took on an anti-feudal stance. The anti-imperialist and progressive movement of May 4, 1919 rejected the foundations of the Confucian and mandarinal old China, and sought the path of modernity. Later in 1945, Mao could also write: "... there are two big mountains which weigh heavily on the Chinese people: one is imperialism, feudalism the other. The Chinese Communist Party decided long ago to remove.[10]" In fact, from the foundation of the People's Republic of China in 1949, a ruthless hunt was conducted against feudalism. At the beginning of the Cultural Revolution in 1966, Mao called to end the "Four Olds" (*Po sijiu*) (old culture, old habits, old thoughts and old ways of Chinese civilization).

### 3.3 Some elements of neo-feudalism in China

The rise of gated comunities of châteaux is indeed the most obvious form of neo-feudalism. But there are other elements of feudalism. There is absolutely no question to say here that China, as a whole, has returned to feudalism. Without at all ignoring the subtleties of the debate on feudalism in China, it is acceptable and sufficient in this study, to stick to a simple position: châteaux are in fact the most obvious symbol of feudalism. The gated communities of châteaux are similar to other observable elements or trends in society, and as a symbol of feudalism come in contradiction with the official communist ideology. How to link this type of residential enclave of luxury with contemporary China?

It should first be noted that the gated communities of châteaux are not an isolated phenomenon in terms of feudalism (or "neo-feudalism"). We observe the revival of some elements of feudalism from the beginning of the strategy of reform and opening. From 1984, historian M.-C. Bergère evoked the return of "Old Man" (1985), that is to say the revival of the old China that Mao had sought to eradicate.[11] Some forms of imperial China tended to be reborn. This is especially true in the field of architecture. More recently, political scientist Zheng Yongnian made the same observation in the politics.[12] He believes that, despite the importance of the Western concept of political party and huge socio-economic changes since the late 1970s, the Chinese Communist Party is a totally Chinese cultural product. It conveys a conception of power similar to that of the emperors in the past. It offers an expression of "organizational emperorship". Zheng studied the mechanisms by which the CPC strives to maintain the continuity of imperial power. John Burns also highlights the forms of continuity between the current nomenklatura and structures of the past.

There is also a particular fascination for the former aristocratic French way of life. If the Chinese have a special attraction to the art of French living, the Chinese elites seem to be fascinated by the lifestyle of the Ancien Regime. Almost all of the gated communities of châteaux in China include the name "château," not "castle," In recent years, various Chinese billionaires have stayed in France and wished on return to build a replica of French châteaux. The best known example is the Château Zhang Lafitte in the suburbs of Beijing. Zhang Yuchen, former head of Beijing's construction bureau, made his fortune in real estate development. There is also the multiplication of wine châteaux (*jiuzhuang*) where the rich Chinese are trying to make their own wine.[13]

Still others have bought châteaux in Bordeaux, such as Château Lafitte Laguens in 2008 or Château Lafitte Chenu in 2010. French châteaux also raise events, such as the exhibition of art and culture in Beijing in 2007. Two hundred works of art exhibited at the Château Zhang Lafitte were selected from 21 French châteaux and museums from the twelfth to the nineteenth centuries : furniture that harks back to the good old days, clocks, watches and other design objects, and manufacturing of fine sculptures and curiosities that demonstrate an exceptional inventiveness. During this exhibition, ten artists, tapestry-weaving experts, wood-carving artists and landscape French designers presented on site samples of their traditional crafts.

The dynastic fantasy is ubiquitous in China. It is observed through the name of the famous wine château and wine Dynasty (Wangchao, Tianjin). But above all it appears that most of the rich in China are children of senior leaders of the Chinese Communist Party. According to the Chinese journal *The World Executive* published in March 2006, among about 3,220 people with more than 100 million yuan of assets, 2,932 are children of high-ranking Communist officials. The English-language Chinese official press takes the term "princeling" to discuss this phenomenon and points out that nepotism is one of the main topics of popular discontent. The term "caste" is increasingly used to describe the social stratification in China, notably the elite. A survey also showed that the rich do not consider themselves only as rich but also as a new aristocracy. We also can note that the book *The Old Regime and the Revolution*, written in 1856 by the famous French political thinker Alexis de Tocqueville, has become very popular in China and is warmly recommended by the Chinese State leaders themselves.[14] Tocqueville promotes the way of a continuous reform.

## Conclusion

Clearly, the gated communities of châteaux in China are a socio-territorial phenomenon profoundly original and unconventional. The very existence of such a residential form marks a profound break with the recent past of contemporary China. It represents a literally unbelievable phenomenon in today's China. It would be very interesting to know if elsewhere in the world it is possible to observe comparable residential forms.

On the one hand, it may appear normal that the rich reside in homes according to their wealth. This phenomenon reflects the massive enrichment of certain segments of Chinese society. On the other hand, the architectural style of the châteaux also encompasses inevitably a history and values of its own. This history and these values are more or less those of feudalism. It is therefore not only extreme forms in the scale of luxury. It is an architectural form belonging to another social and political system, another historical period. These gated communities are probably the most extreme forms of housing inequality in China as the architectural form of the château is not only a luxurious type of habitat associated with high incomes, because there are in China luxury villas more expensive than those châteaux. In contrast, châteaux actually refer to the Ancien Regime in Europe and to a particular social status, that of the nobility. It may appear paradoxical and fascinating that architectural forms desired by some of the super-rich Chinese are not turned towards the future, but to the past. Inevitably, a question arises: is communist China returned to the starting point, the imperial China? Can one speak of a system back on itself?

The interpretation of these gated communities of châteaux in China is not easy. It should fall neither into the over-interpretation nor into the under-interpretation of the phenomenon. The rarity of these residential enclaves, their almost invisibility and the lack of knowledge of the sociology of the residents should not lead us to consider them as insignificant, marginal or politically neutral. Conversely, the historical and political significance of these micro-territories should in no way be over-estimated and lead us to argue that the political system in post-reform China would be feudal. The correct interpretation probably lies between these two pitfalls.

It should be noted that the owners of these châteaux are not lords at the head of agricultural lands and the current situation is very different from pre-communist China. Under these conditions, how to analyze this element of neo-feudalism? Is it just from the elites a nostalgia of imperial China, an aristocratic pure fantasy? In addition, there are not isolated châteaux, but lots. The concentration of these châteaux in real enclaves adds a particular dimension. Could the seclusion of the rich and powerful in specific areas be considered as an ultimate strategy for the authorities to control these elites? On the one hand, the Party permits the rich to live in châteaux, on the other, they are confined in dedicated areas, nearly invisible, most likely to minimize interactions with the rest of society. The gated communities of châteaux, or the invisible neo-feudalism?

## Notes

1  The living castles should be added more than 10,000 remains of castles.
2  Within the county of Dordogne (France), according to J. Secret (1950) *Le Périgord*, Havas.
3  The HOMA Yuzi Paradise is a member of the famous network of luxury hotels Relais & Châteaux.
4  P. Nivelle (2006) "La Chine s'entiche de la copie-propriété" (China chic infatuated copy-ownership), *Libération*, Paris, November 18.
5  Wu Fulong (2010) "Gated and packaged suburbia: packaging and branding Chinese residential development", *Cities*, Vol. 27, Issue 5, October, pp. 385–396. Pow Choon-Piew, Kong Lily (2007) "Marketing the Chinese dream home: gated communities and representations of the good life in (post-)socialist Shanghai", *Urban Geography*, Vol. 28, N° 2, February–March, pp. 129–159.
6  S. Brunel (2006) *La Planète disneylandisée (The disneylandised planet)*, Sciences Humaines Édition, Paris.
7  K. Marx, F. Engels (1973) *La Chine (China)*, 10/18, UGE. K. Marx, F. Engels (2010) *Trois lettres à propos du mode de production asiatique, Juin 1853 (Three letters about the asiatic mode of production, June 1853)*, Strasbourg: La Phocide.

8 Before K. Wittfogel, various writings have evoked the "Oriental despotism", among them the posthumous work of Nicolas-Antoine Boulanger (1722–1759) *Recherches sur l'origine du despotisme oriental, 1761 (Research on the oriental despotism, 1761)*. Reed.: Paris, Hachette, 1972

9 For example, Huang Minlan (2007) "Misunderstandings of 'feudalism' as seen from the difference between the Chinese and Western concepts of 'feudalism'", Xinhua Wenzhai, 20-08. M. Bloch (1939–1940) *La Société féodale (The feudal society)*, 2 vol. (reed. by Albin Michel, in one volume, in 1998).

10 "How Yukong moved mountains", 1945 11 June, in *Little Red Book*, XXI 'Rely on its own forces and fight with endurance', 1964.

11 M.-C. Bergère (1984) "Après Mao, le retour du vieil homme" (After Mao, the return of Old Man), *Vingtième Siècle. Revue d'histoire*, Paris, vol. 1, n° 1, pp. 31–46.

12 Zheng Yongnian (2010) *The Chinese Communist Party as Organizational Emperor*, Routledge.

13 G. Giroir (2013) "The phenomenon of wine châteaux in China: the case of Yantai (Shandong)", paper presented at the Conference of the Association of American Geographers, Los Angeles, April.

14 Zhou Zhou (2012) "Book preferences hint at China's will for mild reform", *China Daily*, 21 November. See also : Nallene Chou West (2012) "Tocqueville in China", 14 September. *CaixinOnline*: <http://english.caixin.com/2012-09-14/100438129.html> (accessed 10 December 2012).

## Bibliography

Bergère, M.-C. (1984) 'Après Mao, le retour du vieil homme' (After Mao, the return of Old Man), *Vingtième Siècle. Revue d'histoire*, vol. 1, no 1, pp. 31–46.

Bloch, M. (1939–1940) *La Société féodale (The Feudal Society)*, 2 vol. (reed. by Albin Michel: Paris, 1998).

Brodsgaard, K. E. and Zheng Yongnian (eds) (2006) *The Communist Party in Reform*, London, New York: Routledge.

Giroir, G. (2002) 'Le phénomène des *gated communities* à Pékin, ou les nouvelles cités interdites' (Gated communities in Peking, or the new forbidden cities), *Bulletin de l'Association de Géographes Français*, Paris, December, pp. 423–36.

Giroir, G. (2003) 'Gated communities, clubs in a club system. The case of Beijing (China)', Paper presented at the International Conference on Gated communities of Glasgow, September, 2003. Available since October 2003 is the website of Department of Urban Studies, University of Glasgow (UK), Centre of Neighborhoods: <www.gla.ac.ak/departments/urbanstudies/gated/gatedpaps/gatedconfpaps.html>

Giroir, G. (2006) 'Yosemite Villas – mirror of emerging capitalism? A gated community in the US in Beijing', Paper presented at the First World Forum on Chinese Studies, August 2004. Published in: 'Yosemite Villas – mirror of emerging capitalism? An American-style gated community in Beijing', *China Perspectives*, Hong Kong, No. 64, pp. 13–23.

Giroir, G. (2006) 'The Purple Jade Villas (Beijing), a golden ghetto in red China', Paper presented at the International Conference of Mainz (Germany), June, 2002. Published in Frantz, K., Glasz, G., Webster, C. (eds) *Private Cities: Global and local perspectives*, London, New York: RoutledgeCurzon, pp. 142–52.

Giroir, G. (2006) 'The Fontainebleau villas (Shanghai), as globalized golden ghetto in a Chinese garden', Paper presented at the International Conference of Royal Geographical Society, London (UK), August 2003. Published in Fulong Wu (ed.) *Globalization and the Chinese City*, London, New York: RoutledgeCurzon, pp. 208–25.

Giroir, G. (2006) '"Hard enclosure" and "soft enclosure" in the gated communities: some empirical evidence and theoretical perspective in China', Paper presented at the International Symposium of Pretoria (South Africa), Territory, Control and Enclosure: the Ecology of Urban Fragmentation, February 28–March 3. Proceedings available on CD; p. 20. In *Sociologia Urbana e Rurale*, Bologna (Italy), 2012, 98, pp. 101–124.

Giroir, G. (2007) 'Spaces of leisure: gated golf communities in China', Paper presented at the International Conference of the Royal Geographical Society, London, August–September, 2005. Published in Wu Fulong (eds) *China's Emerging Cities: the Making of New Urbanism*, London, New York: RoutledgeCurzon, pp. 235–55.

Giroir, G. (2007) 'Socio-territorial fractures in China: the unachievable "harmonious society?"', *China Perspectives*, Hong Kong, No. 3, pp. 83–91.

Giroir, G. (2008) 'Au-delà des gated communities: Phoenix City (Canton), première private city en Chine' (Beyond the gated communities: Phoenix City (Canton), private first city in China), *Urbanisme*, Paris, July–August, no 361, pp. 33–8.

Giroir, G. (2008) 'La réinvention des *hutong* du vieux Pékin dans les *gated communities* suburbaines: le cas des villas Yijun et Guantang' (The reinvention of *hutong* of old Beijing in the suburban gated communities: the case of the Villas Yijun et Guantang), Paper presented at the International Conference of University of Nanterre (Paris), March 2007. Published in C. Vallat (dir.) *Pérennité urbaine, ou la ville par-delà ses métamorphoses (Urban perenniality, or the city beyond its metamorphoses)*, L'Harmattan, Paris, pp. 85–98.

Giroir, G. (2009) 'Chine: nouveaux riches et gated communities de luxe', (China: nouveaux riches and luxurious gated communities) in T. Paquot (dir.) *Ghettos de riches. Tour du monde des enclaves résidentielles sécurisées*, ed. Perrin, Paris, pp. 224–40.

Giroir, G. (2009) 'The phenomenon of gated communities in China: assessment and prospects (1978–2008)', Paper presented at the Sixteenth International Seminar on Urban Form (ISUF 2009), South China University of Technology / Urban Planning Bureau of Guangzhou, Guangzhou (China). Proceedings available on CD; p. 15.

Giroir, G. (2012) 'The gated communities of châteaux in China: back to the neo-feudalism?', 6th International Conference on Gated Communities, Istanbul (Turkey), September, Proceedings available on CD.

Giroir, G. (ed.) (2012) 'Le luxe en Chine' (Luxury in China), *Monde chinois. Asie nouvelle (Chinese World. New Asia)*, special issue, Éditions Choiseul, Paris, p. 141.

Giroir, G. (2012) 'Une nouvelle méthode de géomarketing pour le marché du luxe en Chine : l'étude des gated communities pour riches' (A new method of geomarketing for the luxury market in China: the study of the gated communities for the rich), Venice (Italy), 11th International Marketing Trends Conference, January. Proceedings available on CD; p. 15.

Giroir, G. (2012) 'Riches, gated communities et géomarketing en Chine' (Rich, gated communities and geomarketing in China), 6ème Journées de Recherche en Marketing Horloger (6th Conference of Watch Marketing), Asian Dream, Haute école de gestion, Neuchâtel (Switzerland), 2 November 2011. In Kalust Zorik, François H. Courvoisier (coord.) *Asian Dream. Le rêve horloger (Asian dream. the watch dream)*, Éditions LEP: Lausanne (Switzerland), pp. 35–59.

Giroir, G. (2013) 'Hyper-rich and hyper-luxury in China: the case of the most expensive gated communities', Paper presented at the Asian & Business Management Conference of Osaka (Japan), October 2010. Published in: *Chinese Business Review*, June, Vol. 10, pp. 454–66 and in: S. K. Rai (ed.) (2012) *Global Business in the Changing World*, Excel Books: New Delhi (India), pp 139–152.

Giroir, G. (2013) 'The phenomenon of wine châteaux in China: the case of Yantai (Shandong)', paper presented at the Conference of the Association of American Geographers, Los Angeles, April.

Huang, Minlan (2007) 'Misunderstandings of "feudalism" as seen from the difference between the Chinese and Western concepts of feudalism', *Xinhua Wenzhai*, 20 August.

Huang, Youqin and Setha, M. Low (2008) 'Is gating always exclusionary? A comparative analysis of gated communities in American and Chinese cities', in John Logan (ed.) *Urban China in transition*, pp. 182–202. Malden: Blackwell.

Marx, K. and Engels, F. (1973) *La Chine (China)*, 10/18, UGE.

Marx, K. and Engels, F. (2010) *Trois lettres à propos du mode de production asiatique, Juin 1853 (Three letters about the asiatic mode of production, June 1853)*, Strasbourg: La Phocide.

Nivelle, P. (2006) 'La Chine s'entiche de la copie-propriété' (China chic infatuated copy-ownership), *Libération*, Paris, November 18.

Pow, Choon-Piew and Kong, Lily (2007) 'Marketing the Chinese dream home: gated communities and representations of the good life in (post-)socialist Shanghai', *Urban Geography*, Vol. 28, No 2, February–March, pp. 129–59.

Wu, Fulong (2010) 'Gated and packaged suburbia: packaging and branding Chinese residential development', *Cities*, Vol. 27, Issue 5, October, pp. 385–96.

Wittfogel, K. A. (1957) *Oriental despotism: a comparative study of total power*, New Haven (Connecticut): Yale University Press.

Zheng, Yongnian (2010) *The Chinese Communist Party as organizational emperor. culture, reproduction and transformation*, London and New York: Routledge, p. 254

## 9 The imagination of class and housing choices of the middle class

Case studies in Shanghai and Beijing

*Yu-ling Song*

### Background

China has experienced rapid economic growth within the past decade due to its position as "the factory of the world," and while the rest of the world suffers from an economic depression, she has assumed the role of a stable consuming power. This growth has affected the rise of a new social class benefitting from economic reform originating in the late 1970s, which in turn has allowed them to develop into significant consumers in both the domestic and global markets. This consumptive power has provided them the opportunity to play a crucial role in compelling spatial differentiation in urban China, as evidenced through their housing choices (Fleischer, 2007; Goodman and Zang, 2008). Understanding the consumptive behavior of this new class has become a requisite to master the development of the urban and global markets.

Although there is still debate over whether there is a definitive class as "middle class," it is apparent that one does exist, with an ability for housing consumption and a taste for acquiring social, economic, and cultural capital. It can also be considered as an umbrella term under which titles like "new rich," "new middle class," and "sunrise social class," with these titles usually revealing the group's characteristics for housing choice. Some commentators believe that this class has formed a specific life style influence by particular aesthetics, which has resulted in a social spatial differentiation as well as shaping of exclusive space (Pow, 2007; Zhang, 2010). The driving forces behind this result have been both markets and the intervention of government (Tomba, 2004), which shows that the middle class plays an essential dual-role in accelerating China's market economy while also facilitating a harmonious society.

This group has become increasingly important to China's economic development and social stability, but compared to those that have been enriched through party connections from the beginning of reform, the middle class are believed to be consisting of professionals free from corruption. Therefore, on the one hand, they obtain more social expectation and responsibility,[1] but on the other, they possess superior material conditions, life style, and consumption that are to be regarded within the same group as those who have accumulated huge wealth through personal relationships. Therefore, they are usually judged and criticized strictly under the criterion of social justice and considered as the propellers of the skyrocketing urban housing. From a political economic approach, social justice has a universally agreed-upon meaning, which is that "something to be fought for is a key value within an ethics of political solidarity built across different places" (Harvey, 1996: 360). When Chinese society claims that the harmonious society is the common value and interest of every Chinese, the middle class is usually stig-matized by the burden of social expectations to create a harmonious society. The middle class departs from the key value in Chinese society because they enthusi-astically pursue wealth and enrich themselves through dubious methods. However, there still exists a huge chasm between the reality and the fiction of this class.

The research aims to investigate the middle class, as defined by their profes-sionalism and high education level and who own one or more of housing, through their housing consumption, which includes the process from housing choices to self-identification. Through it, the research explores the diversity of class differ-entiation in the middle class. Eventually, the concept of social justice will be drawn to re-examine the middle class and criticize the inadequate evaluation among the mainstream discourse.

## Literature review

### Social differentiation of middle class in reform China

Although the consumption practices of the middle class have evolved into a major global issue, the existence of this so-called "middle class" in China is still under debate. However, after the reforms in the late 1970s, Deng Xiao-ping's proverb to "let some people get rich first" has been gradually implemented to the point it is incontrovertible that a class benefitting from these reforms has emerged. When class relations and structure transformed within Chinese society, rich people wiped clear the stigma of capitalism that had been prevalent since 1949, and declared the existence of a wealthy class in China (Zhou, 2010). Research into this wealthy class has revealed the diversity found within the group, as various terms like "new rich," "middle class," the "new middle class," and the "sunrise social class" have emerged to aid in identification. Commentators have recognized that these wealthy Chinese emerging from the reforms possess many differences from their Western middle-class counterparts, especially with their influence on politi-cal and social dimensions. Their consumption and taste is also idiosyncratic of China's fast economic development, thus they have developed into the best repre-sentatives of China's transformation. They are perceived as unfettered by the severe constraints of the social system because they actively pursue wealth, share an enthusiasm for the freedom of life, and fear corruption and poverty. They neither feel antipathy toward the government nor intend to substantially affect public policy. The image of "vanguard consumption and rear-guard politics" has provoked a negative response against their wealth under the principle of social justice. On the other hand, they play a significant role in the economic and social development of China. Therefore, the group usually possesses a negative and positive dual-identity (Bian, 2002; Fang, 2005; Unger, 2006; Ha and Liu, 2008; Goodman and Zang, 2008; Gaoyong, 2009).

Lu (2002) proposed an analysis of China's middle class. In the report, Chinese society was divided into ten classes and five corresponding social and economic levels by using the standard of organization or political resources, economic resources, and cultural resources.[2] Among them, the cultural resources[3] were deemed the most important for Chinese people to access to the middle class, and also as the most significant standard to distinguishing themselves from the pre-1990 wealthy class. Professionals with plentiful cultural resources are classified into middle-upper and upper levels (Lu, 2002). But this criterion used for classification also suffered from questioning, as some commentators believed that people who have accessed the new middle class or sunrise social class haven't relied on upgrading their level of culture and knowledge but instead shifted their focus toward underhanded devices to obtain their wealth and power. They have little enthusiasm for political participation and pay little attention to the lower classes. Compared to the Western middle class, there is a major gap separating the two (Li, 2008; Yang, 2011; Liang, 2011).

Some commentators decided to use the new term "new rich" for those who gained their wealth post-1990. This term distinguishes this new class from both the Western middle class, and helps affirm a special (though broad) social class in post-1979. According to their social economy status, their average income is at the middle-upper level (not including off-the-book income), and they accumulate their wealth through professional and technical capacities[4] (Goodman and Zang, 2008). More precisely, the "new rich" refers to people who have benefited from speedy economic growth in the reform era but is not limited to a specific social group or category of people. They still maintain an attachment with the pre-reform era support system and are unable to sever themselves from the social, political, and economic power related to the party-state. This reflects the inherent differences compared to the Western middle class, who possess the characteristics of marketization, democracy, and consumerism (Unger, 2006; Goodman and Zang, 2008). The "new rich" have also accumulated their wealth to some extent through generalized party-state relations. The concept has held a preconception that the party-state relationship is the exclusive element for wealth accumulation in the new rich. However, Huang (2009) compared 1995 1per cent Population Survey and 2000 Census Data for Beijing to point that housing inequality between people with different political statuses was smallest, and *hukou* statuses were more important than education and occupations. It reveals that the political relationship is not really the main element of the inequality of wealth in China. Thus, if "new rich" is a proper concept to describe the group in China, it is still under debate. But they share exactly similarities such as cultural capital, middle-upper level of consumption and professional, so "middle class" is also the relative proper name to distinguish it from the pre-1990 wealthy class. It is thus clear that all of the related research has provided the implication that no matter what the name of the group is, the complexity and differentiation resulted from the social structure exactly exists in the group. In this sense, when the Chinese middle class is treated as a homogeneous group and judged as unjust to Chinese harmonic society, it results as a kind of injustice to them as well. Thus, this paper will continue to investigate how the concept of justice is discussed in the social group.

### Social justice and differences

The notion of "social justice" is a universal principle that is still under continuing debate (Harvey, 1996; Stanley, 2009). John Rawls's (1971) concept of justice has received widespread criticisms from proponents of Marxism and postmodernism because it holds the liberal democratic concept of social justice that treats justice as an individual's right and dealt with only static forms of social inequality, but neglects the deep structural processes that produces injustice (Harvey, 1973, 1996; Dikeç, 2001; Soja, 2010). For him, justice is a universal principle to be applied to every place and people. However, Young (1990) believes that "social justice" is just a deconstruction, but differentiation and universal are both possible and necessary to pose alternative conceptualizations. Therefore, she stressed that individuals be understood as "heterogeneous and de-centered." No social group can be truly unitary in the sense of having members who hold to a singular identity. In her view, conception of social justice "requires not the melting away of differences, but institutions that promote reproduction of and respect for group differences without oppression." Dikeç (2001) argued the "differences" which Young extolled tended to make the certain people marginalized themselves through the use of identities, if they do not try to change their situation. In this sense, he thought the "differences" in Young's idea is only the particularities. Then he drew the "differentialist" project from Lefebvre who believed the movement from the particularities to the differences was the moment of "differing" through political struggle. The action results "the right to difference" which was treated as one of the parameters[5] of social justice. Therefore, facing the differences within the social group and empowering them to suppress the domination and repression, which is from homogenization and stigma and cultivated by the so-called universal values such as "harmonious society," "Chinese dream" and "the precedence in the country's benefits." Therefore, the differentiation among the middle class in China is profoundly necessary to understand. This paper adopts an approach through the prism of investigating housing consumption, the most significant way for middle class to accumulate wealth in post-socialist urban China following the housing reform in 1998.

### Social class and housing choices

The unintentional hegemonic neo-liberalism of China's housing market has provided a possible avenue to accumulate wealth through market mechanisms rather than though party-state relations (Pow, 2009). However, ten years after the advent of housing reform, scores of buyers were purchasing welfare housing at low costs and selling to net more than ten times profit. This allowed them to gain access into the middle class and continue the cycle of wealth accumulation in the housing market (Tomba and Tang, 2008). Not only has purchasing and selling housing become a reliable method in obtaining wealth, it has paved the way for upward mobility for a new generation of Chinese and helped construct a new social self-identity. The middle class who purchase housing as consumption practice has further created a spatial segregation to separate themselves from other classes through their housing choices, which tend to include gated communities emanating a cultural aura of belonging to a wealthy class. Various residential communities occupied by different classes have differentiated spatial characteristics which lend proof to the evidence of the middle class possessing a unique aesthetic vision. Housing choice therefore becomes a dual cultural process of space-making and class-defining (Fleischer, 2007; Pow, 2009; Zhang, 2010). Housing and consumption choices of the middle class have two pointed significances. First, they reveal an evolving approach towards housing choices and consumption. Second, they have created a socio-spatial differentiation as confirmed through the use of housing space.

Within the past ten years, the related discussions on urban housing in contemporary China have focused on the political economic analysis of housing choices (Li, 2000a, 2003, 2004, 2005; Huang, 2003, 2004; Wang and Li, 2004) and the consequent socio-spatial differentiation. This analysis has ascertained the links discovered between social class and urban spatial differentiation (Wu, 2002, 2004; He and Wu, 2005, 2007; Huang, 2009; Li and Song, 2009). The writers further acknowledged that several key factors affect housing choice and spatial differentiation. Huang (2009) believes that the *hukou* (household registration) system, *danwei* (work unit), and city of residence have all caused the inequalities found in housing choices and directly affect the socio-spatial differentiation. With respect to the effects of the *danwei* on the housing choices and accumulation of wealth, Tomba and Tang (2008) also stress that the *danwei* has an important impact on housing choices and spatial differentiation, as participation within a work unit becomes a fundamental factor in obtaining different housing: *danwei* members, although earning a relatively lower salary, own better housing than non *danwei* members. More so, they are usually able to enjoy living in commodity housing in a gated community. Thus even if the middle class possess abundant cultural resources, they need to rely on specific organizations such as the *danwei*, by which they can accumulate wealth rapidly in the housing market. *Danwei* is derived from the party-state system and is closely linked to a series of potential benefits associated with housing. The existing research has illustrated the fact that a party-state relation certainly affects housing choice and wealth accumulation (Bian and Liu, 2005; Zhou, 2006; Logan *et al.*, 2010). Commentators have also pointed out there is evidence of a community of interest being developed between the middle class and the party-state (Goodman and Zang, 2008). Li (2002) emphasizes the party-state system provided a privilege of housing choice that helped a specific class to own houses of better condition. He illustrates that the average living space of party cadres is 30 per cent larger than that of workers and non-members, and that the housing condition of employees in state-owned enterprises was superior to those in collective enterprises. Existing literature reminds us that in the housing reform era near the end of the 1990s, some middle class who still had relations with the party-state received benefits when they engaged in the housing market to earn considerable interest and become winners in the housing reform policy (Logan *et al.*, 2010).

The issue of one's generation has also played an important factor when researchers explored the relationship between class and housing choices. The young generation who entered the labor market in the late 1990s no longer receives welfare housing. Most of them are forced to find alternatives like purchasing housing through market mechanisms. Zhou (2010) argues that the effects of party-state relations on wealth accumulation by the middle class have waned in contemporary China. After 1998 the housing market opened up, and the wealth accumulation of the middle class depended more on the global market, the abundant cultural and economic resources they possessed, and employment with multinationals and joint ventures, rather than relations with the party-state. However, in some provinces or cities where the government dominates the local economy, the young middle class work in the public sector or large enterprises, which still provide privileges in housing choices. Therefore, distinguishing city governance is a possible factor to affect the middle class accumulating wealth through the housing market.

In summation, existing literature states that housing choices are affected by factors such as *hukou*, participation with a *danwei*, the relation with the party-state, city of residence, and one's generation. These factors can be adopted to carefully check the middle class who tend to be homogenized despite the existence of intra-group differences. However, the existing literature concerning the relation between social class and spatial differentiation mostly chooses up-scale housing and inferred that the residents belonged to the same social class, rather than either respectively investigating personal issues including aesthetics, life style, and identity (Fleisher, 2007; Pow, 2007, 2009; Li, 2010) or incorporating a political economic perspective to explore government intervention in housing to consolidate and broaden the middle class (Meng, 2000; Gu and Liu, 2002; Hu and Kaplan, 2001; Li, 2003; Wu, 2002; Tomba, 2004; Tomba and Tang, 2008). Existing work revealing housing choices in China has been explained by either economic or political factors (Meng, 2000; Hu and Kaplan, 2001; Gu and Liu, 2002; Wu, 2002; Li, 2003) or individual life styles (Fleischer, 2007). Few have connected both of them and explored their interaction. Moreover, in research related to the middle class almost no attention has been paid to the consumption patterns by different factors of the middle class despite social and economic dynamics. Few even have done comparative research to demonstrate the variations between different cities under the different characteristics of urban space.

## Research questions and method

The discussion above has prompted the formulation of specific research questions in this paper. Are cultural resources sufficient to argue that the middle class, endowed with their professional expertise, exist independently of the party-state system?

What factors are taken into account when they purchase housing, and how they accumulate wealth through housing consumption? Are there any shared common characteristics of housing choices? How do they identify their social class? This research draws factors which affect housing consumption to analyze the process of housing choices of the middle class. Moreover, the concept of social justice is introduced to criticize the current discourse, as they tend to homogenize the middle class and inappropriately stigmatize them.

To answer these questions, the fieldwork and in-depth interviews were conducted in Beijing and Shanghai from 2009 to 2011. The scope of the research is limited to comparing the middle class in different areas and generations.[6] In this research, the author selected interviewees in Beijing and Shanghai, the two Chinese largest cities, which have also been experiencing the fastest rise in price of housing in the past ten years, to highlight the effects resulting from different areas. Interviewees from the generation of the 1970s and 1980s were chosen to show they have experienced three main periods of housing reform, such as the time of welfare housing, transitional stage of housing reform, and housing marketization. Those selected were born in the 1970s and 1980s, and range from 28 to 42 years old. Snowball sampling was used to generate 32 interviewees in Shanghai and 20 interviewees in Bejing. There are 52 interviewees in total, consisting of 28 women and 24 men. They own one or more units, and also have earned a master's degree or upward. They worked in government departments, research units, and public institutions as well as private and state-owned enterprise, and as executives, researchers, technicians, and so on. Main concepts from the text of the interview were drawn and analyzed, then relation analysis was undertaken between various factors to group the significant types of the middle class found in Beijing and Shanghai.

Some main concepts were extracted by text analysis such as "party-state system" (A), "identity" (B), "sense of place" (C), "mindset of housing choices" (D), and "generation" (E). There are a few sub-concepts subordinate to main concepts (in Table 9.1). The procedure of analysis is: first, choose the sentences implied to the sub-concepts in the text. Second, mark the type of relations (positive '+' or negative '-') between respective sentences subordinate to various sub-concepts. Third, count the total times of positive and negative relation between two sub-concepts. If positive times occur more than negative, the relation of two sub-concept is marked '+'. Finally, respectively extract two sub-concepts with positive relation, and induce to different types of middle class who have various housing choices. As most *danwei* in Shanghai have revoked allotting housing to employees, the relation between housing choices and "party-state system" is absent among analysis in Shanghai, and "characteristics of generation," the significant factor affecting housing choice, is often extracted in the text of interview. Therefore, "party-state system" and "generation" become the important differences between Beijing and Shanghai in factors affecting housing choices. Moreover, it is easier in Shanghai for new-comers to acquire *hukou* than in Beijing, so the interviewees who work and reside in Shanghai all have acquired *hukou*. As a result, there are no interviewees in Shanghai who belong to "non *hukou*/new-comers" (B3).

*Table 9.1* Main concepts and sub-concepts in this research

| Main concepts | Sub-concepts | Note |
|---|---|---|
| A: party-state | A1: housing allotment from work unit (affordable housing)<br>A2: non housing allotment | |
| B: identity | B1: *hukou*/native<br>B2: *hukou*/new-comers<br>B3: non *hukou*/new-comers | |
| C: sense of place | C1: traditional | Beijing: the ingrained belief of the superior location in the city is in upper (north) Haidian, western area (location of emperors' grave)<br>Shanghai: ingrained evaluation of good/bad location: upper/lower corner; inner/outer district; east/west bank of Huangpu River |
| | C2: modern | |
| D: mindset of housing choice | D1: investment | Housing is a significant means of investment. |
| | D2: distinction | Central district is the priority in housing choice. |
| | D3: settle down | They pursue housing to settle down, because they have a permanent job in the city and plan to live there for a long time. |
| | D4: adaptive | They have alternatives for their future, and usually prepare for moving to other cities. |
| E: generation | E1: post '70s generation (born after 1970)<br>E2: post '80s generation (born after 1980) | |

Sub-concepts in this research are clarified into two categories: "resource" and "feeling/attitude", and the matrix was developed under the framework to induce different types of middle class with various housing choices (in Table 9.2).

According to relation analysis, five types of housing choice are induced from the respective combinations of "resource" and "feeling/attitude," displaying an existing positive relation (A1B1, A1B2, A2B1, A2B2 and A2B3) in housing choices of Beijing's middle class (in Table 9.3). Shanghai's middle class also share the same analysis method with Beijing (in Table 9.4). Four types of housing choices are induced according to the respective combinations (E1B1, E1B2, E2B1, E2B2) (in Table 9.5).

From the above analysis, the variety of "resource" and "feeling/attitude" has resulted in different types of housing choices among the middle class. In summary, the middle class in Beijing and Shanghai have exhibited a few types of differences in housing choices, covered by five different types such as moderate

*Table 9.2* The relation analysis in housing choices of Beijing's middle class

| Feeling/ attitude | Resource | | | | |
|---|---|---|---|---|---|
| | *A1* | *A2* | *B1* | *B2* | *B3* |
| C1 | + | + | + | | |
| C2 | + | + | | + | + |
| D1 | + | | + | + | |
| D2 | | + | + | | |
| D3 | | + | | + | |
| D4 | | + | | | + |

Note: '+' means the positive relation between 'resource' and 'feeling/attitude'.

*Table 9.3* Types of housing choices in Beijing's middle class

| | *A1* | *A2* |
|---|---|---|
| B1 | D1C1<br>Moderate investment<br>(I) | D2C1<br>Sectionalism distinction<br>(III) |
| B2 | D1C2<br>Flexible investment<br>(II) | D3C2<br>Pursuing dwelling<br>(IV) |
| B3 | — | D4C2<br>Adaptive<br>(V) |

*Table 9.4* The relation analysis in housing choices of Shanghai's middle class

| Feeling/ attitude | Resource | | | |
|---|---|---|---|---|
| | *E1* | *E2* | *B1* | *B2* |
| C1 | + | + | + | |
| C2 | + | + | | + |
| D1 | | + | + | |
| D2 | | | + | |
| D3 | | | | + |
| D4 | | + | | + |

Note: '+' means the positive relation between 'resource' and 'feeling/attitude'.

*Table 9.5* Types of housing choices in Shanghai's middle class

| | *E1* | *E2* |
|---|---|---|
| B1 | D2C1<br>Sectionalism distinction<br>(III) | D1C1<br>Moderate investment<br>(I) |
| B2 | D3C2<br>Pursuing dwelling<br>(IV) | D4C2<br>Adaptive<br>(V) |

investment (I), flexible investment (II), sectionalism distinction (III), pursuing dwelling (IV), and adaptive. (V).

## Differentiation of the middle class: difference in housing choice

This research groups five types of housing choices belonging to different groups of middle class. Some differences occurred between the middle class of Beijing and Shanghai. In the next session, the paper will engage to illustrate the five types respectively.

### Moderate investment (I)

This type only belongs in Beijing's middle class. Generally, they are native Beijingers who have local *hukou*, and have received housing from the *danwei*. In regards to the characteristics of their housing, they have not only obtained housing from the *danwei* but inherited their parents' housing as well, which was also received from a *danwei*. Their housing is mostly located in the central district, therefore they are used to living in the central city and have a traditional sense of place. Wang Tong (pseudonym) and his family own several welfare housing, due to his parents' employment in a government *danwei*. One house was located in a traditional Chinese compound near the Ministry of Foreign Affairs Department. It was then traded for an apartment in the northeastern district by real estate agent. In addition, they own two houses from the parents' *danwei* that are leased, and are waiting for the appropriate chance to sell for their next investment project. Thus, they are closely monitoring the development of Beijing's real estate market and seeking the appropriate time to make money in the housing market. As native Beijingers who work in a government department, they have built up a close social network, which help them purchase housing at a lower price. Wang Tong perceived the housing prices were rising fast in 2004 year, so he bought a unit through his friends at a lower price because the land belonged to a government department.

This type of middle class obviously grasps the privilege of relations with the party-state system and the advantages of a local social network that enable them to gain progressively sustainable interests from existing lucrative real estate. They do not tend to take big risks in the housing market, but rather use market mechanisms to gradually trade the welfare housing with commodity housing within the central district. In addition to expertise and an abundance of cultural resources, their ample organization and economic resources allowed them to accumulate wealth.

### Flexible investment (II)

In Beijing, the type of middle class that bought housing from *danwei* are normally new-comers with a local *hukou* and a flexible sense of place. With regard to Shanghai's middle class, they are Shanghai natives, born in the 1980s with a relatively traditional sense of place, which allowed them to maintain the idea of an upper and lower area. They have infused flexibility within their strategy of housing investment because they are too young to burden themselves on huge loans.

In Beijing, they usually have purchased housing before being provided them from the *danwei*. The housing, furthermore, tends to be located in the suburbs, so they have leased out their own housing for investment and rented cheaper and smaller housing near their *danwei*. Once they own the housing provided by *danwei*, they then formulate a plan for exploiting it in the future. For them, the location of housing relies on the economic condition and the site of land belonging to the *danwei*. Zhu Ping (pseudonym) is from northern Heilongjiang and decided to live and work in Beijing as a civil servant after she finished her master's degree. The cultural characteristics of tolerance and similar living habits were the main factors that convinced her to settle down. Zhu Ping intended to purchase housing after she married in 2004, but she eventually chose not to when the time arrived. Because the price increased too quickly while the unit was too far away from her work place, she also did not purchase commercial housing. Later, Zhu Ping obtained "affordable housing" at a lower price in Haidian District through *danwei*'s housing system. Although the surrounding area is convenient and full of amenities, she leased it due to its smaller size, relative lack of safety, and noisy environment, and rented an apartment in a quiet, safe, low-density community in Haidian District. For Zhu Ping and her husband, receiving a unit cheaper than market prices through their *danwei*'s housing system would not allow them to accumulate wealth fast but does allow them to dwell in a strange large city that provides temporary relief from the heavy burden of housing. Their flexibility allows them to pursue options beyond a relatively vague idea of where they wish to purchase housing, and though they have consciousness of investment, they tend to have a more easygoing attitude. The priority in their present life cycle is the responsibility for family, such as allowing their parents outside Beijing to live together and arranging a reputable school attendance area for their kids. Those are important issues for them to consider when they will purchase housing in the future.

With respect to Shanghai, the middle class are the younger generation born during the late 80s. They received their wealth from their parents and have also inherited their parents' sense of place as they tend to purchase housing near their parents' neighborhood. Some of their parents provide the down payment, so they usually choose housing in a newly developed district or a relocated residents' community in the urban periphery where housing is affordable and the population is composed of new Shanghaiers with rich cultural resources. The native Shanghai middle class are familiar with the evolution of the city's estate market, and are most likely to purchase housing for investment in the suburbs. Ying Yein (pseudonym) works in a human resources consulting firm as a manager. She married and then purchased housing in the Shanghai World Expo area of Pudong new district in 2004. Five years later, in order to live near by her parents-in-law, she purchased another unit in the same community. Having lived in the central district of Shanghai since childhood, she thinks the new developed district brings more potential in price growth – therefore, recognizing the importance of regional development as a critical key in obtaining value added housing. They realize that housing is a significant means to gain wealth, so they will continue to look for possible opportunities for investment. Although their sense of place is influenced by their parents' traditional perspective, they would rather consider the location from a practical view of potential for development. However, their parents' old housing in the central district is still an area with potential for development, either for investment or living. Furthermore, their parents' old housing in the center of the city is a strong guarantee of their wealth.

### *Sectionalism distinction (III)*

In Beijing, the type of middle class who are native Beijingers have a strong traditional sense of place similar to those in Shanghai born after 1970s, but fail to receive unit from *danwei*. Beijing's middle class of this type usually own more than one housing in the central city. They seek localization when they purchase housing, and insist that living functions should be located in the surrounding neighborhood, as they will not tolerate traveling commuting distances. However, they are successful at building local social networks, which also serve as a resource for them to accumulate more wealth. Li Wei (pseudonym) has been living in Beijing since she was a child. For a single woman, she enjoys living in a prosperous central area of Beijing near the downtown of the World Trade Center. Besides, she also additionally owns two houses in Beijing's central district. She enjoys to engage in collecting information related to the housing market, because she believes housing is the best means for accumulating wealth. Regarding the process of purchasing housing, Li Wei has bought two units of housing respectively in 2001 and 2009 through her father's good friend, a well-known developer in China. The location she chose for her housing was affected by a traditional sense of place, as encapsulated by Chinese proverb "north is upper wind and upper water (shangfeng shangshuei); east is rich and west is honorable (dongfu xiqui)." According to her observations, native Beijingers tend to live in the west in up-scale community while foreign white-collar workers live in the east. Because of her traditional perspective of location, she purchased two units in the east and west respectively. The unit located in a traditionally well-placed area not only satisfies her need for convenience but also her traditional image of Beijing. She is seeking to continue purchase housing for investment.

The middle class of this type have a strong sense of place and identity with Beijing and Shanghai respectively, which affects their housing consumptive behavior. They usually can accumulate their wealth quickly if they play the housing market wisely. They also gain significant potential benefits because of their parents' privileged local networks. Overall, they are relatively intolerant of variations in sense of place and convenience of life. This ideology helps to shape the sectionalism distinction of housing choices.

## Pursuing dwelling (IV)

The type of this middle class found in Beijing have never received housing from a *danwei*, but possess the local *hukou* due to studying or working in government departments or public institutions in Beijing. They have a flexible sense of place when purchasing housing, mainly as a consequence of higher housing prices in Beijing and their retention of saving over a five to ten year span earned from their employment, which allows them to first consider prices. Therefore, all the housing contained within the poorer south as well as the limited affordable housing provided by the municipal government is included in their choice list. Even though their housing tends to be located quite far from the city and thus have to endure longer commutes, they are generally content with tenure in Beijing and happy at obtaining the opportunities that stem from having the Beijing *hukou*. However, they feel indignant at the dual-track housing policy in Beijing, because they believe that the *danwei's* role of providing affordable housing to their employees has provoked a relative deprivation and engendered an unstable society. Shen Weifan (pseudonym) works in a national research unit that does not provide welfare housing. In 2003, he had an urge to purchase housing for living when he had no good economic conditions. His parents paid the down payment of housing for him within the southern third ring, considered the worst location in the traditional sense of place. In spite of painful traffic and a lack of educational resources, he has endured his situation and thinks people living in Beijing are too stressed about the high price of housing as reflected in the idea that "Three families (husband, wife, and their parents) can barely afford to purchase a unit of housing." Therefore, he does not dare to conceive purchasing more housing, and is unhappy about the dual-track housing policy in Beijing. He believes it an unfair system that has caused differences since its onset.

Regarding the middle class in Shanghai born after the 1970s who are newcomers holding a local *hukou*, the majority have settled down in the city after completing a master's program. They have lived in Shanghai for more than ten years and become the "new Shanghai-nese" possessing a flexible sense of place. Their incentive to purchasing second unit is to act as housing for parents visiting in Shanghai. Yan Zao (pseudonym) is from Wuhan. After he graduated from the doctoral program in Shanghai he continued to work in a public institution and married in 2005. His parents paid the down payment for him to purchase a "2nd hand" apartment in Zabei District, located between the outer and inner loop. His *danwei* is in the central area of Huangpu District, 40 minutes by subway from his apartment. In comparison to living in the central district, he is satisfied with having more room and fewer loans. His living quality drastically improved when the subway line extended to his neighborhood. In 2009, Yan Zao purchased a smaller apartment in the same community with the intent of living together with his parents from Wuhan. He bought a car and enjoyed the happy life, but he did not consider purchasing more housing for investment purposes.

For this type of middle class, their main goal for housing purchase in Beijing or Shanghai is to settle down in their respective city. They usually are limited by their economic conditions, or question the inequality of the present housing policy (for those residing in Beijing). Their relatively unstable identity of social class is influenced by their suffering of the heavy burden of high housing prices, as they sometimes negatively perceive themselves as a lower class. Although they believe the two large cities are teeming with cultural resources and are tolerant of new-comers such as themselves, they still perceive a wide gap in social and economic resources as compared with the native middle class. Therefore, it seems inconceivable to them to be grouped together within the middle class.

### *Adaptive (V)*

Another type of middle class in Beijing and Shanghai are those who haven't received housing from a *danwei* nor the Beijing *hukou*. They settled down after completing a master's program and continued to work in a private enterprise in Beijing but not necessarily in a permanently resident capacity. This middle class living in Shanghai were born in the late 1980s. They are new-comers with a Shanghai local *hukou* who have worked in private domestic or transnational enterprises for five to ten years. They have a flexible sense of place and accept an unstable residence situation as economic development in China generated great demand for professionals in different places. The trait both the Beijing and Shanghai types share are that living in a changeable condition has made them more concerned about the price of housing more than the traditional perception of location. Wang Zong (pseudonym), who moved from Jiangxi province to Beijing, believed Beijing was a city full of chances and cultural aura. So he remained in the capital after completing a master's program in university. Since he is the single child in his family, his parents supported him by purchasing housing in Beijing. Although the location did not affect his traditional sense of place, as it was situated in an ingrained superior area, he still purchased a "2nd hand" apartment in the less-traditionally favored south because of the more affordable price and short distance to his work place. Even though the condition of transportation and living were inferior when he purchased his apartment, the subway line had extended to his neighborhood in 2009. For him, having an insight into Beijing's development served as an optimal strategy in housing choice. Holding a non-Beijing *hukou*, he has not decided to permanently live in Beijing, and has kept open the possibility to leave for other cities. However, owning a unit of housing in Beijing when the market was high has allowed him to identify himself as the middle class, even though his housing is located outside the southern Third Road.

Wang Zhengde (pseudonym) worked as a senior engineer in a transnational technical enterprise in Shanghai after she graduated from a master's program in Shanghai. She has rented housing in Shanghai for many years since she migrated from Inner Mongolia to Shanghai, and became tired of dealing with landlords and was eager to purchase housing when the prices were surging. She chose a pre-construction apartment in Minhang district, which is near Suzhou Kunshan, an area with a substantial concentration of Taiwan enterprises that also serves as a prime location for the rental market. In 2009, on the eve of the Shanghai World Expo, she

*Table 9.6* The relationship between factors and types

| Factor | Type | | | | | | | | | |
|---|---|---|---|---|---|---|---|---|---|---|
| | Moderate investment (I) | | Flexible investment (II) | | Sectionalism distinction (III) | | Pursuing dwelling (IV) | | Adaptive (V) | |
| | B | S | B | S | B | S | B | S | B | S |
| Party-state | +++ | | +++ | + | + | + | | | | |
| *Hukou* | +++ | | +++ | ++ | +++ | ++ | +++ | ++ | | + |
| Time to the city | + | | + | + | ++ | ++ | + | ++ | ++ | + |
| Generation | | | | ++ | | + | | + | | ++ |
| Sense of place | ++ | | + | ++ | +++ | +++ | ++ | + | +++ | + |
| Cultural resource of individual | + | | ++ | ++ | + | + | +++ | +++ | +++ | +++ |
| | | | | | | | + | + | ++ | ++ |

Notes: 1. B: Beijing
2. S: Shanghai
3. The number of '+' means the degree of strength in affecting the housing choice and accumulation of wealth. In each type, amount of '+' is 10, by which it shows the effect of each factor.

purchased a used apartment in the World Expo area of Pudong District. She discontinued renting her housing, and eventually established her own place for parents visiting in Shanghai. She usually travels on business both domestically and internationally, so she is familiar with some second-tier cities. According to her experiences purchasing housing in Shanghai, she realized the potential for the development of the housing market in these smaller cities. Therefore, she is open to the chances of working or investing in other cities and leaving Shanghai for settling down in other areas. She is satisfied with her present life in Shanghai, because owning two units of housing in Shanghai have brought her a feeling of safety and security. This type of middle class acquires wealth through their own abundant cultural resources but without the potential benefit from relations with the party-state.

According to the above analysis, the paper continues to illustrate how the factors affect the housing choice and wealth accumulation in each type of middle class (in Table 9.6).

## Conclusions and discussion: reinterpreting middle class from view of justice

This research has illustrated that a differentiation exists within the middle class, as evidenced by their housing choice and wealth accumulation. This middle class is divided into five types according to a different combination of factors, illustrating that even though common themes such as professionalism are shared, differentiation still exists due to the presence of other factors. This paper provides four findings. First, the two factors of "party-state" and "*hukou*" share mutual growth and decline in relation with "individual cultural resource." It means the middle class who are affected more by the factors of "party-state" and "*hukou*" share mutual growth and decline in an indirect relationship with "individual cultural resource." This means the middle class who are affected more by the facto of "party-state" and "*hukou*" in housing choice and wealth accumulation are less affected by "individual cultural resource." It also shows that the young professional middle class are more affected by "party-state" and "*hukou*" in housing choice and wealth accumulation. Second, "party-state" creates the most difference between the middle class in Beijing and Shanghai. The dual-track housing policy in Beijing allows a segment of the young professional middle class to obtain benefits from housing welfare providing by *danwei*. They possess better economic conditions than those who have no housing welfare from *danwei*. In addition to the relationship between *danwei* and the party-state, the parents' identity is a factor relating to party-state relations, which also affects housing choice and wealth accumulation of the young professional middle class. Shanghai middle class of type (II) and Shanghai/Beijing middle class of type (III) have their housing choices affected by the "party-state" as well, because their parents are natives and received welfare housing from their *danwei*. Therefore, the factors of "party-state" and "*hukou*" have included the effects from parents. Third, there is a relationship between the "sense of place" and "*hukou*." For non-native people, they need to hold a relatively flexible sense of place and focus on the potential of an area's development that helps them to accumulate wealth through purchasing housing. The last, the more middle class rely on abundant cultural resources to accumulate wealth, the less clear identity of social class they have. They don't agree that they are the so-called "middle class" or "new middle class" as befitting the general stereotypes found in society. They even believe they have fewer resources to accumulate wealth than their peers around them, especially due to unfair policies such as the dual-track housing policy in Beijing. This relative deprivation persuades them they have a weak identity or consider themselves at a lower level than the generally recognized image. Comparing to Beijing, the middle class in Shanghai within the type (IV) and (V) are more satisfied with their life than those affected by "*hukou*" and the dual-track housing policy which related to "party-state."

According to this study, young professional middle class acquire wealth through different methods, although they are generally considered as the same social class. There is inequality within the middle class, however they are given the same social responsibility and bear the same stigma, particularly under the "social justice" principle. This principle is reflected by moral criticisms of political correctness such as "hating corruption, but not hating rich" (chou fu˘ bu chou fu ). These veiled threats make the middle class uneasy even though they have gained their wealth through reputable means. Harvey (1996) illustrated the concept of "social justice" as something to be fought for as a key value within a class of political solidarity built across different places. However, because of the inequality within the middle class, the key and common value for political solidarity seems empty. This general image of the middle class has papered over the reality of inequality within the social class, which leads members of young professional middle class to suffer from the stigma of being wealthy but still shoulder the responsibility of striving for a harmonious society. Therefore, understanding the differences within the Chinese middle class and transferring the simplistic narratives could be a good strategy to remove the stigma from them and understand that the reform of *hukou* and the housing market is significant in achieving the real just harmonious society.

This research provides the following research to consider the inequality within the young professional middle class by investigating the effects of factors such as "party-state," "*hukou,*" "generation," and "sense of place," and explore the differentiated social justice to examine the class of the middle class. For the young professional middle class, they are not a homogeneous social class. Among them, some own respectable wealth by the conditions such as professionalism, others suffer from stress due to the relative deprivation stemming from the inequalities of certain policies. Therefore, will they contort themselves to the expectations and images of popular society and government and become the bedrock of a stable and harmonious society? It is still a question to be answered.

## Notes

1  According to the analysis of social class in China, 'Report of Contemporary Chinese Social Class Research', by the Chinese Academy of Social Sciences in 2002, China has to expand the middle class for stabilizing the socio-economic development. Then the report of 'The Analysis of Social Development Trend and Forecast in 2011' has demonstrated that the middle class has to be strengthened because they will help China "upgrade" its consumption structure. Those have given the middle class a role to create a stable society and economy in China.
2  Ten social class which include the stewardship class belongs to state and society (organizational resources), manager class (with cultural resources and organizational resources), private entrepreneurs (economic resources), and professional and technical-savvy (cultural resources), staffer class (with a small amount of cultural resources or organizational resources), individual business class (with a small amount of economic resources), and business services staff hierarchy (with very small amounts of three resources), the industrial working class (with very small amounts of three resources), agricultural laborers (with very small amounts of three resources), urban and rural unemployed, unemployment, semi-unemployment (totally short of three resources).
3  This report has defined the cultural resource (technology) as owning the recognized knowledge and skills (identified by a certificate or qualification).
4  Personal annual income is roughly between 60,000 to 500,000 yuan (about 6.15 per cent of the total population, about 80 million people). In addition to income indicators, the political elite, the bourgeois and professionals are included. Regarding the categories of occupation, those are including small-scale enterprises, the management of state-owned enterprises, professor and senior scientists, stockbrokers, real estate, banking and other financial, foreign or private companies white-collar workers, lawyers, accountants, singers, models, designers and athletes.
5  Dikeç (2001) proposed three notions: the spatial dialectics of injustice (the spatiality of justice and the injustice of spatiality), the right to the city, and the right to difference, as the parameters of an 'ideal of égaliberté' (equality-freedom)'.
6  According to the report of China's urban housing prices rankings on January and July 2010, the ranking of cities changed slightly, but Shanghai and Beijing have maintained the top three cities (Sina Real Estate Network, 2010.7.21). Therefore, the housing prices and issues of social spatial justice are often been discussed widespread in a variety of media in the two major cities.

# References

Agnew, J. (2005) 'Space: Place', in P. Cloke and R. Johnston (eds.) *Spaces of Geographical Thought*, London: Sage.

Bian, Yanjie (2002) 'Chinese social stratification and social mobility', *Annual Review of Sociology*, 28: 91–116.

Bian, Y. and Liu Y. (2005) 'Shehui fencing, zhufang chanquan yu juzhu zhilicng—dui zhongguó "wu pu" shuju de fenxi' ('Social stratification, home ownership, and quality of living: evidence from China's Fifth Census') in *She hui xue yan jiu (Sociology Studies)* 3, pp. 82–98.

Dikeç, M. (2001) 'Justice and the spatial imagination', *Environment and Planning A*, 33: 1785–805.

Fang, B. (2005) 'A capitalist paradise', *US News & World Report*, 138(23): 43.

Fleischer, F. (2007) '"To choose a house means to choose a lifestyle." The consumption of housing and class-structuration in urban China', *City & Society*, 19(2): 287–311.

Gao, Y. (2009) 'Gaige kaifang 30nian Beijing jieji jieceng jiegou de bianqian' ('The change of Beijing class structure in the 30 years of reform and opening up') in *Beijing shehui kexue Social (Science of Beijing)* 2, pp. 40–9.

Goodman, D. S. G. and Zang, X. (2008) 'Introduction: The new rich in China: the dimensions of social change', in D. S. G. Goodman (ed.) *The New Rich in China: Future Rulers, Present Lives*, New York: Routledge.

Gu, C. L. and Liu, H. Y. (2002) 'Social polarization and segregation in Beijing', in J. Logan (ed.) *The New Chinese City: Globalization and Market Reform*, Oxford: Blackwell.

Guo, Y. (2008) 'Class, stratum and group: The politics of description and prescription', in D. S. G. Goodman (ed.) *The New Rich in China: Future Rulers, Present Lives*, New York: Routledge.

Ha, B. and Liu, S. (2008) 'Xin shehui jieceng: she hui zhongjian jieceng de zhuti' ('New social stratum: the principal part in the center' in *Hebei shifan daxue xuebao (zhe xue she hui ke xue ban) (Journal of Hebei Normal University (Philosophy and Social Sciences Edition))* 31(5): 38–42.

Harvey, D. (1973) *Social Justice and the City*, London: The University of Georgia Press.

Harvey, D. (1988) *Social Justice and the City*, Oxford: Blackwell Publishers.

Harvey, D. (1996) *Justice, Nature & the Geography of Difference*, Oxford: Blackwell Publishers.

He, S. (2007) 'State-sponsored gentrification under market transition: the case of Shanghai', *Urban Affairs Review*, 43(2): 171–98.

Hu, X. H. and Kaplan, D. (2001) 'The emergence of affluence in Beijing: residential social stratification in China's capital city', *Urban Geography*, 22(2): 54–77.

Huang, Y. (2003) 'A room of one's own: housing consumption and residential crowding in transitional urban China', *Environment and Planning A*, 35: 591–614.

Huang, Y. (2004) 'Housing markets, government behaviors, and housing choice: a case study of three cities in China', *Environment and Planning A*, 36(1): 45–68.

Huang, Y. (2005) 'From work-unit compounds to gated communities: housing inequality and residential segregation in transitional Beijing', in J. C. Ma and F. Wu (eds) *Restructuring the Chinese City: Changing Society, Economy and Space*, London: Routledge.

Huang, Y. (2009) 'Housing inequality in transitional Beijing', *International Journal of Urban and Regional Research*, 33(4): 936–56.

Jiangmen, R. (24 June 2010) 'Zhongguo fangdichan shichang diaokong zhengce zonghui' ('The strategies of regulation of Chinese real estimate market') at http://www.wolai.com/news/2010–06-24/71591/

Johnston, R., Gregory, D., Pratt, G. and Watts, M. (eds) (2000) *The Dictionary of Human Geography* (4th ed.), Oxford: Blackwell.

Li, S. M. (2000a) 'Housing market and tenure decision in Chinese cities: a multivariate analysis of the case of Guangzhou', *Housing Studies*, 15(2): 213–36.

Li, S. M. (2000b) 'Housing consumption in urban China: a comparative study of Beijing and Guangzhou', *Environment and Planning A*, 32: 1115–34.

Li, S. M. (2003) 'Housing tenure and residential mobility in urban China: a study of commodity housing development in Beijing and Guangzhou', *Urban Affairs Review*, 38(4): 510–34.

Li, S. M. (2004) 'Life course and residential mobility in Beijing, China', *Environment and Planning A*, 36(1): 27–44.

Li, S. M. (2005) 'Residential mobility and urban change in China: What have we learned so far?' in J. C. Ma and F. Wu (eds) *Restructuring the Chinese City: Changing Society, Economy and Space*, London: Routledge.

Li, S. M. and Song Y. (2009) 'Redevelopment, displacement, housing conditions, and residential satisfaction: a study of Shanghai', *Environment and Planning A*, 41(5): 1090–108.

Li, T. (2008) *Hexie de yi fu—zhon guo xi xing she hui jieceng diaocha yu fenxi (Harmonious Musical Notation—The Investigation of Chinese New Rising Social Stratum)*, Beijing: Zhongguo fangzheng chubanshe.

Li, Z. (2010) *In Search Of Paradise: Middle-Class Living in a Chinese Metropolis*, Ithaca, NY: Cornell University Press.

Liang, X. (2011) *Zhon guo shehuoi ge jieceng fenxi (The Analysis of Chinese Social Stratum)*, Beijing: Wenhua yishu chubanshe.

Logan, J. R., Bian, Y. and Bian, F. (1999) 'Housing inequality in urban China in the. 1990s', *International Journal of Urban and Regional Research*, 23(March): 7–25.

Logan, J. R., Fang, Y. and Zhang, Z. (2010) 'The winners in China's urban housing reform', *Housing Studies*, 25(1): 101–17.

Lu, X. (2002) *Dangdai zhongguo shehui jieceng yanjiu baogao (The Report of Contemporary Chinese Social Stratum)*, Beijing: Shehui kexue wenxian chu ban she.

Meng, X. (2000) *Labour Market Reform in China*, Cambridge: Cambridge University Press.

Pow, C. P. (2007) 'Securing the "civilized" enclaves: gated communities and the moral geographies of exclusion in (post-)social Shanghai', *Urban Studies*, 44(8): 1539–58.

Pow, C. P. (2009) 'Neoliberalism and the aestheticization of new middle-class landscapes', *Antipod*, 41: 371–90.

Qiu, M. (2007) 'Zhongguo chengshi ju zhufen yi yanjiu' ('A research on residential division in China's cities: a viewpoint of social transformation') in *Cheng shi wen ti (Urban Problems)* 3: 94–9.

Renmin Wan Jiangnan Shibao (2004) 'Zhongguoren shenghuo xianzhuang diaocha: ni shi chengshi de xinfù ma?' ('The survey of Chinese living situation: are you the urban new rich?'), at http://news.eastday.com/eastday/news/news/node4946/node41913/userob-ject1ai696228.html

Shen, J. F. (2002) 'A study of the temporary population in Chinese cities', *Habitat International*, 26(3): 363–77.

Soja, Edward W. (2010) *Seeking Spatial Justice*, London: University of Minnesota Press.

Stanley, A. (2009) 'Just space or spatial justice? Difference, discourse, and environmental justice', *Local Environment*, 14(10): 999–1014.

Tomba, L. (2004) 'Creating an urban middle class: social engineering in Beijing', *The China Journal*, 51: 1–26.

Tomba, L. and Tang, B. (2008) 'The forest city: homeownership and new wealth in Shenyang', in D. S. G. Goodman (ed.) *The New Rich in China: Future Rulers, Present Lives*, New York: Routledge.

Unger, J. (2006) 'China's conservative middle class', *Far Eastern Economic Review*, April: 127–31.

Wang, D. and Li, S. M. (2004) 'Housing preferences in a transitional housing system: the case of Beijing, China', *Environment and Planning A*, 36 (1): 69–87.

Wang, Y. P. (2000) 'Housing reform and its impacts on the urban poor in China', *Housing Studies*, 15(6): 845–64.

Wu, F. (2004) 'Urban poverty and marginalization under market transition: the case of Chinese cities', *International Journal of Urban and Regional Research*, 28(2): 401–23.

Wu, W. (2002) 'Migrant housing in urban China: choices and constraints', *Urban Affairs Review*, 38(1): 90–119.

Xinlang Fandichan Wang (21 July 2010) 'Qi yue zhongguo baicheng fangjia paihangben chulu'('The billboard of housing price in Chinese 100 cities is coming on July') at http://news.dichan.sina.com.cn/2010/07/21/187902.html

Xinlang Wang Guoji Xiangqu Daobao (15 November 2004) 'Zhongguo xinfu jieceng diaocha: guanxin shehui xiangshou shenghuo'('China's new rich class survey: care for the community to enjoy life') at http://finance.sina.com.cn/money/shdkt/20041115/14251155580.shtml

Xuan, G., Xu, J. and Zhao, J. (2006) 'Shanghaishi zhongxin chengqu shehui fènxi' ('Social areas of the central urban area in Shanghai') in *Di li yan jiu (Geographical Research)* 25(3): 526–38.

Yang, J. (2011) *Zhongguo dangdai shehui jieceng fenxi (The Analysis of Contemporary Social Stratum)*, Jiangxi: Gaoxiao chubanshe.

Young, I. M. (1990) *Justice and Politics of Differences*, New Jersey: Princeton University Press.

Zhang, L. (2010) *In Search of Paradise: Middle-Class Living in a Chinese Metropolis*, New York: Cornell University Press.

Zheng, S. and Liu, H. (2004) 'Yi zhufang ziyouhualu pouxi zhufang xiaofei de liangzhong fangshi' ('The analysis of two types of housing and consumption through the owning ratio') in *Jingji yu guanli yanjiu (Economy and Management Studies)* 4: 28–31.

Zhou, X. (2010) 'Quanqiuhua, shehui zhuanxing yu zhongchan jieji de jiangou—yi zhongguo wei duixiang de bijiao yanjiu' ('Globalization, social transformation and construction of middle class—a comparative study of China') in *Jiangsu hangzheng xuebao (The Journal of Jiangsu Administration Institute)* 1: 61–9.

Zhou, Y. (2006) 'Chengzhen zhufang shichang de fenhua he biandong—20shiji 90niandai zhufang xiaofei tisheng de zhuyao yuanyin' ('Heterogeneity and dynamics in China's emerging housing market: factors behind increasing housing consumption in the late 1990s') in *Zhongguo renkou kexue (Chinese Journal of Population Science)* 5: 50–9.

# 10 Living the networked life in the commodity housing estates

## Everyday use of online neighborhood forums and community participation in urban China

*Limei Li and Si-ming Li*

### Introduction

A post appeared on Jiangwaijiang (JWJ), an online neighborhood forum of Riverside Garden, addressing to users to discuss affairs of the housing estate, then and now[1]. It received thousands of views and hundreds of replies. People marveled at how it has changed from a tranquil suburban resort to a full-fledged urban community in a decade. Riverside Garden is one of the earliest commodity housing estates in Panyu, Guangzhou. It was open to market in 1992 and currently accommodates some 12,000 households and occupies an area of 0.81 km². The networked lives epitomized by residents of Riverside Garden serve a prototype of commodity housing estates in urban China, the residential experience in which is a total departure from what previous generations of Chinese urbanites experienced in the work-unit compounds.

China has transformed from a nation of public housing tenants to a nation of private homeowners since the launching of urban housing reform in the late 1980s. Public housing was sold to sitting tenants with subsidized price. Housing market was introduced and leaped forward after the termination of welfare housing allocation in 1998. Until the late-1990s, work units or the state were still the main housing providers. Census data show that in 2000, about 24 per cent urban households lived in privatized public housing and 14 per cent rented public housing. In 2010, these two figures decreased to 13 and 3 per cent, respectively. In contrast, the share of commodity housing owners increased from 9 per cent in 2000 to 22 per cent in 2010. Commodity housing has become the new aspiration for Chinese urbanites.

This transformation to a private housing regime has changed the ways urban residents experience their lives. To many it means an end to their dependence on their work unit or the state, at least in the domestic area. Homeownership has given them a degree of autonomy over housing and community that was not possible before. Commodity housing estates differ from work unit compounds in three aspects: the commodification of community services, private governance, and social composition (Wu, 2005). As markets gain ground and community services are commodified, homeowners have to deal with the developer and the property management company. Housing price filters people from different places with similar social-economic status to the same housing compound. In commodity housing estates it is the shared property interest rather than work-unit affiliation that determines patterns of interaction among neighbors. The traits of anonymity and heterogeneity begin to prevail. Homeowners cherish the newly found privacy, which contrasts control and supervision in the work-unit compound. But the infringements of property rights are common occurrences in the ill-regulated housing market, compelling homeowners to engage in neighborhood activism to defend their rights and even to go beyond the community to pursue public interest. A double movement of privatized living and public sphere activism is a distinctive feature of commodity housing estates in Chinese cities today (Zhang, 2010).

The penetration of the Internet has coincided with the construction of commodity housing estates. The wiring of residential development with local networks has become the norm. Online neighborhood forum, one form of community networks, emerges as the rising social groups of homeowners and homeowners-to-be seek to improve their position in housing consumption and management (Li and Li, 2013). This chapter sets out to understand how people change when they become homeowners, how they integrate the Internet in daily lives in commodity housing estates, and how it affects community participation.

In the next sections, we first discuss the practice of community networks and its effects on community interaction and participation. Then, we describe our research setting, data and methods. Deriving data from two household surveys in Guangzhou, we portrait the profiles of residents in the commodity housing estates in Panyu. We analyze their everyday use of online neighborhood forum and community participation based on ethnographic data of Riverside Garden and JWJ. To conclude, we discuss the socio-political implications of homeownership and community networks in urban China.

## Community networks, neighborhood interaction and community participation

Community is a long-lasting topic of inquiry in social science research. It was first raised against the backdrop of industrialization and urbanization at the end of nineteenth century. Scholars have grappled with the question of whether community is lost or saved. The debates continue with the advancement of new technologies, be it telegraph, telephone, television, or more recently the Internet. The community question becomes more complicated in contemporary networked society with a triple revolution — phenomenal reconfigurations of social networks, the rise of the Internet and the advent of mobile connectivity (Rainie and Wellman, 2012). Early answers to the effects of Internet use on community are pessimistic, reporting that heavy Internet use is associated with reductions in face-to-face contact and social involvement (e.g. Stoll, 1995; Graham and Marvin, 1996; Kraut *et al.*, 1998; Putnam, 2000; Nie and Erbring, 2000). On the opposite of the debate is that the Internet can provide a means and space of sociability and create virtual communities for individuals with shared interests, characteristics, or values (e.g. Rheingold, 1993; Wellman and Gulia, 1999). With the integration of the Internet with everyday life, more studies support the positive effects on social interactions and networks (e.g. Rainie, *et al.*, 2000; Katz and Rice, 2002; Wang and Wellman, 2010). The emerging consensus is that Internet use will simultaneously reduce, create, and reinforce a community (Lyon and Driskell, 2012). The Internet provides new opportunities for social interaction but they may increase privatism by isolating people in their home. A third argument, "community liberated," shifts the focus of inquiry from geographic communities to the study of networks of social relations (Wellman, *et al.*, 1997; Wellman, 2001). The geography of people's social networks are sparsely knit and spatially dispersed instead of being bound up within a single geographic area. With the technologies and heightened population mobility, people may be more embedded in networks that stretch beyond the place rather than connecting to their neighbors (Amin, 2010).

In this chapter we contend that geographic community still matters in the age of global communications. While the Internet can encourage and maintain social ties across great distance, it can also reinforce and regenerate community in the geographic sense (Kitchin and Dodge, 2002; Haythornthwaite and Kendall, 2010). Meanwhile, geographic place can facilitate the formation of online identity (Kang, 2009; Erickson, 2010). We focus on community networks, which create an electronic space supporting by technology infrastructure and applications in a geographic community to provide community-specific information to residents (Virnoche, 1998). Community networks emphasize access to technology, local information and community discussion (Longan, 2002). While anyone connected to the Internet can seek local or non-local information and communication online, the presence of a local portal aggregates information of potential interest to residents and helps to build a critical mass of users within a geographic area (Kavanaugh, *et al.*, 2005a).

There has been a community networking movement in North America (Longan, 2002). It is often initiated by NGOs, universities or business connections, to enhance the civic life or to serve the disadvantaged community. Examples include the Seattle Community Network (Schuler, 1996), the Big Sky Telegraph in Montana (Uncapher, 1999), Netville in Toronto (Hampton and Wellman, 1999), and the Blacksburg Electronic Village in Virginia (Carroll, 2005). Hampton and his collaborators experimentally provided Netvillle with Internet connectivity and a variety of community networking tools and found that: (1) Internet use is associated with larger neighborhood networks, neighbor recognition, greater frequency of online and offline communication among neighbors (Hampton and Wellman, 2003); (2) Internet use helps to build local ties and thus facilitates the organization of collective action and community participation (Hampton, 2003). Longitudinal studies in the Blacksburg Electronic Village show that community network can facilitate civic participation and strengthen social contact and community attachment (Kavanaugh, *et al.*, 2005a; 2005b).

Similar community networks are also found outside North America. Studies in Jerusalem, Israel find that membership in the neighborhood-based electronic forum strengthens neighborhood social ties, and has a positive effect on community involvement and place attachment (Mesch and Levanon, 2003; Mesch and Talmud, 2010). The young and well-educated people in Poznan, Poland, are creating online communities for their housing estates and using them in neighborly relations and real-life actions (Kotus and Hławka, 2010). Similar use of online neighborhood forum is observed in Guangzhou and Xiamen, China (Li and Li, 2013; Huang and Yip, 2012).

Empirical evidences from different countries indicate community networks have the potential to facilitate neighborhood social interactions, enhance community satisfaction, and increase community participation. Community networks evolve with technological progress, be it neighborhood email lists, websites, bulletin boards or online forums, instant messaging, or microblogging. People may change the ways to maintain social ties, but social interactions in geographic community, offline and online, still exist. Physical space and cyberspace interpenetrate. Note that many community networks in North America were externally introduced. This study, however, investigates an internally developed online neighborhood forum initiated and maintained by the residents of a commodity housing estate in Panyu, Guangzhou.

## The research setting

This chapter draws on two data sources. First, two urban household surveys[2] conducted in Guangzhou in 2005 and 2010 respectively provide information on the socio-economic profiles and use of online neighborhood forum of the residents of selected commodity housing estates in Panyu. Panyu is separated from the Guangzhou City proper[3] by the Pearl River in the north. The population of Panyu reached 1.77 million (of whom 43 per cent were migrants), accounting for 14 per cent of Guangzhou's total in 2010 (see Figure 10.1). Due to its proximity to Guangzhou and Hong Kong, Panyu has experienced one of the earliest real estate developments in China. The completion of Luoxi Bridge in 1988 improved Panyu's access to downtown Guangzhou and set residential suburbanization in motion. Developers built homes for better-off families in Guangzhou as well as people from Hong Kong and neighboring cities. These residences offered a full range of community services and a high-quality living environment with a cheaper price than was available in the city. The building boom of commodity housing and mass suburbanization, however, did not come until after the completion of Panyu Bridge and Huanan Expressway in 1999 and Guangzhou's annexation of Panyu into an urban district in 2000. A third bridge linking Panyu to Guangzhou, Xingguang Bridge, was opened in 2007. Two subway lines were extended to Panyu in 2006 and 2010, respectively.

Transportation improvements fueled commodity housing development. Major commodity housing estates were located along the south-north arteries leading to downtown Guangzhou. Figure 10.2 shows the commodity housing space completed and sold in Panyu between 1990 and 2010. The sum of commodity housing floor area completed, sold, and the contracted sales value in Panyu accounted for 21, 22, and 18 per cent of the city total. The exodus of population

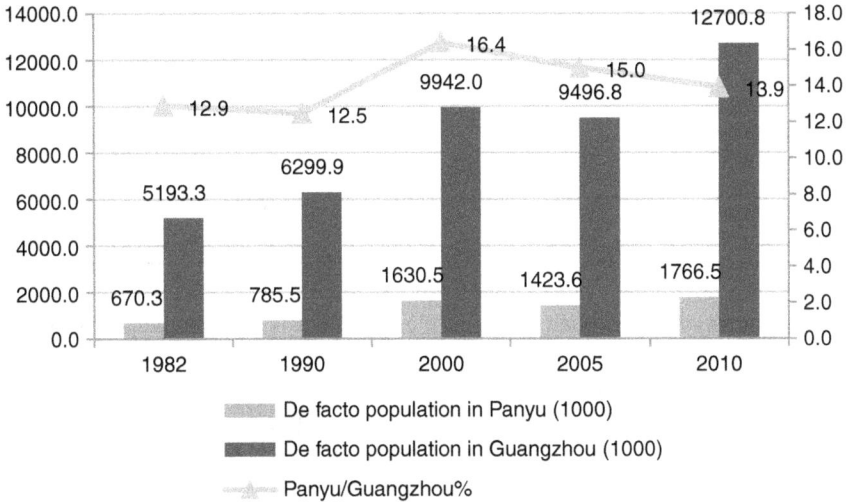

*Figure 10.1* Population of Panyu and its share in Guangzhou.
Sources: Census 1982; 1990; 2000; 2010 and 2005 1% population sample survey.

from the central city and the arrival of well-educated migrants in their home-buying age, sorted by economic affordability, result in the agglomeration of middle-class housing estates in Panyu. Three commodity housing estates were sampled in the 2005 survey, namely, Riverside Garden, Luoxi New Town and Star River. In the 2010 survey, a fourth sample, Clifford Estate was added, to take account of the expanding contiguous built-up area of the city. Table 10.1 lists the distribution of respondents in the two surveys.

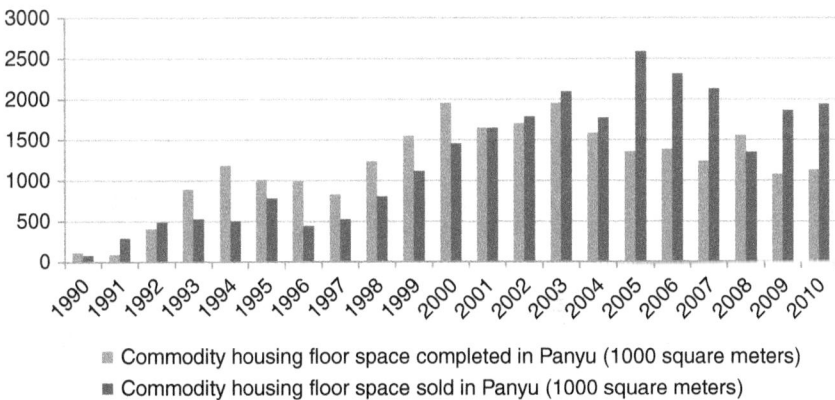

*Figure 10.2* Commodity housing development in Panyu, 1990–2010.
Sources: Guangzhou Statistical Yearbook, 1991–2011.

*Table 10.1* Distribution of respondents in the commodity housing estates of Panyu

| Sampled housing estates | 2005 | | 2010 | |
|---|---|---|---|---|
| | *N* | *%* | *N* | *%* |
| Riverside Garden | 50 | 40 | 25 | 25 |
| Luoxi New Town | 50 | 40 | 25 | 25 |
| Star River | 25 | 20 | 24 | 24 |
| Clifford Estate | – | – | 25 | 25 |
| Total | 125 | 100 | 99 | 100 |

Accompanying commodity housing development is the emergence of online neighborhood forums, which brings together residents living in the same neighborhood to discuss housing and neighborhood related issues (Li and Li, 2013). The second part of our analyses is based on ethnographic data gathered from a commodity housing estate, Riverside Garden, and JWJ, an online forum of the estate established in 2002, one of the earliest neighborhood forums in the country. It was established at the initiative of a few residents of Riverside Garden to provide an Internet platform for community life. It soon gained popularity and recorded heavy traffic. The management group had to solicit donations from users to buy a server to accommodate the rising traffic. As of October 16, 2012, there were 80,790 registered users, 30 per cent of whom had published at least one post. The total volume of posts reached 3.67 million. From 2002 to 2012, JWJ produces 984 posts a day on average. Every registered user publishes about 30 posts and every post receives about 13 replies. Figure 10.3 displays the growth of monthly added posts. According to Alexa Traffic Rank, JWJ attains a rank of 2,125 in Guangzhou[4]. This is quite an achievement considering that JWJ is not a commercial endeavor. Since its inception, it has been financed by users' donations and managed by a group of volunteers without any remuneration. The millions of posts and threads on JWJ over the span of 10 years provide rich information to understand residents' lives and social interactions.

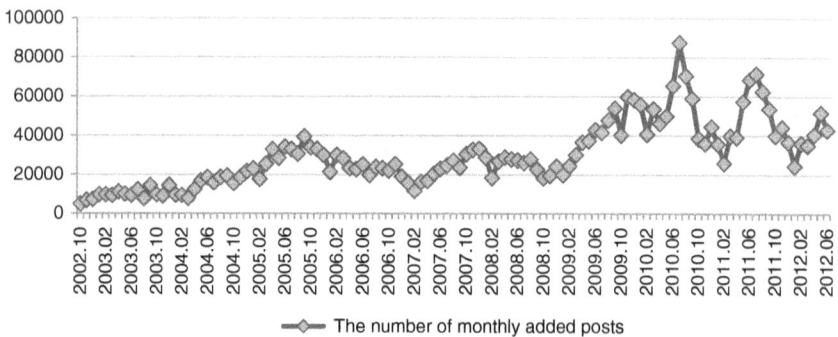

*Figure 10.3* The number of monthly added posts on JWJ, 2002–2012.

Source: Online. Available HTTP: <http://www.rg-gd.net/stats.php> (accessed July 4, 2012).

*Table 10.2* Socio-economic characteristics of residents in 2005 and 2010

| Socio-economic variables | 2005 (N=125) | 2010 (N=99) |
|---|---|---|
| Age (median) | 32 | 37 |
| Sex (per cent male) | 70.4 | 66.7 |
| Marital status (per cent married) | 72.0 | 91.9 |
| Household size (mean) | 2.8 | 3.6 |
| Education attainment (per cent tertiary) | 58.4 | 75.8 |
| CCP (CCP membership) | 17.6 | 30.3 |
| Occupation (per cent working in the high-end service sectors) | 38.4 | 41.4 |
| Work unit type (per cent non-state sectors) | 63.2 | 63.6 |

## Socio-economic profiles of residents in the commodity housing estates in Panyu

The median age of the 2010 sample is 37, five years older than that of the 2005 sample. The share of male correspondents of the 2010 sample is slightly lower than that of the 2005 (67 vs. 70 per cent). Over a span of five years, some residents would have experienced a sequence of marital and fertility events. The share of single people decreased from 25 per cent in 2005 to 7 per cent in 2010, while the share of married people increased from 72 to 92 per cent. Mean household size increased from 2.8 to 3.6. The two samples represent a highly educated segment of the population. About 76 per cent of the 2010 sample and 58 per cent of the 2005 sample received college education, much higher than the Guangzhou average (19 per cent in 2010). The 2010 sample has more Chinese Communist Party (CCP) members than the 2005 sample (30 vs. 18 per cent). As for occupation, the 2010 sample has a slightly higher percentage of people working in the high-end service sectors[5] (41 vs. 38 per cent). A substantial proportion of them (64 and 63 per cent for 2010 and 2005 samples) work in non-state enterprises (see Table 10.2).

Both samples are homeowner-dominated, 82 per cent for the 2005 sample and 93 for the 2010 one. Both far exceed the average homeownership rate of Panyu at the respective times of survey (63 per cent in 2005 and 59 per cent in 2010). The respondents of the 2010 sample live in newer, larger and more expensive apartments, as compared to those of the 2005 sample. The lengths of residence for the 2005 and 2010 samples are 4 and 6 years, respectively (see Table 10.3).

*Table 10.3* Comparison of housing conditions between 2005 and 2010

| Housing conditions | 2005 (N=125) | 2010 (N=99) |
|---|---|---|
| Home ownership | 81.6 | 92.9 |
| Housing age (per cent built in the 2000s) | 31.2 | 77.8 |
| Residential floor area (median, square meter) | 80 | 100 |
| Housing price (median, 1000 RMB) | 390 | 500 |
| Length of residence (mean, year) | 4 | 6 |

*Table 10.4* Comparison of current and previous *hukou* place in 2005 and 2010

| Hukou *place (%)* | 2005 | | 2010 | |
| --- | --- | --- | --- | --- |
| | *Current* | *Previous* | *Current* | *Previous* |
| Panyu | 44.8 | 15.2 | 73.7 | 28.2 |
| Other districts in Guangzhou | 33.6 | 39.2 | 10.1 | 16.2 |
| Outside Guangzhou | 21.6 | 45.6 | 16.2 | 55.6 |

Comparison of the current and previous *hukou* place reveals the migratory status of the residents (see Table 10.4). In 2005, nearly half of respondents (46 per cent) were migrants and only 15 per cent held the Panyu *hukou* before they bought a property here. However, the settlement in Panyu enabled some to have acquired the Panyu *hukou* so that 45 per cent actually held it at the time of survey. In the 2010 sample, 56 per cent were from places outside Guangzhou, but 74 per cent held the Panyu *hukou*.

To recapitulate, the survey findings show that residents of the commodity housing estates in Panyu are mainly highly educated professionals and homeowners in their child-rearing age. Half of them have in-migrated from somewhere else. After settling down in Panyu, many have moved their *hukou* registration to Panyu. The profiles of these residents fit the most wired segment of the population, which partly explains their wide adoption of the Internet. According to the China Internet Network Information Center (CNNIC, 2012), Chinese cyberspace is dominated by people in their twenties and thirties (46 per cent in 2011). Internet use is also positively related to education attainment. Among people with tertiary education, 96 per cent reported that they went online.

## Everyday use of online neighborhood forum and community participation

The two surveys asked questions about the presence and use of online neighborhood forum. About 36 per cent reported that their community had an online forum in 2005, and 32 per cent reported the same in 2010. But the respondents of the 2010 sample were more active users: 21 per cent reported they had registered on the online forum; 8 per cent said they had attended activities organized through the online forum; and 7 per cent stated that they had donated to the online forum[6] (see Table 10.5).

We use JWJ as an example to analyze the everyday use of the online neighborhood forum. There are three types of users: visitors, registered members, and authenticated members. Visitors usually outnumber the registered and authenticated members. Visitors can browse the majority of posts but they cannot contribute unless they provide a verified email address to register. Registered members can post, reply, download files, or send private message to fellow users. Authenticated members enjoy more rights, such as interacting on the exclusive forum and involving in the forum's management. A registered member cannot get an authenticated status until

*Table 10.5* The establishment of online neighborhood forums in 2005 and 2010

| Per cent yes | 2005 (N=125) | 2010 (N=99) |
|---|---|---|
| Does your community have online forum? | 36.0 | 32.3 |
| Have you registered on the online forum? | 3.2 | 21.2 |
| Have you attended activities organized through the online forum? | – | 8.1 |
| Have you donated to the online forum? | – | 7.0 |

he/she meets certain preconditions: having published over 100 posts; and having two moderators, or one moderator and two authenticated users who have gained the status for a year as referees. The referees should meet the applicant in person and have his/her contact information. One person can have only one authenticated ID. Those who have more than one authenticated IDs by deception would be deprived of their authenticated status. These measures assure users that they are interacting with real people and help to circumvent problems arising from anonymity and build trust and community. Users of JWJ address each other "soy sauce (*jiangyou*)," a homophone for "friend of river" in Chinese. Between 2004 and 2012, about 716 registered members had applied for and were granted authenticated membership. One user remarked:

> What distinguishes JWJ from other BBSs (bulletin board systems) is that it is real. There is a real person behind every ID … Certainly JWJ is not my only social network. I have networks from work, school and families. But such a unique community like JWJ is irreplaceable.
>
> (VZ, July 14, 2004)

JWJ creates 20 sub-forums under three themes to cater for different needs. The first is entitled as "I love my home," devoting to housing and community issues. Eight sub-forums are under this theme: Living Room of Riverside Garden, Waste Incineration and Environmental Protection, In the Name of Love, On Housing and Neighborhood, Free Market, Domestic Life, Kids Fun, and Car Pool. The second is named as "To ride one's hobby-horse," which includes 11 sub-forums: Sports Zone, Society, News and History, Photography, Tool Kits, From 9 am to 5 pm, Travel and Outing, Finance and Investment, Literary Writings, English Corner, Films and Music, and Pets. The third is for board management. A content analysis of 3.4 million posts on JWJ reveals its topic distribution (see Table 10.6). The majority of posts are related to housing and neighborhood issues (46 per cent). The second most frequent category, accounting for 24 per cent of the messages, is consumption-related, such as the exchange of unused goods. Leisure and hobbies, and domestic lives, rank the third and fourth (17 and 7 per cent). Mutual help among users is common, such as a car pool. Users also extend their help for the larger society. A sub-forum devoting to charity organization, In the Name of Love, was established in 2003. In 2007, JWJ was awarded "The Advanced Unit on Blood Donation" and one moderator was named "Advanced Individual on

*Table 10.6* Categorical topics of posts and threads on JWJ

|  | Postcounts (thousand) | % |
|---|---|---|
| Housing and neighborhood-related issues | 1540 | 45.6 |
| Shopping and consumption | 820 | 24.3 |
| Leisure and hobbies | 560 | 16.6 |
| Domestic lives | 250 | 7.4 |
| Society, news and history | 100 | 3.0 |
| Mutual help | 60 | 1.8 |
| Board management | 40 | 1.2 |
| Charity | 10 | 0.3 |
| Total | 3380 | 100 |

Source: Online. Available HTTP: <http://www.rg-gd.net/forum.php> (accessed October 17, 2012).

Blood Donation" by the Blood Center of Panyu[7]. The money awarded was donated to the charity fund of JWJ. One user explained why he participated:

> JWJ would report every contribution, expenditure and the distribution process of charity activities. This responsible way can ease the donators' mind. Therefore, I would not only make a donation, but also ask my relatives and friends to participate.
>
> (Big bull, December 5, 2012)

Thousands of posts turn up every day; JWJ tries to organize them in order to mitigate information overloading. In 2005, JWJ set up a sub-forum, Communication Voices, to provide a dialogue platform between the authenticated users and the property management company. The property management company got an ID as "Customer services" to handle complaints and suggestions from residents and to post notices on community issues. The moderator of Communication Voices, a homeowner who has the expertise on property management, specifies that only authenticated members can post and reply on this sub-forum. He urges users to engage in a rational dialogue and avoid posting irrelevant messages, or *guanshui*[8]. Between 2005 and 2012, Communication Voices recorded 7,795 posts. An analysis of the 865 thread titles reveals that customer services or the property management company is the most frequently addressed. Concerns from homeowners, such as problems, complaints, suggestions and demands, rank the second. The most common issues are transportation, including car, parking, roads, and bus; utilities; and security and hygiene (see Table 10.7). Online communications extend to offline activities. Several moderators had three meetings with the property management company to discuss the most concerned issues. Meeting minutes were posted promptly, which aroused users' awareness and responses. Notwithstanding the high thresholds required for participation, the emphasis on accountability contributed to the formation of a critical mass of active users (Granovetter, 1978; Markus, 1987).

> I moved to Riverside Garden in 2003. I have witnessed many changes, be it good or bad. But I have been a free-rider and have yet to do anything for it.

I feel ashamed of myself. Thank you for your efforts to improve our home-stead. Now I would like to offer my suggestions ...

(Big chimpanzee, November 17, 2011)

Observations of online and offline interactions reveal four ways of community participation: common grievances, common threats, common amenities, and common attributes (Li and Li, 2013). The former two are passive responses prompted by rights violation; while the latter two are initiated to serve residents' agendas, be it expressive or instrumental. First, residents participate passively, as a response to rights-violating incidents. The second is the reactions to "common threats," more specifically, events that will inflict negative impacts on the community. The third is initiated by residents to pursue "common amenities" for the neighborhood and even the society at large. The fourth is organized for expressive purposes based on common attributes, such as the same place of origin.

An example of how residents would act when encountering the common threat was their opposition to the construction of a waste incineration power plant. In September 2009, news came out that a waste incinerator would be built in Panyu. Posts calling for resistance appeared on JWJ. A sub-forum, Waste Incineration and Environmental Protection, was created, where residents could discuss strategies, organize resistance actions, and report progress. Several activists held meetings and collected signatures door to door for petition. Then they presented it to the Environmental Bureau of Guangzhou. To arouse public attention, one homeowner toured Subway Line 3, wearing a mask and specially-made T-shirt to protest against the waste incineration on November 8, 2009. She reported her action on JWJ, which received 742 replies and 47,692 views and was cross-posted to other online forums[9]. On November 23, 2009, when thousands of residents took to the street to stage a protest against waste incineration, JWJ witnessed a record of 1156

*Table 10.7* Word frequencies of the thread titles on Communication Voices

|  | Word frequencies | % |
| --- | --- | --- |
| Customer service/property management company | 279 | 32.3 |
| Problems/complaints/suggestions/demands | 175 | 20.2 |
| Car/parking | 140 | 16.2 |
| Utilities(electricity, water, and gas) | 116 | 13.4 |
| Riverside garden | 91 | 10.5 |
| Security guard/security/robbery/break-in | 79 | 9.1 |
| Door/entrance/gate | 78 | 9.0 |
| Roads | 72 | 8.3 |
| Hygiene/garbage/mosquito/rat | 71 | 8.2 |
| Service | 56 | 6.5 |
| Shuttle bus/bus/transportation | 44 | 5.1 |
| Notice/reminder | 36 | 4.2 |
| Total | 865 | 100 |

Source: Online. Available HTTP: <http://www.rg-gd.net/forum.php?mod=forumdisplay&fid=37> (accessed October 22, 2012).

online visitors in real-time. On the next day, JWJ witnessed another record of 3,333 postcounts. In December 2009, another homeowner initiated a face-to-face dialogue with the (Chinese Communist) Party Secretary of Panyu, who then accepted the invitation and came to meet the residents. Facing the continuous resistances, the Panyu District Government gave in and suspended the project[10]. But discussions continue on JWJ. Some residents realize that Not in My Backyard (NIMBY) is not the final solution. They organize workshops and debate ways of disposing waste, post waste classification practices of other countries, and promote green living. They fight against the construction of a waste incinerator in their neighborhood as well as somewhere else.

The story of "soy sauce" bridge illustrates how residents are willing to participate for common amenities. A small bridge connecting Riverside Garden to the subway station was broken. One homeowner took pictures of it and posted on JWJ. In the course of online discussions, someone suggested raising money to replace it. Another user, who is a civil engineer, proposed a solution and offered to do the construction for free. Within ten days, JWJ raised enough money to rebuild the bridge. The original poster was touched and published a message saying that when everyone adds fuel, the flames rise higher.

> I moved to Riverside Garden only a year ago. All my families like our neighbors and environment here. We even find fellow villagers among neighbors. I am more than happy to do a small deed for neighbors.
>
> (Che Guevara, November 9, 2011).

> Thanks for the bridge construction, I get to know many neighbors and we become friends.
>
> (Che Guevara, November 30, 2011)

In certain circumstances, however, it is difficult to reach a consensus about the common amenities. The controversy over the installment of elevators to the nine-story buildings in Riverside Garden is a case in point. People are debating about whether to install an elevator and how much cost occupants on different floors should bear. The major difference lies between the high- and low-floor occupants. Clearly the elevator would bring substantial benefits to the high-floor occupants, who would then not have to climb up many stories of staircase and who would at the same time see the value of their home having appreciated. However, the low-floor occupants have to bear the cost of noise and possible negative impacts on ventilation and lighting, not to mention the future rise in management fee and home value depreciation, at least in relative terms; obviously most of them would not support such an initiative. Ultimately, only one building successfully got the elevator installed. In this case it took the initiators two years to get the agreements from two-thirds of occupants and another one and a half year to get the building permit from the authorities.

Riverside Garden is a commodity housing estate built from scratch. Residents from different places have to adapt their lives in the new neighborhood. One frequent theme of posts is to initiate and organize offline activities based on common attributes, such as games for sport fans and dinner gathering for fellow folks. A jargon, FB[11], is coined to describe the get-together activities organized through online forum.

> JWJ is different from the common Internet platform. Many of us are living in the same neighborhood. There is a good chance to meet each other face-to-face, not to mention the FB activities initiated and organized online. This is the best example of the combination of virtual and real community. Many people like JWJ and treat it as the online homestead. There are also people who don't like JWJ because they encounter unhappy incidents, like their posts being deleted, ID account being blocked, and online arguments.
>
> (Aguang, July 19, 2005)

To avoid trouble with the authorities and keep the forum running, JWJ maintains a degree of self-censorship and refrains from discussing banned subjects, especially politically sensitive topics. Moderators would delete post and block ID when they deem necessary. One moderator explained after he moved a sensitive post:

> JWJ is not a tool to fight tyranny or denounce social injustice or lighten the darkness. It is a space for friends of River to discuss domestic and community issues, to exchange unused goods, to exchange skills about photography, to share food recipes, etc.... In the history of JWJ, more than one friends of River were taken away due to sensitive posts. More than once JWJ received warning from the authorities due to sensitive posts. We don't want to see any of these happening again.
>
> (Scurrying in the wind, October 26, 2012)

## Summary and discussion

Based on survey and ethnographic data from Panyu, Guangzhou, this chapter focuses on middle-class homeowners and examines their networked lives in commodity housing estates and the different ways of community participation. As one of the most wired groups in China, homeowners are familiar with practices of community networking in everyday life. Online neighborhood forum is one of the web applications they use. The household surveys found that over 30 per cent reported their community had an online forum and over 20 per cent had registered on the forum in 2010. They use it to exchange information on housing purchase and local services, to discuss property management, and to organize community activities. Besides the instrumental purposes, they also reach out to the community for expressive needs.

Ethnographic observations on JWJ, an online forum established by residents of Riverside Garden, show four ways of community participation: common grievances, common threats, common amenities and common attributes. These middle-class homeowners have capacity to pull resources to participate in the community affairs, often in a spontaneous and informal way. Many are generous with their money, time, expertise, and efforts to take actions with good causes. Collective actions are not strange to them, the sustained protests against the waste incinerator, the donations and building of the "soy sauce" bridge, the regular charity activities and the decade-long streams of donations and efforts to maintain JWJ, to name just a few. Yet for the majority of users, JWJ is a neighborhood communicative platform for domestic trivia and social interaction. The development of JWJ seems to have been synchronizing with the life courses of many users: from renters to homeowners, from single to married, and from newlyweds to new parents.

As many scholars have observed, Chinese middle-class homeowners are moderate and take actions within the state's restrictions (Cai, 2005; Chen, 2005). They opt for a strategy of carefully separating themselves from any organizations to avoid governments' vigilance. In their efforts to stop the waste incinerator, activists emphasize that there is no organization whatsoever and homeowners act entirely of their own volition. They use the Internet as an organizing agent, to create networks of homeowners, communicate their views and coordinate their actions. Protest and organizational work take place both online and offline, using technologies of different capabilities. The far-flung networks use an assemblage of online forums, instant messaging, texting, blog and microblogging in computers, smart phones, and other mobile devices to function; this allows homeowners to engage in connective actions that are individualized and technologically organized (Bennett and Segerberg, 2012).

Empowered by private homeownership and technologies, Chinese homeowners have carved out a space both online and offline for community participation within the limits tolerated by the state. There is a chance, however, that over time some of them might become citizens, passively or actively, engaging in the civic life of their community and beyond. One homeowner has become more outspoken on the public affairs since he participated in the actions against the waste incinerator. He reflected in an essay titled "We can become a citizen this way", which appeared in a newspaper as well as on the online forums:

> People say an individual cannot achieve anything by oneself. Through my experience last year, I believe it is possible to find a way to communicate with the increasingly open government. Only when more people are concerned with the making and implementation of public policy can the administration transparency be improved.
>
> (Basuo fengyun, December 24, 2010)

## Acknowledgements

This study is supported by Hong Kong Research Grants Council under the General Research Fund (Grant No. HKBU245511) and a grant from the National Natural Science Foundation of China (Grant No.41101134).

## Notes

1 This post was published on November 24, 2012. Online, Available HTTP: <http://www.rg-gd.net/forum.php?mod=viewthread&tid=318581> (accessed December 10, 2012).
2 The two surveys were conducted by a research team of Hong Kong Baptist University led by Prof. Li Si-ming and his collaborators in Guangzhou. A multi-level probability proportional to size (PPS) in respect to population distribution over space sampling strategy was adopted in the two surveys. The two surveys also used largely the same questionnaire, with some revision in the 2010 survey.
3 Panyu has witnessed multiple changes in terms of its administrative status. Panyu had been a county under the administration of Guangzhou since 1975. In 1992, Panyu changed its status from a county to a county-level city. Although it was still under Guangzhou's jurisdiction, Panyu city enjoyed independent power to contract large foreign investment projects and land lease. In 2000, Guangzhou annexed Panyu, together with Huadu, to one of its urban districts. In 2005, the southern part of Panyu was designated as a new district, Nansha. Land area of Panyu decreases from 1314 to 786 square kilometers.
4 Source: Alexa Traffic Rank, Online, Available HTTP:<http://www.alexa.com/siteinfo/rg-gd.net#> (accessed October 12, 2012).
5 Here the high-end service sectors include the Finance, Insurance, and Real Estate sector, Education, Culture, Arts and Radio Broadcasting, Film and Television sector, Scientific Research and Technologies service sector, and Governmental and party organs and social organization, and the Transportation and Telecommunication sector.
6 To provide a rough international comparison, a PEW Internet survey reported that 4 per cent of Americans stated that they belonged to a neighborhood email list or Internet discussion forum for their neighborhood in 2009 (Hampton *et al.*, 2009). Another PEW Internet survey report published in 2010 found that one in five Americans use digital tools to communicate with neighbors and monitor community development (Smith, 2010).
7 See the list from the website of Blood Center of Panyu, Online. Available HTTP:<http://www.pyxz.org/tabid/59/ItemID/13/Default.aspx> (accessed December 5, 2012).
8 In Chinese online forums, a practice known as pouring water, or *guanshui*, refers to posting meaningless, irrelevant messages or remarks.
9 Her post was published on November 8, 2009. Online. Available HTTP:<http://www.rg-gd.net/forum.php?mod=viewthread&tid=175684&extra=page%3D1> (accessed October 9, 2012).
10 Panyu district government has reinitiated the waste incinerator proposal and chose another location, Dagang Town, Panyu. It is planned to build the incinerator in 2013.
11 FB is the initials of the Chinese pinyin for "corruption *(fubai)*," which refers to the offline get-together activities organized through online forum, such as dinner gathering or outing. The bill is split evenly among participants. It is a popular practice in Chinese online forum.

## References

Amin, A. (2010) "Neighbourly bonds", in M. Bunting, A. Lent and M. Vernon (eds) *Citizen Ethics in a Time of Crisis*. London: The Citizens Ethics Network.
Bennett, W. L. and Segerberg, A. (2012) "The logic of connective action: digital media and the personalization of contentious politics", *Information, Communication & Society*, 15(5): 739–68.
Cai, Y.S. (2005) "China's moderate middle class: the case of homeowners' resistance", *Asian Survey*, 45(5): 777–99.
Carroll, J. M. (2005) "The Blacksburg Electronic Village: a study in community computing", in P. van den Besselaar and S. Koizumi (eds) *Digital Cities* (pp. 43–65). Berlin Heidelberg: Springer-Verlag.

Chen, Y. F. (2005) "Ability of action and system restrict: middle class in the urban movement", *Sociological Studies*, 21(4): 1–20 (in Chinese).

CNNIC (China Internet Network Information Center) (2012) The 29th Survey report on the Development of China's Internet, Online. Available HTTP: <http://www.cnnic.cn/research/> (accessed March 28, 2012).

Erickson, I. (2010) "Geography and community: new forms of interaction among people and places", *American Behavioral Scientist*, 53(8): 1194–207.

Graham, S. and Marvin, S. (1996) *Telecommunications and the City: Electronic Spaces, Urban Place*. London: Routledge.

Granovetter, M. (1978) "Threshold models of collective behavior", *American Journal of Sociology*, 83: 1420–43.

Hampton, K. (2003) "Grieving for a lost network: collective action in a wired suburb", *The Information Society*, 19: 417–28.

Hampton, K., Goulet, L. S., Her, E. J. and Lee, R. (2009) Social isolation and new technology, Online. Available HTTP: <http://pewinternet.org/Reports/2009/18--Social-Isolation-and-New-Technology/Overview/Findings.aspx> (accessed April 13, 2012).

Hampton, K. N. and Wellman, B. (1999) "Netville online and offline: observing and surveying a wired suburb", *American Behavioral Scientist*, 43: 475–92.

Hampton, K. N. and Wellman, B. (2003) "Neighboring in Netville: how the Internet supports community and social captial in a wired suburb", *City & Community*, 2(4): 277–311.

Haythornthwaite, C. and Kendall, L. (2010) "Internet and community", *American Behavioral Scientist*, 53(8): 1083–94.

Huang, R. and Yip, N. M. (2012) "Internet and activism in urban China: a case study of protests in Xiamen and Panyu", *Journal of Comparative Asia Development*, 11(2): 201–23.

Kang, T. (2009) "Homeland re-territorialized: revisiting the role of geographical places in the formation of diasporic identity in the digital age", *Information, Communication & Society*, 12(3): 326–43.

Kavanaugh, A., Carroll, J. M., Rosson, M. B., Reese, D. D. and Zin, T. T. (2005a) "Participating in civil society: the case of networked communities", *Interacting with Computers*, 17(1): 9–33.

Kavanaugh, A. Carroll, J. M., Rosson, M. B., Zin, T. T. and Reese, D. D. (2005b) "Community networks: where offline communities meet online", *Journal of Computer-Mediated Communication*, Online. Available HTTP: <http://jcmc.indiana.edu/vol10/issue4/kavanaugh.html> (accessed October 11, 2012).

Katz, J. E. and Rice, R. E. (2002) "Project syntopia: social consequences of internet use", *IT & Society*, 1(1): 166–79.

Kitchin, R. and Dodge, M. (2002) "The emerging geographies of cyberspace", in R. J. Johnston, P. J. Taylor and M. J. Watts (eds) *Geographies of Global Change: Remapping the World*, 2nd edn. Oxford: Blackwell Publishers Ltd.

Kotus, J. and Hławka, B. (2010) "Urban neighborhood communities organized on-line—a new form of self-organisation in the Polish city?" *Cities*, 27: 204–14.

Kraut, R., Lundmark, V., Patterson, M., Kiesler, S., Mukopadhyay, T. and Scherlis, W. (1998) "Internet paradox: a social technology that reduces social involvement and psychological well-being?" *American Psychologist*, 53(9): 1017–31.

Li, L. M. and Li, S. M. (2013) "Becoming homeowners: the emergence and use of online neighborhood forums in transitional urban China", *Habitat International*, 38: 232–9.

Longan, M. W. (2002) "Building a global sense of place: the community networking movement in the United States", *Urban Geography*, 23(3): 213–36.

Lyon, L. and Driskell, R. (2012) *The Community in Urban Society*, 2nd edn. Long Grove, IL: Waveland Press, Inc.

Markus, M. L. (1987) "Toward a critical mass theory of interactive media: universal access, interdependence and diffusion", *Communication Research*, 14(5): 491–511.

Mesch, G. S. and Levanon, Y. (2003) "Community networking and locally-based social ties in two surburban localities", *City & Community*, 2: 335–51.

Mesch, G. S. and Talmud, I. (2010) "Internet connectivity, community participation, and place attachment: a longitudinal study", *American Behavioral Scientist*, 53(8): 1095–110.

Nie, N. and Erbring, L. (2000) *Internet and Society: A Preliminary Report*. Stanford Institute for the Quantitative Study of Society: Stanford University.

Putnam, R. (2000) *Bowling Alone: The Collapse and Revival of American Community*. New York: Simon and Schuster.

Rainie, L. and Wellman, B. (2012) *Networked: The New Social Operating System*. Cambridge, MA: The MIT Press.

Rainie, L., Lenhart, A., Fox, S., Spooner, T. and Horrigan, J. (2000) Tracking online life: how women use the internet to cultivate relationships with family and friends. Washington, DC: The Pew Internet and American Life Project, Online. Available HTTP: <http://www.pewinternet.org/~/media//Files/Reports/2000/Report1.pdf.pdf> (accessed October 10, 2012).

Rheingold, H. (1993) *The Virtual Community: Homesteading on the Electronic Frontier*. Reading, MA: Addison-Wesley.

Schuler, D. (1996) *New Community Network: Wired for Change*. New York: ACM Press.

Smith, A. (2010) Neighbors Online. Washington, DC: The Pew Research Center, Online. Available HTTP: <http://pewinternet.org/Reports/2010/Neighbors-Online/Part-1.aspx?view=all> (accessed October 10, 2012).

Stoll, Clifford. (1995) *Silicon Snake Oil: Second Thoughts on the Information Highway*. New York: Doubleday.

Uncapher, W. (1999) "Electronic homesteading on the rural frontier: big sky telegraph and its community", in M. A. Smith and P. Kollock, (eds) *Communities in Cyberspace*. New York: Routledge.

Virnoche, M. E. (1998) "The seamless web and communications equity: the shaping of a community network", *Science, Technology, & Human Values*, 23(2): 199–220.

Wang, H. and Wellman, B. (2010) "Social connectivity in America: changes in adult friendship network size from 2002 to 2007", *American Behavioral Scientist*, 53(8): 1148–69.

Wellman, B. (2001) "Physical place and cyberplace: the rise of personalized networking", *International Journal of Urban and Regional Research*, 25: 227–52.

Wellman, B. and Gulia, M. (1999) "Virtual communities as communities: net surfers don't ride alone", in M. A. Smith and P. Kollock, (eds) *Communities in Cyberspace*. New York: Routledge.

Wellman, B., Wong, R. Y., Tindall, D. and Nazar, N. (1997) "A decade of network change: turnover, persistence and stability in personal communities", *Social Networks*, 19: 27–50.

Wu, F.L. (2005) "Rediscovering the 'gate' under market transition: from work-unit compounds to commodity housing enclaves", *Housing Studies*, 20(2): 235–54.

Zhang, L. (2010) *In Search of Paradise: Middle-class Living in a Chinese Metropolis*. Ithaca, NY: Cornell University Press.

# Part IV
# Neighborhood governance under housing commodification

# 11 The contentious democracy

## Homeowners' associations in China through the lens of civil society

*Qiang Fu*

## Introduction

The relationship of society, market and state has been a central focus of social sciences research for centuries. As suggested by the history of capitalist societies, the rise of civil society is essentially a beneficial factor and a necessary condition, if not a sufficient condition, for the establishment of a rational legal state (e.g., Keane, 1988; Tocqueville, 1969 [1835, 1840]). Although scholars are still dubious about whether civil society – a concept that originated in the West – can be readily transplanted in a non-Western context (Hann, 1996; Taylor, 1990), the market transition in Eastern Europe actually revitalized this arcane concept and produced enthusiastic yet divergent discussions on the emergence of civil society in socialist countries (Bryant, 1993; Howard, 2003; Kumar, 1993). Yet with the long-standing aversion of communist citizens to civic engagement and the elasticity of the concept itself (Howard, 2003), scholars are still unclear about the underlying mechanism through which civil society can emerge in (post-)socialist regimes.

The question whether and how civil society can emerge from reform-era China is especially valuable to this debate for two reasons. First, the eighteenth-century American and European revolutions were associated with Western religious tradition such as medieval Christendom (Seligman, 1992; Taylor, 1990), thus research on civil society in a country without a Christian tradition can greatly enhance the generality and validity of the concept. Second, different from the abolition of party-state institutions during the market transition in Eastern Europe, the Chinese party-state remains intact, and political power persists in the post-reform era (Bian and Logan, 1996; Nee and Matthews, 1996). Although civil society was historically invoked as a bulwark against "totalitarianism" and the antithesis to party-state relations in Central and Eastern Europe (Kumar, 1993), research on the interplay between state and society shaped by power relations is extremely important for scholars in regarding civil society as an analytical concept in lieu of a normative one (Flyvbjerg, 1998; Kumar, 1993).

This chapter focuses on the development of homeowners' associations (HAs, *yezhu weiyuanhui* or homeowners' committees) as one approach to observing the potential emergence of civil society in China. After China's urban housing reform of the 1990s, the emergence of homeowners' associations is in tandem with the massive transfers of housing property rights in the reform era. Because these grassroots organizations are frequently established by homeowners themselves to protect private/collective property rights and manage residential neighborhoods, their potential link with the rise of civil society draws widely attention from academia (e.g., Read, 2008; Shi and Cai, 2006). By analyzing the establishment, development and conflicts of homeowner associations, this exploratory study examines whether HAs can live up to the expectations of their role in building civil society in urban China.

## The concept of civil society: evolution and debates

Although successful adjudication of civil society depends on a clear and operational definition, debates and skepticism exist about its utility in practice, especially when it is invoked under a socialist context (Howard, 2003; Keane, 1988; Kumar, 1993; Seligman, 1992). Whereas civil society per se is such an elastic term that scholars often avoid proposing a clear-cut definition, a comprehensive and influential definition of civil society (Cohen and Arato, 1994: ix) is given as follows:

> We understand 'civil society' as a sphere of social interaction between economy and state, composed above all of the intimate sphere (especially the family), the sphere of associations (especially voluntary associations), social movements, and forms of public communication. Modern civil society is created through forms of self-constitution and self-mobilization. It is institutionalized and generalized through laws, and especially subjective rights, that stabilize social differentiation. While the self-creative and institutionalized dimensions can exist separately, in the long term both independent action and institutionalization are necessary for the reproduction of civil society.

Although this working definition mentions little about sufficient conditions for civil society, it does suggest several necessary conditions which can be used to direct a further examination: operating in a public sphere, voluntary participation, decisions from rational-critical debates and an institutional core. Next, I evaluate three theoretical dimensions of civil society which were virtually, albeit not unanimously, agreed by civil society scholars to facilitate empirical analyses.

### *The significance of society, market and the state*

One key issue suggested by the civil-society literature is whether society can maintain its relative independence from market and the state. It was not until the end of the eighteenth century that scholars began to emphasize the interaction between civil society and the state. Theorists such as Locke, Kant and Rousseau used the terms *civil society* and *state* (or "political society") interchangeably to contrast with a conceived state of nature or an "uncivilized" condition of human society (Kumar, 1993). Hegel (2008 [1821]: 96–7) made an initial attempt to distinguish civil society from the state when he treated the civil society as the market mechanism in an Adam Smith fashion.

> The civic community is the realm of difference, intermediate between the family and the state.... In this society every one is an end to himself; all others are for him nothing.... The self-seeking end is conditioned in its realization by the universal. Hence is formed a system of mutual dependence, a system which interweaves the subsistence, happiness, and rights of the individual with the subsistence, happiness, and right of all.

As noted by Taylor (1990), the contemporary notion of civil society was inherited from the philosophy of Hegel rather than as a synonym of "political society." Because Hegel categorizes three different terms of family, civil society and the state, civil society refers to those aspects of social life that are independent of the state and the private sphere. Whereas the economic interpretation of civil society adopted by both Hegel and Marx separates civil society from political society, successive scholars, such as Tocqueville and Gramsci, criticize the dichotomy of political society and economic society in defining civil society. They identify civil society as a third region that stands between the "economic structure and the State with its legislation and its coercion" (Hoare and Nowell-Smith, 1971: 208–9). Based on this reasoning, Linz and Stepan (1996) argue that civil society, economic society and political society are three distinct yet interacting arenas of democratization.

### Power relations at work

Moreover, it has been argued that any effort in promoting civil society would be in vain without a concrete understanding of power relations in the public sphere. Although the emergence and relative independence of civil society is regarded as an important condition of democracy, there is a dearth of literature on how collective decisions and actions in civil society are made through "rational-critical arguments rather than mere inherited ideas or personal statuses" (Calhoun, 1993: 273). Habermas (1993) argues that procedural rationality exists if participants in a certain discourse follow five crucial requirements of discourse ethics: generality, autonomy, ideal role taking, power neutrality and transparency. However, Habermas' universalization theory is problematic in practice because it fails to provide a road map for implementing discourse ethics, given specific power relations at work. Without a concrete understanding of power relations in the public sphere such as institutional changes, political violence and rules of law, Foucault (1988) posits that efforts to establish discourse ethics are fruitless. With the transition from *a single dominant factor* (the state or an emperor) to *a plurality of actors* shaping our society, the relations among different actors and the social dynamics through which those actors jointly exercise their power in a specific context become central issues of civil society (Calhoun, 1993).

*Social capital*

The utility of civil society lies in both macro- and micro-level social capital (Lin, 2001, Putnam, 2000). While the term "civil society" is now on the lips of scholars, politicians, NGO leaders and the public, this currently fashionable concept is often accepted unreflectively. Because of the elastic concept of civil society, the need to invoke this concept has been challenged by more recent literature (Kumar, 1993). If civil society targets promoting liberal pluralism, controlling political violence and defending private/collective rights, scholars must articulate the concrete utility of civil society independent of constitutionalism, citizenship and democracy (Kumar, 1993). A reply to this critique is that these ultimate goals, such as democracy and liberal pluralism, can be achieved by the social integration function of civil society in "a public, but not politically structured" sphere (Taylor, 1990). Social integration associated with civil society is different from the aggregation of individuals because the former is related to social networks and communication among citizens (Bryant, 1993; Calhoun, 1993). From an atomized society to an integrated society, Putnam (2000: 338) argues in a Tocquevillian way that civil societies serve as "schools for democracy" such that frequent interactions provide ordinary citizens an opportunity to enhance mutual trust, develop tolerance and practice bargaining skills in the face of powerful rivals in the public sphere; these, in turn, promote macro-level social capital and are beneficial for overall democracy. Underlying the macro-structure of social capital are social resources imbedded in micro-level network structure: interactions, formation of networks and exchanging of resources among connected members (Bourdieu, 1986; Coleman, 1990; Lin, 1982; Lin, 2001).

*Civil society and network forms of organization: a synthetic framework*

In Powell's seminal paper (1990), he posits that network forms of organization (nonmarket and nonhierarchical modes of exchange) represent an effective and reciprocal method of collective action. The importance of network forms of organization is unfolding with the intellectual growth of civil society literature. The significance of society, market and the state suggests that civil society will not be absorbed by either political society or economic society but retain its relative independence. Subsequently, the analysis of power relations not only assumes the independence of civil society but also suggests the importance of understanding relations between civic organizations and others in the public sphere. Finally, the social capital dimension delves into the nature of organizational relations among different entities in the public sphere. More specifically, the social capital dimension of civil society explicitly points to the reciprocal nature of relations between civic organizations and others. In this research, I argue that, with the rise of civil society, relations among civic organizations and other organizations should take on more of a network form than a market or hierarchical structure. As China's urban transformation and its implications on urban housing and housing property rights has been discussed by other chapters, this chapter focuses the HAs and their relations with other entities in the public sphere through the lens of civil society.

## Urban transformation and the rise of homeowners' associations

Massive transfers of housing property rights from work sectors to individuals created a new social stratum, homeowners. Given exorbitant urban housing prices that occurred after 1998, homeowners are regarded as winners of China's economic reform. Meanwhile, the urban housing reform generates a new residential domain, partitioned-ownership (condominium, *qufen suoyouquan*) in a housing complex. Housing complexes dominate urban China due to its high population density. Conflicts and negotiations among homeowners are inevitable, especially when it comes to commonly held amenities of housing complexes, such as parking lots, elevators, roads and gardens.

Most importantly, in the reform era homeowners' (shared) property rights are frequently violated by external forces such as property management companies (PMCs), real estate developers and even government offices. In virtually all neighborhoods in urban China, PMCs directly manage and execute homeowners' shared property and public space. Meanwhile, many PMCs established by real estate developers possess substantial economic resources and maintain good relations with grassroots government officials, who can intervene in neighborhood governance through a variety of administrative and judicial measures. For example, PMCs may appropriate utility fees collected from homeowners. Established neighborhood planning is frequently altered to accommodate economic pursuits of developers without obtaining permission from homeowners. As a single household is always powerless in facing these external forces when a violation occurs and housing is a tremendous financial investment for a Chinese family, both internal conflicts and external violations necessitated the birth of HAs, voluntary organizations created to manage neighborhoods, but perhaps more importantly, to defend homeowners' rights.

The official definition of a homeowners' association in China is given as follows.

> A homeowners association is elected by a homeowners assembly, enjoys the rights and assumes the obligations authorized by a homeowners assembly, executes decisions made by homeowners assembly and is supervised by homeowners.
>
> (Ministry of Housing and Urban–Rural Development, 2009: Article 3)

Unlike small neighborhoods in Western countries, where all homeowners are members of a homeowners' association (HOA), homeownership in urban China only guarantees a seat in a homeowners' assembly, not a homeowners' association, due to the fact that the size of urban neighborhoods in China varies from several hundred to over ten thousand households. Therefore, an HA in China, mainly consisting of five to eleven homeowners elected by the neighborhood majority, is equivalent to an HOA's Board of Directors in the US, who are authorized by homeowners to make decisions for them and are supposed to direct property management companies to carry out these decisions. Based on a three-year field research study conducted in three cities (Guangzhou, Shenzhen and Meizhou) of the Guangdong Province in 2009 and 2011, I next examine the organizational relations between HAs and other entities in neighborhood governance.

## Relations in neighborhood governance

According to Powell's paradigm (1990) about different types of organizational relations, the relations in Chinese neighborhood governance are depicted in Figure 11.1, which is discussed as follows.

### *The relationship between HAs and local government agencies*

Hierarchical relations exist between local governments and HAs because local government agencies can exert substantial influence on HAs through administrative measures. In the absence of *de jure* status and support from local governments, an HA can neither protect homeowners' shared property against external power through lawsuits nor execute its rights within a neighborhood based on homeowners' collective decisions. Almost all of interviewees in the field research acknowledged that governments played a dominant role in determining neighborhood affairs. Given the prominent power possessed by state agencies in China, the judicial branch (different levels of courts) frequently works together with the administrative branch to solve neighborhood conflicts. For example, if no local governments allow an HA to be regarded as a juristic person, an HA cannot directly file a lawsuit against other parties violating homeowners' property rights. To file a lawsuit, an HA must obtain the authorization of the majority of

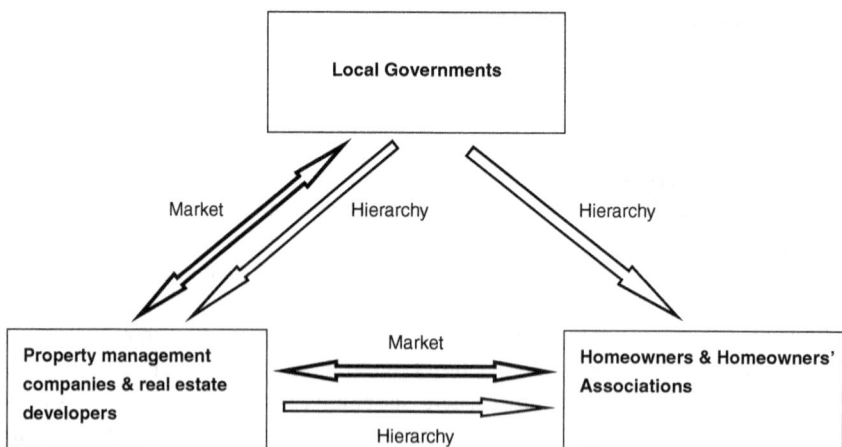

*Figure 11.1* Current organizational relations in neighborhood governance.

homeowners. However, this lawsuit tends to be lengthy and impossible if the court, which embodies the will of local governments, determines that all legal actions need authorization. Meanwhile, an HA needs to register itself in its local government office to acquire HAs' *de jure* status so that it can represent homeowners and make collective decisions within a neighborhood. Due to the recent collective actions organized by HAs, local officials have gradually become aware of HAs' potential to mobilize homeowners. Hence the requirements for registration of HAs have been tightened up. One interviewee commented that the local registration of HAs had changed from informative registration (HAs need to inform local governments about their establishment) to permissive registration (HAs cannot be established unless they satisfy certain requirements of local governments).

### The relationship between HAs and PMCs

It has been observed that the relations between HAs and PMCs are more of hierarchical relations than market relations. Although laws and governmental regulations (Ministry of Housing and Urban–Rural Development, 2009; National People's Congress, 2007) stipulate that PMCs should be employed by homeowners, this is rarely the case in practice because many property management companies are either established by real estate developers or appointed by lower-level governmental agencies to manage neighborhoods. In the absence of effective administrative and legal supervision, real estate developers and PMCs can pursue unjustified benefits, which include: 1) exorbitant monthly management fees; 2) appropriation of revenues generated by homeowners' common property; and 3) tampering with established neighborhood planning.

With regard to market relations in a neighborhood, it is important to distinguish monthly management fees and revenues generated from common property. Homeowners in urban China usually pay monthly management fees to local PMCs as compensation for their services and labor in managing neighborhoods. However, it is frequently observed that property managers disregard governmental regulations and enacts their own standards for management fees in a neighborhood. For example, the management fee of one neighborhood interviewed was twice than that stipulated by the local government. After multiple futile attempts to replace the local PMC through legal and administrative channels, a director commented pessimistically that homeowners paid money to their enemy in order to oppress themselves.

Even if homeowners boycott exorbitant management fees, PMCs can support themselves by lowering standards of property management or appropriating revenues from homeowners' common property, such as parking lots, elevator advertising and other affiliated facilities. In one case, a neighborhood's daily parking fees of approximately 5,000 Chinese *Yuan* were grabbed by the PMC. The actual allocation of revenues from homeowners' shared property is thus determined more by hierarchical relations than by legal stipulations, even though the *Property Management Regulations* in Guangdong (2008: Article 53) stipulates that revenues generated by shared property (such as parking lots) belong to homeowners.

Finally, real estate developers and PMCs can acquire substantial profits by changing neighborhood planning such as parks, gyms and other affiliated facilities and buildings, or reselling these amenities to other parties without permission from a majority of homeowners. In one developed neighborhood, a park collectively owned by homeowners was sold by the real estate developer to another developer for building a primary school designated for use of another nearby neighborhood. Without the consent of homeowners, the real estate developer mobilized substantial administrative forces to make the deal happen.

### Relationship among local governments, real estate developers and PMCs

While strong connections among local governments, real estate developers and property management offices have been well documented in existing research (Read, 2008; Shi and Cai, 2006), not only hierarchical relations but also market relations existed among the three parties. The conflicts between homeowners and PMCs can become drastic when PMCs are established by real estate developers, which usually maintain good relations with local governments. One HA organizer indicated that their efforts for resolving neighborhood problems and protecting homeowners' shared-property rights are widely regarded by other homeowners as futile simply because "the real estate developer is a wallet of the local government." In another instance, hundreds of homeowners had protested their real estate developer in front of the provincial government after the developer-established PMC appropriated funds totaling in the millions. Given strong connections between the real estate developer and a prefectural government in Guangdong province, homeowners had no alternative to resolve this problem other than staging a protest at the provincial government. Without water or power during the summer, homeowners had to live in hotels for almost three months before the provincial government made a decision.

In terms of hierarchical relations, selective involvement of local governments in neighborhood issues can be determined by the priority of goals pursued by local governments. When gangsters or peasants violated homeowners' shared property, local officials were willing to support HAs to reduce local crime rates and satisfy homeowners' collective desires. However, local officials were extremely reluctant to get involved in neighborhood governance if there were conflicts between homeowners and real estate developers. This selective involvement is partly caused by the risk of jeopardizing relations with real estate developers and dampening local GDP growth.

Before HAs can be regarded as a way of building civil society in China, scholars need to examine the current status of HAs, the reality of social capital within a neighborhood, and HAs' power relations with local government offices, real estate developers and PMCs. Built upon the discussion on HAs' relations with other entities in neighborhood governance, I next examine whether the claim that current HAs represent the possible rise of civil society in urban China can stand up to academic scrutiny.

## To what extent can current homeowners' associations be regarded as civil society?

According to the working definition of civil society (Cohen and Arato, 1994) and other mainstream literature on civil society, the rise of civil society should at least possess following four major necessary conditions: 1) operating in a public sphere, rather than private sphere; 2) voluntary participation; 3) collective decisions resulting from rational-critical debates; and 4) an institutional core outside market and state. Although satisfying necessary conditions may not result in the rise of civil society, HAs' failure to satisfy these conditions can falsify HAs' current connections with civil society.

Because HAs are based on homeowners' partitioned ownership and thus operate in a public sphere, they satisfy the first condition. When homeowners' participation in neighborhood affairs is frequently driven by material benefits, (see Fu and Lin, forthcoming) such economic concern contradicts the second condition, i.e., voluntary participation. With regard to the third condition, subordinate roles assumed by most HAs in the power relations across neighborhoods greatly undermine its capability to promote rational-critical debates. Meanwhile, scholars can hardly take it for granted that empowering HAs promotes rational-critical debates. During the field research, it happened that respondents from HAs, local governments and PMCs revealed different and sometimes contradictive accounts of the same episode, which is known as the Rashomon effect (Roth and Mehta, 2002). For instance, local governments sometimes purposefully screened out neighborhood activists from candidates for directors of HAs. In turn, neighborhood activists criticized government officials indulging in rent-seeking behaviors. However, local government officials may feel that an HA controlled by activists can pose serious threat to neighborhood stability. When members in an HA claimed that a real estate developer violated the *Regulations on Realty Management* (2003), they disregarded irretroactivity of law and insisted that the ground floor legally owned by the real estate developer should be returned to homeowners. Even government officials initially overlooked that *Regulations on Realty Management* could not be applied to this case when the HA appealed to local government agencies for support.

As the Rashomon effect happened, how can scholars determine whose claim is *correct* and promotes rational-critical debates? In this regard, juristic laws and administrative regulations, which must be respected by all parties in neighborhood governance, are the benchmark for judging collective decisions. For directors of HAs, their grasp of laws and regulations has already become an important indicator for their competency. One director of an HA criticized that (incompetent) directors of HAs cannot memorize a single article from the *Regulations on Realty Management*. Indeed, a prevalent myth is that dilemmas in neighborhood governance originated from loosely defined shared property rights during China's urban reform. To debunk this myth, it is important to notice that administrative and juristic agencies in

China recently spent huge efforts to define common property rights such that laws and regulations regarding neighborhood governance were properly enacted and timely updated (Ministry of Housing and Urban–Rural Development, 2009; National People's Congress, 2007; State Council, 2003; The Supreme People's Court, 2009b; The Supreme People's Court, 2009a). Therefore, current dilemmas in neighborhood governance are not generated by the absence of laws or obsolete administrative regulations, but by the unabashed flouting of laws and power relations at work. Under this circumstance, these laws and regulations tend to become exam papers one after another testing homeowners' trust in governments and courts. As neighborhood governance succumbs to power without compliance with laws and regulations, homeowners can hardly have rational-critical debates with other powerful entities within a neighborhood.

With regard to the fourth condition, it remains an open question whether current HAs have an institutional core outside economic society and political society. Although the *de jure* status of HAs has been recognized by laws, an internal institutional core regarding the sustainable development of HAs is still far from full-fledged. HA directors found it difficult yet important to establish institutional cores for the sustainable development of HAs. Those important institutional arrangements include, to name a few, nomination, election and re-election, operation, finance and supervision of HAs. As stipulated by the Real Right Law, HAs can virtually make no decisions without the support from at least one-half of homeowners, let alone establish an institutional core in the absence of homeowners' engagement. Therefore, it is dubious whether an institutional core of HAs has already emerged given most homeowners' current disengagement from neighborhood governance.

Based on examination on the four necessary conditions for civil society, current HAs can hardly represent the rise of civil society in urban China. Although HAs operate on public sphere based upon partitioned ownership, homeowners' strong economic concerns, subordinate role in urban governance and lack of social capital undermined voluntary participation, impeded decisions from rational-critical debates and prohibited an internal institutional core of HAs, respectively. Hence, the empirical analysis on current HAs failed to yield a positive answer to the research question whether homeowners' associations can represent the rise of civil society in urban China (see Figure 11.2).

Nevertheless, it is also naïve for scholars to nullify HAs' potential to build civil society in the future, especially given the fact that the rise of civil society is more of a continuous process than a dichotomous outcome. Currently, HAs seem to be weak actors because of the general lack of voluntary participation, mutual trust, solidarity and shared resources. However, as their social capital grows, HAs may gain relative power compared to other actors. As can be seen in Figure 11.3, I conceive the potential of homeowners' associations as a component in the development of civil society in China in two stages. In stage one, the relationships between HAs and other parties in neighborhood governance must evolve from hierarchical and (or) market relations as depicted in Figure 11.1 to network relations in Figure 11.3. Currently, many homeowners' associations remain, to varying degrees, subject to political and

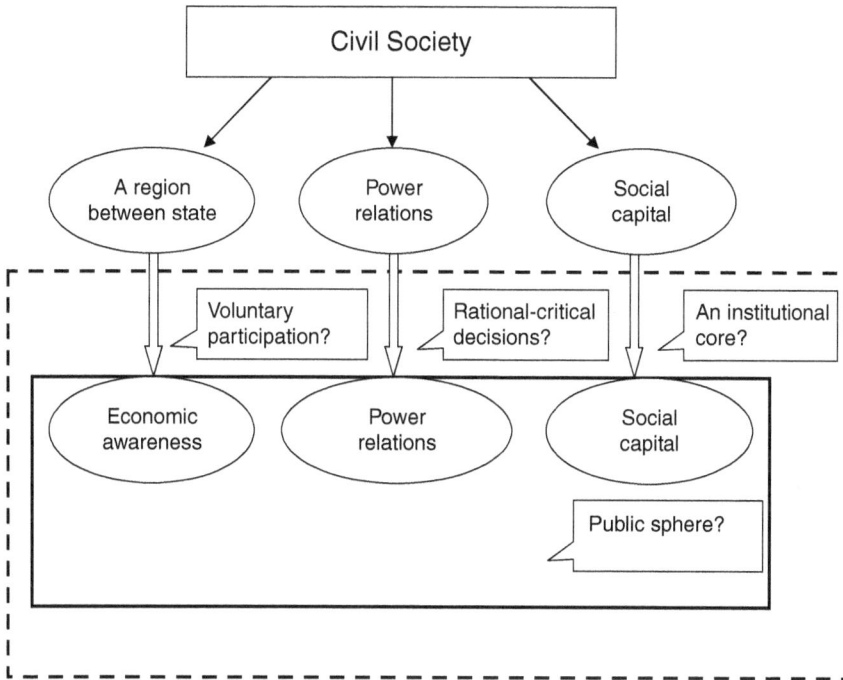

*Figure 11.2* Homeowners' associations and the rise of civil society in urban China.

authoritarian dictates of local government (a hierarchical relation). Meanwhile, homeowners' associations, to varying degrees, are also subsumed under real estate developers and property management companies for the rights to certain common property and for unjustified property management fees (both market and hierarchical relations). I argue that such political and economic constraints must be replaced by equal and mutually beneficial network relations through home-owners' civic engagement in self-governance. After this evolution has taken place, I speculate that, in stage two, HAs may be able to extend their self-interested focus to the broader public sphere, such as development of neighbor-hoods and communities. Subsequently, HAs would actively engage in the building of public and common capital for the benefit of society.

## Civic engagement and network forms of organizations: the potential of homeowners' associations to build civil society

For HAs to become components in a civil society they need to demonstrate compo-nents of civic engagement. Civic engagement, I argue, must contain three elements: 1) the HA needs to collect sufficient social, political and economic capital or resources; 2) it needs to acquire and exercise independent decision making; and 3) it needs to concern others and external social environments, where sentiment

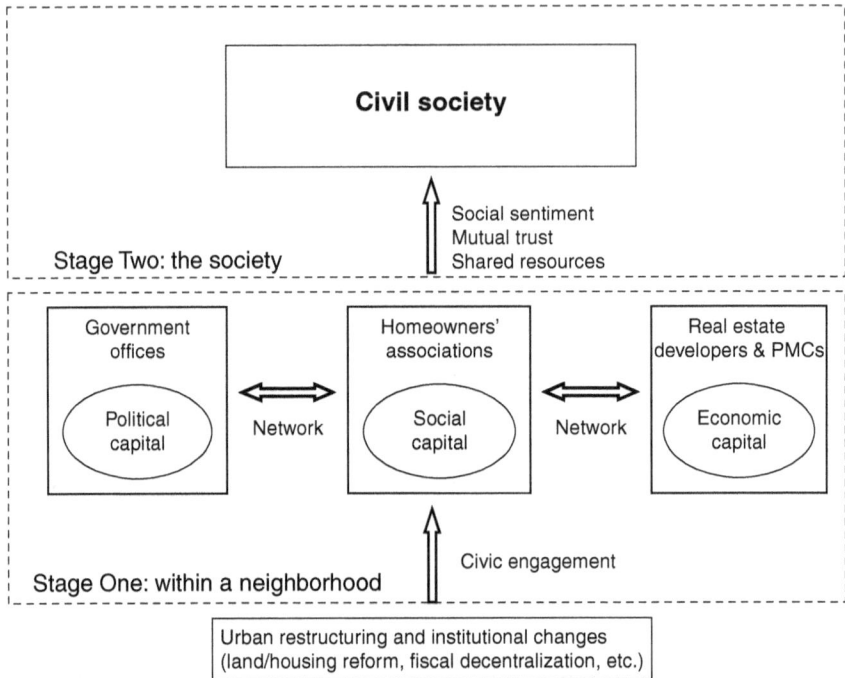

*Figure 11.3* Civic engagement and network forms of organization: the potential of HAs to build civil society.

extends beyond the immediate housing complexes and neighborhoods. At present, at least in Guangdong, the process is at the preliminary stage; HAs remain relatively weak actors in the tri-party relationships, and are primarily concerned with property rights and neighborhood management. However, there is some evidence that the movement toward civic engagement has begun. Prolonged and enduring collective actions organized by HAs across cities have already revealed solidarity within neighborhoods and social capital possessed by HAs. The independent decision making of HAs is widely, albeit not unanimously, accepted as a rule for neighborhood governance. Without the support of at least half of homeowners, any HA stands to lose legal footing in a dispute (National People's Congress, 2007). Furthermore, it remains a provocative question whether the emergence of HAs should be regarded as a governmental device to reduce political tensions in communities or if HAs are controlled and led by political power. To address this question it is essential to realize that those HAs established by local government agencies, real estate developers or PMCs without election by homeowners cannot elicit homeowners' civic engagement to achieve independent decision making and are thus regarded as trivial, incapable and useless in urban governance.

Moreover, I argue that the rise of civil society in (post-)socialist societies was led by neither by the goodwill of political leaders nor the struggles of the disadvantaged, but by serious social problems and constant conflicts embedded in institutional changes (see Fu and Lin, 2013). The emergence of HAs was triggered by problems and conflicts during China's great urban transformation. To address the external problems faced by homeowners, a major reorganization of relations among different parties in neighborhood governance through civic engagement tends to be a viable solution. Regarding the relationship between homeowners and governmental agencies, the massive transfer of housing property rights from the work units (*danwei*) to individuals during the urban housing reform prohibited the direct intervention of political power in neighborhood governance, which occurred frequently before the reform. Instead, the hierarchical relations that existed between individuals and political power in the pre-reform era have gradually evolved toward reciprocal relations between homeowners and local governments after urban housing reform. On the one hand, HAs had assisted local officials collect information in gated communities and persuaded homeowners to cooperate with local development plans, such as environmental protection and rejuvenation of the inner city, in exchange for local officials' support. On the other hand, a local official acknowledged that HAs had greatly reduced administrative costs for local governments because a large share of neighborhood conflicts were handled by HAs instead of by local governmental agencies. In the absence of homeowners' engagement in neighborhood governance, homeowners facing problems in shared property rights had always appealed to local governments for solutions to allocation of parking lots, changes in neighborhood planning, property management and so on, which substantially consumed the administrative resources of local governments.

Likewise, with the development of civic engagement across neighborhoods, I argue that Powell's paradigm about network forms of organization tends to be more relevant to relations between PMCs and HAs. Powell (1990: 302) demonstrated that "intricacies of idiosyncratic, complex, and dynamic exchange" are unlikely to be captured by price systems or markets. Given the complexity of property management in a sizable neighborhood and the relatively short history of property management in urban China, most homeowners lacked knowledge of property management. Accordingly, the asymmetry of information and knowledge in property management precluded pure market links between HAs and PMCs in most neighborhoods, especially in urban neighborhoods where the majority of homeowners failed to fully recognize their shared property rights. During the field research, only a limited number of HA directors who had sufficient expertise in property management, contracts, and related laws and regulations had established genuine market relations with PMCs. As a forerunner of both HAs and property management in urban China, one HA director not only maintained genuine market relations with the local PMC but also instructed staff of other PMCs in property management. Yet, due to most HA directors' lack of expertise in property management, it is extremely difficult for other neighborhoods to duplicate this successful experience and build genuine market relations with local PMCs. Therefore, reciprocity-based cooperation starts when a durable relationship is expected and one side can retaliate against the other side if the latter refuses to cooperate. When PMCs attempted to "exploit the situation" (Axelrod, 1984), homeowners' engagement in neighborhood governance frequently responded to the exploitation by collective actions, such as boycotting property management fees, replacing PMCs, lawsuits, petitions and protests, which may elicit subsequent cooperation from PMCs.

Along with external problems, the potential of HAs to build civil society is also suggested by internal conflicts among homeowners. Because almost all Chinese urban neighborhoods consist of high-rise housing complexes rather than Western-style townhouses, the residential experiences of different households influence and interact with each other through partitioned-ownership properties in a neighborhood (Zhu *et al.*, 2012). For example, improper drainage, unauthorized parking, leaks, pets, housing decoration, furnishing and rehabilitation in a single household can easily inconvenience others. When households paid nominal rents to their work units for housing during the pre-reform era, internal conflicts were largely handled through the hierarchy within a work unit (Lu, 2006). After the urban housing reform, the *danwei*-based hierarchy could no longer address homeowners' internal conflicts (State Council, 1998). Moreover, internal conflicts within a neighborhood can hardly be solved by any of the three dominant social forces in China – political power, market forces or private social network (*guanxi*). As an HA director observed, "No matter how much bureaucratic power you possess or how rich you are, we are all homeowners when we return home." Therefore the changed urban structure and internal conflicts among homeowners also mandate civic participation and generalized trust within a neighborhood.

## Conclusions and discussions

By retrieving three relevant theoretical dimensions (the significance of society, market and the state; power relations; and social capital) in previous literature on civil society, this research demonstrates the importance of network relations in building civil society. After examining the establishment, development and conflicts of HAs, a systematic analysis of the organizational relations across neighborhoods suggests a mismatch between current HAs and standards of civil society originating from Western contexts. Given that network forms of relations are largely absent across neighborhoods, it is dubious that current HAs, which struggle with powerful rivals in urban governance, can represent the rise of civil society in urban China.

However, the logic behind this chapter examining the relevance of HAs to civil society is simple yet fundamental: the rise of civil society is more of a continuous process than a dichotomous outcome. To address persistent problems during China's urban transformation, homeowners' civic engagement in neighborhood governance may lead to a reorientation of relations among homeowners, PMCs and local governments, which can promote the rise of civil society in China. After the housing reform and restructuring of urban space, rival parties began to jockey for power across urban neighborhoods. As long as reciprocal relations are absent across neighborhoods, problems in neighborhood governance will not disappear. As neither market nor state nor private network can provide a satisfactory solution to those problems, civic engagement and subsequent reciprocity-based network relations at each neighborhood in stage one may lead to civil society in stage two when resources are shared across neighborhoods, mutual trust is developed through frequent contacts with others, and, most importantly, social sentiment is formed as individuals become aware of their rights and responsibilities in the public sphere (see Figure 11.3).

## Acknowledgements

I am grateful to Nan Lin, the Community Development Center of South China and our interviewees for their extraordinary support to our field research. I also thank Yushu Zhu, Wenjia Zhuang and participants of the 6th Workshop of Chinese Organizational Sociology (Shanghai, China) and the 2011 Annual Conference of the North American Chinese Sociologists Association (Las Vegas, United States) for their help with this manuscript and valuable comments. This research was supported by the 2009-2010 Lincoln Institute China Program International Fellowship and a summer field research fellowship from Asian/Pacific Studies Institute at Duke University. Direct correspondence to Qiang Fu, Department of Sociology, Duke University, Durham, NC, 27708, USA. E-mail: qf6@soc.duke.edu.

## References

Axelrod, R. (1984) *The Evolution of Cooperation*. New York: Basic Books.

Bian, Y. and Logan, J. R. (1996) Market transition and thepersistence of power: The changing stratification system in urban China. *American Sociological Review*, 61(5): 739–58.

Bourdieu, P. (1986) The forms of social capital. *Handbook of Theory and Research for the Sociology of Education*, 241–58.

Bryant, C. G. A. (1993) Social self-organisation, civility and sociology: A comment on Kumar's 'Civil Society'. *The British Journal of Sociology*, 44(3): 397–401.

Calhoun, C. (1993) Civil society and the public sphere. *Public Culture*, 5(2): 267.

Cohen, J. L. and Arato, A. (1994) *Civil Society and Political Theory*. Cambridge, MA: MIT Press.

Coleman, J. S. (1990) *Foundations of Social Theory*. Cambridge, MA: Harvard University Press.

Flyvbjerg, B. (1998) Habermas and Foucault: Thinkers for civil society? *The British Journal of Sociology*, 49(2): 210–33.

Foucault, M. (1988) The ethic of care for the self as a practice of freedom. *The Final Foucault*, 1–20.

Fu, Q. and Lin, N. (2013) Local state marketism: An institutional analysis of China's urban housing and land market. *Chinese Sociological Review*, 46(1): 3–24.

——— (forthcoming) The weaknesses of civic territonal organizations: Civic engagement and homeowners associations in urban China. *International Journal of Urban and Regional Research*.

Habermas, J. (1993) *Justification and Application: Remarks on Discourse Ethics*. Cambridge, MA: MIT Press.

Hann, C. (1996) Introduction: Political society and civil anthropology. *Civil Society: Challenging Western Models*, 1–26.

Hegel, G. W. F. (2008) [1821] *Philosophy of Right*. New York: Cosimo Classics.

Hoare, Q. and Nowell-Smith, G. (1971) *Antonio Gramsci. Selections from the Prison Notebooks*. London: Lawrence and Wishart.

Howard, M. M. (2003) *The Weakness of Civil Society in Post-communist Europe*. Cambridge: Cambridge University Press.

Keane, J. (1988) *Democracy and Civil Society: On the Predicaments of European Socialism, the Prospects for Democracy, and the Problem of Controlling Social and Political Power*. London: Verso.

Kumar, K. (1993) Civil Society: An inquiry into the usefulness of an historical term. *The British Journal of Sociology*, 44(3): 375–95.

Lin, N., ed. (1982) *Social Resources and Instrumental Action*. Beverly Hills, CA: Sage.

Lin, N. (2001) *Social Capital: A Theory of Social Structure and Action*. Cambridge: Cambridge University Press.

Linz, J. and Stepan, A. (1996) *Problems of Democratic Transition and Consolidation: Southern Europe, South America, and Post-communist Europe*. Baltimore, MD: Johns Hopkins University Press.

Lu, D. (2006) *Remaking Chinese Urban Form: Modernity, Scarcity and Space, 1949–2005*. New York: Taylor & Francis.

Ministry of Housing and Urban–Rural Development (2009) *Yezhu Dahui he Yezhu Weiyuanhui Zhidao Guize (Guidelines for Homeowners' Assemblies and Homeowners' Committees)*. Beijing.

National People's Congress (2007) *Real Right Law of the People's Republic of China*. Beijing.

Nee, V. and Matthews, R. (1996) Market transition and societal transformation in reforming State Socialism. *Annual Review of Sociology*, 22: 401–35.

Powell, W. W. (1990) Neither market nor hierarchy: Network forms of organization. *Research in Organizational Behavior*, 12: 295–336.

Putnam, R. D. (2000) *Bowling Alone: The collapse and revival of American community*. New York: Simon & Schuster.

Read, B. L. (2008) Assessing variation in civil society organizations: China's homeowner associations in comparative perspective. *Comparative Political Studies*, 41(9): 1240–65.

Roth, W. D. and Mehta, J. D. (2002) The Rashomon effect. *Sociological Methods & Research*, 31(2): 131–73.

Seligman, A. B. (1992) *The Idea of Civil Society*. New York: The Free Press.

Shi, F. and Cai, Y. (2006) Disaggregating the State: Networks and collective resistance in Shanghai. *The China Quarterly*, 186: 314–32.

State Council (2003) *Wuye Guanli Tiaoli (Regulations on Realty Management)*. Beijing: Document No. 379.

Taylor, C. (1990) Modes of civil society. *Public Culture*, 3(1): 95–118.

The Standing Committee of the 11th Guangdong People's Congress (2008) *Guangdong Wuye Guanli Tiaoli (Regulations on Realty Management in Guangdong)*. Guangzhou: Document No. 10.

The Supreme People's Court (2009a) *Interpretation of the Supreme People's Court on Several Issues Concerning the Specific Application of Law in the Trial of Disputes over Partitioned Ownership of Building Areas*. Beijing: Document No. 8.

The Supreme People's Court (2009b) *Provisions of the Supreme People's Court on Several Issues Concerning the Application of Laws in the Property Management Cases*. Beijing: Document No. 8.

Tocqueville, A. d. (1969) [1835, 1840] *Democracy in America*. Garden City, NY: Doubleday, Anchor Books.

Zhu, Y., Breitung, W. and Li, S. (2012) The changing meaning of neighbourhood attachment in Chinese commodity housing estates: Evidence from Guangzhou. *Urban Studies*, 49(11): 2439–57.

# 12 Managing the nouveaux riches

## Neighborhood governance in upmarket residential developments in Shanghai

*Xiaoyi Sun and Ngai Ming Yip*

## Introduction

The upsurge of upscale residential neighbourhoods in China has been phenomenal in the last decade. Unlike their counterparts in the developed countries, landed detached houses are preserved for the very few privileged in rich cities in China, apparently constrained by the land lease system as well as the tedious approval procedures in planning and building. Hence the overwhelming majority of the nouveaux riches in urban China can only choose housing constructed by real estate developers in multi-family luxurious apartments or villa in planned gated neighborhoods, being packaged as havens for rich families in pursuing exclusive and luxurious life-styles behind the gates. Despite under current household registration (*hukou*) system, every residential household is enlisted within the "service coverage" of a residents' committee, which in theory also include the richest households. Yet, in practice, it is extremely difficult for residents' committees to penetrate the planned neighbourhoods for the rich. The usual tactics employed by residents' committees in ordinary neighborhoods do not seem to work in high-end neighborhoods. It apparently leaves a gap in a comprehensive system of neighborhood monitoring and social control that is perceived to be vital in the maintenance of social "harmony" (stability). Recent stepping up of social stability measures has driven some local governments to try developing new strategies in extending their control to neighborhoods of the nouveaux riches.

This chapter will look at how residents' committees attempt to incorporate upmarket neighborhoods back to their regulatory framework of local governance. It helps to shed light on how local governments perceive the new challenges of managing neighborhoods of the richest as well as how neighborhood governance can be pushed forward in the context of increasing material affluence. The chapter will focus on upmarket neighborhoods in Shanghai with data collected from social survey as well as qualitative interviews with the property management companies and resident committees as well as participatory observations conducted in upmarket neighborhoods by the authors in seven upmarket residential neighbourhoods (appendix 1). Unfortunately, residents' perspectives are lacking owing to the difficulties in reaching the rich residents in the case neighborhoods.

This chapter will begin with the literature review on gated communities and urban governance in urban China, which will be followed by a brief description of upmarket residential development in Shanghai. Then, the formation of local governance coalition and new strategies of neighborhood governance in Shanghai will be deliberated. The chapter will conclude with a discussion on the implications of such changes, on both the life of the nouveaux riches as well as on neighborhood governance in urban China in general.

## Upmarket residential enclaves in Shanghai: an overview

Shanghai as the economic capital of China leads the country in its development of high-end residential enclaves. Early development of upscale residence began in the city center area. For example, Riverside Arc de Triomphe, located in the then-new financial center of *Lujiazui* overlooking the historic *Waitan* commanded RMB264,000 (US$42,000) per square meter and a villa there even cost RBM200m (US$32m).[1] They both broke the price record in 2009. Other sites of luxurious developments include downtown shopping areas of *Xintiandi* (Luwan District), Nanjing West Road (Jingan District) as well as *Gubei* in Changning District which sprang up with the development of Hongqiao (Airport) Economic Development Zone. In 2009, flats that were sold over RMB100,000 (US$16,000) per square meter were regarded as "luxurious" by the media.

With the economy of China leapfrogged in the early 2000s, the already crowded urban areas of Shanghai could no longer satisfy the appetite of the nouveaux riches for space. Super-luxurious residence began to move to the suburbs, like the Songjiang District. The area of Sheshan in Songjiang, the mountain area that is the closest to Shanghai proper, was exemplary. Initially planned as public tourist resorts in 1996 but unable to attract the private investment it expected, Sheshan was later being rezoned to include 291 hectares of land for villa development.

The Sheshan projects are extravagant. Take the example of the SHJY neighborhood we have visited which sits on a large piece of green land and holds a total of

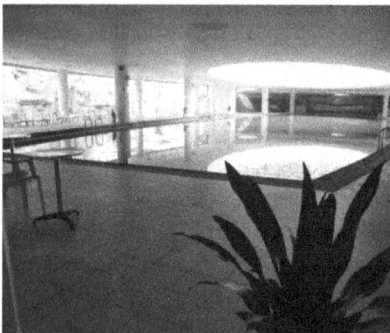

Elaborate club facilities in a high rise       Villas in outskirt Shanghai
neighborhood in Central Shanghai

*Figure 12.1*  Enclaves for nouveaux riches in Shanghai.
Source: Photographs taken by the authors.

65 villas with each villa taking up on an average 2500 m² of land. Another villa in the Sheshan mountain area has set the national record in 2009 when it was sold at RMB205m (USD32m).² With the initial plan as a tourist resort area, facilities like yacht clubs, jockey club, golf courses as well as five-star hotels have already been built. It gave the villa developments a very favorable marketing as well as costing niche. The developers were able to enjoy the comprehensive supporting leisure and livelihood infrastructure but did not have to bear the cost of construction. Therefore, it is difficult not to speculate that the initial plan for tourist resorts was only a camouflage whose real intention was to pave way for super luxury villa projects.

## Enclaves for the nouveaux riches: the pursuit of privacy and sense of community

As landed detached houses (either new built or gentrified) are rare commodities in major Chinese cities, the overwhelming majority of the nouveaux riches in urban China have little choice but to move to residential enclaves developed by property developers, in the form of high-rise apartments or villas clusters, heavily guarded and being enclosed by high walls. The pursuit of privatism and escapism are deep concerns in the gated communities literature. The former expresses the anxiety connected to social changes in the urban context that has been mitigated by the very clear boundaries on physical space the gate has set. The gate, which offers barriers between residents inside and the rest of the city outside, exhibits both as an icon of enclave as well as a symbol of social-spatial exclusiveness. Yet, not only does the privatized public space enclosed by the walls segregate the gated community from its environment, it also reduces inter-neighborhood interaction, which further exacerbates the problem of social segregation (Blakely and Snyder, 1997; Low, 2006).

Escapism connected to gated communities exhibits a sense of retreat, of gated-community residents, "to disengage with wider urban problems and responsibilities, both social and fiscal" (Atkinson and Blandy, 2005: 180). On the one hand, social disengagement is directly linked to the physical enclosure of the community, which is relevant to the context of China. Yet on the other hand, the fiscal disengagement is more indirect in China albeit it is the financial incentives for both the local government and property developers that triggers the proliferation of large-scale gated communities (for developers the benefits in the reduction of land premium and the local government saving in infra-structure investments).

The new commodity housing sector also offers the emerging nouveaux riches distinct life-style residence in which like-minded people are able to create their new identities (Raposa, 2006) and an aesthetic way of living (Pow, 2009). As Pow (2007) remarks, "the general decline in social relations and neighborliness in gated communities reflects the desire for residents to retreat into their own private spaces" (p826). Such communities also deliver enclaves of privatism and escapism, from the threat of crime as well as, more importantly, from the ubiquitous control of the state. Hence, the gate would help to shut off social problems as well as to enjoy the freedom from the depressive omnipresence of state power that allows for the chase for a cozy, autonomous and self-ensuring life-style.

Yet, contrary to gated communities elsewhere, both the morphology and functioning of gated communities in urban China are unique. For instance, the scale of gated developments in China is on an average 15 to 20 times bigger in terms of population than the US (Miao, 2003). Even high-end gated neighborhoods are big in size. For instance, one villa development of our case study neighborhood holds 100 houses and another high-end high-rise development even has 1200 households. The size of the neighbourhood, the diversified and high quality property services the residents' demand as well as the burden of public services such neighborhoods have to shoulder in lieu of state provision have imposed constraints to the pursue of autonomy and freedom. Intensive manpower input as well as the necessary internal rules such developments have to create to make the neighborhood manageable expose residents to intensive surveillance and potential control.

Gated neighbourhoods in urban China also exhibit a different pattern in the sense of community among their residents. Research on gated communities (outside China) has generally agreed that both the interaction and sense of community of residents in gated communities are lower than their counterparts in non-gated communities (Carvalho et al., 1997; Blakely and Snyder, 1997; Blandy et al., 2003). It is even worse in gated communities for high-income households (Wilson-Doenges, 2000). High level of property management services in gated communities which replaces the need for neighbors' interaction or community bonding was to blame, as what the residents need has already been taken care of by property management.

Yet a recent study by one of the authors (Yip, 2012) found contrasting results in Shanghai. Amongst the residents he surveyed, no statistically significant differences was found on the interaction amongst neighbors or on residents' participation of community activities. Despite an apparent difference between sense of community between gated and non-gated communities, such difference is in fact a proxy for the type of housing (commodity vs. sold public housing) (Yip, 2012). The survey data used in Yip (2012) (a survey done in 2007–08 in Shanghai covering 45 neighborhoods in six districts and 1577 households) was re-analyzed for the sense of community in high-end residential enclaves. A scale was constructed to adapt to the special China context and coherent with similar indices that have been used internationally (refer to Appendix 2 for details). Whilst residents who were being surveyed scored a mean index of sense of community at 65.3 against a maximum of 100 points, residents in upmarket villa neighborhoods in Songjiang achieved the highest score of 70.7, which was significantly higher than the scores in both sold public housing and mixed housing (commodity housing and sold public housing) neighborhoods (Table 12.1). The findings of the highest sense of community in upmarket neighborhoods runs contrary to other similar findings in China (e.g. Wu and He, 2005; Forrest and Yip, 2007) and elsewhere (e.g. Wilson-Doenges, 2000; Carvalho et al., 1997; Blakely and Snyder, 1997). Even if there may not be more interaction between

*Table 12.1* Sense of community by neighborhood type

| Neighborhood type | Sense of community score | Difference (villas as the reference group |
|---|---|---|
| Villa | 70.7 | NA |
| Ordinary commodity housing | 68.5 | NS |
| Sold public housing | 65.0 | $p < 5\%$ |
| Mixed housing | 63.4 | $p < 5\%$ |
| Others (temporary housing, housing for relocation) | 67.6 | NS |
| All | 65.3 | |

Note: Posthoc Scheffe test of ANOVA; NA (Not Applicable); NS (Not Significant).

Source: Analysis of household survey by the authors.

neighbours in the high-end neighborhoods, a sense of pride, proximity in their social status and value may bind them more closely.

In addition, connected to the need of escapism and privacy of the nouveaux riches, elaborated security measures appears to be a significant property management service niche for the property management agents in these luxurious residences. Some of such elaborated security measures are in fact comparable to high security installation in top grade office buildings. For instance, in two of the neighborhoods we studied, with a centrally monitored smart-card system being installed, access control was not limited to the front entrance of the neighborhood but to specific floor. Visitors get time limited access granted remotely by the host just enough to reach their host. To reinforce the professional image of security, uniformed security guards are being packaged as paramilitary brigades, not just in their outlook but also the bodily gestures in patrol and stand post (marching, saluting, etc.) as well as the ceremonial regular exercises in explicating their power. Yet the omnipresence of the property management staff, particularly the security personnel and their surveillance installation, have in fact opened up a loophole for the local state to intervene into the private life of the nouveaux riches (which will be elaborated in a later section).

## Residents' committees and neighborhood governance

The economic reform liberalized the economy and attributed to the super-fast growth of China in recent decades. Yet it also brought about a fundamental change on how the society of China is governed. In the socialist era, the "work-unit" (*danwei*) was not only the centre of employment but also the nexus for social service provision, civic and political affiliation as well as bases for cultural identity and attachment (Hua, 2000; Huang and Low, 2008). Yet the *danwei* system was dismantled in the economic reform and this has had serious repercussion on the weakening of social control and public service delivery. To fill the void, local grassroots institutions, like the street offices (*jiedaoban*) and the neighborhood resident committees (*juweihui*) began to play a pivotal role in the revamping the grassroots social control and service delivery system. Such efforts have been packaged in the discourse of the "construction of civilized modernity" (*xiandai wenming jianshe*) in which intervention of the local state in the affairs of residential neighbourhoods has been intensified (Wu, 2005). This may have an impact on the pursuit of freedom, life-style and autonomy of the nouveaux riches in their gated neighborhoods.

After the demise of work-units, urban neighborhoods have been reinvented as important platforms on which social welfare and public services are delivered and social order and stability are maintained. Residents' committees, the state's "nerve tips," are pivotal in such an endeavour (Read, 2000). With very limited administrative resources, these organizations manage to accomplish many administrative tasks in the neighborhoods, such as collecting personal information, conducting national census, implementing birth control, and keeping an eye on potential political dissenters. The secret of residents' committees' capacity of social control and grassroots mobilization lies in the use of local social networks. The officials make an effort to build personal relations with residents in daily interaction. When the officials need residents for cooperation, it would be very difficult for the latter to turn down. More specifically, abstract commitment to the party-state and thin reciprocity between residents' committee officials and residents are regarded as the most important governing mechanisms in "daily authoritarian mobilization" (Liu, 2010).

In the socialist era, abstract commitment to the party-state was rooted in the ideology education of the state-socialist regime that indoctrinated their subjects to achieve a substantial degree of willing participation. As the system of *danwei* wane, residents' committees (and the neighborhood Party branches embedded in the structure) become the only center of loyalty for residents, and the retired *danwei* employees or Party members in particular, who find the nostalgic recollection of egalitarian communist ideology in Mao's era memorably appealing. The wide support from these neighborhood loyalists – such as block captains, retired Party members, residents' representatives – forms a significant basis for residents' committees' grassroots mobilization capacity (Yang, 2007). Slogans like "serve the neighborhood and residents," "make a contribution to the country," as well as "this is party members' obligation" are particularly effective for mobilization (Guo and Sun, 2013).

Thin reciprocity, on the other hand, has been the other important mechanism through which residents' committees manage to penetrate urban grassroots (Read, 2003: 29). Residents' committee officials make an effort to build personal relations with their constituents through face-to-face familiarity or occasional chatting in everyday life. The officials also offer small favors to residents, such as providing free blood pressure tests or giving out free detergent to every household. Beneficiary residents would appreciate the favors. When the officials ask the residents to cooperation, the residents would realize that it is time to return the favor.

Yet such strategies are more effective in old and poor neighborhoods (like sold public housing neighbourhoods) because the residents in those neighborhoods have no other alternative resources but to depend on residents' committees for livelihood and better living environment. For instance, the residents' committee subsidizes property management services for the residents, and in turn, those residents show a high degree of identity towards the officials (Interview 20120626). Such strategies, however, do not seem appealing for the nouveaux riches residing in upscale housing enclaves. Small favors provided by the residents' committee are not at all attractive to the rich residents, and the residents who mostly work in the private sector do not show strong identity toward the Party. At the same time, high security measures in high-end residential enclaves also make it hard for residents' committee officials or block captains to get contact with residents and set a hurdle to their daily works.

The inability for the residents' committee to penetrate upscale neighborhoods poses a pressure for the respective local governments. On the one hand, it limits their capacity in discharging their routine duties, on the other hand, it presents a blind spot in the paramount mission of maintaining social "harmony" (stability) as they know little of what happen in such upscale neighborhoods, not to mention the capacity to levy control if something goes awry. Pilot measures have been attempted to penetrate upscale gated enclaves. Zhu and Guo (2011) describe an effort made by a residents' committee in Changning District in Shanghai to target neighbourhoods with high concentration of residents from overseas (perhaps the most difficult neighborhoods to penetrate). With no conventional social networks of block captains to fall upon, the residents' committees approached the property management companies of the neighbourhoods in jointly organized activities targeted at international residents. This proved to be largely effective and opens up a new way for residents' committees to penetrate into neighborhoods of the nouveaux riches. Yet, given the nature of property management companies as profit-seeking neighborhood service providers, there seems to be little incentive for them to let local residents' committees take the advantage. This is often the case in other liberal countries. However, the unique socio-political milieu at the neighborhood of urban China has created a local symbiotic eco-system in which property management companies are being induced to cooperate with the local residents' committees to achieve a win-win game.

## The local governance coalition and the exchange of favour

It is well documented that nexus of rent-seeking local-state-business coalition has been created by the entrepreneurial impulse of local state which is being reinforced by the unchecked exercise of state power (Duckett, 1998; Zhu, 2004). Property developers have been notorious in this endeavour in which local government (in the case of Shanghai, the District government that holds such power) in manipulating planning parameters and land leases to maximize their benefit in the extraction of the exchange value of urban lands (Wu, 2002) as well as in the exploitation of displaced residents in urban redevelopment (Shin, 2008; Zhang, 2002). They are also being accused of taking advantage of the underdeveloped regulations in infringing the property or the consumer right of homeowners (Yip, 2013). Given the close association between the property management companies with the developers of the respective neighborhoods (the former usually being the subsidiary of the latter), it is not surprising for the property management agents to have maintained good relations with the respective local government.

Unlike their counterparts in upper-tier municipal governments, which are connected to the state-business nexus by material interests, the lowest tier of local governments at the neighborhood does not have such benefit as they were already being forced to reframe from any profit-generating business. It is instead their shared goal for operational efficiency with the property management agent at the neighbourhood level that has driven them to establish a local governance coalition. In this respect, a symbiotic working relationship would help to facilitate the political mission of residents' committee in maintaining social harmony and stability. The residents' committees desperately need the property management agents, particularly those in upscale neighborhoods, in helping them to penetrate upscale neighborhoods as well as in sharing the legwork of their mandatory and ad hoc duties. The property management agents in return, would take advantage of the pseudo-state power of the residents' committees in getting an upper hand in their interaction with the residents or relevant state agencies. Our fieldwork in Shanghai offers a number of illustrations on these synergies.

With traditional approaches of thin reciprocity and mobilization by loyalty to the party-state unattractive to the nouveaux riches, upscale neighbourhoods present as a hard-to-access, if not no-go areas, for the residents' committees. A high desire for privacy, coupled with the excessive security measures, set further hurdles for residents' committees even if they are determined to break the fortresses of the rich. In such respect, assistance from the property management agents is instrumental. For instance, in the JNHT and YZFH neighborhoods we studied, property management agents helped to arrange appointments with resident visits and accompanied residents' committee official in the visits, which were otherwise inefficient for the residents' committee. Trust on the property management agents, generated by their professional services and frequent contacts with residents have apparently dwarfed the confidence residents used to associate with the legitimate power of state officials.

Yet even with the help of property management agents, personal contact with individual residents on a large scale is not always possible owing to the suspicion of the individuals for unsolicited visits from government officials. In conventional neighborhoods, services rendered by residents' committees, confirmation of their household registration for birth or marriage certificates, application to state school, etc., would generate the opportunities for residents' committees to meet with their residents. Yet many rich residents in upmarket neighborhoods do not have such needs. Hence, there are quite a lot of residents the residents' committees have no excuse to meet in verifying the information they obtained. This limits the comprehensive information-gathering work of the residents' committee and weakens the maintenance of the surveillance mechanism in the neighborhood.

To counteract the lack of direct contracts with residents, residents' committees in Shanghai have attempted to exploit recent special events in generating such opportunities. For instance, Shanghai municipality has taken advantage of the World Expo 2010, in making home deliveries of free gifts of the event (free Expo and Metro tickets) to residents. This created the opportunities for residents' committees to make fact-to-face contact with residents and collect the intelligence on the households. This worked remarkably well particularly for hard-to-contact upmarket neighborhoods as the event was highly publicized and the gifts were regarded as a benevolent gesture of the government. Revealed by a residents' committee official of the upmarket YZFH neighborhood in the effort in reaching the once thought to be unreachable residents of foreigners in his neighborhood,

> The EXPO gift bags created a good opportunity as foreign residents were also eligible. Normal local resident in Shanghai can be traced by the household registration book but foreigners cannot. Sometimes we asked for their information from the property management company yet we were unable to verify such information. We volunteered to deliver the bags to them and they often happily accepted. This helps to open conversation with them.
>
> (Interview20120827).

In return, property management agents often get the help of residents' committees when the property management agents encounter difficulties in dealing with their residents. They are reluctant to employ tough measures, worrying that it would agitate their "boss" and risk losing the management contract. The issues may involve small thing like restricting dog keeping to serious conflicts between the residents and the property management agent. In mediating minor disputes, besides acting as an independent third party, the residents' committees could also manipulate their authority as pseudo-state officials as well as guardians of public interests and play the role of "bad guys" that the property management agents are uncomfortable to act. Remarked by a property manager we interviewed,

> Residents left their stuff in the hallways and just reacted perfunctorily to our request to remove them but never actually act. RC official could take a sterner stand by accusing them sabotaging their campaign on civilized neighbourhood (a competition that tied to the residents' committee's performance) and threatened to take tougher action. Residents would usually comply immediately. How can I act tough when my job depends on the satisfaction of the residents? I can only rely on the RC to deal with such issues.
>
> (Interview20111223)

Maintaining a symbiotic relations with the residents' committees would put the property management agents better connected to and perhaps better protected by the local government or at least better informed of likely moves of the government that would affect their business. For instance, property manager in the SHJY neighborhood in Sheshan revealed of the company being left out as an "orphan," ignorant even of the on-spot inspection of the city property management bureau, as their history of being part of the tourist administration of Sheshan before the rezoning made them not fully integrated into the local township network (equivalent of the street office in Shanghai city proper). Their subsequent deliberate effort in getting closer cooperation with the local residents' committee has greatly enhanced their connection with the government and facilitated their business (Interview20120828).

By far the most crucial value of the residents' committee emerges at the time when there is the survival of the property management agent at stake. Again, the apparently neutral position of the residents' committees and their presumed position as guardian of public interests would help in their lobbying on the behalf of the property management agent. The moral imperative of maintaining neighborhood harmony may also service to lure residents to treat the property management agent more leniently. In fact, residents' committees' reluctance to abandon a long-term partner in neighborhood governance is apparent. Not to mention that stable and effective teamwork needs time to foster and the transition to a new management agent per se already risks uncertain turbulence. In fact, residents' committees would be keener to protect property management agents that are connected with the developer, despite the latter are often prime targets of action when homeowners engage in dispute with the developers on substandard building quality of their home. Residents' committees would worry that driving out such property management agents would instead cut off the connection with the developer altogether and hence reduce the incentive of the developer to strike for a settlement as there is no need to do this in order to keep the business of their subsidiary company.

### Governing upmarket neighborhoods

Forming the local governance alliance is just the first step in enhancing the governing capacity of residents' committees in neighborhoods of the nouveaux riches. With the pressing need to maintain social stability, what the residents' committees need is not merely intelligence on what their residents are but also down to the day-to-day monitoring. It is even better if they have closer allies in the neighborhood whom they can mobilize as helping hands to their campaigns.

For instance, as property management services in Shanghai is highly dependent on migrant workers for the lower end of the labour force, managing the so-called "people from outside" (*wailai renkou*) posed not only an issue of the control of crime but was also central to the measures in containing the threat from outsiders. This is done in ordinary neighborhoods by keeping updated records of all residents via the household registration system. Yet it poses a challenge to both the residents' committee and property management agents in upmarket neighbourhoods as their super rich clients rely heavily on migrant workers even to do their housework. Yet they have little intention to fully cooperate with the property management agent in detailed records of these employees. One housing manager we interviewed described such complexity.

> One homeowner in my neighborhood hires 15 employees including drivers, cook, housemaids and gardeners. Yet some of them may work for several households in the neighbourhood at the same time. Some of them live in the house but others don't and we even don't know which house they stay for the night. Actually it is impossible for the police to control them.
>
> (Interview20120828)

With recent step-up of security control, the local police has asked the property management company to keep more detailed information of the domestic employees of their homeowners and even better to keep track of their daily mobility records. The property management agent had to devise more innovative ways in extracting such intelligence. The housing manager we interviewed explained the details of their simple but effective design in ensuring they have full information on the identity as well as pattern of mobility of the domestic workers.

> Their domestic employees need a key card to go into the neighborhood – a different key card for regular or temporary workers (for renovation or repair works etc.). People need to deposit their key card upon entry to the neighbour-hood, so we can [get] ideas on who stay overnight and to ensure all holders of temporary key cards have left by the end of the day.
>
> (Interview20120828)

Of course, a better way for residents' committees in managing the neighborhoods of the nouveaux riches is to set up local networks they can mobilize, the same as they usually do in ordinary neighbourhoods. Yet this is not easy given the background of the homeowners of such neighborhoods. However, the extensive exist-ence of extended families in urban China makes this possible. Regardless whether it is out of obligation (filial piety) or necessity (underdeveloped elderly care), it is not uncommon even for rich families to live with their elderly parents. This is in sharp contrast with families in most economically advanced countries. In fact, many upmarket apartments (or even villas) are occupied only by the elderly parents of the rich owners (perhaps they do not want to rent out their investment properties and need someone to take care of them). As the background of these elderly residents are in no way different from that of an ordinary neighborhood, it gives the residents' committee golden opportunities to deploy the working approach they are good at.

The residents' committee officials all too well recognize the need for personal, social as well as ideational identity of these elderly members of rich families and the strategy of employing a mix of personal touch and a sense of pride in serving the neighborhood have been employed to motivate these loyalists (Guo and Sun, 2013). Again, as they do in ordinary neighborhoods, leisure activities in building close personal relationship have been intertwined with the creation of formal duties for them in the neighborhood in instilling the loyalty to the neighborhood (and the local party branch). We were in fact amazed by the success of the residents' committee in the JAFJ, a city-center neighborhood which sells at about RBM55,000 (USD$9,000) per square meter, in building up such a network. The day we visited the neighborhood, we were shown around in the neighborhood by a team of elderly women, elegantly dressed which may reflect their affluence, who were fluent both in the political rhetoric of community building as well as every details of their neighborhood. In fact, the residents' committee was able to assign five loyalists to each building (around 10 such buildings) in the neighborhood, a level that only conventional neighborhoods (sold public housing) were able to achieve. Apparently, the neighborhood party branch has a trustworthy and skillful brigade of loyalists they can mobilize. Such approach was equally applicable to other upmarket neighborhoods, though its efficiency depends on whether a critical mass of loyalists can be established.

Whilst networks of loyalists would enhance the discharge of routine duties of residents' committees, they would not give the residents' committees the legitimate organizational platform in penetrating these upscale neighborhoods. There is no other alternative but the homeowners' association which (at least in theory) has the undisputable decision making power in neighborhood governance (which includes hiring and firing of the property management agent). Hence, the most ideal situation, from the residents' committees' point of view, is to have the homeowners' association under their full influence. Despite under the current property management law, homeowners' associations are already put under the monitoring and supervision of their local residents' committee, it is not as convenient as putting their cronies to the positions. It is the safest way in which the interests of the residents' committee (and their local governance alliance, the property management agent) can be better protected. The party secretary of the JAFJ residents' committee, revealed this implicit intention when she described the mobilization to install the director of the homeowners' association in the neighborhood,

> Sometimes he (the homeowners' association director) complained about the troublesome governance affairs in the neighborhood. I have always told him that he must keep going as long as I am still in the position. As a Party member, you are supposed to dedicate your whole life to the cause of Communism. I am not asking you to dedicate your whole life. I just ask you to dedicate a little (time and energy)…As a result, members of our homeowners association are upright and integral and very supportive to the work of the property management company.
>
> (Interview20120827)

Of course this approach is very much dependent on whether the residents' committee homeowners' associations can be successfully set up in high-end gated enclaves. However, this is not always easy. In fact, out of the seven neighborhoods we studied, only three of them have established homeowners' associations. The property manager in JLHT described of the difficulties,

> We tried to establish a homeowners' association. But the homeowners were either overseas or rich who did not want to engage in the neighborhood affairs which were perceived by them as time consuming and not very meaningful. Out of 547 housing units in our neighborhood, we could even not manage to recruit five owners (the threshold to form the preparation group).
> (Interview20120823)

In fact, such failure may partly be attributed to the lack of enthusiasm of the property management agents, who would shoulder all the legwork of mobilizing homeowners in forming the homeowners' association. For many property management agents, a neighborhood with no homeowners' association may be easier to manage. They can "divide and rule" rather than to struggle with one powerful opponent. To keep the necessary power balance in the neighborhood governance coalition, they also like to see the homeowners' association to be under their influence, not that of the of residents' committee. As a housing manager we talked to subtly framed his role as homeowners' representative,

> Our director of the homeowners' association goes on business trips all the time and sometimes won't be back for one or two months. We mainly contact him through email. But RCs rarely use electronic means. They are still far behind our management model. So our company is the bridge between the homeowners' association and the RC. Actually both sides do not have much time to talk face to face. Normally we represent the homeowners to attend the meeting and negotiate with government departments, and then bring back the governmental policies to the neighborhood.
> (Interview20120828)

## Conclusions

Upmarket residential enclaves for the nouveaux riches are thriving in urban China. Regardless whether they are villas in spacious and scenic landscape at the fringe of the city or high-rise apartments at city centers, prestigious and leisure life-style as well as safety and autonomy are the usual selling points of such developments. Restrictions in land leasing and the tedious planning and construction approval system would have made stylist independent housing all but impossible in major cities, nouveaux riches families have little choice but to reside in large-scale neighborhoods developed by real estate developers. Whilst extravagant facades, elegant landscaping, ostentatious club house facilities are the usual hallmarks, intensive property management and particularly super elaborated security services are the essential features in these upmarket gated communities.

Yet contrary to what is commonly found in gated neighborhoods elsewhere of loose communities in which escapism is a common quest of most their residents and the well-provided property management services make even the functional inter-actions between neighbours unnecessary, there is evidence in Shanghai that upmar-ket gated communities have, instead, a stronger sense of community. Of course, a sense of community can be boomed by the strong social capital in the neighborhood of long-term and intensive interaction among neighbours, yet it can also be a product of a sense of togetherness generated by the clustering of like-minded people who enjoy a particular kind of life-style and autonomy. More empirical research has to be conducted to uncover the underlying processes of such patterns.

Although the pursuit of privatism and autonomy may be what attracted the nouveaux riches to these upmarket residential enclaves, the social and political reality does not seem to allow a comparable level of freedom and autonomy their counter-parts in the Western world are able to enjoy. The omnipresent local state, in its attempts in monitoring every milieu detail of people's daily life, has been striking hard to crack the defense of the upmarket gated communities. The first breakthrough is perhaps getting the cooperation and support of the property management agents that act as a de facto first line of defense against external threat. Through such help, local police and residents' committees are then able to install additional device in monitor-ing the renters as well as domestic workers in the households. Getting the cooperation of and perhaps, full influence on, the homeowners' association is another direct but harder route of accessing such neighborhoods. Yet with a change of working strategy of the local residents' committees, some success has been achieved.

Recently, innovative means in penetrating upmarket neighborhoods have been attempted. Whilst special events and activities that targeted the special interests of wealthier residents are being tried out, a more effective means is to directly incor-porate the residents as loyalists of the residents' committees. Whereas the younger and more educated residents in such neighborhoods are not easy to be attracted by conventional working approaches of the residents' committees, the elderly members of their family are. It is not uncommon for the nouveaux riches to stay with their elderly parents and they have background, taste and perhaps value system no differ-ent from their counterparts in ordinary neighborhoods. This has become a break-in point for forward-looking and innovative residents' committees in Shanghai.

A local neighborhood governance coalition by the residents' committees and property management agents is by far the most instrumental vehicle for the resi-dents' committees to penetrate into the neighborhoods for the nouveaux riches. This is facilitated by the mutual benefits such coalition would produce on the operation efficiency of both parties. Yet, to residents in such neighborhoods, their over-reliance on intensive property services and their taste for extravagant secu-rity measures may have instead invited a Trojan horse that may threaten their quest for privacy and freedom from state interference.

This paper argues that the ubiquitous presence of local state power is also trying hard to penetrate the enclaves of the nouveaux riches. This is regarded as critical to their mission in maintaining social stability and the hegemony of state power at the grassroots. Empirical evidence shows that some success has been achieved. Yet what are missing in our empirical study are the perspectives of the nouveaux riches on whether they perceive such penetration as irrelevant nuisance or whether it presents a real threat to their pursue of freedom and autonomy.

*Appendix 1*  Basic information of the seven case study upmarket residential enclaves

|  | Price RBM (US$) / m² | Housing type | Total units | Floor area per unit (m²) | District | Rental |
|---|---|---|---|---|---|---|
| SMHB | 40,000 (6,400) | Flat & villa | 937 | 135–560 | Pudong | 50% |
| JAFJ | 55,000 (8,800) | Flat | 1200 | 116–158 | Luwan | 50% |
| JLHT | 65,000 (10,400) | Flat | 547 | 118–328 | Luwan | 60% |
| YZFH | 90,000 (14,400) | Flat | 430 | 101–312 | Luwan | 60% |
| JNHT | 40,000 (6,200) | Flat | 700 | 70–170 | Changning | 50% |
| CSJ | 75,000 (12,000) | Villa | 46 | 271–876 | Changning | 10% |
| SHJY | 80,000 (12,800) | Villa | 100 | 310–480 | Songjiang | 0% |

Source: Interviews and the internet.

*Appendix 2*  Components of index for sense of community

| *Index components* |
|---|
| 1   I feel like being home in the neighborhood |
| 2   I like the neighborhood |
| 3   I am proud of telling other people that I live in this |
| 4   I will regret it if I am forced to leave the neighborhood |
| 5   Neighbors in this neighborhood are willing to help each other |
| 6   Most of the residents in the neighborhood have good spirit of involvement |
| 7   I am interested in things that happen in the neighborhood |
| 8   I am concerned about the image of the neighborhood |
| 9   I have a strong sense of responsibility towards the neighborhood |
| 10  I feel good if I have done meaningful things for the neighborhood |
| 11  I believe anything that is beneficial to the neighborhood is also beneficial to me |
| 12  In general, relationship between residents in the neighborhood is good |
| 13  In general, background of residents in the neighborhood is homogeneous |
| 14  Residents in the neighborhood share similar values |
| 15  I am concerned on how my neighbors comment on my behaviour |
| 16  I am an important figure in the neighborhood |
| 17  Residents believe that they can contribute positively to the functioning of the neighborhood |
| 18  Environment in the neighborhood is conducive to children's activities |
| 19  Environment in the neighborhood is conducive to the growth of young people |
| 20  Environment in the neighborhood is conducive to the life of old people |
|      Test for reliability of the scale- alpha=0.868 |

# Notes

1   The news report "13 Luxury Houses in Shanghai Reached over 100,000 Yuan," http://shbbs. soufun.com/news~-1~3481/81548126_81548126.htm (accessed November 29, 2012).
2   The news report "One villa in Sheshan Mountain Area Sells at 205 Million Yuan and Becomes the Most Expensive Residence in China," http://sh.xinhuanet.com/2009-03/17/content_15973007.htm (accessed November 29, 2012).

# References

Atkinson, Rowland and Blandy, Sarah (2005) 'International perspectives on the New Enclavism', *Housing Studies*, 20 (2): 177–86.

Blakely, Edward J. and Snyder, Mary Gail (1997) *Fortress America: Gated communities in the United States*, Washington, DC: Brookings Institution Press and Cambridge, MA: Lincoln Institute of Land Policy.

Blandy, Sarah, Lister, Diane, Atkinson, Rowland and Flint, John (2003) 'Gated communities a systematic review of the research evidence', Paper represented at the *ESRC Centre for Neighbourhood Research*, Paper 12, 1–65.

Carvalho, M., Varkki, R.V. and Anthony, K.H. (1997) 'Residential satisfaction in condominium exclaves (gated guarded neighbourhoods) in Brazil', *Environment & Behaviour*, 29: 734–68.

Duckett, J. (1998) *The Entrepreneurial State in China: Real estate and commerce departments in reform era Tianjin*, London & New York: Routledge.

Forrest, Ray and Yip, Ngai-ming (2007) 'Neighbourhood and neighboring in a Chinese city: aspects of local social relations in contemporary Guangzhou', *Journal of Contemporary China*, 16 (50): 47–64.

Guo, Shengli and Sun, Xiaoyi (2013) 'Activists' networks and institutional identification in urban neighborhoods', in Ngai-ming Yip (ed.) *Neighborhood Governance in Urban China*, Cheltenham, UK: Edward Elgar.

Hua, Wei (2000) 'A return from the work-unit to the community system: fifty years of urban local management system change in China', *Strategy and Management*, 1: 86–99. (*Dan wei zhi xiang she qu zhi de hui gui: zhong guo cheng shi ji cheng guan li ti zhi wu shi nian bian yu*)

Huang, Youqin and Low Setha, M. (2008) 'Is gating always exclusionary', in Logan, John R. (ed.) *Urban China in Transition*, Malden, MA; Oxford: Blackwell Publishers Ltd.

Liu, Wei (2010) 'Practicing logic and double dimension of the neighborhood politics in block's daily life—a community residents committee-centered analysis', *Zhejiang Social Sciences*, 4, 2010. (*Jiequ linli zhengzhi de dongyuan lujing yu erchong weidu – yi shequ juweihui wei zhongxin de fenxi*)

Low, Setha (2006) 'How private interests take over public space: Zoning, taxes, and incorporation of gated communities', in Setha, Low and Neil, Smith (eds) *The Politics of Public Space*, Chapter 5. Abingdon; New York: Routledge.

Miao, Pu (2003) 'Deserted streets in a jammed town: Gated communities in Chinese cities', *Journal of Urban Design*, 8 (1): 45–66.

Pow, Choon Piew (2007) 'Constructing a new private order: Gated communities and the privatization of urban life in post reform Shanghai', *Social and Cultural Geography*, 8 (6): 813–31.

Pow, Choon-Piew (2009) 'Neoliberalism and the aestheticization of new middle-class landscapes', *Antipode*, 41 (2): 371–90.

Raposa, Rita (2006) 'Gated communities, commodification and aestheticization: The case of the Lisbon metropolitan area', *GeoJournal*, 66: 43–56.

Read, B. L. (2000) 'Revitalizing the State's urban "nerve tips"', *The China Quarterly*, 163: 806–20.

Read, B. L. (2003) 'Democratizing the neighborhood? New private housing and home-owner self-organization in urban China', *The China Journal*, 49: 31–59.

Shin, H. B. (2008) 'Living on the edge: Financing post-displacement housing in urban redevelopment projects in Seoul', *Environment and Urbanization*, 20 (2): 411–26.

Wilson-Doenges, Georjeanna (2000) 'An explanation of sense of community and fear of crime in gated communities', *Environment and Behaviour*, 32 (5): 597–611.

Wu, Fulong (2002) 'China's changing urban governance in the transition towards a more market-oriented economy', *Urban Studies*, 39 (7): 1071–93.

Wu, Fulong (2005) 'Rediscovering the gate, under market transition: From work-unit compounds to commodity housing enclaves', *Housing Studies*, 20 (2): 235–54.

Wu, Fulong and He, Shenjing (2005) 'Changes in traditional urban areas and impacts of urban redevelopment: A case study of three neighborhoods in Nanjing, China', *Tijdschrift voor Economische en Sociale Geografie*, 96 (1): 75–95.

Yang Min (2007) 'Community as State Governance Unit: A case study on residents' community participation and cognition in the process of community building campaign', *Sociological Studies*, 4: 137–64. (*Zuowei guojia zhili danwei de shequ – dui chengshi shequ jianshe yundong guocheng zhong jumin shequ canyu he shequ renzhi de gean yanjiu*)

Yip, N. M. (2012) 'Walled without gates: Gated communities in Shanghai', *Urban Geography*, 33 (2): 221–36.

Yip, N. M. (2013) 'Introduction: The context of neighborhood governance', in Yip, N. M. (ed.) *Neighbourhood Governance in Urban China*, Cheltenham: Edward Elgar.

Zhang, T. (2002) 'Urban development and a Socialist pro-growth coalition in Shanghai', *Tingwei Zhang*, 37 (4): 475–99.

Zhu Guohong and Guo Shengli, (2011) *Chinese International Communities in Globalization – Empirical Studies in Changing District in Shanghai*, Shanghai: Shanghai People's Publishing House. (*Quanqiuhua Beijing xia de zhongguo guoji shequ: shanghai changningqu shizheng yanjiu*)

Zhu, J. (2004) 'From land use right to land development right: Institutional change in China's urban development', *Urban Studies*, 41 (7): 1249–67.

# 13 Uneven "right to the city"

## Theorizing the new communal living space and a new form of urban politics in China

*Lili Wang*

## I. Introduction

Conflicts around the built environment at the neighborhood level have been extensively documented and analyzed in the West, especially in the United States (Purcell 2001; McKenzie 1998; Cox and Jonas 1993; Davis 1992; Davis 1991; Cox 1983; Cox and McCarthy 1982; Cox 1981). In China, this form of urban politics is relatively new, yet no less intense:

> "Interests of Homeowners Embezzled, Professor Defending Rights Beaten Bloody";
> "Conflicts between Developers and Homeowners Escalated, Complaints Regarding Commercial Housing Hard to Resolve";
> "Eighty per cent of Guangdong Communities Don't Have Homeowners' Committees, Defending Rights Risks Bloodshed."

Since the end of the 1990s such startling newspaper headlines have become frequent. Even the Western media have scented the new tensions (French 27 January 2008; Fan 26 January 2008). This form of urban politics, i.e. the scuffles and wrestling between homeowners (often led by Homeowners' Committees, HCs hereafter[1]) and various other interest groups, e.g. developers and property management companies (PMCs hereafter), who fight over the communal living space, is quite new in China. Before being commoditized, housing was provided by work-units, and the politics of the living space unfolded around and was subordinated to politics in the workplace (Friedmann 2005; Wu 2005). During the reform, however, the work-unit system collapsed; and both housing provision and community maintenance were commodified. The old fabric woven by work-units was disrupted while new social networks were and still are in formation. It is in this destruction and construction that a new form of urban politics – a politics centering on the new residential neighborhood – is emerging and growing to shape the everyday experience and politics of contemporary Chinese urbanites.

Despite its significance, this new form of urban politics remains understudied in the English-language literature. There are little more than ten journal articles and book chapters, all of which are written by political scientists and sociologists (Yip *et al.* 2011; Huang 2009; Wasserstrom 2009; Shi 2008; Read 2008; 2007; Zhu and

Ho 2008; Zhu 2007; Liu 2007; Zhu and Wang 2007; Shi and Cai 2006; Cai 2005; Tomba 2005). These usually take the form of case studies and try to answer three major questions: 1) What leads to these conflicts? 2) What contributes to the success or failure of homeowner resistance? And 3) What is the role of the state in these conflicts and how can state-civil society relations be characterized in China? These are crucial questions and existing studies do provide insights about them. The literature nevertheless suffers from three major shortcomings. First, it looks into a very limited spectrum of cases of homeowners' resistance and thus fails to grasp the complexity of the phenomenon. It is, for example, a little disappointing to see four of those ten or so articles studying the same community's resistance in Guangzhou (the Lijiang Garden, 丽江花园). Second, existing studies tend to focus solely on the strategies and results of homeowners' resistance and scarcely look into how such conflicts are integrally related to much broader historical changes. In those rare instances where they do (Shi and Cai 2006; Read 2007), the analysis is rather brief, so brief that the ontologically complicated history is reduced to one dimension – the commodification of housing in China. Third, since the literature is mostly concerned with the political and sociological aspects of the conflicts, a geographical perspective on the issue is yet to be provided.

This chapter aims to address these three shortcomings. First, based on extensive and close reading of Chinese online news[2] and existing scholarship in both English and Chinese, it tries to present a more comprehensive and complex picture of the conflicts around the living space in Chinese cities. Second, it contextualizes the new form of urban politics with respect to the broader transition of China's urban political economy, which is characterized notably by: 1) the commodification of land; 2) the commodification of all the use values embodied in the residential space, including housing, community maintenance, and public utilities; 3) the transformation of community governance; and 4) the establishment of private property ownership. Built on such solid empirical observation and historical contextualization, the third goal of the chapter is to adopt a relational geography approach informed by thinkers like Henri Lefebvre, David Harvey and Doreen Massey to theorize the emerging communal living space and the new form of urban politics in China. As such, communal living spaces are conceptualized simultaneously as spaces of profits, spaces of utility, and spaces of governance. The following three sections are devoted respectively to these three tasks. The gist of the chapter is to delineate another approach to the unevenness of China's urban residential landscape other than mapping or quantifying the material difference as has been fruitfully done by other authors in the book. This approach focuses on Chinese citizens' differentiated power to shape their own lives, their "uneven rights to the city" (Harvey 2008: 23), and aims to understand how such differentiated power is a product of multiple social transitions that stretch over time and space.

## II.  The new form of urban politics: concrete complexity

Taking note of the objects of disputes, the conflicts between homeowners and opposing interests can generally be placed into seven categories.

*1) Disputes about residence quality: the housing unit and*
*the neighborhood as a whole*

It is not uncommon for developers to fail to deliver on the promises made in advertisements or in the contract signed before housing is handed over to the buyer. The violations are of a motley variety. For example, building materials and techniques are defective, causing water leaks or cracks in walls; the promised kindergarten or lovely lake never turns up but gives way to additional buildings for more profit. The frequent result is that disappointed homebuyers argue with developers for rightful compensation.

*2) Disputes about residence quality: the surrounding environment and NIMBYism*

The threat of the location of unfavorable land uses close to the neighborhood has been another source of conflict. Such unfavorable land uses include, for example, a garbage-processing plant, an incinerator (Watts 23 January 2009), a maglev train (Fan 26 January 2008; French 27 January 2008), or a cemetery (Shen 21 December 2005). In such instances the mentality of NIMBYism (Not In My Back Yard) plays strongly among homeowners, underpinned by concerns with personal health and the quality of the neighborhood environment.

*3) Disputes about residence quality: property management services*

Conflicts arise also, and frequently, because of the malfunction of PMCs. These housing and neighborhood service providers may not be able to guarantee community safety, may fail to take good care of the landscape of the neighborhood, often charge exceedingly high management fees, may resist disclosing how the funds are utilized, may refuse to leave even after their contract is terminated by the HC, and so forth.

*4) Disputes about residence quality: the provision of utilities*

By utilities I refer to a set of services such as water supply, heat supply, gas supply, sewage disposal, and garbage disposal, etc. With the rapid expansion of cities at the periphery, the supply of utilities often suffers from inadequacy or instability. Meanwhile, the marketization of many such services tends to create antagonisms between home-owner-consumers and public–private utility providers, especially over the pricing of utilities.

*5) Conflicts over the ownership and use of communal property*

Communal property includes all the space outside the private living space, e.g. an elevator within a building, a community center, public parking space, green open space, civil air defense works within the community,[3] and so forth. These public spaces tend to be misappropriated in various ways by developers, PMCs, or even local governments. For example, elevators are used for advertisements; the community center is leased out to collect rents, etc. This type of conflict is also one that has attracted attention in the English-language literature.

*6) Conflicts over the Housing Special Maintenance Fund (HSMF)*

According to the *Management Methods of Housing Special Maintenance Fund* implemented in February 2008, the HSMF is a special fund used to repair, renovate and maintain the public space of housing, and public facilities and equipment (Article 2). This is a considerable amount of money, equivalent to two to three per cent of the total real estate value of the neighborhood. According to the *Management Methods*, the fund is owned by all homeowners in the neighborhood, and after a Homeowners' Assembly is formed the HSMF should be transferred to the Assembly and managed by it (Article 15). PMCs, however, often refuse to complete the transfer and continue maintaining control over a substantial amount of HSMF. Other than coercive seizure, PMCs also frequently misuse the HSMF without notifying homeowners.

*7) Conflicts over rights of administration and representation*

Conflicts also arise within a neighborhood as different groups compete for the right to represent and manage the neighborhood. Competition often takes place between HCs and RCs. Although both of them are allegedly "autonomous community organizations," RCs are more like a helper and subordinate to local governments.[4] Competition also exists between the developer/PMC-backed HC and the homeowners'-supported HC. The major issue is who is legitimate? Legitimacy has a double meaning here: "legitimate" in terms of the ability to represent homeowners' interests and "legitimate" in the eyes of the state.

## III. Contextualizing the new form of urban politics

This brief survey exemplifies the diverse forms of conflict around the communal living space in Chinese cities and the interwoven social relations involved. A critical scholar, however, needs to go beyond immediate empirical observation and reflect upon how the examined phenomenon is linked to changes at wider scales. This section analyzes how the transition in four internally related fields of China's urban political economy works to create and shape the new form of urban politics in China.

### The commodification of land

Before the reform, land was allocated by the state and did not have a price. In the early 1980s local governments started to charge foreign investors rent for using land in the four Special Economic Zones; they also used land as their share of investment in early joint-venture enterprises. In 1986, the *Land Administration Law* was approved and came into force, confirming the separation of land use rights and land ownership, which created the necessary legislative support for land-leasing. In 1988, the *Constitution* was revised to legitimize transactions of land use rights (Lin and Ho 2005; Chen 2011). Since then, a land pricing and leasing system has been in effect. Space and location are as a result monetized. The commodification of land is the very condition for the formation of a dynamic and differentiated housing market; it is also the precondition for the rapid industrialization and urbanization of China, which then substantially expands the social demand for private housing (Dowall 1994).

### The commodification of housing, neighborhood maintenance, and utilities

Even before the late 1990s, there were policy efforts to develop a private housing sector. First, some public housing was "sold" by the government as a way of raising money (Zhou and Logan 1996). Second, private (including foreign) capital was allowed in selected cities to develop private housing so as to accommodate housing demands stemming from the prospering private sector. However, the size and scope of this housing market was still restricted.

The turning point came in the late 1990s, when the Asian Financial Crisis severely impacted the state sector of China and necessitated its reform. Tens of thousands of state-owned enterprises (SOEs) were privatized, and the onus of providing welfare to workers, including housing, was shed off by SOEs and transferred to the market. In 1998 the State Council issued a scheme to encourage private housing provision through the market and to completely disband the public allocation of housing (He and Wu 2009). Around the same time, public housing underwent extensive privatization (Lee and Zhu 2006; Wang 2005; Wang, *et al.* 2005).

The rise of private housing is coupled with the emergence of property management companies, which perform housing and community maintenance that used to be carried out by the housing department of the local government or SOEs (Wu 2005). In 1981, the first PMC in China, the Shenzhen Property Management Company, was founded (Yu and Wang 2000). Property management is no longer a government function but a profit-generating service sold and purchased on the market.

Since the early 2000s the provision of public utilities has witnessed increasing involvement of private capital as well. In 2002, the then Ministry of Construction promulgated *Principles of Accelerating the Marketization of Public Utility Projects*, which allows private capital, domestic and foreign, to invest in public utility projects (Meng *et al.* 2011). Since then private capital has taken active roles in investing public unities in various ways (Zhong *et al.* 2008).

### The transformation of neighborhood governance

#### Governance at the city level

Faced with the problems of a highly centralized and stale economy and severe deficit in late 1970s, the Chinese Communist Party (CCP) embarked on a series of liberalization reforms including, notably, governance decentralization. In 1980 a central-local fiscal "contract" system was implemented to greatly increase local autonomy in arranging investment and expenditure. In 1994 the new tax-sharing system, while reinforcing the central government's ability to extract tax, decentralized decision-making power even further (Yeh and Wu 1996; Wu 2002). Examining the direct and intensive involvement of Chinese local authorities in economic development, Duckett (1998) has described them as "entrepreneurial states."

The repercussions of decentralization for China's new form of urban politics have been rather apparent. First, the devolution of substantial welfare provision responsibility to the locality and the 1994 fiscal reform that reduces the local sharing of tax revenue have given rise to a local boosterism, pressing local governments to secure extra-budgetary revenue to finance local development. Second, city governments are given the power to sell land use rights in order to earn such extra-budgetary revenue (McGee *et al.* 2007: 18; Wu 2002). In fact, Chinese cities have become increasingly reliant on – if not trapped in – this land-based finance (Tian and Ma 2009). The local government thus has "good" reasons to side with developers, their "clients" and "partners," in resolving the conflicts around the living space.

*Governance at the neighborhood level*

Accompanying the decentralization of power from the central government to local governments is the strengthening of the functionality of street-level or neighborhood level government units, i.e. Street Offices and RCs. For example, in 1991 the central government initiated a "Community Building" movement, wherein the RC's role "as providers of services and sponsors of social and civic activities has been greatly augmented" (Read and Chen 2008: 326). These base-level governments, however, commonly experience shortages of work-funds (Friedmann 2007; Wu 2002). They thus sometimes collaborate with local developers and PMCs to misappropriate neighborhood space so as to increase income. In these cases they make themselves the targets of homeowners' resistance (Chao 2004; Zhang and Liu 2005; Cai 2005).

In addition to the state-dominated neighborhood governance institution is the HC, nowadays the leading organization for homeowners' activism. In general, the HC is supposed to be a homeowners' self-administration organization, representing all homeowners in a territorially identified neighborhood and acting to protect their interests in all kinds of conflicts with other interest groups. The legal definition of HCs can be found in the two milestone pieces of legislation implemented in 2007, the *Real Right Law* (Article 75) and the *Regulations on Property Management of 2007* (Article 15). Even though the two laws have greatly advanced the legalization of HCs, HCs still suffer from an ambiguous legal status. As explained in Fu's chapter in this book, the HC has never been formally defined by law as a juristic person (法人), and is thus unable to sue opposing groups (Chen 2003). This is deemed by Chinese scholars a major institutional impediment to homeowners' activism (Chen 2006; Xu 2007). For this and various other reasons, HCs remain a minor and weak form of civic engagement in Chinese cities.

In sum, urban governments, their neighborhood subsidiaries (Street Offices and Residents' Committees), and HCs, all assume certain governing authorities over the socio-space of the neighborhood. In addition, PMCs, quite likely converted from previous off-shoots of local housing authorities, also hold the mentality of "governing" – rather than "servicing" – the neighborhood (Wu 2005; Wang, *et al.* 2005). These different bodies of governance often come into conflict with each other with respect to the everyday and the future of the neighborhood.

*The establishment of private property ownership*

China's housing reform in late 1990s created massive homeownership in a relatively short time frame. In 2007 the homeownership rate in China was estimated to be 75 per cent (Walker and Buck 2007). Today it may well exceed that number. The legislation and ideology of private property ownership, however, has been a simmering process extending over about 30 years. Table 13.1 lists critical legal documents that illustrate the transformation of ownership schemes in China since 1982. When private ownership was officially written into the *Constitution* in 2004, it was received as an epochal moment in Chinese history, "laying down a new marker in the nation's swift march away from the doctrinaire Communism of its founders" (Cody 2004). The *Real Right Law* implemented in 2007 is by far the most important legislation that directs the resolution of disputes about the communal living space. It stipulates how public space and HSMF should be managed, how the expense of maintaining the building and its affiliated space and the revenue generated from them should be allocated, and confirms the legal right of homeowners to fire a PMC. Although still unclear about the power over space among different governing bodies and among homeowners, it lays down the legislative condition for homeowners' activism.

******

To sum up, it is within the context of the entrenchment of capitalist relations of production of the built environment, the changing institutions of neighborhood governance, and the establishment of the private property regime that the new form of urban politics comes into being and assumes the diverse forms discussed in section II.

## IV. Theorizing the communal living space in Chinese cities

*Relational geography*

Relational geography is gaining increasing popularity in human geography (Parker and Sites 2012; Sheppard 2008; Murdoch 2005; Castree 2003, 2002; Harvey 2006, 1996). It takes different forms with varying emphases by different authors, but first and foremost, it means the inseparability of the spatial and the social. Space is not just a container or a residual of social processes; it is instead integral to them. As Lefebvre eloquently narrates,

> ... sociopolitical contradictions are realized spatially. The contradictions of space thus make the contradictions of social relations operative. In other words, spatial contradictions "express" conflicts between sociopolitical interests and forces; it is only in space that such conflicts come effectively into play, and in doing so they become contradictions of space.
>
> (Lefebvre 1991: 365)

In addition to the integrality of the social and the spatial, the relational approach is also characterized by the essential interrelationship between processes *across space and time*. Lefebvre, for example, contends that social space is multiple as

*Table 13.1* The historical evolution of the legal system as regards property ownership in China, PRC (adapted from Chen 2011)

| Year | Laws/regulations | Critical stipulations |
|---|---|---|
| 1982 | *The Constitution* | Two forms of ownership allowed: state ownership and collective ownership |
| 1986 | *The General Principles of Civil Law* | Property rights established related to ownership, including:<br>1) Contract responsibility operational rights (承包经营权)[1]<br>2) SOEs' operational rights<br>3) Rights arising from "neighborhood relationship" |
| 1986 | *The Land Administration Law* | Land ownership allowed<br>1) in cities, by the state<br>2) in villages, by rural collectives |
| 1988 | *The Constitution* | "The right to use land may be transferred according to law' |
| 1990 | *The Right to Use State-Owned Land in Cities and Towns* | Methods of acquiring state-owned land for real estate development described<br>The maximum terms of these land use rights set, e.g. the term for residential use is 70 years |
| 1993 | *The Constitution* | China is now practising "socialist market economy" (rather than "planned economy on the basis of socialist public ownership") |
| 1994 | *The Law on the Administration of Urban Real Estate* | Regulates property transactions |
| 1998 | *The Land Administration Law* | Protects arable land<br>Regulates the supervision and inspection of land requisition<br>Mandates compensation for displaced peasants |
| 1999 | *The Constitution* | The individual and private sectors declared to constitute "important" components of the socialist market economy |
| 2004 | *The Constitution* | "The lawful private property of citizens shall be inviolable" |
| 2007 | *The Real Right Law* | "The 'real right' (物权) mentioned in this Law means the right of the right-holder to control directly specific things to the exclusion of others, and includes ownership (属有权), rights of use and enjoyment over things (用益物权) and security rights over things (担保物权)" |

Note: [1] This is the basis for the rural reform and early decentralization reforms in SOEs in 1980s, which subdivide tasks among peasant groups or worker-groups through the contract responsibility system.

well as intertwined – it crosses multiple scales. Indeed, it is the outcome of dynamic, contesting processes of many currents or tendencies (Lefebvre 1991: 97, 110, 266). Harvey holds a similar view in his explication of a relational "dialectics" and "relational space." In *Justice, Nature and the Geography of Difference*, he writes that "dialectical thinking emphasizes the understanding of processes, flows, fluxes, and relations. ... Dialectical reasoning [should] ... transform the self-evident world of things ... into a much more confusing world of relations and flows that are manifest as things" (1996: 49). In a similar vein,[5] Massey (1999a, 1999b, 2005) proposes an approach that centers on the openness and non-linearity of time and space. Her approach emphasizes: 1) the chance juxtaposition of spatial-temporal relations, i.e. the messy, contingent, and constantly changing configuration of space-time as multiple trajectories and narratives come together, and: 2) the non-linear feedback dynamics following that juxtaposition.

### *A relational conceptualization of the communal living space in Chinese cities*

As illustrated above, the relational approach conceives space in terms of multiple social processes and conditions working together, which necessarily extend over time and space. Guided by this approach I abstract – the abstraction is solely for analytical convenience and does not presume a mechanical separation of ontologies – the communal living space as relational spaces of profit, utility, and governance respectively (see Figure 13.1). Each category of space emerges out of the everyday experiences of multiple social actors, but also embodies the social changes occurring at wider scales, including the commodification of housing and related services, the transformation of governance, and the establishment of property ownership in discourses and practices, as discussed in earlier sections. As Lefebvre's famous quote states: "the urban, defined as assemblies and encounters, is therefore the simultaneity (or centrality) of all that exists socially" (Lefebvre 1976: 15).

Conflicts often arise at the interfaces of these different social relations. Quite straightforwardly, spaces of utility (and the social actors involved) are repeatedly confronted by spaces of profits (and the social actors involved). The Marxist perspective well illustrates how such confrontations are firmly rooted in the contradiction between the dual roles of the communal living space – as a commodity for capital and as a necessary shelter for workers' social reproduction (Cox 1981; Harvey 1978). The concrete expressions of the contradiction are however diverse, as homeowners come into conflict with different sections of the "profit" regime. Meanwhile, the multiple governance structures implicated in the relational spaces of governance often entail divergent interests and varying degree of legitimacy and resources to govern. Such a situation does not aid in problem-solving but rather complicates and aggravates problems.

Moreover, as the relational approach suggests, the social relations encountered in the communal living space should be firmly contextualized with respect to broader socio-spatial processes. Section III has illustrated how the contradictions between the relational spaces of utility, of profit, and of governance are products of historical changes that go beyond the physical boundary of the neighborhood. Notably, the transformations of governance at the municipal level and at the base-level have rendered such government units not just subjects of governance but also subjects of profit. The precarious positionality of HCs as a governing body of neighborhood politics is also shaped by specific historical processes, including myriad legislative efforts to establish and refine private property rights in Chinese.

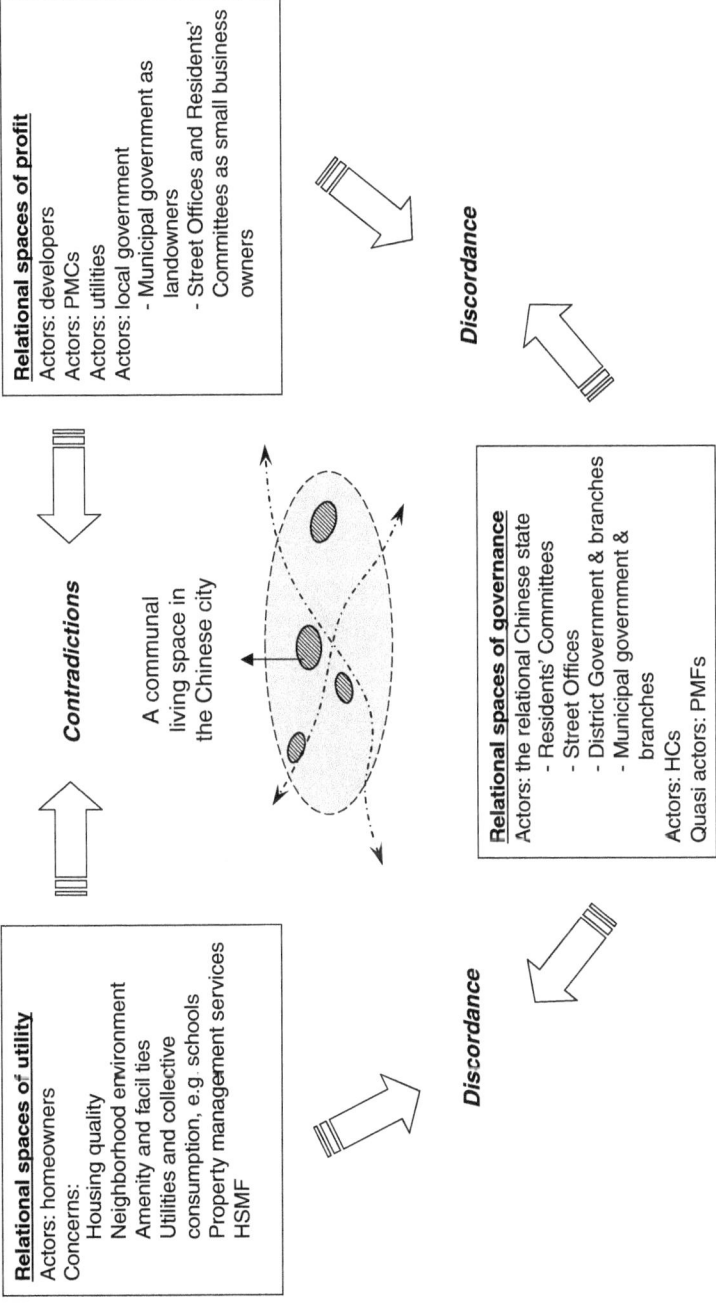

**Relational spaces of utility**
Actors: homeowners
Concerns:
 Housing quality
 Neighborhood environment
 Amenity and facil ties
 Utilities and collective
 consumption, e.g. schools
 Property management services
 HSMF

*Contradictions*

A communal
living space in
the Chinese city

**Relational spaces of profit**
Actors: developers
Actors: PMCs
Actors: utilities
Actors: local government
 - Municipal government as
 landowners
 - Street Offices and Residents'
 Committees as small business
 owners

*Discordance*

**Relational spaces of governance**
Actors: the relational Chinese state
 - Residents' Committees
 - Street Offices
 - District Government & branches
 - Municipal government &
 branches
Actors: HCs
Quasi actors: PMFs

*Discordance*

*Figure 13.1* A relational conceptualization of the communal living space in Chinese cities.

## V. Conclusion

The uneven landscape of dwelling emerging in Chinese cities is not only manifested in and approachable by mapping socio-spatial stratification or segregation. One should also look at the finer differences within a broad category of dwelling – the privately propertied communal living space. This research is an attempt at such a task. It does so by examining growing conflicts and struggles around the communal living space between homeowners and developers, PMCs, utilities, and sometimes local governments. Based on an extensive literature review, it accomplishes three tasks: 1) to show the diversity and complexity of such conflicts; 2) to put the subject matter in its diverse historical contexts; and 3) to develop a new theoretical framework to understand the new politics of the communal living space in China. It then shows that it is at the intersections and encounters of various social relations in such propertied communal living spaces that differences and inequalities emerge and forcefully get played out. Empirically, inequality is embodied in the uneven rights over the various utilities of dwelling, and the differential power of homeowners in managing the public space in face of the abuses of developers, PMCs, and other profit-oriented groups. Indeed, it is about the uneven "right to the city" in Harvey's terms – the collective power to reshape the urban process (Harvey 2008: 23).

## Acknowledgements

I would like to express my deepest appreciation to my advisor, Professor Kevin R. Cox, who has always been supportive and stimulating to my research. I am also thankful for the valuable comments from the participants in the "Housing, Land, and Urban Transformation in China" session in the Annual Conference of the Association of American Geographers (February 2012, New York), and in the "Polarized Residential Landscape in Transitional Chinese Cities" session in the International Conference on Spatial and Social Transformation in Urban China (December 2012, Hong Kong). My sincere gratitude is thus extended to the organizers of both sessions, Professor Si-ming Li and Youqin Huang, who are also the editors of the book, for their hard work of organizing and editing as well as inviting me to participate in this book project. Finally, I would acknowledge with much appreciation the Mershon Center for International Security Studies at the Ohio State University, which supported my field work related to this research in summer 2010.

## Notes

1  Another contributor to the book, Qiang Fu, uses HAs to denote the organizations of homeowners. I opt not to use HAs in that it can also abbreviate "Homeowners' Assemblies" and create term confusion.
2  Due to the lack of any formal survey data about the issue, the study is based on close reading of second-hand materials, especially a large number of news articles on the internet. The author uses the Baidu News Search Engine (http://news.baidu.com/advanced_news.html) to explore and retrieve available online sources. The search was

performed in December 2011. The search criteria are defined as follows: 1) Search keywords: homeowners (业主) *and* rights-defending (维权); 2) Search scope: search these key words in the title rather than the content of news so as to increase the relevance of results. After weeding out dead links, repeated coverage of the same case and entries that did not involve any substantive "case studies" or included a case but with no sufficient empirical information, the list comprised around 400 cases. It should be noted that data generated in this way by no means represent the real spatial-temporal dynamics of the conflicts around the living space in Chinese cities; it is not intended for that end. It is however believed that such an extensive review of online news enables a solid qualitative understanding of the evolution of those conflicts and the general pattern of social relations implicated in them.

3   For example, according to the *Shanghai Civil Defense Regulation* (revised in 2003), any newly planned civil-use building should build underground space that can be used as an air-raid shelter during wartime (Article 36). Normally, civil air defense works are also used for underground parking. Article 33 of the Shanghai regulation stipulates that air civil defense works are managed by whoever invests in them, and the gains generated by these works go to the investor. In newly built residential communities, while these works are constructed by developers, the cost of construction is mostly transferred to homeowners through the payment for their housing. In most cases, however, such spaces are taken by the developer as they are the owners and "sold" to car owners in addition to the condominium.

4   Residents' Committees often execute orders of the Street Office, which is then commanded by the District Government. They are designed to provide more diverse services and perform policing and overseeing duties at the neighborhood level, as what the work-units did in the socialist era (Read and Chen, 2008).

5   One should certainly never overlook the difference between Harvey and Massey's approaches. At one point Massey (1993) heavily criticized Harvey for understanding urban change solely in terms of capitalist accumulation and contradictions (Harvey, 1978). As Harvey became more and more involved in relational thinking the two scholars' approaches can be said to converge. Yet the notable difference that still persists is how Massey (1993) highlights other social dimensions, e.g. gender and race, in addition to class to understand the formation and reformation of place, while Harvey is still emphatic of the centrality of production and class while acknowledging the importance of other dimensions.

# References

Cai, Y. (2005) "China's moderate middle class: the case of homeowners' resistance", *Asian Survey*, 45(5): 777–99.

Castree, N. (2002) "False antithesis? Marxism, nature and actor-network theory", *Antipode*, 34: 111–46.

Castree, N. (2003) "Differential geographies: place, indigenous rights and 'local' resources", *Political Geography*, 23: 133–67.

Chao, L. (2004) "The benefit gambling in community autonomy: the Zhongqing Garden of Nanjing as an example", *Society*, 4: 31–3 (in Chinese).

Chen, A. (2011) "The law of property and the evolving system of property rights in China", in G. Yu (ed.) *The Development of the Chinese Legal System: Change and Challenges*, New York: Routledge.

Chen, W. (2003) "On the legal status of the estate owner's committee", *Journal of Political Sciences and Law*, 20(5): 39–41 (in Chinese).

Chen, Y. (2006) "Ability of action and system restrict: middle class in the urban movement", *Sociological Studies*, 21(4): 1–20 (in Chinese).

Cody, E. (2004) "China amends constitution to guarantee human rights", *The Washington Post*, Sunday, March 14, 2004. Online. Available HTTP: <http://www.washingtonpost.com/ac2/wp-dyn?pagename=article&contentId=A57447-2004Mar14> (accessed June 20, 2012).

Cox, K. R. (1981) "Capitalism and conflicts around the communal living space", in M. J. Dear and A. J. Scott (eds) *Urbanization and Urban Planning in Capitalist Society*, London and New York: Methuen.

Cox, K. R. (1983) "Residential mobility, neighborhood activism and neighborhood problems", *Political Geography Quarterly*, 2(2): 99–118.

Cox, K. R. and Jones, A. E. G. (1993) "Urban development, collective consumption and the politics of metropolitan fragmentation", *Political Geography*, 12(1): 8–37.

Cox, K. R. and McCarthy, J. J. (1982) "Neighbourhood activism as a politics of turf: a critical analysis", in K. R. Cox and R. J. Johnston (eds) *Conflict, Politics and The Urban Scene*, New York: St. Martin's Press.

Davis, J. E. (1991), *Contested Ground: Collective Action and the Urban Neighborhood*, Ithaca and London: Cornell University Press.

Davis, M. (1992) *City of Quartz: Excavating the Future in Los Angeles*, London and New York: Verso.

Dowall, E. D. (1994) "Urban residential redevelopment in the People's Republic of China", *Urban Studies*, 31(9): 1497–516.

Duckett, J. (1998) *The Entrepreneurial State in China: Real Estate and Commerce Departments in Reform Era Tianjin*, London and New York: Routledge.

Fan, M. (2008) "Shanghai's middle class launches quiet, meticulous revolt", *Washington Post*, Saturday, January 26, 2008. Online. Available HTTP: <http://www.washingtonpost.com/wp-dyn/content/article/2008/01/25/AR2008012503500.html> (accessed June 20, 2012).

French, H.W. (2008) "Ordinary citizens seeking a place at the decision-making table in China", *The New York Times*, Sunday, January 27, 2008. Online. Available HTTP: <http://www.nytimes.com/2008/01/27/world/asia/27iht-shanghai.1.9523501.html> (accessed June 15, 2012).

Friedmann, J. (2005) *China's Urban Transition*, Minneapolis: University of Minnesota Press.

Friedmann, J. (2007) "Reflections on place and place-making in the cities of China", *International Journal of Urban and Regional Research*, 31(2): 257–79.

Harvey, D. (1978) "Labor, capital, and class struggle around the built environment in advanced capitalist societies", in K. R. Cox (ed.) *Urbanization and Conflict in Market Societies*, Chicago: Maaroufa Press.

Harvey, D. (1996) *Justice, Nature and the Geography of Difference*, Oxford: Blackwell.

Harvey, D. (2006) "Space as a keyword", in N. Castree and D. Gregory (eds) *David Harvey: A Critical Reader*, Malden, MA and Oxford: Blackwell.

Harvey, D. (2008) "The right to the city", *New Left Review*, 53: 23–40.

He, S. and Wu, F. (2009) "China's emerging neoliberal urbanism: perspectives from urban redevelopment", *Antipode*, 41(2): 282–304.

Huang, R. (2009) "Protecting the rights of homeowners: urban resistance in a Shanghai neighbourhood", paper presented at ISA International Housing Conference, Glasgow, 2009.

Lee, J. and Zhu, Y. (2006) "Urban governance, neoliberalism and housing reform in China", *The Pacific Review*, 19(1): 39–61.

Lefebvre, H. (1976) *The Survival of Capitalism: Reproduction of the Relations of Production*, London: Allison and Busby.

Lefebvre, H. (1991) *The Production of Space*, trans. Donald Nicholson-Smith, Oxford: Basil Blackwell.

Lin, G. C. S. and Ho, S. (2005) "The state, land system, and land development processes in contemporary China", *Annals of the Association of American Geographers*, 95(2): 411–36.

Liu, C. (2007) "How does morality evaluate public works? Justifications in a community-based environmental dispute in Shenzhen", *Chinese Sociology and Anthropology*, 40(2): 35–64.

McGee, T., Lin, G., Marton, A., Wang, M. and Wu, J. (2007) *China's Urban Space: Development under Market Socialism*, London and New York: Routledge.

McKenzie, E. (1998) "Home-owner associations and California politics – an exploratory analysis", *Urban Affairs Review*, 34(1): 52–75.

Massey, D. (1993) "Power-geometry and a progressive sense of place", in J. Bird (ed.) *Mapping the Futures: Local Cultures, Global Change*, New York: Routledge.

Massey, D. (1999a) "Space-time, 'science' and the relationship between physical geography and human geography", *Transactions of the Institute of British Geographers*, NS 24: 261–76.

Massey, D. (1999b) "Spaces of politics", in D. Massey, J. Allen and P. Sarre (eds) *Human Geography Today*, Cambridge: Polity Press.

Massey, D. (2005) "The elusiveness of place", in D. Massey (ed.) *For Space*, London and Thousand Oaks, CA: Sage.

Meng, X., Zhao, Q. and Shen, Q. (2011) "Critical success factors for Transfer–Operate–Transfer urban water supply projects in China", *Journal of Management in Engineering*, 27: 243–51.

Murdoch, J. (2005) *Post-structuralist Geography: A Guide to Relational Space*, London and Thousand Oaks, CA: Sage.

Parker, S. and Sites, W. (2012) "New directions in urban theory: introduction", *Urban Geography*, 33(4): 469–73.

Purcell, M. (2001) "Neighborhood activism among homeowners as a politics of space", *Professional Geographer*, 53(2): 178–94.

Read, B. L. (2007) "Inadvertent political reform via private associations: assessing homeowners' groups in new neighborhoods", in E. J. Perry and M. Goldman (eds) *Grassroots Political Reform in Contemporary China*, Cambridge, MA: Harvard University Press.

Read, B. L. (2008) "Accessing variation in civil society organizations: China's home-owner associations in comparative perspective", *Comparative Political Studies*, 41(9): 124–65.

Read, B. L. and Chen, C. M. (2008) "The state's evolving relationship with urban society: China's neighborhood organizations in comparative perspective", in J. Logan (ed.) *Urban China in Transition*, Malden; Oxford: Blackwell.

Shen, X. (2005) "Cemetery to be built near new housing, homeowners of Southern Bank Garden raise the flag of resistance", *Xinhua News*, December 21, 2005. Online. Available HTTP: <http://www.zj.xinhuanet.com/newscenter/2005-12/21/content_5863409.htm> (accessed October 20, 2012).

Sheppard, E. (2008) "Geographic dialectics?" *Environment and Planning A*, 40: 2603–12.

Shi, F. (2008) "Social capital at work: the dynamics and consequences of grassroots movements in urban China", *Critical Asian Studies*, 40(2): 233–62.

Shi, F. and Cai, Y. (2006) "Disaggregating the state: networks and collective resistance in Shanghai", *The China Quarterly*, 186: 314–32.

Tian, L. and Ma, W. (2009) "Government intervention in city development of China: a tool of land supply", *Land Use Policy*, 26: 599–609.

Tomba, L. (2005) "Residential space and collective interest formation in Beijing's housing disputes", *The China Quarterly*, 184: 934–51.

Walker, R. and Buck, D. (2007) "The Chinese road", *New Left Review*, 46: 39–66.

Wang, Y. (2005) "Low-income communities and urban poverty in China", *Urban Geography*, 26(3): 222–42.

Wang, Y. P., Wang, Y. and Bramley, G. (2005) "Chinese housing reform in state-owned enterprises and its impacts on different social groups", *Urban Studies*, 42(10): 1859–78.

Wasserstrom, J. N. (2009) "Middle-class mobilization", *Journal of Democracy*, 20(3): 29–32.

Watts, J. (2009) "Chinese protestors confront police over incinerator plans in Guangzhou", *The Guardian*, Monday, January 23, 2009. Online. Available HTTP: <http://www.guardian.co.uk/environment/2009/nov/23/China-protest-incinerator-guangzhou> (accessed October 20, 2012).

Wu, F. (2002) "China's changing urban governance in the transition towards a more market-oriented economy", *Urban Studies*, 39(7): 1071–93.

Wu, F. (2005) "Rediscovering the 'gate' under market transition: from work-unit compounds to commodity housing enclaves", *Housing Studies*, 20(2): 235–54.

Xu, Q. (2007) "The power redistribution in transitional society – an analysis of the predicament of homeowners' rights-defending", *Academia Bimestris*, 2: 123–8 (in Chinese).

Yeh, A. and Wu, F. (1996) "The new land development process and urban development in Chinese cities", *International Journal of Urban and Regional Research*, 20(2): 330–53.

Yip, N. M. and Jiang, Y. (2011) "Homeowners United: the attempt to create lateral networks of homeowners' associations in urban China", *Journal of Contemporary China*, 20(72): 735–50.

Yu, X. and Wang, H. (2000), "Sociological reflection induced by Owners' Committee", *China Civil Affairs*, 10: 13–14 (in Chinese).

Zhang, L. and Liu, L. (2005) "Property management as a new public space: the tension between an over-powered state and an underprivileged society in China", *Society*, 114–63 (in Chinese).

Zhong, L., Mol, A. P. J. and Tao, F. (2008) "Public–private partnerships in China's urban water sector", *Environmental Management*, 41: 863–77.

Zhou, M. and Logan, J. R. (1996) "Market transition and the commodification of housing in urban China", *International Journal of Urban and Regional Research*, 20: 400–21.

Zhu, J. (2007) "Space, power, and the construction of community identity: a case study of a residents' movement in a Shanghai neighborhood", *Chinese Sociology and Anthropology*, 40(2): 65–90.

Zhu, J. and Ho, P. (2008) "Not against the state, just protecting residents' interests: an urban movement in a Shanghai neighborhood", in P. Ho and R. L. Edmonds (eds) *China's Embedded Activism: Opportunities and Constraints of a Social Movement*, London and New York: Routledge.

Zhu, J. and Wang, C. (2007) "Seniors defending their rights: strategies and culture in collective action: the home-owner rights movement in Lijiang Garden, Guangzhou", *Chinese Sociology and Anthropology*, 40(2): 5–34.

# Index

For Product Safety Concerns and Information please contact our EU
representative  GPSR@taylorandfrancis.com
Taylor & Francis Verlag GmbH, Kaufingerstraße 24, 80331 München, Germany

9 781138 069220